About Christopher Ruddy

"Chris Ruddy is tenacious. His reporting is serious and compelling."

William S. Sessions
former Director, Federal Bureau of Investigation

"Has turned in more scoops on Foster's death than any other."

Britain's *Independent*

"A serious reporter who has raised important questions."

Edward I. Koch
former Mayor, City of New York

"Relentless."

The Wall Street Journal

"Sharp, quick, and in command of the facts."

Investor's Business Daily

"The right background for a sleuth . . . Ruddy broke the key stories."

Chicago Sun-Times, London *Telegraph*

"Two-thirds of Americans still are not sure [Vince Foster committed suicide] . . . in large part because of the work of this man, investigative reporter Christopher Ruddy."

"60 Minutes"

"Ruddy trod where others fear to tread."

Kenneth Chandler
Editor, *The New York Post*

ABOUT THE AUTHOR

Christopher Ruddy is the only reporter in America investigating on a full-time basis the death of former deputy White House counsel Vincent W. Foster Jr. He began his probe as an investigative reporter for the New York Post in 1993, and continues today as a journalist with the Pittsburgh Tribune-Review. He is also a Media Fellow at the Hoover Institution on War, Revolution and Peace. He received the Western Journalism Center's Courage In Journalism Award. His reports were the basis of a feature on CBS-TV's "60 Minutes." In 1992, as editor of the New York Guardian, he broke a number of national stories, one of which led to the withdrawal of a PBS documentary — the first time PBS has disavowed one of its own projects. At the New York Post, Ruddy broke several stories that received national attention about abuses of Social Security programs. Ruddy holds a B.A. *summa cum laude* in History from St. John's University in New York and a Master's Degree in Public Policy from the London School of Economics.

VINCENT FOSTER:
The Ruddy Investigation

Articles written by Christopher Ruddy
and reprinted with the permission of

THE NEW YORK POST

and the

PITTSBURGH TRIBUNE-REVIEW

ISBN: 0-9652342-0-7

Contents

Acknowledgements

There are countless people who have helped to make this story and my investigation happen. I offer my sincere thanks to them for helping me tell this unfolding story.

Especially, I want to thank Joseph Farah and the Western Journalism Center for making this whole project possible. My thanks to Cindy and Mike of the Center for their help in organizing this compilation. Also, thanks to Becky and Gretchen for their work on the design and layout.

One reporter I am grateful to is Ambrose Evans-Pritchard of London's Sunday Telegraph. He has pursued several stories, including the Foster one, with vigor and courage.

My first set of stories appeared in The New York Post. I am grateful to its editor, Ken Chandler, for giving me that opportunity. I still think it was a minor miracle the original articles were published.

George Beidler, my editor at the Pittsburgh Tribune-Review, has been supportive throughout the investigation. I am appreciative of all his help, as well as the support of the publisher, Richard M. Scaife, and the whole staff of the Tribune-Review.

I have called many experts and officials for background information and their help is demonstrated in my work. Particularly I would like to thank Vincent Scalice and Professor Thomas Scorza. Other sources, I am sure, would prefer that they not be acknowledged here. I trust that I will acknowledge them at a later date when their stories can be fully told.

"Mrs. Z.," during two critical points in the story, came to my assistance. I hope my work here, in a small way, is a continuation of her husband's great legacy to the American people.

A private citizen, Hugh Sprunt, has contributed greatly with his Citizen's Independent Report on the Foster case. I highly recommend it.

Reed Irvine and Accuracy in Media have devoted tremendous energy to this case.

And of course, James Dale Davidson, editor of Strategic Investment, has gone above and beyond the call of duty in helping to bring the facts of this case to the public.

Foreword

Having investigated thousands of homicides during the past 35 years, beginning with my work at the New York City Police Department, I can say with some degree of certitude that the official story offered about the death of Vincent W. Foster Jr. makes little sense.

Earlier this year I was hired by the Western Journalism Center to examine certain aspects of Foster's death and the finding of his body at Fort Marcy Park in Virginia. After a comprehensive examination of the crime scene, official documents and pertinent FBI laboratory reports, I and Fred Santucci, also formerly with the New York City Police Department, concluded that "the overwhelming evidence" indicated Foster's body had been moved to the park.

Numerous points of evidence, such as the many multi-colored carpet fibers found all over Foster's clothing, including his underwear, are indications of such movement. Fort Marcy is not carpeted.

The easy dismissal of circumstantial and forensic evidence in the case by authorities and the media is worrisome.

"60 Minutes," no less, used a Congressman as an expert witness to dismiss forensic evidence. For example, the Congressman made the ridiculous assertion that carpet fibers came to be found all over Foster's clothing because the Park Police had mixed all over Foster's clothing in the same evidence bloodied items and non-bloodied items.

If this was true, why then did the FBI lab find carpet fibers on Foster's suit jacket and tie—items found in his car and bagged separately?

The carpet fibers first came onto the clothing, the Congressman asserts, because Foster walked across carpets.

While this phenomenon of "jumping" carpet fibers happened, we are expected to believe not a speck of soil or grass stains found their way on Foster's shoes, though Foster was said to have walked over 700 feet through the park to the spot

he was found.

In tests conducted by myself and my associates, including one of the nation's top forensic scientists, Dr. Richard Saferstein, we found soil on three pairs of shoes walked in the park—and one pair was walked just several feet around where the body was found.

There are dozens and dozens of inconsistencies like these that Christopher Ruddy has brought to light.

A few inconsistencies should arouse suspicion. The evidence strongly indicates that murder can not be ruled out in the death of Vincent Foster.

Christopher Ruddy has conducted, as his articles demonstrate, a thorough investigation into the death and official handling of the case. He has done the type of work the police and the FBI should have done.

Ruddy has stuck to the fair questions about the death and the official handling. He has not offered any conspiracy theories. He has asked the question police are trained to first answer when coming upon a suspicious death: *How* did Foster die? Only after this question is answered can we ask competently *why* Vincent Foster died.

The failure of the Park Police and federal authorities to treat the case as a homicide, as police procedure demands, is baffling.

In my experience, I have never seen a case so poorly handled and investigated, especially since there is so much evidence of foul play.

Vincent Scalice

Vincent Scalice is a veteran New York City Police homicide investigator. He is an expert in crime scene reconstruction, identification and forensic analysis. He served as a consultant to the House Select Committee on Assassinations.

Editor's Note

The Western Journalism Center has been proud to support the work of investigative reporter Christopher Ruddy. In fact, we consider his exhaustive and relentless work on the Vincent Foster case a model for future projects.

You will find his work thorough, sobering and challenging. You will be stunned not only by the magnitude of an apparent cover-up surrounding the details of a high government official's death, but by the failure of the establishment news media to cover what is certainly one of the most important stories of our time.

While the rest of the media have shown little interest in uncovering the facts of the case, Ruddy's work has been more intensively scrutinized than any other reporter's in the last 25 years. He has been the target of slanted and malicious attack stories in some of the same major newspapers that have ignored the Foster case. The denouement of this disinformation campaign was a hatchet-job by Mike Wallace of "60 Minutes" in October 1995. Yet, despite the scrutiny and the double-standard to which Ruddy's work has been subjected, he has proven irrepressible. Why? Because he has truth on his side.

After two years, Ruddy's prolific reporting has withstood the two most important measurements of investigative journalism: time and accuracy.

In your review of this compilation of Ruddy's articles you will see how, time and again, his reports were proved right by unfolding events. For instance, on March 7, 1994, he reported that the police had none of the crucial crime scene photos. He came under sharp criticism for that report. Later, it was revealed the police have only a handful of Polaroids. All of the key photos have vanished or been destroyed.

Since this is a compilation of essentially raw news reports, you may detect some minor factual inconsistencies. Like any reporter, Ruddy uses the best available information. For example, in early stories, Ruddy refers to a report in the Boston Globe suggesting Foster was left-handed. When he learned of the Globe's error, Ruddy became the first reporter to state that Foster was indeed right-handed.

Also, a section entitled "Darkwater" appears in this book. Some of the articles in this section may or may not have anything to do directly with Foster's death. They were included, however, because of what they reveal about the milieu from which those currently in power come from, and the darker, more serious aspects of corruption and abuse of authority.

Joseph Farah
Executive Director
Western Journalism Center

Mr. Farah is former editor-in-chief of the Sacramento Union and a veteran reporter and news executive.

Preface

The Story That Won't Die: The Death of Vincent Foster

By Christopher Ruddy
DECEMBER 1, 1995

In mid-September 1995, Fort Marcy Park was cordoned off as FBI agents and other forensic experts began one of the most intensive bullet searches in the bureau's history.

Across the Potomac from Washington, Fort Marcy's pastoral setting soon became adorned like a Christmas tree: geometric lines of string stretched out across the park mapping possible bullet trajectories; red stakes marked an extensive grid system as field experts scanned the ground with sophisticated metal detectors. Still more agents stood in a cherry picker crane as they searched trees — all this in an apparently vain effort to find the bullet with which Vince Foster is said to have shot himself.

On July 20, 1993, Deputy White House Counsel Vincent W. Foster, Jr. was found dead there, lying on one of the obscure park's steep, earthen berms. The official claim is that Foster had killed himself after taking a 1913 Colt .38 revolver, pressing the four-inch barrel deep against the back of his mouth, and firing. Finding the gun still in his hand, the U.S. Park Police quickly ruled the death a suicide. Some say too quickly.

Independent Counsel Kenneth Starr has kept the case open. Starr hired forensic scientist Henry C. Lee to re-examine the case. Lee, an expert witness in the O.J. Simpson trial, asked that the FBI begin the search, the third probe by the Feds for the bullet. Locating the bullet would counter evidence that Foster may have been murdered or committed suicide elsewhere and his body moved to the park.

Like finding the bullet, answers to explain the death of Foster, a boyhood friend of the President's and a Rose Law Firm partner of Hillary Rodham Clinton, seem equally elusive.

In the summer of 1995, both Speaker Newt Gingrich and Banking Committee chairman Sen. Alfonse D'Amato (R-NY) challenged establishment wisdom that the report of the first Whitewater Special Counsel, Robert Fiske, had closed the case. In June 1994, Fiske wrote "the evidence overwhelmingly supports" the conclusion Foster took his own life.

Gingrich told a press breakfast in July that he was "not convinced" Foster took his own life.

D'Amato reversed his position of 1994 when as ranking minority member of the Banking Committee he signed off on Fiske's conclusions after a single day of hearings. In 1995, D'Amato told New York's WCBS radio that if Foster shot himself it would have been "impossible" for the gun to remain in his hand as it did. On PBS's "Charlie Rose" program, D'Amato said legitimate questions as to whether the body was moved needed answers.

To add to the ruckus, D'Amato shot off a press release in mid-September announcing the committee would subpoena former White House aide Helen Dickey and Arkansas trooper Roger Perry. D'Amato said there was "a clear discrepancy" between Perry's account and that of the White House. Perry claims that while on guard duty at the Governor's mansion, Dickey called from the White House early on the evening of Foster's death — well before the White House claims to have known of the death — to advise that Foster had shot himself in his car on the White House parking lot.

Dickey now denies that and says she called Perry after 10 p.m. that evening. A confidential Secret Service memo written on the night of Foster's death gives some corroboration to Perry's account, stating ". . . U.S. Park Police discovered the body of Vincent Foster in his car . . . a .38 cal. revolver was found in the car."

The body wasn't found in the car, and the Secret Service now says the memo was an honest mistake. Like so many nagging questions about the death, this discrepancy is apparent from official records — not a product of wild conspiracy theories.

The cumulative result two years later is stunning: a recent Time/CNN poll asked, "From what you know, do you think Vincent Foster . . . committed suicide or do you think he was murdered?" Twenty percent of respondents said Foster was murdered, and another 45 percent responded "not sure" — nearly two-thirds of the public has yet to accept the official version.

Suicidal depression?

The sheer number of discrepancies in the case has made it the story that won't die. Talk radio, Internet bulletin boards and alternative media are still abuzz about the death.

Standard police procedure is to first treat every suicide as a homicide. That wasn't done here. "It seems to me that we made that determination prior to going up and looking at the body," senior Park Police investigator Cheryl Braun said, admitting the police's verdict was reached before detectives had even inspected the death scene.

"You look for inconsistencies, things that don't fit with what you would normally expect," explained Vernon Geberth. Geberth has been part of over 5,000 death investigations, starting with the New York Police Department and now as an expert witness. He has authored the standard text on homicide investigations, "Practical Homicide Investigation."

"A high number of inconsistencies should raise an investigator's antennae and raise suspicion," Geberth said, referring to the critical area of concern for police investigators: the crime scene. A careful examination of the scene permits an investigator to distinguish a real suicide from a staged one — a murder made to look like suicide — an occurrence Geberth said is happening with increasing frequency.

But in Foster's case the scene was not the primary basis for a suicide conclusion. For example, the U.S. Park Police, which had exclusive jurisdiction over the case, didn't even bother to send the gun for testing until a week after they ruled the death a suicide. Instead, the police relied heavily on Foster's state of mind and his "depression" for their ruling.

The official story is that Vincent Foster was busy working in his West Wing office one hot July Tuesday. He had lunch brought to his office: a cheeseburger, fries and Coke. After eating his lunch, leaving only the onions, he took his suit jacket, told his secretary, "I'll be back," reminded her of the M&Ms still left on his table, and left. Foster was last seen alive exiting the West Wing

at about 1 p.m. by a Secret Service guard.

His body was found at around 6 p.m. at Fort Marcy Park. Expressing shock the next day, White House officials said Foster's death was unexplained and that he had not behaved unusually. That story soon changed. Foster, the man the President called the "Rock of Gibraltar," was clinically depressed, the White House said, upset over critical editorials in the Wall Street Journal and Congressional inquiries over the Travel Office scandal.

A note torn into 28 pieces, leaving no fingerprints and said to have been written by Foster, was found almost a week after his death, expressing these and other concerns.

Foster's wife, Lisa, who believes her husband took his own life, has said she was not aware he was depressed before his death. He appeared to be under stress, she said, recalling that her husband began compulsively rubbing his hands together. At one point his heart was pounding so hard, he thought it was coming out of his chest.

The family's Little Rock doctor, Larry Watkins, had just prescribed the anti-depressant trazadone for Foster the day before his death. Watkins told the FBI that the trazadone was prescribed mainly for insomnia. His statement reads: "He did not think that Foster was significantly depressed nor had Foster given the impression that he was 'in crisis.'"

Lisa Foster's failure to detect the depression was remarkably similar to statements made to Fiske's investigators by her husband's close friends and associates. Former Rose Law Firm partner Webster Hubbell told the FBI that he "did not notice Foster acting differently in the days or weeks before his death."

Testifying before the Senate in the summer of 1995, Hubbell completely reversed direction, stating that Foster "seemed to be depressed." Hubbell remarked that Foster even believed his phone was tapped.

Other evidence of depression, Fiske said, was Foster's "obvious" weight loss. Yet medical records show Foster actually gained weight while at the White House, jumping from 194 pounds just weeks before joining the White House to 197 pounds at his autopsy (which didn't include the weight of lost blood).

Insomnia, compulsively rubbing his hands, believing the phone is tapped, rapid heartbeat — are these signs of suicidal depression or are they signs of anxiety? If Foster was afraid, what did he fear? What worries led him to purchase a special alarm system for his Georgetown home shortly before he died?

The Park Police, and later Fiske, relied heavily on the nebulous aspects of Foster's state of mind, while seemingly ignoring unusual circumstances of Foster's death and the forensic evidence derived from the crime scene — the area in which police typically concentrate their efforts.

Scene inconsistencies

Foster left no suicide note. According to homicide expert Vincent Scalice, the torn note is not a suicide note because "it doesn't mention final departure, death, farewell to loved ones, or harm to oneself." Foster bid no farewell to his wife of 25 years or his three kids. The meticulous lawyer made no special financial arrangements for them — leaving them his standing life insurance money of about $1,000,000 — not a considerable sum considering their living standards.

Other linkages to the suicide also aren't there: Foster had no history of visiting Fort Marcy Park. Foster's face was splashed across newspapers and TV screens after his death, yet no one came forward to claim they had seen him alive at the park, or even around Washington that fateful afternoon. From the time he left the White House, five hours of his life are simply, and inexplicably, unaccounted for.

Unaccounted time, unusual place, no suicide note, no farewell, no financial arrangements — each in itself does not prove Foster did not commit suicide — but any Baker Street Irregular can appreciate their importance in light of the questionable aspects of the crime scene.

Foster was found, by all accounts, lying amidst dense brush in a supine position on a steep hill, his head almost touching the ridge's crest. His body was found in a neat position: arms at his side, legs extended straight, head and face straight up. Lead Fairfax County paramedic Sgt. George Gonzalez, among the first to find the body, said he had never seen a gunshot-to-the-head death leaving the body so pristine, as "if it was ready for the coffin."

The police said the neat arrangement of the body was one sign there was no struggle — evidence consistent with a suicide. This is true, but signs of struggle would not be the only evidence to determine that the death was a suicide.

Gonzalez and others noted the relatively small amount of blood loss from the head. EMS worker Kory Ashford told the FBI he had cradled Foster's head in his arms as he placed him in the body bag: he did not get blood on him, did not even wash his hands after the task. He said he couldn't remember an exit wound or seeing blood, and upon return to his station, classified the death in his report as he saw it: a homicide.

An FBI lab report notes several blood drainage tracks emanating from Foster's nose and mouth, but no excessive bleeding. Fiske's experts concluded that Foster's heart had to have stopped almost instantly after the gunshot fired (not impossible, but unusual).

The gun, perhaps the most crucial scene evidence, was found in Foster's right hand, held close to his right thigh in almost the classic cowboy position. Foster was right-handed. The thumb was still in the trigger mechanism. Homicide expert Geberth said it is "rare" for the gun to remain in the suicide's hand. "Under ordinary circumstances, the gun is away from the person," he said, pointing out the gun's explosive recoil and the natural reflexes of the body.

Was the gun ever owned by Foster? Investigators have equivocated on this point, but the bottom line is that no family member has ever positively identified it. The gun was believed to have come from Foster's father's gun collection. Foster's children and a nephew, intimately knowledgeable of the collection, told the FBI that the gun positively was not in the collection. The antique Colt, which the Bureau of Alcohol, Tobacco and Firearm's lab said was made from the cannibalized parts of two or more guns, had two serial numbers, traceable to Seattle, Washington 1913. (In a recent profile in The New Yorker, Mrs. Foster said the gun was Foster's, something she was unable to do in two previous federal investigations.)

The revolver was found loaded with two rounds, one fired, the other unspent. No matching ammunition was found in either of Foster's homes.

The fired bullet was never found. No one heard the fatal shot.

Though the FBI asserted the gun's barrel had to have been pressed deep against the back of the mouth, no blood, tissue or blowback material was visible on the gun. The explosion left no gunpowder on Foster's tongue, and the recoil didn't chip or damage any teeth.

The FBI lab found some DNA material at the very tip of the gun, from blood or saliva, that was inconclusively matched to Foster — a rather tenuous link.

And multiple test firings in the FBI lab found that Foster's index fingers, hence his hands, had to be "in the vicinity of the (front) cylinder gap when the gun was fired." Minus the jargon, Foster shot himself, neither hand on the gun's grip, with both hands clasped around the sides of the gun's cylinder. "It doesn't make any sense," Dr. Vincent Di Maio explained. Di Maio, medical examiner for San Antonio, Texas, considered one of the nation's top firearms forensics experts, suggested such gunpowder residue patterns were "not con-

Continued on next page

sistent with suicide."

Just the gun, and the list of inconsistencies at the crime scene grows: the blood, the failure to identify the gun, the matching ammo, the position, the lack of powder burns, the noisy shot that no one heard — all are strangely inconsistent with the death.

If Foster didn't shoot himself with that gun, who did? Where? How did he really die? These are questions investigators should have asked. Their answers lead to other, logical questions about the strong evidence that the body was moved to the park.

Failure to find the bullet is one piece of evidence the shot wasn't fired there. FBI blood track analysis found that Foster's head was in as many as four separate positions after death — but that doesn't jibe with Fiske's pathology team's conclusion Foster died almost immediately with prompt heart cessation. Foster's head might have been moved by an emergency worker checking a pulse, as Fiske conjectures, but that doesn't explain multiple head movements, including one where blood drained from Foster's nostril to above his ear — moving up his face and against the gravity of the hill.

Investigators noted no blood splatter or tissue above Foster's head, though the bullet is said to have exited the top of the back of his head while he was in a sitting position. The medical examiner at the scene noted only a small amount of blood behind the head. He said that the blood was "matted and clotted under the head." Had the wound been covered at some point?

Trace analysis of Foster's shoes at the FBI lab found not a speck of soil on his shoes or clothing despite a 700-foot-plus trek through the heavily wooded park. No grass stains were mentioned. No soil—yet almost every garment of clothing, including his underwear, was covered with multi-colored carpet fibers.

Fort Marcy isn't carpeted, but an independent study found that the micaflecks are present on all vegetation in the park. The discovery of such flecks on Foster's clothing means nothing more than Foster's body was lying on top of vegetation, according to experts that have reviewed the matter. Fiske had dismissed the absence of soil on the basis of flecks of mica found on the clothing. The soil in the park, Fiske noted, is micaceous. He didn't bother checking out the fibers.

A good detective, it is said, never jumps to conclusions and always asks good questions. If the bullet is ever found, it will help fill in just one piece of a large puzzle of the mysterious death of Vince Foster — a puzzle that grows ever larger as the third of a trio of federal investigation continues; it is Starr's turn. Three balls, two strikes. The batter is still up but it's the most precarious of all possible counts. ■

Chapter One

A Memo: The Unanswered Questions . . .

A MEMO:

The Unanswered Questions in the Foster Case

By Christopher Ruddy

Herein follow some of the critical issues involved in the death of Vincent Foster and subsequent investigations. This memo identifies almost a hundred significant problems with the case. There are dozens of issues that have not been included in this memo.

It has been over two years since the highest ranking federal official in more than 30 years died under very suspicious circumstances.

One doesn't have to be a conspiracist to ask serious questions about the high number of inconsistencies that challenge whether the death was a suicide or to note the mishandling of the case by the Park Police, Special Counsel Robert Fiske, Independent Counsel Ken Starr, and the FBI.

A Time/CNN poll conducted in July 1995 showed that 20 percent of Americans believe Foster was murdered, and another 45 percent don't accept the suicide ruling at this point—65 percent of Americans don't buy the official version. In response to another question, 45 percent said they believe a cover-up took place in the death investigation of Foster.

One need not be a conspiracist to believe that if the original Park Police investigation was mishandled, and that subsequent investigations uncritically reviewed the original investigation, the results of a hundred superficial investigations would come up with the same, possibly faulty, conclusions.

In fact, former FBI Director William Sessions has charged that the investigation into Foster's death by the Park Police was "compromised from the beginning."

Critically, the Foster case is about the proper administration of justice and the public's right to know.

Few of us knew what a decent, stable, conscientious and devoted family man Vincent Foster was, which makes the suicide theory even more preposterous.

But a cursory review of the evidence and handling of the case demonstrates that there is much more to the death than the public has been told.

The Circumstances
- No suicide note
- Another torn note was found in a briefcase that previously had been searched
- Three handwriting experts, including one from Oxford University, concluded the note was a forgery
- A note which never mentioned suicide and torn into 28 pieces was found almost a week after his death
- No fingerprints were found on the torn note
- No farewell to his family, or final arrangements made for them
- No history of visiting Fort Marcy Park
- Large amount of unaccounted time from when last seen alive until body found five hours later

The Body
- Body so neatly arranged, arms at sides, head straight up, as "if it was ready for the coffin," according to two paramedics
- Found on steep slope amidst dense brush, unusual surroundings in which to commit suicide
- Little blood loss from a gunshot wound to a living person's head

The Gun
- In two probes, family couldn't positively identify the gun as Foster's
- Two rounds found in gun, no matching bullets at home
- No fingerprints, though gun found in hand
- No visible blood splatter or blow-back on gun
- No one heard the fatal shot
- No gunpowder found on tongue
- Recoil didn't chip or damage teeth, though barrel said to have been pressed against back of mouth
- Gun remained (unusual) in hand
- Two homicide experts say the gun was "staged" in hand
- Powder burns on both hands indicate neither hand on grip when fired—seven leading experts say firing position "inconsistent" with suicide

Park Police Investigation
- Improperly treated death from arrival at scene; police procedure says treat all suicides as homicides first
- Didn't bother to interview park neighbors or regular visitors
- Failed to take statements from all persons found in park
- Key witness says the representation of her statement in police report was "untrue"

Continued on next page

Continued from page 3

- Didn't seal Foster's office, though he died during workday
- Gave away key crime scene evidence, such as his beeper and papers, within hours after the death
- Gun not sent for testing until one week after official ruling of suicide
- Lead investigator had never handled a homicide case before
- Police claimed they conducted metal detector search, yet FBI later found 70 pieces of metal (including 12 modern bullets) in same area of search—even some right on path where body was found
- Police underexposed key 35mm crime scene photos, other Polaroids missing
- Never conducted fiber suction of Foster's clothing
- Didn't analyze Foster's shoes
- Relied on autopsy of Virginia medical examiner, who has been challenged in two suicide rulings—in one case the murderer later confessed
- In violation of their own procedures, no police present at the death scene attended the autopsy

The Fiske Investigation

- Foster's death investigation was exempted from the grand jury, no one was interviewed under oath (unusual)
- Confidential witness who discovered the body stated FBI badgered him to alter his testimony on critical issues
- Patrick Knowlton, a witness who officials said was the first to spot Foster's Honda in the parking lot, claims the FBI "lied" in his witness statement; they claimed he could not identify a man he saw in the park; he says he can.
- Claimed that everyone known to have been in Fort Marcy that evening was interviewed; this is not true. Still not interviewed are an Hispanic-looking man, a dark-haired man, a blonde-haired man, and "volunteers" working on a park trail
- Fiske ignored witness statements of couple in the park who said two men, not Foster, were in and around his car just before body was found; said police misrepresented their statements; Fiske omitted their critical testimony from his report
- Canvass of neighborhood was never conducted by Fiske
- Implied on page 36 that medical examiner saw a large pool of blood under Foster's body; medical examiner denied this
- Person who found the body asked a park maintenance worker to call 911; Fiske never bothered to have maintenance worker identify this person
- Fiske investigation leaked conclusion of suicide by April 4 to the Wall Street Journal, yet records show no real investigation had taken place, including FBI lab reports or autopsy review

- The body was never exhumed
- Falsely claimed that there was "no evidence" Whitewater was a concern of Foster's before his death
- Two professionals claimed Fiske's FBI team never conducted an excavation of about half of a ton of soil where Foster's body was found—as the FBI claimed in their report
- Evidence uncovered during Starr probe showed that FBI investigation had used distorted copies of original photos for analysis
- Fiske claimed Foster was depressed citing, among other things, Foster's "obvious" weight loss. Medical records demonstrate Foster actually gained weight while working at the White House
- Fiske failed to include in his report key testimony from White House aide Thomas Castleton that he saw Foster leave his office with a briefcase
- Ignored as many as five witnesses who said they saw a briefcase in Foster's Honda at Fort Marcy. Suppressed Castleton's FBI interview statement from Congress
- Failed to follow-up on testimony from a CNN make-up artist who overheard a conversation between Clinton and an aide indicating Clinton knew of the death *prior* to the time he has claimed. Fiske suppressed the make-up artist's testimony by not turning it over to Congress

Missing Evidence

- All the 35mm crime scene photos
- Seven Polaroids taken at the scene by Park Police officer; he says other photos don't match scene he saw
- Other Polaroids taken of blood on ground after body was removed
- No X-rays even though autopsy report and police report state they were taken
- Government claims to have no set of fingerprints for Vincent Foster

Starr Investigation

- Promised to review Fiske probe, but put the same FBI agents in charge of reviewing their own work
- Lead prosecutor of Foster case, Miquel Rodriguez, resigned after being thwarted in conducting full probe
- Rodriguez was told to conclude case at early stage of the investigation
- Rodriguez was denied the right to bring experts outside the FBI to explore inconsistencies
- Witnesses were allowed to review evidence before testifying
- Took more than nine months to conduct a canvass of neighbors around park
- Starr summons three witnesses before grand jury after London Telegraph reported he had never interviewed them—though Starr's investigation was over a year old and published reports said he was

---

ready to close case

- Allows grand jury begun under Fiske, where key evidence was presented by Rodriguez, to expire and replaces it with new grand jury; he was allowed under law to keep grand jury for another year
- Photographic evidence of a wound or trauma to Foster's neck has been ignored
- FBI agents refused to draw map of Fort Marcy Park; grand jury proceedings took place without use of map
- Testimony of four witnesses and photographic evidence that a briefcase was in Foster's car have been ignored
- Evidence that the gun in Foster's hand was moved or switched has been ignored
- Evidence that Park Police were not truthful in previous testimony of finding men in orange vests in the park, as well as other park visitors, has been ignored
- Evidence that White House knew of death earlier than stated has been ignored
- Has regularly, and unusually, failed to challenge claims of attorney-client privilege by several Clinton aides—including former counsel William Kennedy
- Two Arkansas State troopers claim Starr's investigator attempted to have them change their testimony as to when they were notified of Foster's death
- Investigators used unusual tactics and false pretenses in an attempt to undermine the credibility of witness Knowlton
- Starr's investigators were able to get a couple who told the FBI under Fiske they saw two men in and around Foster's Honda, to change their stories. The couple now say they saw no one around the Honda
- Starr hired O. J. Simpson defense expert Henry Lee to help close
- Starr hired Dr. Brian Blackbourne, the San Diego Medical Examiner, to help close the case. Blackbourne is a former deputy and close friend of the lead pathologist who ruled on the case for Fiske
- Starr's Washington deputy, Mark Tuohey, quit Starr's office to join the Washington law firm that represents the Rose firm before Starr's very own firm

Movement of the Body

- Medical examiner said there was little blood under the body
- Medical examiner also said blood had matted or congealed on back of head, indicating possible covering of wound
- FBI blood analysis noted only blood drainage from head, not excessive bleeding—one indication gunshot may not have been cause of death
- Though bullet exited top of back of head while in sitting position, no blood tissue or splatter was seen above head
- FBI analysis found not a trace of soil on shoes or clothing, though Foster allegedly walked nearly 750 feet through park and sat down on dirt path
- FBI report omitted any mention of grass stains that should have been apparent on Foster's shoes.

- FBI analysis found mica particles on clothing, consistent with body having been moved and placed on dense foliage
- Neat arrangement of body unusual for violent death
- Blood tracks indicated Foster's head moved as many as four times after instant death
- Eyeglasses found 19 feet downslope from Foster's head, a physically impossible result of the claimed gunshot
- FBI found carpet fibers all over Foster's clothing and underwear, indicating body may have come into contact with one or more carpets before delivery to park
- Fired bullet never found, despite exhaustive searches
- Foster's car keys not found in his pockets at Fort Marcy

Location of Body

Evidence indicates the Park Police misrepresented the location of the body's discovery at the park:

- Fairfax County paramedic Gonzalez told reporter Ruddy that the body was lying on a slope well past the first cannon. The police report gives another location: directly in front of a second cannon a few hundred feet away.
- A Park Police officer told Ruddy the body was by the first cannon area
- Gonzalez and the police officer were unaware of the second cannon hidden deep in the park
- Polaroids that depict heavy vegetation around the body don't match the second cannon site, where the ground is visible
- Second cannon site has been a dirt path for over two decades; a Gannett news report stated that the pathway was a dirt one the day after the death. Yet not a trace of soil was found on Foster's shoes or clothing
- Tests conducted by two police experts found significant soil deposits on shoes and clothing of a test model at second cannon site
- Experts note that a leaf identified as *magnolia acuminata* in ABC News Polaroid is commonly found by first cannon site; no such leaf was found by second cannon site
- Doctor Haut's FBI statement indicates cannon was 10-20 yards behind body, which is consistent with Gonzalez's and police officer's account of first cannon site
- Haut sketched a map of body near first cannon site; map is similar to one drawn by Gonzalez
- Fairfax EMT worker Kory Ashford told Ruddy he could not remember cannon's location in park. Later, Ashford draws detailed map for the FBI depicting two cannons
- Park regular Robert Reeves and maintenance supervisor Ty Brown said the body was found near the first cannon
- Maintenance worker who called 911 disputes transcript of call, which has him locating body near the last cannon"; he said he only knew of one cannon

Examining the Crime Scene

This is a representation of the Foster crime scene at Fort Marcy Park. Foster was found lying amidst dense brush on the side of slope. He was found face-up, head-up in a neat arrangement. Detectives begin their investigation with the death scene. Certain tell-tale clues, or "inconsistencies," help them determine whether the death is a suicide, or a murder made to look like one. Italics indicate the remarks made by Vincent Scalice and Fred Santucci, two homicide experts formerly with the New York City Police Department.

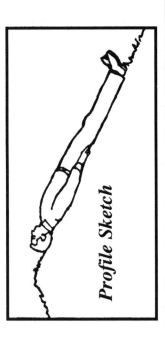

Profile Sketch

1. Location of Body—should be consistent with the person. Foster had no history of visiting the park, no one saw him alive in the park, no one heard the gunshot. *We found the placement of the alleged suicide unusual, as he was found amidst dense brush. Failure to link Foster to the park with past visits, or with witnesses that may have seen him alive, and the fact that no one heard the shot are inconsistencies.*

2. Blood Loss—should be consistent with wounds. Gunshot wounds typically involve heavy blood loss, blood splattering, pools of blood. Officials noted small amount of blood loss, and only blood drainage from Foster's mouth and nose. Foster's white shirt appeared neat and clean. *Small blood loss resulting from a gunshot to the head is one indication that the death may have been caused by other means.*

5. Body's Position—should be consistent with position of body when shot was fired. Officials say Foster fired the gun while in sitting position and was thrown back into neat position. Two paramedics found the death scene suspicious. The body, they said, appeared "ready for a coffin." *The head, arms, and legs appear too neatly arranged for a violent gunshot death.*

6. Exit Wound Splatter—should be consistent with location and nature of exit wound. Officials claim that the bullet exited the top rear portion of Foster's head leaving a large, jagged exit wound. Of 20 officials present at scene, including the lead police investigator and the medical examiner, no one noted blood splatter or other tissue above the head. After the body was removed, no bone fragments were found. *The exit wound noted in the autopsy should have resulted in blood and gelatinous matter falling in the area above the head. It should have been readily apparent to scene observers. Failure to find such material is one indication the shot was not fired there.*

7. Blood Pooling—should be seen around body. None was. Fiske report claims pool of blood was under body. *A pool of blood from the exit wound would be consistent only with blood drainage from the head. Blood pooling should have been evident from both entry and exit wounds.*

6

8. Clothing and Shoes—should have been examined for scene consistency. *If Foster had walked to the spot, soil and grass stains should have been visible on shoes.* The FBI lab found no soil on shoes. *The shoes should have been physically inspected. Soil and grass stains, as well as other matter, should have been visible to the naked eye.*

9. Indications of Struggle—should be looked for, such as disruption to clothing, body, or vegetation. Investigators said they found none. The first person to find the body said the area of vegetation below the body appeared matted and trampled.

10. Indications of Scene Tampering—should be looked for. Foster's eyeglasses were found with gunpowder on them 19 feet from where his head lay. The glasses, officials claim, bounced down the incline onto the other side of the ravine. *It is physically impossible for the eyeglasses to have moved 19 feet, or any significant distance from the body, as a result of the gun's explosion.*

3. The Gun's Position—should be consistent with the firing of the weapon. Officials claim he held the gun with both hands, pressed the barrel deep against the back of his mouth and fired. *Red flag indicating possible foul play: the gun does not usually remain in suicide's hand. During simulations at site, we determined, even if Foster's thumb had been stuck in the trigger guard, the gun and both hands would have been thrown outward, in a flailing motion with the arms resting more perpendicular to the body. Palms should have fallen upward. In our 50 years combined experience investigating homicides, we have never seen a gun so neatly arranged in a suicide's hand. We believe the gun was staged.*

4. Gun's Appearance—should be consistent with wound. The gun appeared clean to witnesses. *If the barrel had been placed in contact with the body, as claimed, blood and blowback material should have been apparent on gun.*

INSET

13 feet away from shoes.

Diagram by C. Ruddy
Drawing by G. Slater

7

Chapter Two

Breaking the Story: Reports from The New York Post

Doubts Raised Over Foster's 'Suicide'

By Christopher Ruddy
FOR THE NEW YORK POST
JANUARY 27, 1994

Interviews with some of the first people to see Vincent Foster's body after it was found in a Virginia park have raised new questions about the "suicide" of the White House deputy counsel.

The questions involve the position of Foster's body; the fact that the gun was still in Foster's hand and had no blood on it; the small amount of blood on and near the body; and the swiftness with which the death was declared a suicide.

Fairfax County paramedic George Gonzalez, who says he was the first rescue worker to see Foster's body last July 20, told The Post he found several things about the death scene "strange."

For one thing, Foster's body was laid out perfectly "as in a coffin," Gonzalez said in his first public interview about the mysterious death.

"I found it peculiar: Every extremity [of his body] was straight, as if it was ready for the coffin," said Gonzalez, a paramedic for 13 years.

He said a .38-caliber Colt revolver was in Foster's right hand—even though experts say handguns used in suicides often are "catapulted" up to 20 feet away from a body.

He said Foster's arms were resting perfectly straight alongside his body.

Gonzalez said he was surprised to find so little blood at the death scene of someone who appeared to have placed a .38 in his mouth and pulled the trigger.

"The face was white and pale, and only a thin trickle of blood oozed from one corner of his mouth," he said.

"Usually a suicide by gunshot is a mess," said Gonzalez, who claimed he has examined a number of suicide victims who shot themselves in the mouth.

Kory Ashford, an emergency service technician who helped put Foster's body in a body bag, also said he does not remember seeing any blood.

"I can't even recall an exit wound," Ashford said, explaining that typically there would be a "mess" under the victim's head.

Park Policeman Kevin Fornshill, the first police officer at the scene, said everything, including Foster's white shirt, "was really neat," with no blood on it.

The apparent contradiction—a scarcity of blood in a death involving a gunshot wound to the head—raised the possibility that Foster may have been killed elsewhere and that his body was dumped in the park, according to homicide experts contacted by The Post.

The pathologist who conducted the autopsy said the wound had been "self-inflicted," but the autopsy results haven't been made public.

The results will be sent to special Whitewater counsel Robert Fiske, who will look into Foster's death as part of his investigation.

Another key question involves the gun.

Gonzalez remembers looking carefully at Foster's hand.

"His hand was wrapped around the grip of the gun," he said.

"The fingers were cyanotic—or pooling blood," he said, which is an indication of death.

He said the barrel of the gun was perfectly perpendicular to Foster's leg.

His account of the positioning and condition of Foster's body was corroborated by other witnesses who examined the body and scene.

Two witnesses said the first cops who came upon Foster's body took a cursory look at the crime scene and declared the White House official an apparent suicide.

"They saw the gun," Gonzalez said of the cops' snap judgment.

The Post took Gonzalez's detailed observations to a medical examiner and several present and former New York City homicide investigators.

They said they would not have been so quick to come to a conclusion about Foster's death, because killers often try to make murders look like suicides.

"You treat it as a homicide, particularly if it is a VIP, like this case, until you can prove otherwise," said a city detective with more than 20 years experience with homicides.

"The dead body is the most accurate and honest witness you have, if you know how to 'interrogate' it," he said.

Almost all experts consulted by The Post said it would be impossible to render a judgment on Foster's death, particularly since the autopsy and other crime scene reports have not been released.

But all said some aspects of the crime scene—as described by Gonzalez—baffle them.

"This is a head wound. Usually there's tremendous amounts of blood, blood all over the place, it would be a mess," said a detective considered the city's best.

"There should be pools of blood . . . Look at the gun—if it was the instrument of death, there would be blood on it. A .38 makes a powerful explosion. There's a backwash of

Continued on next page

Continued from page 11

blood and tissue."

Gonzalez and a law enforcement official described the gun as clean.

The experts also said it was highly unusual that Foster was clutching the gun.

"In my 30 years in dealing with homicides, I've never seen someone shoot themselves in the mouth and still hold the gun perfectly at his side," said a retired detective who spent most of his career investigating murders.

A prominent forensic pathologist added: "Normally when a person commits suicide, the gun doesn't end up in their hand. If the individual is gripping the gun, that would lead to thinking that possibly someone put the gun in his hand."

Also questioning the position of the gun was Vernon Geberth, a former city detective who wrote a nationally recognized homicide investigation textbook.

"Under ordinary circumstances, after the firing, the gun is away from the person," Geberth said, acknowledging that there are "rare" instances when the gun remains in the suicide's hand.

Experts said a suicide gun can end up 20 feet away—thrown by a reflex action of the person committing suicide.

Witnesses surmised that Foster was sitting or lying in the park when the fatal shot was fired.

"It's hard to explain how he shot himself—putting the barrel in at a right angle to his arm—fired it, and [had] it land still in his hand at his side," a detective said.

Forensic experts and homicide detectives said the key to answering many questions could be found in the bullet—if the cops ever find it.

The White House did not respond to several requests for comment. ■

Key Questions Leave Experts Wondering

By Christopher Ruddy
FOR THE NEW YORK POST
JANUARY 27, 1994

Expert detectives can often distinguish a suicide from a murder by asking—and finding the answers to—a number of key questions.

Here are their unanswered questions about the death of White House lawyer Vincent Foster:

Was the suicide victim familiar with the weapon?

Police say the 1913 Colt .38-caliber revolver found in Foster's hand was the gun used, based on powder residue on Foster's hand.

But the Foster family has not positively identified the gun as his.

Is the victim's time accounted for on the day of his death?

The autopsy report put the time of death between 4 and 5 p.m. Foster left the White House at 1 p.m., leaving up to four hours unaccounted for.

Did anyone hear the gunshot?

Police say no, but they apparently did not question all homeowners and workers in and near the park.

Were there nearby witnesses?

Police say no one besides Foster apparently was in the park at the time of his death.

But The Post has learned that a blue Mercedes-Benz was parked, unattended, on a short roadway leading to the park when police and ambulances arrived just after 6 p.m.

It was still there a half-hour later.

Police say the Mercedes was simply disabled. A spokesman couldn't explain why that information was withheld from the press at the time of Foster's death.

Was a suicide note found?

No suicide note was found on his body, according to officials.

The White House gave police a note—torn in 27 pieces—that had been found in Foster's briefcase. They said it had been overlooked during an earlier police search.

The note detailed Foster's anguish over a number of issues, but made no mention of suicide. ■

Cops: Foster Gun Was Never Tested

By Christopher Ruddy
FOR THE NEW YORK POST
JANUARY 28, 1994

The gun found in Vincent Foster's hand after his reported suicide might not have been tested to determine if it was the weapon used in the White House deputy counsel's death.

"We may not have done a ballistics test," Maj. Robert Hines, a spokesman for the U.S. Park Police, told The Post.

The agency had reported after Foster's death that the Washington Metropolitan Police performed tests confirming the gun killed Foster.

The district police routinely do such testing for the federal service.

But the district police's ballistics unit told The Post this week that had not happened.

"No, we did not test that gun," the head of the unit, George Wilson, said.

Questioned about the conflicting reports, Hines told The Post yesterday: "We will no longer be providing you with information. You will have to FOIA all requests from now on"—submit formal requests under the Freedom of Information Act.

The Post reported yesterday that aspects of the Foster death were inconsistent with suicide.

Homicide investigation experts said that even without the bullet, ballistics tests could be helpful.

A test would show that the gun worked. And any unused ammunition should be fired to compare the gun's powder with the powder burns and stippling (a tattooing effect) in the victim's mouth, retired New York detective Vernon Geberth explained.

Park police say the bullet exited the back of Foster's head and was lost in the woods. A second bullet was found in the revolver.

Geberth, whose book "Practical Homicide Investigation" is considered the bible on homicide forensics, said: "The last thing you want to classify a death as is suicide. Death investigations are analytical. Don't jump to conclusions."

Just because a gun is found in the victim's hand, he said, "Who says that it is the gun that is fired?"

But Geberth said he could not draw any conclusions without an autopsy report and police file.

Dr. James Beyer, the Virginia medical examiner who conducted the autopsy on Foster's body, said that the finding of suicide was made by the Park Police.

Foster's body was found on July 20 in Fort Marcy Park, just across the Potomac River from Washington. The park falls under the jurisdiction of the Park Police.

Park police said they did not canvass the neighborhood around the park.

"There are no homes around there, it's secluded," Hines said.

But from where Foster's body was found, one can see directly down a gully into the front yard of a home where a large construction project has been going on since before Foster's death. ■

Editors note: *As a result of this story the Park Police admitted they had in fact sent the gun for testing to the BATF (Bureau of Alcohol, Tobacco and Firearms) laboratory in Rockville, Maryland. The gun was sent, however, a week after the police officially ruled and closed the case.*

More Questions About Foster's 'Suicide'

By Christopher Ruddy
FOR THE NEW YORK POST
JANUARY 31, 1994

Who was the man in the white utility van?

This is one of the many nagging questions that remain unanswered in the official account of the "suicide" of deputy White House counsel Vincent Foster.

The mysterious man in the white van was the first person known to have seen Foster's body—which was found on a ridge in Fort Marcy Park in Arlington, Va.

At about 6 p.m. on July 20, park worker Francis Swann was in the parking lot of a maintenance facility two miles away from the park when the man in the van appeared.

Swann was sitting with a co-worker on the tailgate of his truck "having a beer after work" when the white van pulled up, Swann told The Post in his first press interview.

Swann said the driver was a heavyset white man in his mid-40s, with graying hair, who was dressed in work clothes "like a utility worker."

Speaking through the van window, Swann said, the man told him: "There's a dead body by the cannon up in Fort Marcy. Will you call the Park Police?"

Then, Swann said, the man drove off, but "not in a rush."

Swann said he went to a pay phone in the parking lot and called 911.

He didn't write down the van's license plate number—and doesn't even remember what state it was from.

Swann said he wondered why the man didn't make the call himself—and recalled joking with his co-worker about it, saying: "Maybe he didn't want to spend the quarter."

Rescue workers said Foster's body was not visible from the main trail that runs through Fort Marcy Park.

That means the unknown driver had to have been out of his van and off the main trail to have seen the corpse.

The U.S. Park Police said they have been unable to locate the driver.

If he were located, he could tell police if others were in the park at the time, if he had seen Foster alive and if he heard the fatal shot.

Another key unanswered question is whether Swann's call was the only one made to 911.

Police insist it was.

But George Gonzalez, a Fairfax County, Va. paramedic dispatched to Fort Marcy Park, said he distinctly remembers that a 911 call was made by an unidentified woman.

Warren Carmichael, a spokesman for Fairfax County's 911 dispatch unit, told The Post that Swann's call was the only one on record.

"We only keep the first call that comes in," he said.

Carmichael said the Park Police had a tape of Swann's call, but—like all his unit's 911 recordings—it was destroyed 30 days after the emergency.

He said he was "pretty sure" there were no other calls about Foster.

Another question—one that forensic pathologists and homicide experts find particularly puzzling—involves the positioning of Foster's hand and the gun that was found in it.

They wonder how the gun came to be clutched in Foster's hand—with fingers around the grip—after he had apparently used his thumb to fire a single fatal shot into his mouth.

They note that using the thumb to fire a suicide shot is normal—but it's highly unusual for the gun to then end up clutched in a normal position.

Last week, The Post reported that homicide experts found it strange that Foster's .38 Colt revolver had ended up clutched in his hand, which was lying neatly alongside his body.

They said in most cases the gun would be thrown from the hand either by reflex or by the force of the gun blast.

The White House, besieged by calls for comment about the questions raised by The Post, referred reporters to Dr. Cyril Wecht, a Pittsburgh pathologist.

Wecht told The Associated Press:

"You can get, in many of these instances, an instantaneous, spasmodic reflex, which is entirely involuntary, and the hand will clutch an object, in this case a gun."

He added: "Often, the fingers will tighten around the weapon."

But his explanation doesn't jibe with the Park Police account that Foster had fired the gun with his thumb.

Wecht, a former Democratic Senate candidate, fielded questions about Foster's death for the White House without benefit of the autopsy report.

The Post asked Dr. Lester Adelson, longtime medical examiner for Cleveland and a highly respected pathologist, if Wecht's explanation meshes with the Park Police account of Foster's death.

Adelson, who also hasn't seen the autopsy, said:

"I think that if a person shot himself in the mouth with a .38, he is not going to be able to carry out purposeful acts.

"Nature is honest. Use common sense," Adelson reasoned, questioning whether Foster could fire the gun with his thumb and then change his grip and move the weapon to his side.

Yet another question is why Foster would choose to die in Fort Marcy Park.

Experts say that there is usually some logic behind the selection of a suicide site. ■

Editor's note: *Paramedic Gonzalez said in his original interview some of Foster's fingers were found around the grip. Several witnesses told the FBI that the gun's position in the hand, as depicted in a Polaroid, did not match the scene they originally saw—an indication the gun may have been moved or switched.*

Ex-Chief: Politics Kept FBI Off Foster Case

By Christopher Ruddy
FOR THE NEW YORK POST
FEBRUARY 3, 1994

The FBI was kept out of the investigation into Vincent Foster's alleged suicide because of a "power struggle within the FBI and the Department of Justice," former FBI Director William Sessions says.

The decision about the investigative role of the FBI in the Foster death "was . . . compromised from the beginning," Sessions claimed in a handwritten statement he gave to The Post yesterday.

After Foster's death on July 20, the Justice Department put the U.S. Park Police in charge of the investigation.

Sessions said the FBI did not get involved in the probe for political reasons.

"The relationship between the White House and the FBI at the time of Mr. Foster's death should be looked at in the context of known events which had political implications," Sessions said.

Sessions—fired by President Clinton the day before Foster's suicide—noted that there had been a long-standing "power struggle within the FBI and the Department of Justice."

He said Foster, as the top deputy in the White House counsel's office, "was deeply involved in [the] relationships and events" involving the dueling bureaucracies.

One of those "events," he said, was the Travelgate scandal—when FBI agents were "summoned to the White House without my knowledge" as part of a bid by Clinton aides to oust veteran White House travel staffers in an abortive bid to make way for Clinton cronies.

The White House later admitted erring in getting the FBI involved and in publicizing its involvement.

"The White House and Justice Department were clearly in a politically awkward position" with the FBI 'Travelgate' investigation in July 1993 when Foster's body was discovered, Sessions wrote The Post.

Floyd Clarke, who was named acting FBI director the day before Foster died, "had been long involved with the Department of Justice to affect the power shift at the FBI," Sessions said.

And that, Sessions implied, is why Clarke let the Park Police head the investigation.

Calls for comment to the White House and the Justice Department

Judge William S. Sessions

were not returned.

A number of law enforcement officials questioned why the FBI did not take on the investigation.

"In view of the nature of this case, the FBI should have been involved," William Roemer, former head of the FBI's Organized Crime Strike Force, told The Post.

Roemer blasted the bureau for "allowing the tail to wag the dog."

"[Attorney General Janet] Reno and Clinton had undue influence, the FBI would normally be finding reasons to get involved in a high profile case," Roemer said, questioning the reasoning behind the Park Police's lead role in the

Continued on next page

Continued from page 15

probe.

Other law enforcement officials echoed his sentiments.

"The Park Police are not much more than traffic control and night watchmen," said Gene Wheaton, a retired investigator with the Army Criminal Investigations Division.

In his dealings with the Park Police during his 22 years with the Army CID, Wheaton said, they were known as the most "pliable" of law enforcement agencies and had almost no experience in "professional investigations."

Last year, the Park Police criminal investigations unit probed 35 deaths. The agency refused to provide a breakdown on how many were homicides, suicides or natural deaths. ∎

Experts: Park Cops Bungled the Probe

By Christopher Ruddy
FOR THE NEW YORK POST
FEBRUARY 3, 1994

U.S. Park Police failed to follow standard investigative procedures in probing the circumstances surrounding the death of deputy White House counsel Vincent Foster, law enforcement experts told The Post.

The Park Police, by quickly classifying Foster's death a suicide, violated a cardinal investigative rule, the experts said: Don't jump to conclusions.

Making a snap judgment that Foster's death was a suicide was a violation of textbook procedure—which laid the groundwork for further violations.

"In the Vince Foster case nothing was done right, as far as the public record shows," said Gene Wheaton, an investigator for 22 years with the Army's Criminal Investigation Division.

Experts stress that any death should be considered a possible homicide until it is proven otherwise by forensic and autopsy reports and other evidence.

The Park Police conducted only a cursory search in Fort Marcy Park in Arlington, Va.—apparently because they believed Foster's July 20 death was a suicide.

Witnesses said police did not follow textbook procedure and do a "hand and knee" search of the area around his body, or use metal detectors to search for the bullet that was fired into Foster's mouth and exited through the back of his head.

They also didn't dust Foster's car for fingerprints, or canvass the neighborhood around the park, or interview regular park visitors.

And they were apparently unaware that there was a rear park entrance—closer to the death scene than the main entrance.

Their sloppy on-site investigation was duplicated off-site when they delayed securing Foster's office for at least 12 hours—if not longer.

And they also didn't run ballistics tests on the gun found in Foster's hand—tests that experts say would show whether the 80-year-old weapon was operable.

Park Police officials have defended the probe that followed the discovery.

"It seemed definitely a suicide," said one of the first law enforcement officials to arrive at the scene of Foster's body.

"It was a perfect place to commit suicide. It's very peaceful there in the woods," another investigator, Park Police Officer Kevin Fornshill, told The Post. ∎

Editor's note: *The Park Police would later claim they did dust some areas of Foster's car and found eight prints of unidentified origin.*

The Park Police spokesman also claimed no metal detector search for the bullet had taken place—though the police claimed otherwise later.

Fumbling Feds Change Story On Foster 'Suicide'

By Christopher Ruddy
FOR THE NEW YORK POST
FEBRUARY 10, 1994

The U.S. Park Police has quietly revised its theory about exactly how Vincent Foster died—but its latest account of his "suicide" still doesn't jibe with the official autopsy report, The Post has learned.

Initially, Park Police investigators said the former deputy White House counsel inserted the barrel of a gun in his mouth and pulled the trigger.

Confronted with medical evidence that showed this almost certainly could not have happened, the investigators now have a new conclusion—that Foster held the gun a few inches away from his mouth and fired.

But that's equally inconsistent with the medical evidence, according to experts consulted by The Post.

The Park Police would not comment.

Foster was found dead July 20 in Fort Marcy Park in Arlington, Va.

The Park Police, put in charge of the investigation by the Justice Department, first said Foster put the barrel of an 80-year-old .38 caliber Colt Army service revolver into his mouth and fired.

If a suicide victim put a gun inside his mouth, experts say, there likely would be:

■ Thick quantities of gunpowder around or inside the wound.
■ Trace residue of gunpowder on his tongue.
■ Broken or damaged teeth.
■ Blood on the gun barrel.

But none of these conditions existed when Foster's body was found. "The entrance wound [inside the mouth] would be seared with a black margin, a heavy deposit of black soot, the size of a silver dollar, with a hole in the center," said Dr. Vincent Di Maio.

Di Maio, medical examiner for San Antonio, Tex., and a leading expert on wounds caused by firearms, said the only reason soot would not be found around the wound is if "the barrel is jammed really tight against the palette."

But then, he said, soot would be found inside the hole made by the bullet—and that was not the case, according to the autopsy report.

Di Maio said he has not been involved with the Foster case and was speaking in general terms.

The Park Police's revised theory—that Foster fired the gun a few inches outside his mouth—also fails to hold up, according to pathologists consulted by The Post.

They agreed that if a gun were held outside Foster's mouth and fired, there would likely have been powder and burn marks on his face and damage to his lips.

According to one veteran New York City homicide detective, there's only one possible way Foster—holding the gun either inside or outside his mouth—could have committed suicide without leaving evidence that an autopsy would turn up.

That would be if the gun had been equipped with a silencer, which extends the barrel, absorbs the blast and reduces the soot discharged.

But experts say suicide with a silenced weapon is extremely rare. And there was no silencer on the gun found in Foster's hand, or near Foster's body.

The Park Police maintain that the Colt, which lay clutched in Foster's hand alongside his hip, is the weapon that caused his death.

But the gun has not been positively identified as Foster's by his widow, according to Park Police.

Experts also point out that because of its age and the fact that its history is unknown, the weapon fits the description of a "drop gun."

A "drop gun" is an old, nondescript and untraceable revolver that can be "dropped" by someone at a staged suicide or crime.

The gun found in Foster's hand "was an old, reconstituted gun that had cannibalized pieces of other guns used to replace parts of it," Jack Killoran, a spokesman for the federal Bureau of Alcohol, Tobacco and Firearms, told The Post.

Park Police have said one of the key reasons they ruled Foster's death a suicide is that his thumb bore an indentation from the trigger.

A person pointing a gun backward, into his mouth, would pull the trigger with his thumb.

But Di Maio said he has never heard of a case in which a permanent imprint was made on a finger by simply pulling a trigger.

"It's virtually impossible," he said.

An imprint on the thumb would be plausible if Foster had been found still clutching the trigger in "cadaveric spasm"—a spasm caused by instant death, according to Vernon Geberth, a leading authority on death investigations and author of the standard police text on the subject.

But police said when Foster's body was found, his thumb was not on the trigger—it was caught under the trigger guard. ■

Top Docs Cast New Doubt On Foster 'Suicide'

By Christopher Ruddy
FOR THE NEW YORK POST
FEBRUARY 17, 1994

Leading pathologists dispute the U.S. Park Police's conclusion that an indentation on late White House counsel Vincent Foster's right thumb is evidence that he committed suicide.

Police claim the indentation proves Foster pulled the trigger of the 1913 Colt .38 that was found in his hand in Fort Marcy Park in Arlington, Va., last July 20.

They contend that Foster pointed the gun toward his mouth and pulled the trigger with his thumb.

But leading pathologists and forensic experts told The Post they were surprised that the existence of the indentation was presented as a key element in the official suicide ruling.

"I wouldn't call it on that," Dr. Vincent Di Maio told The Post.

Di Maio, medical examiner for San Antonio and a leading expert on firearms and their effects on the human body, said it's "virtually impossible" to find an indentation on the thumb from a single depression of a trigger.

Di Maio said he had never heard of such a case.

Other leading forensic pathologists agreed.

"Try it yourself," suggested Dr. Charles Petty, former chief medical examiner of Dallas.

He explained that the skin's resilience would make any indentation from a single moment on the trigger impossible to see—even at the moment of death.

"You're no more likely to see it than you would find an imprint of the steering wheel on the hand of someone who died in a car accident," Petty said.

Yet another expert said an impression on the thumb would likely not occur even if, in foul play, a gun were put into someone's hand and the thumb manipulated to pull the trigger.

"I wouldn't expect it," said Dr. Richard Mason, medical examiner of Santa Cruz, Calif., who specializes in firearms forensics.

"You might get a bruise from the recoil, but not an imprint."

The pathologists agreed that there are circumstances that could create an indentation or impression on the thumb of a deceased person.

First, acids from a corpse's "sweat" can "rust the skin," Di Maio said.

"The acids can actually dissolve metal, which can impregnate themselves in the hand," he explained.

Foster's right thumb, according to the police, was under the gun, trapped between the trigger and the front of the trigger guard.

Foster's other fingers clutched the top part of the gun's cylinder and the handgrip.

The pathologists said the weight of the gun—very likely two pounds—lying on top of Foster's thumb for several hours before his body was taken away would have created this effect.

Another explanation, they said, would be a rare phenomenon known as cadaveric spasm—which occurs in instantaneous death.

But the doctors believe cadaveric spasm is unlikely in Foster's case because he was not found depressing the trigger, and his arm and fingers had moved after the gun was fired.

In concluding that Foster's death was a suicide, the Park Police cited forensic tests that, the agency contends, prove powder burns on Foster's hands match the powder found in his mouth.

"There is no such test," Di Maio said.

Other pathologists agreed.

They said only ballistic tests using the fired bullet could confirm that the Colt fired the fatal shot.

Police never found the bullet that exited the back of Foster's head. ∎

Editor's note: *Despite the fact there is no forensic evidence that the simple act of depressing a trigger leaves a permanent impression, the police and others continue to cite this as primary evidence supporting suicide.*

Park Cops Have Botched a Death Probe Before

By Christopher Ruddy
FOR THE NEW YORK POST
FEBRUARY 17, 1994

When the U.S. Park Police ruled that Vincent Foster killed himself, it wasn't the first time the agency declared a suspicious death a suicide without conducting a proper investigation.

Its probe into Foster's death bears striking similarities to its handling of the 1991 death of Terry Todd Wright, a 20-year-old soldier assigned to the National Security Agency.

Wright's "suicide" stunned his family because he had no known history of mental or social problems.

Although Wright's death is still classified as a suicide, Congress last fall passed a resolution calling for a Defense Department review of its procedures in investigating suicides and for the reopening of questionable deaths like Wright's.

A retired Army investigator who took part in the probe of Wright's death is convinced the young soldier did not die by his own hand.

"The investigation does not support a suicide," Trent Smith told the Philadelphia Inquirer.

Smith said the Army never challenged the suicide finding because the Park Police was the "lead agency" in the investigation.

The Park Police was "very, very unprofessional" in handling the Wright case, said David Zucchino, a Pulitzer Prize-winning investigative reporter for the Inquirer.

"They (the Park Police) didn't bother to gather crucial evidence. They assumed it was a suicide from the very beginning."

Experts say police should treat every suicide as a possible homicide—and should not declare a suspicious death a suicide until all possible evidence is gathered and all necessary tests are conducted.

But the Park Police declared the death of Foster and Wright suicides from the start.

A passer-by found Wright's body lying on a dirt road running through park land adjoining Fort Meade in Maryland.

Officials said Wright had rested the butt of a .22-caliber rifle on the ground and fired it upward into his head.

The passer-by noticed the gun had no marks left on it by the dirt road, and the dirt bore no marks from the fired butt.

The passer-by also observed that Wright was wearing thick gloves that would have made it difficult for him to pull the trigger.

In addition, Wright's glasses remained perfectly placed on his nose, despite the jarring shot to his head.

Similar evidence was found in Fort Marcy Park in Arlington, Va., when Foster's body was discovered.

In both cases, evidence inconsistent with suicide was ignored.

In the Wright case, Zucchino said the Park Police didn't do basic things like questioning people living nearby or lifting fingerprints from the victim's car.

The Post has reported that the Park Police didn't canvass homes near Foster's body and didn't dust his car for fingerprints. ∎

Cops Made Photo Blunder at Foster Death Site

By Christopher Ruddy
FOR THE NEW YORK POST
MARCH 7, 1994

The U.S. Park Police never took a crucial crime-scene photo of Vincent Foster's body before it was moved during the investigation into the death of the White House deputy counsel, FBI sources told The Post.

The embarrassing blunder—corroborated by a Park Police source—was one of several routine crime scene procedures inves-tigators neglected to follow in Fort Marcy Park in Arlington, Va., in the Foster case, FBI sources said.

And, the sources noted, the break with standard police procedure came in an investigation involving the highest ranking federal official to die under suspicious circumstances in more than 30 years.

According to FBI sources, the Park Police also:

■ Failed to test Foster's shoes for residue.

A member of the Fairfax County, Va., Fire and Rescue squad previously told The Post Foster's shoe bottoms were "very clean."

According to an FBI source, this was apparent to law enforcement officials at Fort Marcy Park on July 20 of last year, the night Foster died.

A residue test would have shown whether Foster had walked in the park—or if his body had been carried there after he died elsewhere.

■ Failed to make impressions of footprints around Foster's body.

The impressions would have indicated if Foster had been alone, or if others were with him or had carried him.

■ Failed to conduct fiber sweeps of Foster's clothes and his car.

The sweeps would have revealed whether Foster's body had been carried, and if someone else had driven his car.

"It's extremely important, everything should have been vacuumed for trace evidence," said Vincent Scalice, a nationally recognized crime scene expert.

But the worst police omission of all in the mishandled investigation, experts say, was the failure to take a crime scene photograph of the body.

"Photographs should have been taken of Foster before his body was moved, and of his car, and of the relative positions of each," an FBI source said.

Although FBI officials were at Fort Marcy Park after Foster's body was discovered, the Park Police were in charge of the investigation.

"Crime scene photographs are permanent and comprehensive pieces of evidence," notes Vernon Geberth in "Practical Homicide Investigation," considered the authoritative text on death probes.

Geberth was incredulous that a crime scene photo of Foster's body had not been taken.

"I can't believe it. Who's to say this was a suicide?" he asked.

"If this is true, this is the most sloppy death investigation I have ever heard of."

Standard police practice requires that the scene of any death by accident, suicide or homicide be photographed, he said.

"It's imperative. It's a basic requirement. It's extremely important in an investigation because it shows the body's position and other patterns which can never be recreated."

"It's unspeakable. I can't imagine any competent investigator would not take crime scene photographs," said Robert Ressler, a retired FBI official who is considered a leading forensic expert on staged homicides.

Ressler said the only excuse for not taking a photograph is if the person is still alive and has to be moved.

Ressler said the absence of the photographs will make any investigation into Foster's death difficult.

A spokesman for the Park Police refused to comment on charges that his agency mishandled the crime scene investigation.

Meanwhile, The Post has learned that Roderick Lankler, the special deputy prosecutor in the Foster investigation, in a bid to recreate the crime scene, has interviewed several rescue workers who were among the first to find Foster's body. ■

Foster Coroner Has Been Dead Wrong on Suicide Before

By Christopher Ruddy
FOR THE NEW YORK POST
MARCH 8, 1994

The Virginia pathologist who conducted the autopsy on deputy White House counsel Vincent Foster was proved wrong on one previous suicide ruling and is being challenged on another.

The first "suicide" turned out to be a homicide—and the killer later confessed.

The autopsy was done by Dr. James Beyer, the 76-year-old deputy chief medical examiner for northern Virginia, who last year determined that Foster's death was "consistent with a self-inflicted wound."

The U.S. Park Police, whose investigation into Foster's death has been sharply criticized, have relied heavily on Beyer's autopsy. Park Police officials declined to comment yesterday.

But two families who had "suicide" cases ruled on by Beyer are skeptical of his work.

"I feel he did an incomplete job, and that's scary," Pam Easley told The Post. "He has caused us a lot of pain."

Easley's 21-year-old son, Tim, was found in his apartment with a knife through his heart in 1989. Four years later, Easley's girlfriend admitted killing him.

Beyer had ruled the death a suicide. Pam Easley became suspicious when she saw that the autopsy report said Tim had "gray" hair. His hair was dark brown.

"I made a mistake . . . The hair color is not altered after death," Beyer explained later in a letter.

At Tim's funeral, his mom and others noted—and photographed—a significant cut on the back of his right hand that was not mentioned in Beyer's report.

"The cut on the hand is definitely *ante mortem* (before death) and I cannot understand how any competent forensic pathologist would miss it. It is a classical 'defense' wound, suffered while trying to avoid the knife," concluded another pathologist, Dr. Harry Bonnell.

Bonnell, chief deputy medical examiner for San Diego, Calif., reviewed the available records and evidence at the mother's request.

Bonnell also stated that the knife's entry spot and its trajectory to the body were "inconsistent' with a self-inflicted wound.

Beyer told The Post he had no reason to question the trajectory of the wound.

He also said the cut on Easley's right hand was "consistent with a needle mark"—though he noted no such mark on his report. He said it was likely caused by rescue workers, but he had no records for the mark, and no explanation for why other incisions made by rescue workers were noted.

Forensic pathologists consulted by The Post said an examiner should make a note of everything, even if it's caused by medical assistance.

A needle mark, they said, would be extremely important in an apparent suicide because a victim might be drugged in a faked suicide.

A second family is still questioning Beyer's handling of their son's death.

"My wife and I can't measure the pain," said Thomas Burkett.

In December, 1991, Beyer ruled the death of Burkett's 21-year-old son, Tommy Jr., as "consistent with a self-inflicted wound."

"The basic forensic evidence and the opinion of the medical examiner indicate a suicide," Fairfax County, Va., police spokesman Warren Carmichael said, adding that there are no plans to reopen the case.

But a second autopsy conducted for the family, by Dr. Erik Mitchell, former chief of pathology in Syracuse, detailed serious omissions.

The second autopsy noted trauma and discoloration to Tommy's right ear—which could indicate he was beaten before a shot was fired into his mouth. The Burketts said the ear was so "disfigured and bloody," they thought he had been shot there.

Beyer never noted the trauma to the ear.

Beyer also failed to identify a fractured lower jaw, which could also indicate a beating.

The second autopsy also revealed that the lungs had not been dissected, although Beyer's report claimed they had been.

And the second autopsy found no trace of gunpowder in the mouth. Beyer left blank the section for "powder burns" on the gunshot-wound chart.

In an interview with The Post, Beyer did not challenge the findings of the second autopsy, beyond pointing to his earlier report: "All that I identified at the autopsy was the perforating gunshot wound to the head."

The Burkett case is similar to Foster's: Both were found with guns in their hand, both had little or

Continued on next page

Continued from page 21

no powder burns in their mouth, and there were numerous inconsistencies at the crime scene.

As for the Foster case, Beyer says he "considered it a full autopsy."

But other pathologists have questioned Beyer's actions on such a high-profile case: He did not visit the crime scene at Fort Marcy Park; he did not review crime-scene photos; and was not aware of the caliber of the gun before he rendered his judgment.

Beyer admits to having a medical condition with "some impairment of the upper and lower extremities on the left side" due to a "cerebral-vascular accident," he said.

"It has not impaired my ability to perform an autopsy," he said.

According to the American Medical Association, Beyer began practicing medicine in 1946 and received his certification for forensic pathology in 1970. Beyer said he has always practiced pathology, but was late in taking the test for certification. ■

Foster File Shocker

2nd set of papers taken from safe after mad scramble for combination

By Christopher Ruddy
FOR THE NEW YORK POST
MARCH 9, 1994

White House officials frantically scrambled to get the combination to Vincent Foster's office safe soon after his death—and ultimately removed a second set of files, The Post has learned.

White House counsel Bernard Nussbaum's removal of one set of Whitewater files from Foster's office has been widely reported.

But the disappearance of a second set of papers—including some also related to Whitewater—wasn't previously known.

Three separate White House sources told The Post that Clinton aides were scrambling—like "cats and dogs," as one put it—as they tried to get into Foster's safe just hours after his death.

Foster's body was found in Fort Marcy Park in suburban Arlington, Va., at about 6 p.m. on July 20.

As previously reported, a few hours later, Nussbaum—accompanied by First Lady Hillary Rodham Clinton's chief of staff, Margaret Williams, and long-time Clinton aide Patsy Thomasson—entered Foster's office and removed Whitewater files that were not in the safe.

But The Post has learned that Nussbaum also asked a White House security officer on night duty for the combination to Foster's safe.

Nussbaum was told that the security staff didn't have the combination, a White House source said.

Combinations are controlled through top secret clearances in the Office of Administration, which is run by Thomasson.

The Office of Administration staffer in charge of security—including the safeguarding of combinations—was out of town that night, a law enforcement source said.

Later, during the wee hours of July 21, a senior White House aide—not Nussbaum—succeeded in opening Foster's safe, according to another law enforcement official who is assigned to the White House. It's not clear how the combination was obtained.

The safe was opened before most

Patsy Thomasson, *Presidential Assistant*

White House personnel reported to work on the morning of July 21, the source added.

Several documents, including papers relating to Whitewater, were removed from the safe and turned over to President and Hillary Clinton's personal lawyer, David Kendall, the source said. Then the safe was relocked.

Foster, who was deputy White House counsel, also handled the Clintons' private legal matters, including Whitewater.

Word that the safe had been

opened apparently did not reach most White House officials, including senior members of the White House counsel's office—and they continued to scramble for the combination, a source said.

They were so anxious to be the first to see the contents of the safe that the counsel's office refused to let Park Police—who were handling the investigation into Foster's death—search the office on the morning of July 21.

The Park Police agreed to return the next day.

On the afternoon of July 21, members of the counsel's office were again asking White House personnel for the safe combination, claiming that "Bill Kennedy needed to get into Mr. Foster's safe,"

another source said.

William Kennedy is a former law partner of Mrs. Clinton and Foster at the Rose Law Firm in Little Rock. He is associate White House counsel—the No. 3 post in the counsel's office.

But the combination could not be given out, a source said, because Foster had taken the rare step of authorizing only himself to have access to the number.

Usually, White House staff members with safes share the combination with their staff or secretary.

The FBI's most highly decorated former agent told The Post that the revelation about entry into Foster's safe after his death underscores questions about a possible cover-up.

"The safe is crucial—it's an A-1 priority," said William Roemer, former head of the FBI's Organized Crime Strike Force.

He was sharply critical of the failure by federal authorities to secure Foster's office immediately after his death.

"It raises the question [of] a cover-up," Roemer said, adding that the entry into the safe appeared to be "self-serving, to protect documents which could have shed light on either a suicide or homicide."

Repeated calls to the office of Patsy Thomasson and the White House Press Office for comment went unreturned. ■

It's a Safe Bet Foster Had One

By Christopher Ruddy
FOR THE NEW YORK POST
MARCH 10, 1994

WASHINGTON—The White House claimed yesterday that deputy counsel Vincent Foster did not have a safe—but two Post sources said he did and would testify about it if subpoenaed.

The Post reported yesterday that a second set of files was hastily removed from Foster's office safe shortly after his death last July 20.

The report said former White House counsel Bernard Nussbaum,

who removed other files from Foster's office, tried futilely to get the combination to Foster's safe, but another senior official later got it, opened the safe and took the papers.

The papers were turned over to David Kendall, the Clintons' private lawyer, sources told The Post.

White House chief-of-staff Mack McLarty questioned that account, telling reporters: "I don't think there was a safe, as I understand it. To the best of my knowledge, there was not."

But two Post sources reiterated that there was a safe in Foster's office.

The sources—who described a frantic scramble by White House staffers seeking the safe's combination—requested anonymity.

But both said they would be willing to testify if subpoenaed by special Whitewater counsel Robert Fiske.

One source suggested the safe may have been removed after Foster's death.

Bush administration officials said there was a safe in the deputy counsel's office while George Bush was president and John Schmitz was his deputy counsel. ■

Foster's Secret Apartment Hideaway Revealed

By Christopher Ruddy
FOR THE NEW YORK POST
MARCH 11, 1994

Former Deputy White House Counsel Vincent Foster shared a secret apartment with several senior administration officials at the time of his death, The Post has learned.

"It was like a clubhouse, a place to kick back, have a drink, hide out," a White House source told The Post.

The source, who asked not to be identified, said the apartment was known among a tightknit group of Arkansans—including Foster.

The source said the apartment was "not far from the White House. Maybe just across the [Potamac] River [in suburban Virginia]." Other sources said they believed the apartment was in the Crystal City development in suburban Virginia.

The July 20 death has been ruled a suicide, but the Whitewater special prosecutor's office has opened the probe.

The Park Police report on Foster's death does not mention Foster having an apartment, but a police source said the White House told investigators about the apartment—two facts which trouble one leading homicide expert.

"You have to go back immediately to his office and any residence after his death," said Vernon Geberth, a leading national homicide forensic expert.

"Even if this was a suicide you still have to look at all the immediate events leading up to the death."

Geberth also said the failure of the Park Police to interview administration colleagues who shared the apartment and neighbors indicated that they had conducted a "less than thorough investigation."

Foster left the White House at 1 p.m. on the day of his death. His body was found at approximately 6 p.m. The autopsy report said Foster died between 4 and 5 p.m., leaving at least three hours of unaccounted time.

Foster's second apartment has been the source of Washington gossip and speculation for months, and it has grown in significance after a series of articles in The Post challenged the suicide ruling.

A prestigious investment newsletter said Sen. Daniel Moynihan's office indicated that Foster had committed suicide in the undisclosed apartment and that his body was moved to Ft. Marcy Park, in Arlington, Va., several miles away.

Moynihan's office vehemently denied the report in the newsletter put out by Johnson, Smick International, a D.C.-based consulting firm headed by Manuel Johnson, a former Federal Reserve board member.

White House spokesman Dee Dee Myers denied there was any secret apartment and called the newsletter report "a complete fabrication."

The exact location of the apartment was not known. But a source told The Post Foster visited the rental-leasing offices of Lincoln Towers, 850 North Randolph, Ballston, Va., weeks before he died.

The source said Foster was seeking an apartment in the luxury high-rise development and was shown several and filled out "a traffic card"—a questionnaire interested renters are asked to fill out.

The management company at Lincoln Towers refused comment. ∎

Chapter Three

A Special Report on the Fiske Investigation of the Death of Vincent W. Foster Jr.

A Special Report by Christopher Ruddy

As a reporter for The New York Post, I authored a series of articles on the death investigation of Vincent Foster, former deputy White House Counsel.

Since the release of the Fiske report of June 30, 1994 on the Foster death investigation, I have received a number of requests for comment. Herein, lies my detailed analysis. I have chosen to produce this information in this manner since a newspaper format would be inappropriate, and the pending hearings make this information timely and important.

Christopher Ruddy
July 18, 1994

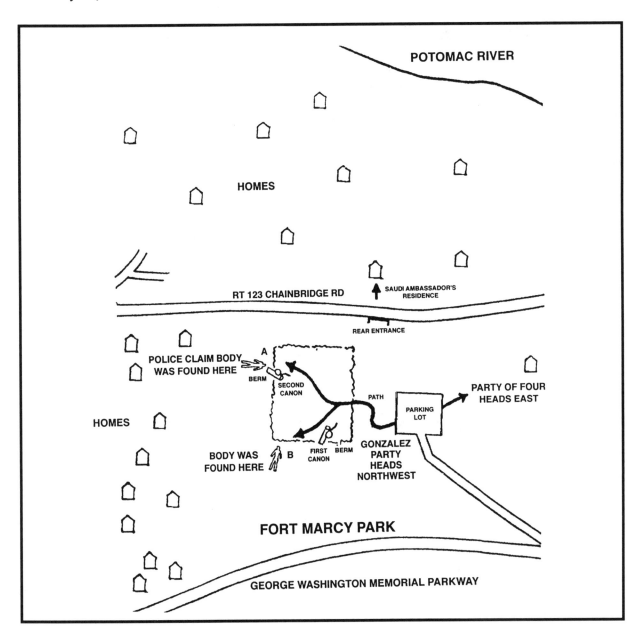

"Stretch your talents, grasp beyond the closest branch, take a risk, stick your neck out, speak your mind, challenge the status quo and conventional wisdom. Do not just accept responsibility. Chase it down."

—Vincent W. Foster Jr., May 8, 1993, Commencement
Address, University of Arkansas Law School

THE COVER UP

When Sgt. George Gonzalez, a lead paramedic, reported for duty to cover for an absent member of the Fairfax County (Va.) Fire & Rescue Station No. 1 on July 20, 1993, little did he know that fate would make him privy to one of the biggest cover-ups in American history.

For just a couple of hours into that sweltering evening, Gonzalez, and at least 20 other officials, would have intimate knowledge of the spot where Vincent Foster's body was found in Fort Marcy Park — and the subsequent knowledge that the Park Police participated in a cover-up by changing the location, in their official reports, by a couple of hundred feet.

What Gonzalez and his fellow officials know could incriminate many of the federal officials involved in investigating the death of Foster, then deputy White House Counsel. There is powerful evidence that these officials obstructed justice by:

■ issuing false reports;

■ lying to the press and public;

■ committing a number of other federal offenses, including intentionally misleading Special Prosecutor Robert Fiske, his staff — and the FBI.

Revelation of this cover-up would also seriously impugn the credibility and legitimacy of the U.S. Park Police, whose forensic and physical evidence constituted a major part of the Special Prosecutor's report on the cause of Foster's death.

Late on a January night six months after Foster's death, Gonzalez detailed the circumstances of his death to this reporter; this unrehearsed testimony remains the most comprehensive, accurate and honest account of what happened at Fort Marcy Park in McLean, Va., following a 911 call reporting a lifeless body in that park.

In reviewing my notes of that interview, I noted that Gonzalez's recall of details was sharp. He remembered, for example, a Mercedes Benz at the park's entrance with hazard-lights blinking — something a police officer who followed him into the park couldn't remember, even though the Fiske report confirms Gonzalez's account. And Gonzalez vividly recalled the two small cars in the parking lot.

And Gonzalez's description of the crime scene — the highlight of my first major article on the event in The New York Post, which is generally acknowledged to have prompted the broadened probe by Special Counsel Robert Fiske into Foster's death — parallels the findings of that probe, as follows:

- Foster's body lay on the side of a hill, face-up.

- He wore suit pants, a dress shirt, but no tie or jacket.

- The top shirt was unbuttoned.

- Blood trickled from the side of his mouth.

- Flies were buzzing around his eyes and orifices.

- A gun was in his right hand.

- Every limb was straight, as if Foster was "ready for the coffin," in Gonzalez's words.

Everything Gonzalez said was in agreement with Fiske's findings — except for two all-important details: the body's location, and who discovered it.

Gonzalez and the Fiske report are in agreement that at approximately 6 p.m. on July 20, 1993, Gonzalez's paramedic unit, consisting of himself and two other rescue workers, arrived at the parking lot of Fort Marcy Park, followed closely by a Park Police Officer. A Fairfax County fire truck carrying three other rescue workers also arrived.

The rescuers quickly separated in the lot: Gonzalez, a Park Police Officer and Todd Hall of Gonzalez's unit, took a looping northeast trail through the park; the four others took the south trail through dense brush and woods, moving away from the fort.

Gonzalez's testimony and the Fiske report are in agreement that Gonzalez moved quickly up the park's northeast trail, a distance of about 200 feet, and entered the main clearing of the historic fort around which the park was established. Here, in the fort, there are two cannons, and Gonzalez came upon the first one and searched to the left of it, while a Park Police Officer and Hall probed on the other side of the clearing.

Here we come to the part where Gonzalez's original account to me differed from what he subsequently told Fiske's staff.

Picture Fort Marcy, a small parcel of land wedged between two east-west thoroughfares: the George Washington Parkway on the south and Chainbridge Road on the north. Close to Chainbridge Road in the middle of the parcel, the wooded land rises to form a roughly squarish plateau measuring a few hundred feet in length and width; this is the original fort, one of a number that President Lincoln authorized as a bulwark against attack of the Capitol during the Civil War.

On two sides of this tiny fort the land falls away sharply, forming steep embankments, sometimes called berms. During the Civil War, numerous cannons sat perched overlooking the berms, giving the defenders maximum effectiveness. Again, only two of these Civil War era cannons remain.

The first sits in the southeast corner of the square closest to the park's parking lot. The other rests in the opposite, northwest corner, hidden by brush and earthern mounds. They are referred to in the Fiske report as, respectively, the "first" and "second" cannon.

In that January interview, Gonzalez told me he moved past the first, south cannon and found nothing. But as he moved "at least 20 feet" along the southern berm that the cannon overlooks, he came upon the body, lying on the berm itself. (This spot is now wildly overgrown because the park's grounds have not been maintained, as the main entrance to the park has been closed since December, 1993).

But the Fiske report locates the body directly in front of the second, west cannon — a couple of hundred feet away.

Moreover, Gonzalez told me that upon discovering the body, he shouted to the two other searchers on his team, who, he said, were still in sight. That precludes them from being by the second, west cannon, which, as indicated above, was not visible from that spot.

Gonzalez told me he moved down the berm and checked Foster for life signs, closely examining his eyes and then his fingers, to see if they were cyanotic (pooling blood). They were. Foster was dead. And Gonzalez emphasized — keep this detail in mind — that it's important never to assume death but to carefully verify it.

The Fiske report has a significantly different version of the discovery, stating that "[Park Police Officer Kevin] Fornshill was first to arrive at the body." And the location is given as approximately ten feet in front of the second, west cannon.

The Fiske report has Gonzalez arriving after the two others had found the body. It then states that *Todd Hall* probed for life signs by checking Foster's pulse. Hall "found none," the report states.

Gonzalez now claims he never saw Hall check the pulse, but just assumed Foster was dead. He, the lead paramedic — who, remember, had emphasized to me the necessity of verification — now says Foster's condition was "obvious."

Gonzalez flip-flopped. Which version is true?

The evidence supports his original contention that the body was down the berm from the first, south cannon, a couple of hundred feet from where the Fiske report had it.

This is not a matter of verbal confusion; Gonzalez backed up his account of the events by drawing a map and sketching out in my notebook several diagrams of the scene. The map details the looping trail from the parking lot to the fort's main clearing, a distance of about 200 feet. He marked the cannon he saw as he moved to the left. He drew his path past the cannon some distance and marked an "x" as the point at which he found the body. He clearly stated the body was *not* in front of the cannon, and remembered such a seemingly insignificant detail as a curve-shaped hollow at the top of the berm, which he drew in my notepad.

Gonzalez drew a picture of what he thought was a little used, brush-filled pathway down the berm where he said Foster's body was lying. He also drew a cross-section of the body on the berm, indicating that the feet of the body were pointed toward the George Washington Memorial Parkway, which runs parallel to the berm.

A Park Police Officer present at Fort Marcy that night, speaking on condition of anonymity, corroborated Gonzalez's general description of the body and its location. He told me the body was well past the first, south cannon, motioning with his hand, as he indicated the body was not near the cannon. He, too, described Foster's feet as pointing toward the parkway.

If Foster's body was lying on the berm by the first, south cannon, it would be on a north-south alignment, with the feet pointing toward the parkway several hundred feet west.

If, on the other hand, it was where the Park Police and Fiske officialy locate it, it would be on an east-west alignment, with the feet pointing north toward woods and an out-of-sight development of homes.

More unrehearsed testimony corroborates Gonzalez's original account and that of the above-cited unnamed Park Police Officer.

Kory Ashford, an EMS technician who arrived before nightfall at 8:45 p.m. to place Foster's body in a body bag, claimed he didn't even remember seeing a cannon — which is consistent with the fact that if Foster's body was where Gonzalez originally had it, the first south cannon would have been off to the side — out of Ashford's direct line of sight — as he made the path from the clearing's entrance tot he body. Were the body where the Fiske report had it, it is difficult imagining Ashford wouldn't have noticed the cannon, since it sits prominently over the berm where the body supposedly was.

The location of the body is disputed only because the Park Police curiously omitted what every death investigation requires: key crime scene photographs.

In my March 7 New York Post article, I noted that the Park Police had failed to take a "crucial crime scene photograph," or series of photos, that would depict the entire crime scene, including shots of the *whole body and its surroundings*, as well as "relationship photos," pictures that would show where the body was relative to such landmarks as a cannon or the deceased's car, which was found in the parking lot.

"It's extremely important in an investigation (to have such photos) because it shows the body's position and other patterns which can never be re-created," said Vernon Geberth, a former lieutenant commander of New York City's homicide division. Geberth, author of the authoritative police text "Practical Homicide Investigation," noted that such indispensable photos, for one thing, allow police to re-create the scene of death and establish if homicide was staged to look like suicide.

That Post article was widely misinterpreted as stating the police had no photographs; this was not the case The Park Police have claimed that these photos were taken, but the film was not properly developed. The Fiske report noted that 35 mm shots were taken — but they were "underexposed."

In the absence of these crucial photos, the police took 13 Polaroid photos, which show only close-up shots of Foster's body, according to a source who has seen them. One of these photos was leaked to ABC News; it showed Foster's right thumb inserted into the trigger guard of a .38 Colt lying next to his thigh. The photo also shows *thick quantities of vegetation* around the gun, hand and body.

This photo, as well as some that were not released, corroborate Gonzalez's original statements of the location of the body and undermine the Fiske report. The path on the berm directly in front of the second, west cannon is *devoid* of vegetation, and the sides of the pathway, where Foster's arm was supposedly reclined, has only small amounts of vegetation and foliage — a condition inconsistent with the photos.

In early April, Fiske's staff excavated for a bullet in the place where they believe Foster's head lay, which was directly in front of the second cannon. But film footage of the berm taken prior to the excavation indicates the path had no real foliage, and little plant growth on either side.

Further, a journalist who visited the site the day after Foster died says the berm does not match with the photo shown on ABC. John Hanchette, a reporter for Gannett Newspapers, was at the fort, together with another reporter, around 1 p.m. the day after Foster's death. Neither had any idea where the body had been discovered so they began a search until they found what they believed to be the site.

"The (Park Police) were sloppy," Hanchette recalled in describing the area of the second, west cannon. "They left rubber (crime scene) gloves all over the place."

Hanchette said he and his colleague further confirmed the spot where they found a "bloodstain in the dirt," which he said had dried. He said the spot was on the slope directly in front of the second, west cannon, just where the police claim Foster's body was found.

Hanchette remembers his colleague putting a stick into the dirt and confirming the color as "red." He assumed the blood to have been Foster's.

Asked if the photo released by ABC News matches the area where the bloodstain was found, Hanchette replied: "No, it does not. I thought it (the photo) was fishy."

Hanchette said the photo was "too verdant" for the area he remembers seeing, where the landscape clearly shows bare ground.

Lieutenant Bill Bianchi of Fairfax Fire & Rescue was present when Kory Ashford put Foster's remains in a body bag. He told me he saw a bloodstain "on the grass."

Yet Hanchette saw a bloodstain on dirt, not on grass.

However, Gonzalez said — and the Polaroids verify — that the body was on top of vegetation.

The truth is that Foster's body was on top of grass on the berm by the first, south cannon. It left a residue of blood on the grass. The Park Police changed the location of the body in their official report. Furthermore, someone re-created a second crime scene by the second, west cannon — complete with bloodstain.

The Park Police report, which has not been released, places the body in still another, third location. According to a source, that report, "Tab 46: The Initial Mobile Crime Lab Report of the Scene of Death," states that Park Police crime-scene technician Peter Simonello places Foster's body approximately 20 feet west of the cannon axle, in an east-west alignment. This contradicts Fiske's report, which said that the body was some 10 feet north in an north-south alignment.

These discrepancies point to an apparent attempt to falsify the facts relating to the body's discovery. Why?

We might look to Watergate — where we still do not know for sure why the original burglary took place. We only know that it happened — and that a massive cover-up ensued to hide the truth.

Similarly here: We don't know yet why they changed the location of Foster's body; we just know that certain parties have falsified the location of Foster's body — and that a concerted effort is being made to hide this fact and other truths.

Gene Wheaton, a former Army Criminal Investigation Division agent with 25 years experience in homicide investigations, suggests the key to understanding the cover-up is to place the events in the context of July 20, 1993.

Wheaton, who spent several weeks in Washington investigating the Foster case, says that the Park Police at Fort Marcy that night recognized the Foster "did not commit suicide." He suggest they may have wanted to move the official location in order to hide the real crime scene. "Maybe Foster's body, neatly arranged in the middle of knee-high brush, looked like a strange location to kill oneself," he speculated.

He also suggested that because the police did not find the bullet that went through Foster's head, they may have feared someone else would find it — a possible explanation for the ruse of the second cannon site, complete with rubber gloves and a bloodstain.

As for Fiske, he attempts to substantiate the second cannon site through a confidential witness identified as "CW" throughout the report. CW testified he found the body directly in front of the second, west cannon.

Wheaton thinks CW's testimony strains credulity. For example, CW claims he stopped at the park because he had to urinate badly — and then walked several hundred yards through the heavily wooded park before doing so, accidentally coming upon the body.

CW claims he then told a park maintenance worker to call 911. (In an off-air interview with radio talk show host G. Gordon Liddy, CW was insistent that he did not see a gun in Foster's hand; according to Fiske's report, he later said he wasn't sure — an equivocation.)

The 911 call came about after CW left the park in his white van, and drove north on the parkway several miles from Fort Marcy to a park maintenance facility. He drove into the lot and encountered two park workers. CW told them he found a body in Fort Marcy and asked them to notify the Park Police. CW then drove off.

One of the park workers, Francis Swan, called 911 and reported the discovery of a body.

A transcript of the 911 call quotes the park worker: "There's ah, ah, have, ah, ah, this is, is a body, this guy (CW) told me was a body laying up there by the last cannon."

The park worker repeated: "The last cannon gun."

Walking from the parking lot, the second, west cannon is the "last cannon." CW gave the wrong location of the body, which was by the first, south cannon.

If Foster's death was not a suicide, CW, by placing the body in the wrong location, would become a prime suspect for the police.

FISKE AND THE TRUTH

The facts about this case are not elusive; over 20 Park Police and Fairfax Fire & Rescue personnel are aware of the location of the body.

Yet the weighty "Report of the Independent Counsel in re Vince Foster, Jr." does not contain the truth. Why?

For one thing, many of those present at Fort Marcy Park that night were probably not even asked about the body's location. And of those that were, perhaps they believed that telling the truth wasn't all that important on this seemingly minor point.

But there was a way that Fiske could have gotten to the truth on this "minor point."

"If they (Fiske's staff) were suspicious, it would amount to putting people under subpoena before a grand jury," said Vernon Geberth as to why the strong possibility of cover-up was not explored. "He (Fiske) accepted the fact it was a suicide from the beginning."

According to Geberth, standard police practice requires that every suicide investigation first be treated as a homicide investigation, until proven otherwise; why did Fiske not look into this alarming departure from standard police procedure?

In a press release accompanying the report, Fiske stated, quite obscurely and without explanation, only that the "investigation into Mr. Foster's death was not a grand jury investigation."

But Geberth, in commenting on the grand jury process, said: "If he (Fiske) was inclined to believe there was a cover-up, you put everyone — medical examiner, emergency medical workers, police, witnesses — under subpoena to get sworn testimony under oath. What doesn't jibe with official reports, you charge those (who gave such false information) with either issuing false reports or perjury."

Fiske did in fact impanel two grand juries: one in Washington, one in Little Rock. *But neither the Washington nor the Little Rock grand juries heard testimony concerning Foster's death nvestigation.*

Fiske, in his report, tells of extensive interviews his office conducted. And a footnote to that section attempts to justify his not using the grand jury in the way Geberth thinks it should have been used: It maintains that if those interviewed gave false answers to his FBI staff, they "would be prosecutable under Title 18, United States Code, Section 1001."

Section 1001 states that intentional lying or misleading of federal investigators, such as those of the FBI, is a prosecutable offense. However, experts say, that code is rarely invoked and carries little practical weight.

"Thousand and one (Section 1001) is very, very, very, very seldom used," noted William F. Roemer, Jr., a 35-year FBI veteran who headed the Bureau's Organized Crime Strike Force in Chicago and is the FBI's highest decorated former agent. "I have never heard it applied. We never observed it.,

"If Fiske had the power (of subpoena) and he didn't use it, something could be inferred from that." Roemer added, "I would certainly use the hammer, because sworn testimony is a powerful lever — to put witnesses before a grand jury with the threat of perjury charges hanging over them."

"On the surface, it appears there could have been a lot of disinformation given (Fiske's investigators)" Wheaton added, agreeing with Roemer on the need for using a grand jury. Wheaton, who has read the Fiske report, suggested that using sworn testimony would lessen the possibility conflicting information might have been fed to the investigators to confuse them.

THE CORNERSTONE OF THE INVESTIGATION

Fiske's conclusions that Foster committed suicide rely heavily on an autopsy performed by the Virginia medical examiner, Dr. James Beyer, shortly after the body was discovered.

Incredibly, 91 pages of Fiske's almost 200-page report are resumes trumpeting the qualifications of Dr. Beyer's medical and pathology team. The actual report on Foster's death is only 58 pages. Even more incredible, the one resume that really counts is absent: that of Beyer himself.

A number of newspapers, including The New York Post, The Washington Times, and several Virginia newspapers, have seriously challenged Beyer's credentials and abilities.

Beyer, 76, has been under fire for two "suicides" he ruled on; in one case, medical evidence suggested the deceased had been attacked, and in the other case someone later actually confessed to killing the deceased.

That confession came about after the family of 21-year-old Tim Easley challenged Beyer's findings that the young man had taken his own life. At his funeral, the family noted and photographed a cut on Easley's hand that Beyer had not noted on the autopsy report.

"The cut on the hand is definitely ante mortem (before death), and I cannot understand how any competent forensic pathologist would miss it," said Dr. Harry Bonnell, who reviewed the case. Bonnell is chief deputy medical examiner of San Diego, Calif. "It is a classic 'defense' wound suffered while trying to avoid (a) knife" attack.

Beyer admitted, during an interview with me, that he saw the cut, and that he failed to note it. He said it was "consistent with a needle mark." (Would, say, a needle mark on Foster's body have been important enough to note?)

Bonnell also challenged Beyer's assertion that Easley could have stabbed himself, noting that the trajectory of the knife was "inconsistent" with a self-inflicted wound.

In the other case — one that has striking parallels to the Foster matter — Beyer ruled that 21-year-old Tommy Burkett's death was "consistent with a suicide."

Burkett, like Foster, was found dead of an apparent gunshot through the mouth. After Burkett's survivors noticed that Beyer had failed to note a "bloody and disfigured ear" on his autopsy, they had the young man's body exhumed for a second autopsy, which was performed by Dr. Erik Mitchell, former chief of pathology for Syracuse, N.Y.

Mitchell found not only trauma to the ear, but other crucial evidence that Beyer had failed to note: a fractured lower jaw, which indicated the deceased may have been beaten first. That second autopsy also revealed the Burkett's lung had not been dissected, as Beyer claimed in his report.

Beyer, in several interviews with me, emphasized that the U.S. Park Police ruled the death of Foster a suicide. He did not.

His autopsy report doesn't say that the wound was self-inflicted; rather the cause of death is simply stated: "Perforating gunshot wound mouth-head."

Nevertheless, Beyer's report is the basis for Fiske's independent pathology report — signed off by four prominent pathologists: "The post -mortem findings demonstrated in this case are typical and characteristic of such findings in deaths due to intentional, self-inflicted intraoral gunshot wounds."

The pathologists determined certain critical findings *based almost exclusively on Beyer's notations:* that there was no sign of a struggle or injury on Foster's body; that the bullet path described by Beyer was accurate in that it passed through Foster's brain stem and out the upper-rear of Foster's head, disabling the brain stem and causing instantaneous death (clinical death followed shortly after) with cardiovascular activity ceasing immediately; and that toxicology tests were accurate, an no drugs had incapacitated Foster. [Fiske's Independent Pathology team stated that Foster's brain stem was disabled by the bullet, causing his heart to cease pumping promptly. but pathologists I consulted indicated the heart, operating on an independent electro-impulse system, does not cease pumping simply because the brain stem is disabled. Disabling the brain stem immediately stops lung activity, as the lungs are controlled by the brain. The heart is oxygen sensitive, and deprived of oxygen, the heart ceases pumping typically anytime from 30 seconds to two minutes after the bullet is fired. In other words, Foster's heart should have pumped more than several times after the shot was fired, causing blood to gush out of the entrance wound onto his mouth, face and shirt. Greater blood loss would have been expected from the exit wound at the rear of the head.]

Two critical issues — the legitimacy of the Park Police's original investigation and the integrity of the autopsy report — seriously undermine the credibility of the Fiske report on Foster's death. Despite the blatant discrepancies pointing to a cover-up, there has been, to date, no indication that Fiske is taking any of the normal steps to resolve the case, such as exhuming the body or using subpoena power.

OTHER PROBLEMS IN FISKE'S FINDINGS

The Fiske report raises, and either casually dismisses or ignores other serious questions:

1. According to the evidence, Foster's head had to have assumed four distinct positions after his supposed instantaneous death.
(The pathologists believe Foster's heart stopped almost immediately, which would explain the lack of visible blood on the front of his body.)

> a) There was a bloodstain on Foster's right cheek, presumably from touching his shirt, which the report said was blood-soaked in the shoulder.

> b) The report said the head was tilted slightly to the right because blood tracks had run from the right side of his mouth and nose.

> c) The report also said because blood had run from the nose to where it was seen on the temple area above the ear — in the sloping position he was perched on the steep berm — the head would have had to be tipped slightly backward.

> d) Finally, the report notes the Polaroid photo shows the head to be looking generally "straight-up."

Fiske accepts the premise that Foster's head was touched by what he believes to be an early observer. Even if this occurred, the evidence of four different head positions is ignored.

2. Why, despite the claim that the investigation was thorough, were not elementary investigative practices followed?

Standard police procedure calls for questioning neighbors, passersby and everyone else in the vicinity of deaths that are even remotely suspicious. Apparently, Fiske's staff failed to do this.

Several weeks ago, The London Telegraph reported that it had canvassed the many homes abutting and near Fort Marcy Park. The newspaper discovered that neither the Park Police nor Fiske's staff had ever conducted a house-to-house canvass. (The Fiske report notes only that it interviewed security personnel at the Saudi ambassador's residence, which is directly across the street from the rear entrance to the park. The Fiske report refers to the rear entrance as a "pedestrian" one, but motorists frequently park on the shoulder of the road by the rear entrance, and then enter the park.)

3.   Why was the gun in Foster's right hand, if, as The Boston Globe reported and the Park Police confirmed, he was left-handed?

4.   Why is evidence that might be conflicting left out of the Fiske report?

For example, Fiske treats CW as credible — yet in his original testimony to G. Gordon Liddy, he stated that he found a wine cooler bottle near the body and that he saw a wine cooler pack in Foster's car.

The Fiske report makes no mention of this seemingly significant testimony, nor does it explain why it was omitted from the list of official evidence.

5.   Why were key observations by the emergency workers left out of their Fairfax official reports?

In a footnote, Fiske states that both Fairfax EMS workers Gonzalez and Richard Arthur doubted the suicide ruling because they believed they saw additional wounds on Foster's head and neck. Yet no mention was made in their Fairfax County reports of such wounds.

(In Gonzalez's discussions with me, he never mentioned the wound, citing primarily the issue of the lack of blood. "Usually a suicide by gunshot is a mess," he told me. "Have you ever had pork brains for breakfast?" he asked rhetorically, in making the point that there should have been a mess of blood and flesh on Foster's face and shirt.)

6.   Why does a lab report attached to Beyer's autopsy findings indicate no drugs were found — yet, an FBI analysis found traces of an anti-depressant, as well as valium (benzodiazepine)?

7.   Did the Park Police ever conduct a search for the bullet?

"Tab 55" of the Park Police report indicates a search was conducted for the bullet and none was found — yet, nine months later when an FBI team searched the area near the second, west cannon where the police claim the body was discovered, 12 contemporary bullets and 58 metal Civil War artifacts were found.

In March 1994, Park Police told Congressman Robert Dornan they conducted a thorough sweep of the area with sophisticated metal detectors. Why was the FBI able to find so much metal in an area the Park Police said they had swept?

8. Why did Fiske's staff accept the fact that a note allegedly written by Foster was found in his office in his briefcase — when the Park Police themselves, as reported in The new York Times, claimed they searched the briefcase and found no such note, seriously challenging the White House account?

9. Why did Foster check out a White House beeper if he did not plan on returning? Who tried to contact him?

The Washington Post reported that it is not standard practice to carry a White House beeper, yet Foster's was found at Fort Marcy.

The Fiske report states that the beeper was found on Foster's person, but an official at Fort Marcy that night had me the beeper was on the passenger car seat.

The Fiske report states that the beeper was found in the off position.

Yet a statement by Major Robert Hines, spokesman for the Park Police, directly contradicts the Fiske report.

"He (Foster hadn't been answering it (his pager)," Major Robert Hines told media critic Reed Irvine in a taped interview on March 9. Hines also admitted that the White House "had been on that day (he died)" trying to contact Foster.

Curiously, the beeper is not listed on the official list of evidence of items handed over by the Park Police to Fiske's FBI staff.

10. How did Foster's glasses "bounce" 13 feet?

The police and Fiske say Foster's bouncing eyeglasses were found 13 feet below Foster's body on the berm. Because gunpowder was found on Foster's glasses, the Fiske report concludes that Foster's eyeglasses "were dislodged (from Foster's head or shirt pocket) by the sudden backward movement of Foster's head when the gun was fired, after which the glasses *bounced down the hill*" (emphasis added) — all of this happened, mind you, while Foster was in a *sitting* position.

A visit to the berm will show that the berm is steep enough to allow the glasses to slide (and remember, they say the site had dense foliage).

* * *

The explanations in the Fiske report still leave the public with a high number of unusual occurrences, or a "preponderance of inconsistencies," as Wheaton calls them. Among them: the gun still in Foster's hand; a gun still not positively identified by his family; a gun with only two bullets (no matching ammunition was found in Foster's home); the lack of visible blood and the unusual, immediate cessation of the heart; the neat position of Foster's body; the lack of powder burns in Foster's mouth; no broken teeth despite the barrel having been placed deep into his mouth; the fact that Foster, a devoted family man, made no arrangements for his family, or even said a good-bye; the fact that no one heard a shot; the fact Foster had chosen a park he had never visited before; and the fact no soil was found on his clothes or shoes.

OBSTRUCTION OF JUSTICE

Fiske pledged that, in addition to examining the issue of the alleged suicide, he was going to look into the serious charge that the White House had kept the FBI out of the investigation and had assigned it instead to the far less qualified and less-experienced Park Police.

Fiske, who curiously did not use the grand jury for this critical part of his investigation, devotes just a little over a half page in explanation. While admitting that the circumstances of Foster's death could have come under FBI jurisdiction, he explained that since "a preliminary inquiry by the FBI ... failed to indicate any criminal activity, the FBI's inquiry into this matter was closed."

But in a two-page letter sent to me by Judge William Sessions, the former Director of the FBI, Sessions wrote that the FBI was kept off as the lead investigative agency because of a "power struggle (between) the FBI and the Department of Justice" at the time of his firing.

"The decision about the investigative role of the FBI in the Foster death was therefore compromised from the beginning," Sessions wrote, noting specifically that Foster's death tool place "the day after my termination" and on the same day Judge Louis Freeh had been "proposed" as Director. Freeh took office several weeks later.

The day of Sessions' firing, The Wall Street Journal ran a lead editorial called "What's the Rush?" It began: "So the gang that pulled the great ravel-office caper is now hell-bent on firing the head of the FBI." The paper thought it strange that Sessions had to be fired — when he had offered to resign once a replacement had been confirmed by the Senate.

Fiske doesn't seem to have turned up any obstruction issues, yet there seems to be no explanation for charges, such as those published in The Washington Times, that "Mr. Sessions' statement corresponds with those of current and former FBI and Justice Department officials who told The Times of interference by the White House and Justice Department in the Bureau's work in the Foster investigation."

Similarly, ex-FBI notable William Roemer said that "(Attorney General Janet) Reno and Clinton had undue influence. The FBI would normally be finding reasons to get involved in a high-profile case" like this.

And former Army CID agent Gene Wheaton concurs, describing the Park Police as being the "most pliable of federal law enforcement agencies."

When I asked the Park Police for a breakdown of their approximately 35 death investigations that were suicides, homicides or natural deaths, they could not provide it.

CONCLUSION

As soon as Fiske accepted the Park Police testimony at face value, the results of his report became inevitable. He chose not to use his subpoena power. He accepted the autopsy report without question.

With the same type of acceptance, Fiske would have us also believe that "there is no evidence that any issues related to Whitewater, Madison Guaranty or Capital Management Services played any part in (Foster's) suicide." Perhaps he is right: Whitewater had no connection.

Perhaps he is wrong.

* * *

In the end, we the ordinary citizens, are left at Vincent Foster's transitory resting place, Fort Marcy Park.

Fort Marcy brings us to the period of civil war when rivers of blood were spilled so that we might preserve our unique experiment in "government, of, by and for the people" — one where justice would reign supreme and no man, no group of men, no matter how powerful or highly placed, would be above the law.

How paradoxical, how utterly tragic, then, if that tiny square of earth should now stand as a symbol of violation of that noble ideal.

Chapter Four

Did Vincent Foster Fire the Gun?

A Special Report by Christopher Ruddy

Did Vincent Foster Fire the Gun

By Christopher Ruddy

One of the most crucial pieces of evidence in a homicide investigation is the weapon.

In a case of suspected suicide by gunshot, police are trained to examine carefully the gun's location, ownership, gun powder residues and other forensic details which can help investigators prove either suicide or murder.

Despite two federal probes into the death of Vincent W. Foster, then deputy White House counsel, questions challenging the official ruling of suicide continue to be asked.

Many of these questions relate to the gun, an antique 1913 .38 Colt Army service revolver found in Foster's hand when his body was discovered lying in Fort Marcy Park, Virginia, on July 20, 1993.

Some of the issues raised by critics of the official suicide ruling include:

- The fact that no fingerprints were found on the gun, even though the gun was found in his hand;

- The unusual location of the gun, still loosely clasped in Foster's right hand, when typically the gun is found away from the person;

- The position of the gun in Foster's right hand, especially since Foster was left-handed;*

- The uncertainty that Foster even owned the gun, and the family's failure to positively identify the weapon;

- The Park Police's failure to find the fired round at the Park, and the fact no matching ammunition was found in Foster's homes;

- The strange location of gun powder residues found on Foster's hands; and

- The fact no visible blood or blowback material was seen on the gun.

When U.S. Park Police homicide investigators came upon Foster's body, they had clear warning signs that should normally arouse suspicions of a possible homicide; among the most evident was the

---

* Foster was in fact right-handed. This was misreported in the *Boston Globe* in March 1994.

neat appearance of Foster's body, the small amount of blood, and perhaps most compelling, the fact the gun was still in Foster's hand.

"Under ordinary circumstances, after the firing, the gun is away from the person," Vernon Geberth explained. Geberth is the author of the authoritative text, "Practical Homicide Investigation."

Experts say the gun, due to normal reflex actions of the body, can literally be thrown many feet away from the body.

But in Foster's case, his right hand was found loosely clasped over the top frame of the gun with his right thumb sticking out of the trigger guard. The police have surmised that Foster placed the Colt's 4-inch barrel into his mouth, and depressed the trigger, using his thumb.

The Park Police have claimed that the gun's position led them to believe, in fact, that Foster had committed suicide.

No matter what conclusions police draw from the crime scene, standard police practice calls for treating all suicide investigations first as homicides, until the facts prove differently.

A number of tell-tale signs reveal that the Park Police did not follow this standard procedure. The Park Police, for example, did not conduct a routine door-to-door canvass of homes around the park. Nor did they preserve crucial crime scene evidence such as Foster's beeper and personal effects -- all of which were returned to the White House within 24 hours of Foster's death.

But the most telling sign that the police were not prepared to follow police procedure was their treatment of the Colt revolver.

On August 10, the Park Police officially ruled Foster's death a suicide. Amazingly, they did not send the Colt for any testing until August 12, two days *after* they ruled on the death.

For six months the Park Police, through their spokesman, had said the gun went through ballistics tests at the D.C. Metropolitan Police ballistics labs. That was later found to be untrue. The Park Police had sent the gun neither to the D.C. police nor the premier gun-testing labs at the FBI. Instead, the Park Police forwarded the Colt to the Bureau of Alcohol Tobacco and Firearms for examination.

Technicians at the ATF labs in Rockville, Maryland, checked the gun for operability and powder residue patterns. The gun worked, and the ATF said the residue patterns were consistent with powder patterns found in photographs of Foster's body.

ATF spokesman Jack Killoran described the Colt as an "old,

reconstituted gun that had cannibalized pieces of other guns used to replace parts of it."

The ATF found two serial numbers on the gun, which were traceable to a Seattle, Washington, purchase in 1913.

According to Larry Wilson, considered the foremost expert on antique Colt pistols, the hybrid Colt found in Foster's hand fits the general description of a "drop gun."

A drop gun is typically an old, untraceable gun, left at a crime scene by a criminal who wishes to confuse police investigators.

Wilson said a careful review of markings on the Colt could help determine for sure if the gun is indeed a drop gun. To date, the ATF has not released its full report on the Colt.

Questions about Foster's actual ownership of the gun persist because the family cannot positively identify the gun.

The Park Police have stated that Foster's wife Lisa could not identify the gun as having been Foster's.

Photographs of the Colt were shown to Foster's sister, Sharon Foster Bowman, who resides in Little Rock.

Bowman told a Little Rock architect that the Colt "looked like a gun she had seen in her father's collection," noting a "wavelike" design on the hand grips.

The Fiske report states that Vincent Foster had removed guns from his father's home in 1991, after the father's death.

The Fiske report also states that "Lisa Foster stated that the gun looked similar" to a gun brought from Arkansas to the Foster's Washington home. On the night of Foster's death, Lisa found a gun in a closet, but it appeared different than the one she remembered bringing to Washington.

A footnote in the Fiske report states "Foster's children did not recognize the gun as one they had seen in their home."

Even though gun owners typically buy bullets by the box, no matching ammunition of the Colt's .38 caliber type was found in either of the Foster's homes, according to the Fiske report. (The antique Colt was found with only one bullet in its cylinder. A shell casing from a fired bullet was also found.)

In the absence of family identification, forensic evidence should help investigators link the weapon to the victim.

For example, the fired bullet could be matched through ballistics tests with the one remaining bullet in the cylinder. This test could, at least, prove that the Colt was not just a drop gun, but had been the source of the head wounds.

But the Park Police never found the bullet. Originally the Park Police spokesman, Major Robert Hines, said that the Park Police had not conducted a search for the bullet. That story was revised by the Park Police, who claimed they had conducted a thorough metal detector sweep of the area around Foster's body.

Curiously, Fiske's investigators conducted a similar sweep in the area the Park Police claim as the location of the body's discovery. Fiske's team found 70 pieces of metal in the same area, including 12 modern-day bullets, as well as some Civil War relics.

Without a comparative ballistics test, Fiske ties the gun to Foster by the fact that the FBI labs found DNA material from either blood or saliva at the tip of the Colt's barrel. The DNA material was consistent with Foster's DNA type, which is shared by only 6 percent of all Caucasian males.

Fiske's Independent Pathology Team deemed the DNA evidence as "strongly supportive evidence that associates the weapon with the deceased."

While the DNA evidence does not prove Foster fired the gun, it strengthens the case that the gun was the source of the shot fired through his head.

The DNA is not conclusive. If one accepts, for example, that Foster's death was staged to look like a suicide, the Colt could have been placed in Foster's mouth by another person. If one believes that officials have engaged in a cover-up as to the circumstances of Foster's death, a smattering of blood taken from a blood sample of Foster's could have been placed on the gun's barrel.

Other powerful forensic evidence indicates Foster did not fire the gun.

When a gun is fired, a blast of heat and powder is released through openings in the gun. In the case of the Colt, the FBI found the blast is released at the end of the gun barrel, called the muzzle, and from the front cylinder gap, a small space between the gun's barrel and the cylinder which holds the bullet.

The autopsy notes that gunpowder residue was found on Foster's right hand, in the area of the thumb, right index finger, and the web area between the index finger and the thumb. Powder residue was also found on the left hand, in the vicinity of the index finger.

Based on these residues, Fiske's pathology team concluded that

"Mr. Foster's index fingers were in the vicinity of the cylinder gap when the weapon was fired."

But one noted expert on guns and their interaction with the human body says that such powder residues are inconsistent with Foster having fired the Colt himself.

"(Foster's grip) is an extremely unnatural and awkward grasp, totally inconsistent with what both experience and logic show us to expect of a suicidal person with a gun in their hand, directed at themselves," writes Massad Ayoob, after analyzing the forensic evidence relating to Foster.

Ayoob, Executive Director of the Lethal Force Institute, is considered one of the nation's most prominent experts on such matters. Ayoob was an expert witness for many law enforcement agencies, as well as the States of California and Michigan.

Ayoob also suggests that Foster's grip, based on powder residues, also violates the actions of a "deliberate suicide," someone who really wants to kill oneself and who would employ the "strongest possible grasp on the gun."

Ayoob says normally a person who commits suicide by firing the gun using their thumb, as was allegedly the case with Foster, would normally place their remaining four fingers on the back of the gun's handgrip.

But powder residues on Foster's hand indicates Foster would have placed his thumb on the trigger, and then placed his four remaining fingers over the gun's cylinder, grasping above the gun's frame.

This not only would be unnatural, according to Ayoob, but dangerous since Foster's large hands would have put his smallest finger in harm's way of the gun's hammer.

Also, Foster's fingers could well have interfered with the cylinder's action.

The Park Police have suggested that Foster used his strong left-hand to grasp the gun's grip tightly, while using the right thumb to fire the gun. Ayoob accepts this possibility, but says that gunpowder residues on the left hand do not support this hypothesis.

Gun powder residues on the left hand indicate the hand was not on the hand grip. As the Pathologists' report notes, the left index finger, hence, Foster's left hand, was in the vicinity of the front cylinder gap.

If Foster didn't fire the gun, who did?

Ayoob's Analysis of Gun Power Residues

Using a Colt .38 revolver similar in size and dimensions as the one found in Foster's hands, Ayoob explains how gun powder residues don't support the conclusion Foster fired the Colt. The various models use a hand similar in size to Foster's.

PHOTO ONE:

This was the exemplar gun used, a Colt Official Police .38 Special revolver with four-inch barrel, produced circa 1955. It is fundamentally identical to the Army Special. Colt introduced the Army Special in 1908, and changed its name to Official Police in 1928.

PHOTO TWO:

This Colt Official Police duplicates the dimensions of a four-inch barrel Colt Army Special. Barrel length (measurement includes portion that is screwed into frame) is four inches. Overall length of the revolver is approximately nine and one quarter inches.

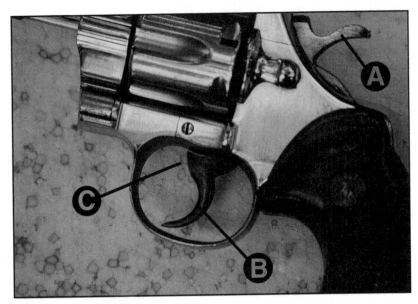

PHOTO THREE:

Hammer **(A)** and trigger **(B)** of the exemplar Colt .38 in regular position, that is, at rest, and uncocked. The parts in question would return to these positions after a shot had been fired and pressure had been released from the trigger.

The "notch" on the upper portion of the trigger, above where the trigger finger would be, is visible in this photo **(C)**.

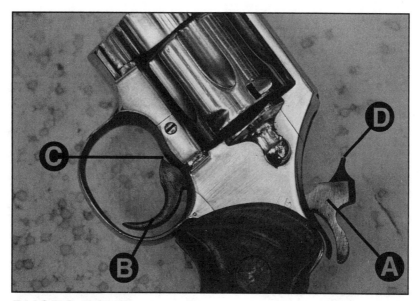

PHOTO FOUR:

Exemplar revolver in its cocked, or single action, position. Hammer **(A)** has been manually drawn to the rear until locking in the cocked position. The trigger **(B)** had also been drawn back. Now a very short, light-pressure movement is all that is required to be exerted to the rear on the trigger to fire the cocked revolver.

Note that the notch at the upper portion of the trigger **(C)** is clearly visible here. When the gun is fired and pressure is released from the tripper, the trigger will rebound forward. This gap or notch at top of trigger can now close on either a fold of skin or glove material, etc.

Note also the hammer mounted firing pin **(D)**. Anything that gets between it and the frame of the revolver will keep the firing pin from reaching the primer (or "cap") of the cartridge, and will cause the gun to fail to fire.

PHOTO FIVE:

How the Army Special or Official Police mechanism would appear at the moment of firing. Conventional grasp is shown. As trigger is moved all the way to the back, the hammer is released and snaps forward under pressure of the mainspring. Driven by the hammer it is mounted to, the firing pin's tip strikes the primer of the cartridge, firing the round.

Note that at this instant the trigger, at its maximum rearward position, has also maximally opened the notch at the top of the trigger, where thumb of the deceased was allegedly caught.

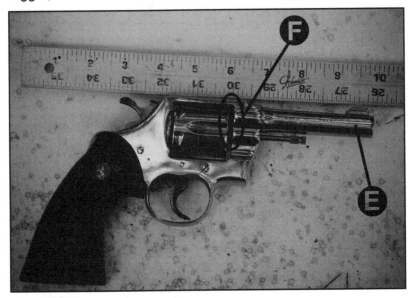

PHOTO SIX:

Exemplar Colt .38 revolver is seen from the right. The two points where sufficient gas, unburnt powder, and other debris to create the gunshot residue (GSR) described in this case can escape the gun, are the muzzle of the gun **(E)** and the gap between the barrel and cylinder. The gap is at the point marked **F**.

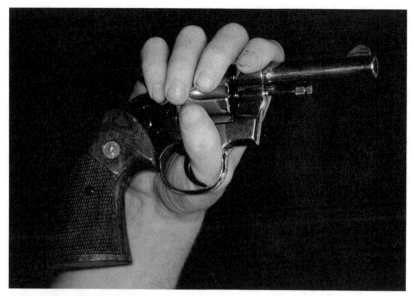

PHOTO SEVEN:

The alleged manner Foster fired the gun: As the hypothetical question was described to me over the phone by Chris Ruddy, this is the sort of grasp that would be necessary for GSR (powder burns) to be on the edge of the right index finger with the thumb on the trigger.

The exemplar revolver is shown with the action at rest, that is, with the trigger forward in the double-action position. A long and heavy rearward pressure on the trigger would have to be exerted to fire with this grasp in double-action mode.

There are several things that would contraindicate a hypothesis that the deceased shot himself with such a revolver from such a grasp:

I. As the trigger is drawn toward the back of the trigger guard for the long, heavy firing stroke, the hammer is rising and ultimately falling, and the cylinder is rotating. A grasp firm enough to stabilize the gun would probably bind the cylinder, preventing rotation and "jamming" the revolver, that is, preventing it from firing.

II. Downward pressure of the thumb, i.e., toward the heel of the hand, is required to fire the gun from this grasp. This is an unnatural movement of the thumb, and the thumb is mechanically disadvantaged in attempting to perform it. It would be extremely awkward, and highly unlikely, that even a physically strong man would attempt to fire double action with this grasp.

III. It is also very easy for the little finger of a large man's hand to block the necessary rise of the hammer during a double-action pull of the trigger. This would again "jam" the gun, preventing it from firing.

The hand in this and subsequent photos is that of a six-foot-three adult male with proportional size hands.

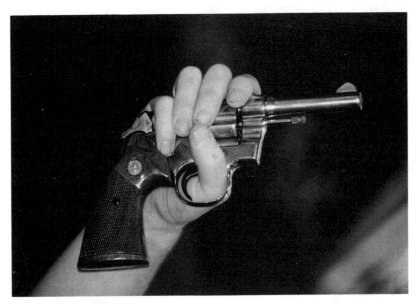

PHOTO EIGHT:

If the hammer of the revolver had been cocked into single action mode, then it would have been possible (but still extremely awkward) to grasp the gun as shown and activate the trigger with the thumb.

However, note that with this grasp, with the index finger positioned near the barrel cylinder gap to account for GSR (powder burns) found on that digit, we now see that the proportional-size right hand on a six-foot-three male has now positioned the little finger between the hammer and its firing pin, and the frame.

If the trigger was pulled from here, the little finger would be pinched painfully (possibly with enough force to leave a postmortem artifact if death took place a few moments later), and the gun would not have fired with that pull of the trigger since the little finger would have blocked hammer and firing pin, "jamming" the Colt .38.

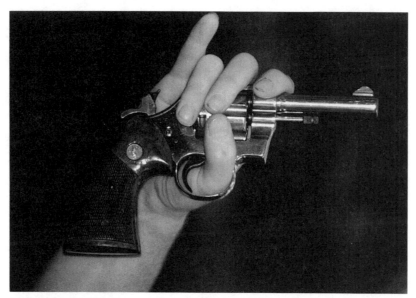

PHOTO NINE:

To fire in the hypothesized position with the fingers grasping around the cylinder, something like the grasp seen in this photo would be necessary. The little finger would have to be extended outward in this "tea with the queen" gesture. This does not in any way alleviate the awkwardness of the unnatural movement of pressing the thumb essentially downward to force the trigger back and make the gun fire. It is also inconsistent with the forcible grip one would expect of a right-handed man about to commit suicide with the right hand.

It is my understanding from the information furnished me that there was no fingerprint evidence from the dominant left hand on the gun . . . that there was no gunshot residue on the dominant left hand . . . and that the gun barrel was inserted sufficiently far into the mouth of the deceased that there was not room for a large hand to stabilize the gun barrel outside the mouth.

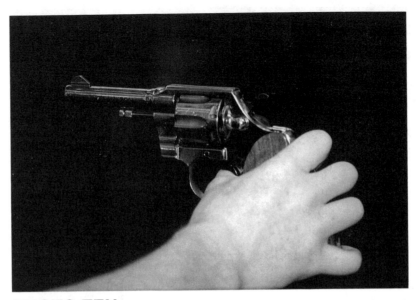

PHOTO TEN:

If the suicidal subject chooses not to simply hold the gun normally and either bent the wrist or point the gun upward to achieve an angle for an intraoral gunshot wound, this is the most likely grasp.

Wrist remains relatively straight. Gun is turned in the hand, with the thumb replacing the index finger on the trigger and the fingers curled around the back of the grip frame instead of around the front.

This allows the most naturally solid hold and most natural leverage with which to fire the gun using the thumb instead of the normal trigger finger. It has been documented on numerous occasions of individuals shooting themselves. By contrast, I have never seen or heard of a case where the handgun was grasped as in photos Seven through Nine.

The photo shows the hammer of the unloaded revolver as it, and the trigger, would be oriented in the instant that a shot was fired from this position. As the trigger rebounded forward when the muscles of the hand went slack, the trigger is positioned to catch the flesh of the thumb in the trigger notch as described.

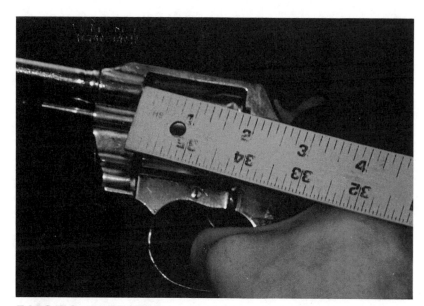

PHOTO ELEVEN:

With the gun held in the typical position in which a suicidal subject would use the thumb to activate the trigger, we can see that the index finger of the right hand (subject is six-foot-three, proportional hand size) is nearly four inches from the barrel/cylinder gap.

This is the grasp seen in Photo Ten.

Chapter Five

The Investigation:
Reports from the
Pittsburgh Tribune-Review

Opposites Join Call for Starr to Probe Foster's Death

By Christopher Ruddy
FOR THE PITTSBURGH
TRIBUNE-REVIEW
DECEMBER 19, 1994

Calling speculation about the death of Vincent W. Foster Jr. "a cancer on the American political process," Rep. Barney Frank, D-Mass., has joined such political opposites as the Rev. Jerry Falwell in demanding that the new independent counsel come to his own conclusion about Foster's death.

Late last week, Frank, a staunch liberal who is known as a maverick, revealed the contents of a letter he wrote to Kenneth Starr, the independent counsel in the Whitewater case. He urged Starr to decide "whether you are accepting Mr. Fiske's conclusions, or whether you believe that those conclusions should not stand without further investigation."

Robert Fiske was the original special counsel in the case. Though a Republican, his findings and methodology were widely criticized in conservative quarters, and he was eventually replaced by a three-judge panel.

Last June, Fiske concluded that Foster, the deputy White House counsel who was closely linked with the Whitewater case, had died by his own hand in Fort Marcy Park, Arlington, Va.

Frank's letter and his public pronouncements increase the chances for a new investigation into the matter. That is surely unwelcome news for the White House, which has publicly requested that Starr not review matters Fiske had investigated.

FRANK'S ABOUT-FACE

Frank, who, along with virtually all other Democrats in Washington, had accepted the Fiske report as final, did an about-face during an appearance on the TV show "Nightline."

"I've changed my position now," Frank told the show's host, Ted Koppel. "I am going to insist that Mr. Starr tell us: Does he think Mr. Fiske was right or not, because I think it is a cancer in the American political process to allow this kind of absolutely irresponsible suggestion that somebody murdered Vince Foster to go ahead."

Both on that show and in an interview with the *Tribune-Review* Friday, Frank emphasized that he believes Foster's death was a suicide. But, he said "a continued vicious, despicable effort . . . by a whole lot of people on the right wing" requires that Starr make his own conclusion.

He added that even a thorough investigation by Starr might not satisfy the "extremist fringe."

Frank stressed both in his interview and in his letter to Starr that Fiske's conclusions are not binding on Starr. In the letter, he reminded the new special counsel that under the Independent Counsel Law signed by President Clinton in June, "it is within your mandate to reopen any aspect" of the Fiske investigation, including the Foster conclusions.

FISKE REPORT CRITICIZED

Fiske's report on Foster's death has been widely criticized for his failure to employ a grand jury investigation and not putting potentially biased witnesses under oath. He empaneled grand juries for all aspects of his Whitewater probe except the investigation into Foster's death.

On his "Nightline" appearance, Frank was critical of the Rev. Falwell and *New York Times* columnist William Safire for their pronouncements in the Foster case.

Falwell has been promoting a videotape called *The Clinton Chronicles*, more commonly known as the "Falwell tape," which intimates that Foster was murdered. It cites a number of unusual circumstances about the death, such as the finding of the gun in the deceased's right hand when he was left-handed.

Attempts to reach Falwell for comment were unsuccessful.

The Clinton Chronicles is not put out by any organization controlled by Falwell. It is produced by Citizens for Honest Government, a non-profit group in California. The group recently published a book version of the tape in which a chapter is devoted to questions about Foster's death.

Frank's criticism of Safire centered around the influential columnist's use of the phrase "mysterious circumstances of (Foster's) death."

FBI SUPPORT

But critics of the Fiske report have received support among some members of FBI and other law-enforcement circles.

"Something can be inferred" from Fiske's failure to invoke his power of subpoena, said William F. Roemer Jr., former head of the FBI's Organized Crime Force, who handled bureau investigations for 35 years.

Roemer, the bureau's most-decorated living former agent, said an investigation employing a grand jury could have easily produced a totally different result.

Similarly, Thomas Scorza,

Continued on next page

Continued from page 63

professor of legal ethics at the University of Chicago and a former federal prosecutor, said he found Fiske's failure to use a grand jury "real odd."

"You don't have a grand jury on just one aspect of the Whitewater case. It should be taking evidence on every aspect," he said.

Scorza also pointed out that employing a grand jury greatly reduces the chances of a cover-up, since the threat of perjury charges puts people "at risk for spinning and fibbing and not telling the whole truth."

NO EXPLANATION

Fiske, in his report, offered no explanation as to why he chose not to employ a grand jury in the investigation.

Roderick Lankler, a New York City criminal-defense attorney who served as Fiske's deputy and who led the Foster investigation, said it would be "inappropriate" to comment on that matter because of the continuing investigation.

Starr has said he is reviewing the entire Fiske investigation. He has not announced which aspects, if any, of the investigation he may reopen.

A petition attached to *The Clinton Chronicles* book asked readers to demand of Starr and their elected representatives that "the independent counsel reopen the investigation into the death of . . . Foster and convene a full grand jury investigation into the death. . . ." ■

Mystery Grows over Foster Death Scene

By Christopher Ruddy
FOR THE PITTSBURGH
TRIBUNE-REVIEW
JANUARY 12, 1995

Evidence is mounting that a U.S. Park Police report misidentified where White House Deputy Counsel Vincent W. Foster Jr.'s body was found in Fort Marcy Park in Virginia.

The official version places the body more than 200 feet from the spot several observers—including the only trained medical professional on the scene the evening of July 20, 1993—have identified as the actual site.

In an interview last weekend, the Virginia medical examiner who viewed the death scene the night Foster died said the body was found near what is known as the park's first, or southwest, cannon.

The statement contradicts the conclusions of Robert Fiske, the former independent counsel who investigated Foster's death as part of the Whitewater probe.

Medical Examiner Dr. Donald Haut said that when he entered the open area of the fort just off the parking lot, "The only cannon I took notice of was off to the left."

The cannon cited by Haut is commonly referred to as the "first cannon."

Haut said Foster's body was on the western embankment, an area over which the first cannon pointed. He said the body was about 10 to 20 yards past the cannon—matching the earlier account of Sgt. George Gonzalez, the lead paramedic for Fairfax County Fire and Rescue.

Gonzalez said in a published interview last year that in response to a 911 call he was the first to come upon Foster's body. He said he found the body lying on a slope "at least 20 feet" past the only cannon he saw.

The cannon, according to Gonzalez, overlooked the fort's western embankment.

Gonzalez drew a map and several diagrams to support his claim. Previously, Haut had drawn a similar map for Accuracy in Media.

But Park Police reported the body was discovered just 10 feet in front of a second cannon's barrel, an area located deep in the northeast corner of the park. However, one Park Police officer, speaking on condition of anonymity, corroborated Gonzalez's earlier account of the body's location.

Ironically, Gonzalez has since changed his story and now supports official police claims that the body was found in front of the second, or northeast, cannon.

Last year, Gonzalez indicated he was unaware of the existence of a second cannon in the park.

But the discrepancies don't end there.

Haut also challenges another aspect of the official findings.

According to the Fiske report: "At approximately 7:40 p.m., Dr. Donald Haut, the Fairfax County medical examiner, arrived at the scene to examine the body. At that point, Foster's body was rolled over and those present observed a large pool of blood located on the ground where Foster's head had been. Haut observed a large exit wound in the back of the skull."

"There was not a hell of a lot of blood on the ground," said Haut. "Most of it had congealed on the back of his head."

Haut said he was never interviewed by Fiske's investigators, though the June 30, 1994, report by the special counsel stated Foster's death had been "fully and thoroughly investigated."

In the end, Fiske concluded the White House aide committed suicide at the spot where police claim they found the body.

TWO CANNONS, TWO SITES

The distinctly different terrain surrounding the two cannons leaves little room for confusion by witnesses.

The second, or northeast cannon, where police claim the body was found, is hidden deep in the corner of the park by earthen mounds and brush. The area around the cannon is accessible by several hilly paths.

Many park visitors "don't know about this (second) cannon," said Robert Reeves, who frequents the park and is perhaps more familiar with the area than any other outside observer.

Although Reeves was never interviewed by Fiske's investigators or Park Police, his knowledge might have proven invaluable to them.

Had authorities spoken to Reeves, they might have avoided a nine-month search for the driver of a white van who first alerted a park maintenance employee about Foster's body.

Through talk show host G. Gordon Liddy, Fiske's investigators eventually were able to identify the man and obtain his services as a confidential witness.

Reeves said he frequently sees the man driving his company-owned white van through the park and would have been able to immediately identify him by name to police.

Reeves, a retired career soldier who served in the Korean and Vietnam wars, has frequented the park since the late 1960s, considering it his second home. He began to take a proprietary interest when "someone left a total mess"

following a Fourth of July celebration.

At the time of Foster's death, Reeves was recuperating from surgery. He returned to his regular park rounds about a week after the body was found. He was told by park service employees "that Mr. Foster died by the area of the first cannon."

Sometime later, Reeves recalled, he came upon a television crew filming near the second (northeast) cannon. When he informed them that they must be filming at the wrong location, a crew member showed him a Park Police diagram indicating the site was the correct one.

Bewildered, Reeves turned to Tyrone Brown, the park's maintenance supervisor, and asked him if the site to which the TV crew had been directed was the right one. Brown said no, Reeves recalled.

"It was by the first cannon," Reeves said Brown told him.

In a telephone interview, Brown confirmed that he told Reeves the body was found near the first cannon. He said he was never interviewed by Park Police or officials from Fiske's office.

"The area that I believe he died at used to have a cannon . . . the first cannon," Brown said.

The cannon was removed by the park service in recent months and a metal anchor marks the location. Though Brown was not at Fort Marcy the night Foster died, he said he had been told by officials of the location.

NO PHOTOS

Homicide experts say all questions about the location of the body could be answered by the crime scene photos. Unfortunately, there are no such photos.

Last year, FBI sources said no "crucial crime scene" or series of photos showing the whole body and its surroundings or the body's relationship with landmarks were found.

The Fiske investigation acknow-

ledged that key crime scene photos taken on 35mm film had been "underexposed" in Park Police labs. Police investigators were left with only 13 Polaroid close-ups of Foster's body. These have not been released by investigators.

Congressional sources and the Fiske report said the Polaroids show dense foliage around the body. Directly in front of the second, or northeast, cannon, the officially designated site, is a dirt path devoid of vegetation.

Reeves said it has been that way since he began visiting the park. The area, he said, is well-shaded from sunlight and has less vegetation than other parts of the park.

Fairfax County paramedic Gonzalez originally said he found the body lying in "knee-high brush." Lt. Bill Bianchi of Fairfax Fire and Rescue recalled seeing a bloodstain "on the grass" after Foster's body had been removed. Those descriptions, consistent with the Fiske report, are more evidence that the body was located near the first cannon, with its heavy vegetation, rather than on the dirt path, as police now claim.

SHOES, CLOTHING

Another problem with the officially designated death site is the FBI's finding, through a microscopic analysis, that there was an absence of soil on Foster's shoes and clothing. Had Foster walked from his car in the parking lot to either of the two cannons, he would have traversed 400 to 600 feet of wooded area with exposed soil.

Fiske's report speculates that the 200-pound Foster sat down on exposed root stems in the dirt path before firing the weapon. The report also states that Foster was found face up, meaning his entire backside was in contact with the soil.

"It's impossible," said Reeves, when told about this. For Foster to reach that northeast spot with clean shoes, he said, "either he was carried or he crawled."

Continued on next page

Continued from page 65

In April, Fiske's investigators conducted an exhaustive search at the second cannon site for bone fragments from Foster's head and for a missing bullet. Neither was found.

The absence of soil, bone fragments and the bullet are just some of the loose ends in the official findings on Foster's death.

Among other unresolved issues are:
■ No fingerprints were found on the gun.
■ Blood tracks indicated Foster's head had moved several times after death.
■ There was no note mentioning suicide, nor did the methodical Foster make final arrangements.

CRITICISM

Law enforcement experts have criticized Fiske for accepting the Park Police version of events without question and for his failure to employ his Washington, D.C.-based grand jury to look into the Foster case.

Thomas Scorza, professor of legal ethics at the University of Chicago and a former federal prosecutor, described Fiske's failure to use a grand jury as "real odd," and said such a measure would have reduced the chance of a cover-up. He said the threat of perjury charges puts people "at risk for spinning and fibbing and not telling the whole truth."

Scorza said it would be natural for a grand jury to examine the issue of the body's location, but stressed the importance of putting under oath everyone at the park that night and others knowledgeable about the scene. Between 20 and 30 people have direct knowledge about the location of the body at Fort Marcy Park.

Fiske's investigators and the Park Police also have come under criticism from law enforcement experts for failing to engage in the most rudimentary of police procedures. One such basic procedure they ignored was a sweep of park regulars like Reeves and the many homes around Fort Marcy Park.

"Canvassing is a time-consuming investigative procedure that is part of just old-fashioned spade work," said Vernon Geberth, a former lieutenant commander in New York City's homicide division and author of the standard police text on homicide investigations, "Practical Homicide Investigation."

"The process involves not just interviewing neighbors and park regulars like Reeves, but coming back at the exact time of the death even months later to locate anyone who might have knowledge of the case," he said.

Geberth was surprised that no one ever conducted a canvass, which he considers absolutely "basic" in such a case. ■

Editor's note: *Though Haut said he had not been interviewed by Fiske, documents released after this report showed that FBI investigators had, in fact, interviewed him.*

Forensic Experts Doubt Foster Suicide Finding

By Christopher Ruddy
FOR THE PITTSBURGH
TRIBUNE-REVIEW
JANUARY 18, 1995

Leading forensic and firearms experts have cast serious doubts on the official suicide ruling in the case of Deputy White House Counsel Vincent W. Foster Jr. in July 1993—strongly suggesting that Foster might not have fired the gun that is said to have killed him.

Based on the FBI's analysis of the death weapon's residue-emitting characteristics and on such residue found on Foster's hands, the experts concluded that if Foster actually fired the fatal shot, he would have had to have held the gun in a highly unusual position, with both hands on the forward part of the gun—neither hand being on the grip when it was fired.

Earlier this month, Independent Counsel Kenneth Starr convened a grand jury to review the Foster case. The Associated Press reported that Starr has been reviewing the "thoroughness and competence" of the investigation into Foster's death in a top-to-bottom review of the case. Such a review, according to law enforcement experts, should touch upon discrepancies involving the apparent suicide weapon.

Foster's body was found in Fort Marcy Park, Arlington, Va., with an antique 1913 Colt Army service revolver in his right hand. He had supposedly placed the gun's 4-inch barrel deep into his mouth and fired it using his right thumb and hand.

Massad Ayoob, who heads the Lethal Force Institute, noted that holding a gun with neither hand on the hand-grip constitutes "an extremely unnatural and awkward grasp totally inconsistent with what both experience and logic show us to expect of a suicidal person."

Ayoob, who has served as a forensic expert for the states of California and Michigan, said that gunpowder residue found on Foster's hands indicate he wasn't a "deliberate suicide."

"It looks like someone faked it," he said, suggesting that a gun may have been placed in Foster's hands and then fired, in order to leave "gunpowder residue on his hands." This, he said, might lead relatively inexperienced investigators to conclude Foster had fired the gun himself.

Ayoob conducted a detailed analysis of the shooting using a replica of the death weapon wielded by someone with hands comparable in size to those of the 6-foot-4 inch tall Foster.

Ayoob concluded that not only would the gun have been difficult to fire according to the scenario suggested, but that Foster's hands would have interfered with the gun's operation. With his hands pressed across the cylinder he would have inhibited its necessary rotation, and the fourth and fifth finger of his right hand would have likely prevented the hammer from striking the bullet.

Dr. Richard Mason, who specializes in firearms forensics and is the pathologist for Santa Cruz, California, is similarly bothered by the unusual residue deposits on the deceased's fingers. It "doesn't make any sense," he said. "I wonder if they came to erroneous conclusions."

UNUSUAL MARKS

Challenges to the findings on the part of experts have been prompted largely by their readings of the report of Special Counsel Robert Fiske and FBI findings in the case.

When the apparent death weapon was fired in the FBI laboratory, soot and smoke-blast were emitted from the gap between the front of the cylinder (referred to as the front cylinder gap) and the gun's frame, as well as from the muzzle.

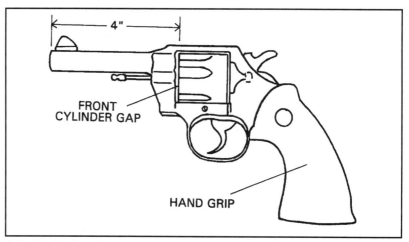

Colt .38 Service Revolver found in Foster's hand. The FBI lab found that gun powder is discharged from the barrel's muzzle and the front cylinder gap when the gun is fired. Residues on Foster's index fingers indicated both hands were in the vicinity of the front cylinder gap when the gun was fired.

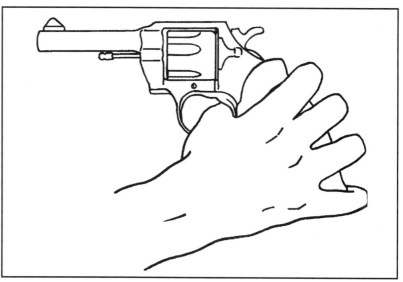

A typical suicide will fire a gun in this manner. The fingers grasp the gun's handgrip to stabilize the gun, and allow for a natural pull on the trigger.

Because the muzzle was deep in Foster's mouth, any visible residue found on his hands could not have come from the muzzle but rather from the front cylinder gap.

This was established in an "Independent Pathology Report" that was appended to the Fiske Report of June 30, 1994.

"With the barrel of the revolver placed into the decedent's mouth," the report noted, "the only source of such gunpowder would be the gap between the cylinder and the frame of the weapon. Multiple test firings of the revolver in the FBI laboratory

conclusively demonstrated that gun powder residue escapes from its cylinder gap."

According to the autopsy and its photographs, a heavy deposit of soot was found on Foster's right index finger and the web area between it and his right thumb. A similar deposit was found on his left index finger on the side nearest his thumb.

Because of these deposits, Fiske's pathologist panel was prompted to conclude "that Mr. Foster's index fingers were in the vicinity of the cylinder gap when the weapon was

Continued on next page

Continued from page 67

fired"—meaning that neither hand could have been on the weapon's grip.

Similarly, an FBI analysis attached to the Fiske report states that soot marks on Foster's right hand are consistent with circumstances "when this area of the right hand is positioned near the front of the cylinder . . ."

This indicates that as Foster pulled the trigger with his right thumb, his four right fingers, which are usually placed on the back of the hand-grip to stabilize the revolver, were instead inexplicably wrapped around the cylinder and the top of the gun frame.

A visible line of gunpowder residue was also found on Foster's left index finger, indicating that the left hand was also near, or on, the gun's cylinder.

Strangely, the FBI laboratory analysis omitted any mention of the heavy soot found on Foster's left index finger.

FOUL PLAY

Dr. Vincent Di Maio, medical examiner for San Antonio, Texas, is regarded as one of the nation's leading firearms forensic experts. He pointed out how difficult it would be to fire a weapon with both hands forward of the grip and trigger. "It doesn't make any sense," he said. "It would be such an awkward way, you'd have to contort yourself to do this. It is not consistent with suicide."

Another expert who questioned the suicide scenario was Dr. Martin Fachler, who headed the U.S. Army's Wound Ballistics Laboratory in San Francisco for 10 years before retiring. "It's almost impossible to pull the trigger without some counter-pressure," he said, referring to the need to brace the weapon against the force of the trigger pull.

Fachler said he could "not see how any person left to their own devices" would use the weapon in

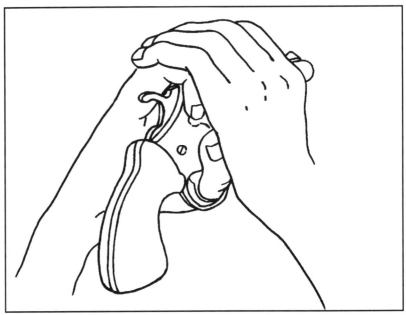

Based on residue deposits, Foster's hands were likely configured in a manner similar to this. Neither hand is on the hand grip, making the gun unstable. The palms of the hands, pressed against the cylinder of the gun, would interfere with the cylinder's rotation. Foster's large hands would likely have put his two smallest fingers in jeopardy of the gun's hammer when it was fired. The thumb would have to depress the trigger in an unnatural movement.

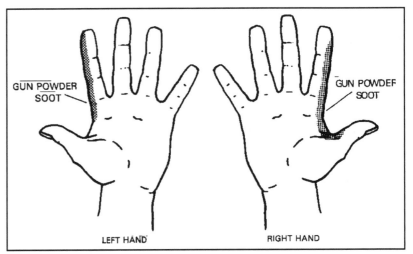

Foster was found with heavy powder burns on the index fingers of his left and right hands. The FBI lab concluded both of Foster's hands were in the vicinity of the front cylinder gap when the gun was fired.

this manner. "If you ask is this an indication of foul play, I have to say, yeah, maybe it is."

Still another expert with similar misgivings was Robert Taubert, 33-year veteran of the FBI who conducted extensive research on weapons as a firearms expert with the FBI Swat Team. "I never heard of anyone gripping a gun like that," he said.

Taubert reviewed both the FBI analysis and the review of that analysis conducted by Ayoob. In re-enacting the shooting as it supposedly occurred, he noted that he "had a lot of problems actuating the trigger" because of "the awkwardness of the grip."

Taubert concluded that the both-hands-up-front scenario was "completely unnatural." Only someone who had never seen a gun fired, even in a movie, might try to do it that way, he said.

Vincent Scalice was yet another expert who found the gun residues, and the grip they implied, "not consistent with suicide."

Scalice spent 35 years with the New York City Police Department, where he worked major homicide cases as a crime-scene expert. He was a consultant to the House Committee on Assasinations, which debunked a number of theories relating to the death of John F. Kennedy.

All four forensic pathologists who served on Fiske's team were contacted about the gunpowder residue discrepancies. Calls were referred to the Independent Counsel's office or went unreturned.

POLICE FAULTED

Scalice faulted the U.S. Park Police, who handled the Foster investigation, for not following standard police procedure, which is to treat such a death as a homicide until established otherwise.

The Park Police, an agency that investigates only around 35 deaths per year, has asserted that it followed such a procedure.

But Scalice said the testing of the gun and powder residue on the hands would be "critical" aspects of a homicide investigation. He added

that, had he worked on a case involving the type of residues in the Foster death, he would have assumed that there was a "strong possibility that it was an actual homicide."

The Park Police did not send the gun for testing until two days after they officially declared Foster's death a suicide, on August 10, 1993.

Homicide experts say that killers are becoming increasingly sophisticated in staging suicides, including the deliberate firing of a gun to leave powder marks on a victim's hand to fool investigators.

"In some parts of the country, it's become a license to kill," said Vernon Geberth.

Geberth, author of the author-itative police text "Practical Homicide Investigation," said experienced investigators look for "inconsistencies" with what one would expect from a typical suicide.

In the Foster case, not only does the powder residue not fit, but there are a number of other inconsistencies involving the gun alone: no fingerprints were found on it; the fired bullet was never found; the gun could not be positively identified by Foster's family; no matching ammunition was found for the gun in either of the victim's two homes; and no visible blood or blow-back material was found on the gun.

LAPSES CITED

The then-Republican minority report to the Senate Banking Committee report on its Whitewater hearings noted "variances" in Park Police procedure, assigning blame for them on "interference by staff from the White House."

Among the lapses in police procedure noted in that minority report and by law enforcement experts:

■ Failure to retain as evidence Foster's beeper, turning it over to the White House within hours of his death. (A Park Police officer said in an interview in January 1994 that Foster's beeper was found in his car, but the Fiske report stated it was found on his body.)

■ Similar failure to retain other critical evidence such as personal belongings and papers found at Fort Marcy Park the day after his death, returning this evidence to the White House.

■ Failure to conduct a standard canvass of residences surrounding Fort Marcy Park and failure to interview individuals who frequent the park.

■ Failure to immediately secure Foster's office as a crime scene.

■ Delay in testing of the gun, and failure to conduct a vacuum sweep of Foster's clothing and shoes. ■

Foster's Death Site Strongly Disputed

By Christopher Ruddy
FOR THE PITTSBURGH
TRIBUNE-REVIEW
JANUARY 25, 1995

As irregularities in the investigations of the death of Deputy White House Counsel Vincent W. Foster Jr. come to light, doubts are mounting over the location where U.S. Park Police say his body was found in Fort Marcy Park, Arlington, VA., July 20, 1993.

A park maintenance worker who was asked by a passerby who discovered the body to call 911 has disputed key parts of the 911 transcript. That document shows the worker locating the body at what was subsequently designated the official location in the report of Special Counsel Robert Fiske.

The worker, Francis Swann, who never saw the body, was asked to make the call by a man driving a white utility van.

According to official reports, Swann and a co-worker were standing in the parking lot of a parkway maintenance facility, which is some two miles from the park, when the unidentified man drove up asking that they report the body to authorities. Neither of the men noted the license plates of the van.

Swann says he immediately went to a pay phone and made two calls. First he called Fairfax County's 911 service. Then he made a call to U.S. Park Police.

DISPUTED 911

In two separate interviews conducted with Swann, he reviewed transcripts of those calls. Both times he categorically denied statements attributed to him in the first of the two calls, to Fairfax's 911, that quote him as identifying the location of the body near a "last cannon."

Following is an excerpt from the Fairfax 911 transcript:

Swann: There's ah, have ah, this is a body, this guy told me was body laying up there by the last cannon.

911 Dispatcher: Last what?

Swann: Huh?

911 Dispatcher: There's a body laying near what?

Swann: There's a man laying up there by the last cannon gun.

Dispatcher: Cannon.

Swann: Yes, they have cannon up there. Those big guns.

In both interviews, Swann emphatically denied that he could have used the term "last cannon," since he believed there was but one cannon in the park.

"He (the van's driver) said *a cannon*. There's nothing but one cannon up there," Swann insisted. "Just one."

There were actually two cannons in the park but Swann was unaware of the second one, which is in the northeast corner of the park obscured by brush and hilly terrain. Several of the officials who came to the park the evening of Foster's death were also unaware of that second cannon.

Swann was unaware the official Park Police report located the body in front of that second or "last" cannon.

Swann is a veteran Park Service employee whose tenure dates back to the Kennedy administration, when he was assigned to maintenance at the White House. His recollection is important because it contradicts the police claim that Foster's body was lying 10 feet directly in front of the second cannon.

A growing number of observers dispute that. They position the body some 200 feet away in the general area of the "first" cannon—the only one most visitors to the park are aware of.

According to Fairfax County Police spokesman Warren Carmichael, the 911 tape in question was transcribed and given to the Fiske investigators. A copy of that transcript shows it was transcribed March 9, 1994, shortly after Fiske began his probe. An FBI report says agents took possession of the original tape April 21.

KEY WORD MISSING

In a Park Police memo of July 20, 1993, labeled "Sequence of calls and transmissions," a Park Police sergeant notes that at 6:03 p.m., minutes after Swann called Fairfax 911, a park service employee (Swann) called the Park Police "to say a white contractor-type van pulled into Turkey Run (maintenance facility) and a w/m (white male) advised them of a dead body by the last cannon in Fort Marcy."

But a careful read of the Park Police 911 transcript of Swann's call to that department shows that Swann, consistent with his recollection, had never referred to any "last" cannon, nor had he referred to a cannon in any way that indicated there was more than one.

This is the pertinent part of the police transcript:

Swann: He (the van driver) said you got a dead body down there at the Fort Marcys [sic].

Police: OK, did he (the van driver) say it was in the parking lot or back in the woods or —

Swann: He said it was back up

there by the cannon.

Swann's recollection is also buttressed by the statements of numerous Fairfax County rescue workers interviewed by Fiske's staff. None of them said that, when they arrived at Fort Marcy Park that night, they were directed to a "last" or "second" cannon—even though the 911 dispatch reads to that effect today.

For example, paramedic George Gonzalez states in his deposition to Senate Banking Committee investigators, "the report (911 dispatch) was that it (the body) was at the first cannon, excuse me, the report was that it was at a cannon."

Another rescue worker, Richard Arthur, said he reviewed the 911 dispatch after he returned to his McLean fire house. He described as "weird" the fact that the 911 dispatch didn't identify a specific cannon, and gave no other details as to the body's placement.

CW CHANGES LOCATION

Swann's statements draw the focus back on the van driver, an enigmatic figure whom the Fiske report names as the first person to discover the body. In that report, he is designated "CW," or confidential witness.

CW is also important because, if foul play was involved, police normally treat the person discovering the body as a suspect.

In the Fiske report, CW is key to corroborating the Park Police's placement of Foster's body directly in front of the "second" cannon's barrel.

But since the report was issued, on June 30, 1994, CW has been saying something quite different.

"I'm going to say this," said CW in a taped telephone interview conducted by Reed Irvine, "I still recall him (Foster) being to the right of the cannon, not directly in front of it." Irvine is chairman of the conservative media watchdog group Accuracy in Media.

On the tape, which was made available to the Tribune-Review,

CW was insistent that the body was not where the police said it was. Though not disputing it was near the "second" cannon, he said it was on a slope close to a maple tree to the right of the cannon.

CW told Irvine that FBI agents had persuaded him that the body was found on a slope directly in front of the cannon.

CW altered his account when confronted by Irvine with the fact that the area directly in front of the second cannon is a well-worn dirt path—inconsistent with the heavy foliage under and around Foster's body, as originally described by CW and other witnesses, and recorded on Polaroid photos.

An FBI analysis found no soil on Foster's shoes and clothing, strongly supporting the conclusion that the body could not have been in front of the second cannon, where the soil is almost totally exposed and bare.

Greg Howland, a National Park Service historian for Fort Marcy Park, said that the dirt path on which Foster's body was said to have been found has for years been bare, shaded ground, etched by root.

Howland's description of that dirt path is consistent with a Gannett news report, as well as the statements of other knowledgeable persons. In his FBI statement, CW denies the dirt path even existed.

CW AND FBI

CW first came forward as a critical witness to G. Gordon Liddy, who hosts a popular syndicated radio talk show on Virginia's WJFK. Liddy says he first verified CW's credibility as best he could and then helped publicize CW's version of events.

CW told Liddy that when he discovered the body there was no gun in either hand. Officials say the body was found with a 1913 Colt revolver in the right hand.

Liddy said that once he began publicizing CW's account, FBI agents contacted him, asking to meet his witness. Liddy said that he

persuaded CW—who intimated Foster had been murdered and that there was a high-level cover-up—to meet with the agents.

Apparently Fiske's staff was anxious to accept CW's account at face value, because the FBI agents working under Fiske never bothered to have park worker Swann, who made the 911 call, positively identify CW.

According to Swann, FBI agents never showed him a photo or a lineup to ensure they had the right witness, even though it was Swann who placed the critical 911 call.

Swann said he believed his co-worker, Chuck Stough, had identified CW. Stough refused to comment on this, stating, "I was informed by the FBI I can't disclose information."

In an FBI report of Stough's identification of CW, he states only that CW "could have been him."

The identification by Fiske's staff of CW appears to have been something of an afterthought—since CW was presented to Stough June 22, 1994, just a week before the report was released and over two months after Fiske had been treating CW as a credible witness.

A number of homicide experts said the failure of Fiske's investigators to have the identification made by Swann, who was the actual 911 caller, was an indicator of a less-than-thorough investigation.

"It's not enough," said Vernon Geberth, referring to the FBI's interviewing of Swann's co-worker rather than him.

"It's only common sense, you don't interview just one when two were present," he said, explaining that "you want the witness, the person who called 911 and said there was a dead body, to ID the man. It's basic police work."

Geberth, a former lieutenant commander in the New York City Police Department who investigated over 5,000 homicides, stressed that "it's important to take each point to *Continued on next page*"

Continued on next page

Continued from page 71

its ultimate conclusion. Apparently it wasn't done here."

Experts say that a positive identification and thorough investigation of CW should have been routine—especially since his testimony had major discrepancies.

CW BADGERED?

CW himself has taken exception to his testimony as represented in the Fiske report—but only after the report had been out a few weeks and evidence began to emerge that he, like the Park Police, seemed to have given the wrong location of the body.

"He was absolutely furious" when he read the Fiske report, said Liddy about CW.

And, although he says his life is in danger, CW has embarked on a bold, if anonymous, campaign to criticize the report, appearing on radio, television and before print journalists.

CW has said that FBI agents badgered him to change his testimony, asking him as many as 25 times if the gun he failed to see might have been hidden by foliage. The Fiske report states, "CW has further stated that the natural foliage in the area made it difficult to see Foster's hands."

Liddy, a former FBI special agent and supervisor whose program draws a large number of Washington law enforcement professionals, feels that the FBI investigation was far below bureau standards. Liddy, based on information he obtained from sources in the bureau, has been critical of the assigning of senior FBI agents Larry Monroe and William Colombell to the case, pointing out that neither has substantive homicide experience.

Susan Lloyd, a spokeswoman for the FBI's Washington field office, provided no information on either agent's homicide experience, stating that because both agents had been assigned to the Independent Counsel's office, she could not comment.

FISKE FAULTED

Dismissing any suggestion that Colombell might have mishandled a witness, a ranking FBI source added: "He is known as a crackerjack investigator, a very successful field agent and field supervisor." He said Colombell has had a "distinguished" career, and approximately five years ago had been promoted from the Baltimore office to Headquarters.

Several former and current FBI sources rejected criticism of the two agents, both of whom are highly regarded, suggesting that higher bureau officials erred in allowing Fiske's staff to put the agents before the Senate Banking Committee, where the agents drew several conclusions about Foster's death. These conclusions, sources said, should have been offered by Fiske or his attorneys.

"It gave the appearance we were covering these things up," said another bureau source, who explained that bureau policy is not to draw conclusions but to pass evidence to prosecutors.

Sources criticized Fiske and his staff for not giving the agents subpoena power and for not having them thoroughly investigate such essential matters as Foster's whereabouts on the day he died, possible motives for his suicide, and trace evidence on his clothing.

As for CW's complaints about badgering, several FBI sources expressed doubts, since he had gone through his witness statement line by line with the agents involved, and then signed it.

Irvine, who had championed CW, now finds his credibility "very dubious," and wonders, as do several experienced investigators, if CW is merely an innocent bystander or has deliberately been misleading federal investigators, for example, on the body's location.

Irvine questions CW's account on how he found Foster's body. CW said he entered the park to urinate and came upon the body—but to get to that site, he would have had to walk through 600 feet of heavily wooded park where there are many areas of seclusion. ■

Park Police Challenged In Journalist's Death Case

By Christopher Ruddy
FOR THE PITTSBURGH
TRIBUNE-REVIEW
MARCH 5, 1995

WASHINGTON—Robert Corley Groves was at the top of his profession in December 1988.

On an overcast afternoon, the 29-year-old lead investigative news producer of ABC's "World News Tonight" was sitting in his BMW at a red light with a fellow ABC News producer, Emma Gilbey, preparing to turn east onto Independence Avenue here.

As the car entered the intersection to make the turn, the BMW was suddenly broadsided on the driver's side by a U.S. Park Police car that, according to court records, "ran the red light at an excessive rate of speed."

Gilbey was knocked unconscious as the collision hurled the BMW across the intersection. She suffered multiple injuries but survived. Groves did not.

Taken by helicopter to Washington Hospital Center, Groves was pronounced dead after an hour of feverish efforts to resuscitate him.

The Park Police's handling of the case involving the death of this award-winning news producer is another example of an investigation by this law enforcement agency that raises questions about its commitment to uncovering the facts. Court records, eyewitnesses and other evidence seriously challenge the Park Police version of events in this auto accident.

In the Groves case, Park Police have been accused by various individuals of:

■ possible fabrication of a witness statement.

■ withholding statements from a critical witness.

■ altering a crime scene diagram.

■ possible destruction of accident-scene evidence.

■ attempting to smear the victim's character.

The Park Police are already under intense scrutiny by Independent Counsel Kenneth Starr, who is probing several aspects of the death of White House Deputy Counsel Vincent W. Foster Jr.

Evidence indicates Park Police may have inaccurately represented—by a couple of hundred feet—the site where Foster's body was discovered in a McLean, Va., park. Former special counsel Robert Fiske concluded Foster committed suicide at the location noted in Park Police reports. Several witnesses have challenged that story.

Park Police were given exclusive jurisdiction over the Foster investigation shortly after his body was found in Fort Marcy Park, a road-side facility across the Potomac from Washington.

In addition to policing parks, the 600-member force—which describes itself as an urban police department—has broad jurisdiction over traffic and criminal investigations in and around the District of Columbia.

This federal police service, established in 1791, is one of the nation's oldest law enforcement bodies and is an agency of the Department of the Interior.

CIVIL CASE

As a result of court records and eyewitness testimony, questions surfaced about the official explanations of the circumstances of Groves' death.

Despite the Park Police denial of any wrong doing, three years later in a civil case brought by the Groves family, a federal judge sided with the plaintiffs.

Groves was killed Dec. 8, 1988, at 2:30 p.m., when his BMW was struck by a Park Police cruiser driven by officer Ronald Robinson.

The collision, according to court records, "virtually demolished the left side of Mr. Groves' car."

Robinson, a three-year member of the force, said that just before the collision, as he approached the intersection, he slowed his vehicle.

When he spotted a truck running a red light, he carefully started across the intersection with flashing lights and his manual siren in operation before colliding with the BMW, he said. (The driver of the truck was never apprehended.)

But this version of events has been challenged by several eyewitnesses.

Shortly after their son's death, Asa and Una Groves of Miami hired the Washington law firm of Williams and Connolly to sue the Park Police in federal court.

On Oct. 28, 1991 after nearly three years of legal wrangling, U.S. District Court Judge Stanley Sporkin awarded the Groves family $1.25 million in damages. Sporkin ruled that Robinson had "recklessly and carelessly entered the intersection without exercising due regard to those travelers who were abiding by the law . . ."

According to the court's findings, "Instead of stopping at the red light to verify the intersection was clear before he entered it against the traffic signals, officer Robinson accelerated into the intersection . . . at an excessive rate of speed."

ACCIDENT DIAGRAM

The journalist's parents believe
Continued on next page

Continued from page 73

the approach to the Park Police investigation was largely motivated by some agency officials' fears that the matter might be turned over to a grand jury, resulting in Robinson possibly being charged with vehicular homicide.

Court depositions indicated the police were aware of the possibility that their fellow officer could wind up before a grand jury.

For example, there was the issue of the critical accident-scene diagram—which was eventually altered by Park Police. It originally showed skid marks indicating Robinson was traveling at an excessive speed, perhaps as fast as 60 mph.

A Washington, D.C. police detective reviewing the case testified that "90 percent" of such cases go before grand juries, "especially (those) involving a police officer."

The Groves case was never presented to a grand jury because, according to the detective, the Park Police were able "to straighten their story" concerning the skid marks.

How this change came about was explained in a deposition by Park Police officer Roxanne Brown.

"I was contacted by the Metropolitan Police Department traffic-homicide detective, who said that he had been contacted by the U.S. attorney, who stated that there was an error in the accident diagram for officer Robinson's case, and that if the error was not corrected, that officer Robinson was going to have been placed in front of the grand jury," Brown said.

The D.C. detective claimed the diagram was recognized as being erroneous when it was reviewed at the U.S. Attorney's Office because it showed a curved line of skid marks.

He said skid marks don't curve and that the absence of "scuff marks"—marks made by tires after a collision—for the police car supported the conclusion that the diagram was in error.

Subsequently, a Park Police accident reconstruction expert made a new diagram after visiting the scene. Park Police said the revamped drawing was "a more correct accident diagram."

In the revised diagram, part of what had been designated as skid marks was redesignated as scuff marks. In addition, the length of the skid marks was reduced. These facts together transformed what was originally 59 feet of skid marks to 35 feet, in effect reducing Robinson's rate of speed.

One prominent expert on accident reconstruction is surprised that the diagram could be determined to be in error by someone not present at the scene, as was the case here.

Frank Laine, retired commanding officer of New York City's police Accident Investigation Squad, said it would "not be unusual" for a diagram to show skid marks curving, or to show an absence of scuff marks for a car after a collision—countering police claims that they could tell the original diagram was in error just by looking at it.

At the time of the accident, the Park Police Criminal Investigation Branch was headed by Maj. Robert Hines.

Hines, a respected figure in the Washington law enforcement community, is now spokesman for the department.

Hines recalled the accident, but said he was aware only that the case had been fully investigated. Court records indicate Hines had little if any involvement in the case. He was unaware of any controversy involving the case.

He said the decision of whether to present the case to a grand jury rested solely in the hands of the U.S. Attorney's Office.

The officer who drew the original diagram stated that his first rendering of "the length of (the) skids showed his speed to be in excess of 60 mph."

The officer, in his deposition, said

he agreed his original rendering of the accident scene was wrong and that the new diagram was more accurate. He also acknowledged that he was trained to know the difference between skid marks and scuff marks and that the original markings were witnessed by two other officers on the scene.

The police also claimed that a videotape of the scene as well as "crush data"—which indicate the speed of a vehicle by the damage done—supported the revised diagram.

But the plaintiffs charge the video did not clearly establish the length of the marks and was therefore ineffectual in that regard. A reconstruction expert hired by police stated that crush data showed the impact to be 40 mph—still in excess of the 30 mph speed limit.

SAW POLICE CAR

The testimony of eyewitness Michele Mirabelli was one of a number of things that sharply challenged the police version of events.

As Mirabelli recalled in a court deposition, she was stopped for a red light at the intersection where the collision took place when she saw in her rear-view mirror a police car approaching the intersection "very fast." At the same time, she noticed the BMW slowly moving into the intersection to make a left turn.

She recalled thinking: "Oh, my God! (That police car's) not going to stop!" Mirabelli said she did not remember seeing flashing lights or hearing a siren. She said the cruiser did not slow down before entering the intersection.

Judge Sporkin found that Robinson had slowed approaching the intersection. Nonetheless, the judge noted, "The Park Police Review Board found that the accident was preventable," adding that Robinson "failed to use a continuous siren as he should have . . . ."

Robinson claimed to have activated both the flashing lights

and his manual siren as he entered the intersection. The manual siren would only work as long as the officer depressed a button on his dashboard.

After the collision, the Park Police officer exited his car while radioing for emergency assistance. He then began directing traffic. Mirabelli was surprised that he did not come to the assistance of the injured passengers, who were being helped by two U.S. Park Service employees and some passers-by.

Mirabelli said she pulled alongside a Park Police officer and told him she was a witness. She said she was simply told to "move on"—as, she claimed, other witnesses were told to do.

"No," she protested to the officer, according to the deposition, "I witnessed this accident."

She added that the officer "didn't look very concerned."

Encouraged by another passer-by, Mirabelli pulled to one side and stayed at the scene.

Soon she was greeted by a plainclothes Park Police officer, who, after establishing that she had been driving in the same direction as Robinson, said, "The light was green, wasn't it?"

"Sir, the light was not green, it was red," she replied to the question. After the accident, she was contacted by the Park Police and met with a detective in the presence of her husband, a Washington attorney.

At that interview, Mirabelli stuck by her account. The detective countered her assertions by stating that the passenger Gilbey said she heard the siren and saw the lights. Mirabelli's husband then asked the detective to leave, upset by the detective's manner.

During the interview, the detective made a reference to one of the Groves' attorneys at Williams and Connolly. Mirabelli's husband noted this and later contacted the

Robert Groves

firm. He learned that his wife's name had not been provided to the firm by the Park Police.

STATEMENT FABRICATED

As for Gilbey's alleged remarks that she saw flashing lights and heard a siren, she claims police fabricated her statement.

While still awaiting emergency treatment at the hospital after the accident, she said she was approached by a Park Police officer who insisted she give a statement.

"Here I was on a stretcher," she recalled, "I just had a concussion and knew nothing that was going on." She said she gave in to the officer's demands and provided a statement.

The officer, in his deposition, claimed he asked Gilbey if she was able to give a statement. He said she told him that she was and he took a brief statement, but left after she told him she was experiencing some discomfort.

When she later learned she was quoted as saying the cruiser had flashing lights and siren on, she denied it.

Other witnesses corroborated Gilbey's recollection.

In his court deposition, lead Park Police investigator Robert Johnson said although Robinson told him at the scene that he had activated his

emergency lights and siren, he was prompted to broach the subject again because "witnesses told me that they didn't see any emergency red lights or any emergency visibar being activated."

Johnson said upon his arrival at the scene, he turned off the emergency lights on Robinson's car, but he said it was unclear when those lights were turned on.

In court, the Park Police version of events rested largely on an account given by the two U.S. Park Service employees who were in the area and eventually assisted the injured motorists. The park workers said they saw a white van cross the intersection, apparently the vehicle that Robinson said ran the red light. The park service workers said the van was followed by a police car that stopped before entering the intersection. However, they said they heard no siren.

The two park service workers later received letters of commendation from the Park Police for their assistance to the victims at the scene.

CHARACTER 'SMEARED'

Asa Groves feels that Park Police defamed his son.

"They did a lot to smear Bobby," he said.

He said tests indicated a controlled substance in the bloodstream of his son, who had no history of drug or alcohol abuse. It was later revealed that these residues were from drugs administered by medical personnel after the accident.

Another "drug" trace was consistent with Groves having had a hamburger with poppy seeds at a Burger King that afternoon.

"When they tried to say Bobby had drugs in his blood, it was just unbelievable, shocking," said Gilbey, who added she was horrified

Continued on next page

Continued from page 75

that her colleague would be victimized that way. "He was the straightest guy I ever knew."

Despite the focus on Groves' potential drug use, the Park Police never checked Robinson's blood for drugs and alcohol. Maj. Hines acknowledged that "normally, in a case like this, a driver would have their blood checked," adding that it was probably not done in this case because Robinson is a police officer. Robinson is still a member of the Park Police's investigative unit.

The park police also brought out that Groves was driving with a suspended license. The action had been taken in response to unpaid parking tickets by the State of Florida during Groves' relocation from Miami to Washington.

At the trial, Judge Sporkin found that "Robert Groves was truly an extraordinary young man who accomplished much in his 29 years."

STILL DISTURBED

Six years after the accident, Michelle Gillen, a former colleague of Groves is still disturbed by Park Police behavior in the case.

She recalls visiting the accident scene two days after the crash, where she was horrified to find parts of a police car, including lights and wires, mixed in with beer cans and other trash in a nearby garbage can.

Standard police procedure is to preserve all such evidence— something that Park Police claim to have done in this case, despite Gillen's discovery.

Gene Wheaton, an expert on police procedure and a former U.S. Army criminal investigator, thinks that at the very least, the Park Police handling of the Groves case was "sloppy."

Wheaton, who has reviewed two other homicide cases involving the organization, suggested that Park Police standards may be lower because they are "highly political," having patrons in high places, and have thereby escaped much media and public scrutiny.

Gillen suggested that, while many of Groves' colleagues were obviously aware of the irregularities surrounding his death, many felt that their professional code prevented them from working on the case of someone to whom they were close.

Groves' parents have donated much of their court award to Miami University's Robert Corley Groves Memorial Television Broadcast Studio.

"Regardless of circumstances, and even with lights and siren on, a police officer can't just blast through an intersection," said accident expert Laine. "Due caution must be used and the safety of innocent civilians always come first." ∎

Groves: 'A Consummate Journalist'

By Christopher Ruddy
FOR THE PITTSBURGH
TRIBUNE-REVIEW
MARCH 5, 1995

Robert Groves, according to his colleagues, could easily have been an on-camera personality—he had the looks, personality and articulateness—but he was drawn to the investigative end of journalism.

"Bobby was a consummate journalist," said Michelle Gillen, who was a reporter and anchor for Miami's Channel 10 when she first met Groves in 1984.

Groves had originally approached her three years before his death, offering to work for nothing on uncovering a story about abuse of the elderly at state-run agencies.

Gillen agreed, and their collaboration resulted in a seven-part series called, "Florida: State of Neglect."

The series led to reforms in the state's programs for the elderly and won the team one of broadcast journalism's most coveted prizes, the Alfred I. DuPont-Columbia University Award.

By the time Groves left Miami in 1988 for ABC, he had collected a long list of prizes, including five Emmys. Gillen moved on to NBC as a national correspondent.

Grove's mother said she'd harbored hopes of her son becoming a national on-air correspondent.

"He was full of life, 6 feet 4, blond hair, blue eyes," she recalled with obvious pain.

Gillen, who had hoped to continue working with Groves, was sure that he could easily have landed a more glamorous job on the air. But "Bobby wasn't ego-driven," she explained; rather, "he had this tremendous desire to help people through his stories."

In accepting the Dupont Award, Groves told the audience that investigative reporting "is the backbone of what our industry is all about." His resume listed the areas he most wanted to look into: official corruption, organized crime, drug trafficking, to name a few.

At the time of death, he'd been

working for five months as associate investigative producer of ABC's "World News Tonight," heading up investigative features for the network.

Grove's death came as "a shock" to the entire staff, recalled Christopher Isham, senior news producer for the show. He described Groves as a "first-rate reporter, with a first-rate inquisitive mind, great communication skills, who carried himself well."

He "would have gone far," said Isham, adding that he "could easily have held my job."

Several colleagues and friends pointed to the irony of Grove's death—under the very sort of circumstances that would have intrigued him as an investigative journalist.

"Bobby would have loved this case," said John Terrenzio, who at the time was executive producer of NBC News.

To this day, Terrenzio, now with Disney's Tri-Star Productions, is baffled by the Park Police handling of the case. "There was no way they could possibly be wrong in anything they did—that was their attitude," he said.

"The drug thing was ridiculous, the [not exceeding the speed limit] was ridiculous, their not testing their guy [Robinson] for drugs was ridiculous," said Terrenzio, who sat through part of the trial and testified at it.

Groves is said to have carried a poem in his pocket every day to review at random moments. One that he might well have taken along, an eerie one in light of his death, was written by Groves himself, "A Loving Journey":

As I sit in Love's arrest, I watch carefully the winging bird landing softly on a withered branch.

Broken-rooted, the branch snaps, the bird falls quietly into the snow's gentle arms, cushioned and embraced.

Our loving bird rises and with a quick shake once more, takes to heaven's highway, looking down carefully.

The snow shows where our bird has been; acres of uninterrupted white have one little nest, one spot to prove life was there. ■

Park Police Probe Left Parents Uneasy

Crime Scene Photos Questioned in Soldier's Death, Foster Case

By Christopher Ruddy
FOR THE PITTSBURGH
TRIBUNE-REVIEW
MARCH 6, 1995

What some observers consider the mishandling by U.S. Park Police of the investigation of a soldier's death in 1991 may have ramifications for the probe into the 1993 death of White House Deputy Counsel Vincent W. Foster Jr.

In both cases the Park Police investigation led to a finding of suicide. There are possible irregularities in both deaths, however, that challenge such rulings—at least to the extent that the purported suicides occurred in the manner portrayed.

Park Police determined in 1991 that Terry Todd Wright, a 20-year-old soldier assigned to the National Security Agency, killed himself.

But a key witness, Eugene Hyatt, contends photographs taken of Wright's body were staged.

Hyatt, who runs a federal hunting program on land near where Wright's body was found, said he discovered the corpse at the side of a dirt road running through property adjoining Fort Meade, Md.

Hyatt said an Army photographer used by the Park Police to record the death scene removed Wright's baseball cap before taking the photos. This, according to Hyatt, was done in the presence of three police officers, including one he described as "a ranking officer."

Hyatt said the cap was removed shortly after he remarked to police that its neat appearance on the head was inconsistent with a jarring "suicide" gunshot on the head.

Photographs of the scene in the Park Police file—copies of which were obtained by the Tribune-Review—clearly show Wright's hat off the top of his head, but trapped behind it in a disheveled manner.

Gene Wheaton, a 25-year veteran of the Army's Criminal Investigation Division before retiring, criticized the Park Police, noting that once death has been established, the scene must never be tampered with—"it's one of the most basic things."

"If it was done," said the well-known homicide expert, "it was a crime."

Wheaton and other experts stress

Continued on next page

Continued from page 77

that photos are critical in a death investigation since they show body positions and other evidence that can never be recreated.

Wheaton also said there was no reason to remove the hat even, for example, to get a clearer view of the face and head.

Death scene photographs are also a factor in the investigation of Foster's death. Several police officers who were at Fort Marcy Park in McLean, Va., when his body was found have challenged the factualness of the photos later shown to them.

In statements to the FBI, they questioned the position of the gun supposedly used by Foster to kill himself, and the amount of blood found on the front of the body.

Park Police officer Christine Hodakievic was one of those at Fort Marcy on the evening of July 20, 1993, when Foster's body was discovered. She was shown a Polaroid photograph of the body that night by Park Police Sgt. Robert Edwards.

During the subsequent investigation by then-Special Counsel Robert Fiske, she was shown several photos of the scene. The FBI account of her statement reads:

"Hodakievic, after viewing these Polaroid photographs, stated that in her opinion they were not identical to the Polaroid photograph that was initially shown to her by Sgt. Edwards. She reiterated the fact that the photograph Sgt. Edwards showed to her was consistent with her observations, specifically that there was no blood on the decedent's face, nor any blood on the decedent's shirt."

Hodakievic was called to testify before the grand jury convened by Independent Counsel Kenneth Starr, who took over the investigation following widespread doubts about the Fiske report.

Recently she was summoned by the grand jury to testify a second time.

PARALLEL CASES

In both the Foster and Wright cases there may be reason to question the official finding of suicide.

Perhaps the most compelling reason is that in each case the position in which the body was found was inconsistent with such death.

In Foster's case, the body was so neatly laid out, with arms at the side and a powerful gun still in hand, that a paramedic was moved to say it was as if it had been prepared "for the coffin."

In Wright's case, police state that he'd rested the butt of a .22-caliber rifle on the ground and fired it upward into his head.

But passer-by Hyatt, for one, had problems with that scenario. For example, the rifle left no marks on the dirt road and he saw no dirt marks on the rifle. In addition, Wright was wearing thick gloves and would have had difficulty fitting a finger into the trigger guard, he said.

Most remarkable of all to Hyatt, Wright's "glasses and hat were on perfectly straight."

The Wright case gained national attention in 1993 when David Zucchino of the Philadelphia Inquirer identified 40 questionable military suicides of recent years.

Wright's supposed suicide was only one of these to be investigated by the Park Police.

Zucchino, a Pulitzer Prize-winner, characterized the Park Police's investigation as "very, very unprofessional."

"They didn't bother to gather crucial crime-scene evidence," he charged. "They assumed it was a suicide from the very beginning."

Officials of the U.S. Park Police could not be reached for comment.

Standard police procedure calls for all apparent suicides to be treated as homicides until the facts prove otherwise.

In the Foster case, too, police apparently failed to follow this basic

rule. They did not, for example, canvass the neighborhood surrounding the death scene for leads, nor did they originally submit the supposed death weapon for testing—a step that was taken only after the suicide ruling.

FAMILY SUSPICIOUS

Sidney and Carlos Wright of Albertville, Ala., parents of Terry Todd Wright, have protested the ruling of a suicide.

Though initially accepting the finding—despite the fact their son had no history of psychological problems and had just received a promotion—they "became suspicious when the police kept changing the location where they body was found," said Sidney Wright.

He charged that police gave various versions of his son's death: He was found next to a tree in one story; next to his car in another; he was found squatting, according to one report, and prone in another.

The Wrights say the Park Police were helpful—until the couple began questioning the circumstances of their son's death.

Carlos Wright said the Park Police have steadfastly refused to release to them an original "suicide" letter—they were provided a copy—written by their son.

The couple claim the police have also declined to have the handwriting analyzed, failed to bring investigating apparatus to the scene, allowed Army investigators to take their son's car away and military investigators to throw into a dumpster items from the car that might have constituted critical evidence.

Park Police procedures in death investigations have become a major focus of Starr's probe.

Earlier this year, he convened a grand jury and began taking depositions from Park Police officers and emergency personnel present at Fort Marcy Park the night Foster's body was found.

The Associated Press quoted lawyers for Park Police officers as saying that these officers were assured by Starr's staff they were not targets of the probe.

Thomas Scorza, a professor of legal ethics at the University of Chicago and a former federal prosecutor, said such assurances could be an indication that the prosecutors have a theory of wrongdoing at a high level.

He cautioned that the assurance to lower-level personnel does not exonerate them; rather, it indicates only that higher officials are more culpable.

Scorza pointed out the gravity of perjury charges against any medical personnel or police officers who don't "tell the truth."

"They could be very severely punished, especially if this is a potential murder case."

In such a situation, Scorza noted, the federal code provides that any such perjurers would have "aided and abetted" the crime, and could be subjected to life imprisonment.

Scorza was skeptical of a recent report in USA Today and The Wall Street Journal that Starr had basically concluded the case and was ready to declare it a suicide.

"It doesn't make any sense," said Scorza, suggesting that such action, given standard grand jury workings, would be decidedly premature. ■

Press Leaks Indicate Fiske Conclusions Were Preordained

By Christopher Ruddy
FOR THE PITTSBURGH
TRIBUNE-REVIEW
MARCH 22, 1995

Recently released documents of the official investigation into the death of Vincent W. Foster Jr. suggest that Special Counsel Robert Fiske's conclusion of suicide was preordained.

On April 4, 1994, the Wall Street Journal published a story headlined "Fiske Is Seen Verifying Foster Killed Himself."

The Journal scoop, quoting lawyers familiar with the case, stated Fiske's staff is "expected to release a report this month declaring the death of White House aide Vincent Foster was a suicide."

Seemingly corroborating the report was Fiske's deputy counsel, Roderick Lankler, who told the Journal that "he hoped to release the report in mid-April."

The report on Foster's death, in fact, was not released for another three months.

But the timing and accuracy of the Journal's story as to the suicide conclusion, followed as it was with a spate of similar stories in other media, raises suspicions that Fiske's staff announced their conclusions before any substantive aspects of the investigation had taken place.

Documents released by the Senate Banking Committee this past January demonstrate conclusively that by April 4 the investigation into Foster's case was at the most preliminary of stages.

"The Wall Street Journal had a stifling effect on independent press inquiry of the case," according to conservative media critic Reed Irvine. "It said Fiske has already made this conclusion, and if anyone else questions it, you're marginalized as a conspiracist."

Irvine, chairman of Accuracy in Media, has actively challenged official versions of Foster's death, faulted the Journal for being

Special Counsel Robert Fiske

"patsies" for both the White House and Fiske's staff, who "apparently didn't want anyone looking into the matter."

Fiske was officially appointed special counsel on January 20, 1994. On February 23, Fiske appointed Lankler, a New York criminal attorney, to head up the Foster probe.

On February 28, in a letter
Continued on next page

Continued from page 79

presented in federal court to block the release of a Park Police report on Foster's death, Fiske promised a "thorough and complete investigation" into the case. He noted that forensic experts and pathologists were to be retained, and added that the matter would be reviewed by two former homicide prosecutors, Lankler and Russell Hardin Jr.

A team of seven FBI agents was assigned to the Foster case. Those familiar with the investigation say what was billed as a homicide probe only began to pick up steam by mid-March.

Records demonstrate that by the end of March, Fiske's FBI investigators had only conducted interviews with most of the Fairfax County emergency fire and rescue workers who were present at Fort Marcy Park, where Foster was found dead on July 20, 1993.

Their testimony supported earlier published statements about the unusual circumstances of the death, notably that there was little blood, the gun was still in Foster's hand, and the appearance of the body was neat.

One EMS worker even coded the case as a homicide on his official report.

A careful examination of the Fiske report shows that Fiske's conclusions relied heavily on Foster's depression and an independent pathology review of the autopsy conducted by Dr. James Beyer, the Virginia medical examiner. But records show that the bulk of FBI interviews of Foster's friends and family that would describe Foster's state of mind, and the independent pathology review, took place in May and June, well after the Journal's article and shortly after a similar report in May was published by Reuters.

Press leaks by Fiske's staff didn't stop with the Journal. On May 4, 1994, a Reuters wire story indicated "Whitewater Counsel to Report Foster Killed Himself."

The Reuters story reported " . . . Fiske has told associates his report, accepting the official police version that Foster committed suicide last year because he was depressed, may be released by the middle of May."

By May 6, the Reuters story had received wide confirmation, with corroborating reports in the Washington Post and Boston Globe. But chronological developments in the Fiske investigation are in black and white, laid out in a two-volume set, produced by the Senate Banking Committee and just released this past January.

Here's how a chronology of major developments compares with press reports of a suicide conclusion:

■ On April 4, the very day the Journal piece ran, an FBI team working for Fiske begins the rudimentary task of searching for the missing bullet. It is not found.

■ On April 6, Fiske's staff reviews a transcript of an interview with Dr. Beyer, conducted a week earlier by one member of Fiske's pathology team. The report draws no conclusions and simply reiterates the autopsy results already stated in the police report.

■ An interview with Dr. Donald Haut, the medical examiner who visited Fort Marcy on the night of Foster's death, is conducted April 12. (In a January 12 article in the Tribune-Review, Haut was quoted as stating he gave no FBI statement. Documents released on January 23 indicate that he had.)

■ By April 20, Fiske's investigators interview a White House Secret Service officer who last saw Foster leave the White House's West Wing.

■ The lead Park Police investigator for the case is interviewed April 27. Five other officers present at the scene that night will be interviewed over the following five days.

■ Five days after the Reuters story appears on May 4, Mrs. Foster is interviewed for the first time.

■ Foster's own physician isn't interviewed until May 16.

■ Documents in May and June reveal that investigators only then begin to focus on Foster's friends and colleagues in developing their theory of Foster's state of mind.

■ Perhaps the clearest evidence that Fiske's investigators had pre-drawn conclusions is found on the dates of the critical FBI reports. Those FBI forensic reports are first dated May 9, over a month after the Wall Street Journal report, and several days after the Reuters report.

■ The independent pathology report is undated, but clearly makes reference to the FBI lab reports—indicating it too was completed well after press reports had said the Foster case was closed.

Vincent Scalice, a former New York City police crime scene expert with 35 years experience on major homicide cases, said no legitimate conclusion could have been drawn based on early interviews with police and rescue workers, that is, before April 4.

"The fact is that the observations of people on the scene are inconsistent with suicide," he said.

Scalice said the FBI lab reports would be "critical" in making any judgment in a case like this, but added "they don't lend support to the suicide conclusion, either."

One report demonstrates, for example, that Foster fired the gun with neither hand on the gun's hand grip—something Scalice and some of the nation's top forensic experts view as implausible, whether Foster was left- or right-handed.

In March 1994, the Boston Globe reported that Foster was left-handed, even though the gun was found in his right hand. The Globe reported, according to the Park Police chief, that "Foster, as is common in suicide by handgun, used two hands to put the gun to his mouth."

Contrary to the clear implication of that news report, Foster was right-handed, according to several Little Rock sources close to him.

Blood tracks as well as unusual

carpet fibers also counter the official version, Scalice said.

"In police work you never jump to conclusions. Every lead has to be followed up on, especially in a case like this," Scalice said, adding, "It wasn't done here. That's obvious."

A recent spate of reports bears an eerie resemblance to last year's Wall Street Journal and Reuters reports. Last month the Journal ran a page one story, "There May Be Less To Whitewater Case Than Meets The Eye," stating that the present independent counsel, Kenneth Starr, had concluded Foster's death was a suicide. A similar story appeared in USA Today.

Despite the press reports, several legal experts indicate that it would be highly unlikely that Starr could draw any conclusions at this stage of the grand jury process. A number of homicide experts indicate that a suicide conclusion at this point would carry little weight unless a second autopsy was conducted on the body.

Efforts to reach Fiske for comment were unsuccessful. Lankler has referred all inquiries on the matter to Starr.

A source close to the Starr investigation has told the Tribune-Review that the independent counsel has not drawn a conclusion of suicide at this point. ∎

Fiske Probe Leaves Trail of Unanswered Questions

By Christopher Ruddy
FOR THE PITTSBURGH
TRIBUNE-REVIEW
MARCH 29, 1995

WASHINGTON—As Independent Counsel Kenneth Starr conducts a grand jury investigation into the death of Vincent W. Foster Jr., the original probe by special counsel Robert Fiske has also come under scrutiny by Capitol Hill Republicans.

Fiske turned up no proof of wrongdoing when probing Foster's death. Likewise, he found no evidence that administration officials obstructed the Resolution Trust Co.'s investigation of links between Bill and Hillary Clinton and the failed Whitewater real estate partnership with Madison Guaranty, a failed Arkansas savings and loan.

"Fiske was not an aggressive investigator," Sen. Lauch Faircloth told the Tribune-Review this week, explaining why he wants the banking committee to revisit areas covered by Mr. Fiske's probe, including aspects of Foster's death.

"It's noteworthy that Starr has used the hammer of a grand jury to look into Foster's death," said Faircloth, a freshman Republican Senator from North Carolina who has gained considerable national prominence for being one of Clinton's toughest critics on Whitewater-related matters.

For starters, Faircloth wants to resummon Park Police Capt. Charles Hume before the banking panel. Hume supervised the police probe of Foster's death.

During hearings last summer, Hume was scheduled to appear before the committee, but didn't show. At the time, the committee was told Hume was on vacation and could not be reached.

A number of Republican senators were anxious to hear from Hume because, in a pre-hearing deposition, he had been candidly critical of White House interference in the investigation.

Faircloth also shares the desire of banking committee chairman Alfonse D'Amato to investigate why documents were removed from Foster's office after his death.

Capitol Hill interest in Foster's death has escalated since the empanelment of Starr's grand jury in January. The seating of the grand jury has highlighted what some view as serious lapses in Fiske's investigation.

Fiske, asked to comment on criticisms of his probe, told the Tribune-Review: "We put out our report. I'm not going to comment beyond it."

FOSTER'S WHEREABOUTS

One of the most perplexing questions about Foster's death, apparently an issue of concern for Starr's staff, is Foster's whereabouts after he left the West Wing of the White House on July 20, 1993, at approximately 1 p.m.

The Fiske report read: "At about 1:00 p.m., (Foster) came out of his office holding his suit jacket, without a briefcase. He told (Linda) Tripp (an executive assistant to White House counsel Bernard Nussbaum) that there were still some M&Ms on the tray if she wanted them. He said, 'I'll be back,' and then left."

Foster's body was found by officials after 6 p.m. His car was first sighted in Fort Marcy Park at about 4:30 p.m.

The coroner who conducted the original autopsy specified no time of death. Fiske's pathology team said Foster could have died "within

Continued on next page

Continued from page 81

the broad range of when the deceased was last seen alive to the time the body was discovered."

But in standard homicide cases, approximate times of death are usually much more specific.

One way to determine time of death is by examining stomach contents and digestion.

The Park Police report quotes Dr. James Beyer, the Virginia medical examiner during the autopsy, as stating that Foster "had eaten a large meal" and that Beyer believed Foster had eaten "2-3 hours prior to death."

Beyer indicated the food "might have been meat and potatoes."

The official White House story is that Foster ate a cheeseburger, French fries and a coke in his office shortly before 1 p.m.

Three scenarios can be drawn from the facts outlined so far and based on the fact that stomach digestion is completed within three hours.

The first theory is that Foster ate lunch in his office, went soon thereafter to the park, and then shot himself, explaining the "large meal" found in his stomach.

A second scenario would be that Foster left the office at 1 p.m. and went to an undisclosed location. Within 2-3 hours the meal he had eaten at the office was completely digested, so he ate another large meal before going to the park and shooting himself.

A third scenario is that Foster didn't eat lunch in his office, as officials claim, and that he had lunch after leaving the office either somewhere on the White House campus or elsewhere. He then died shortly after eating lunch.

This third scenario would suggest that Foster was somewhere outside his office for several hours before he died.

It has been confirmed that Foster left his office about 1 p.m.

But the long lapse in time from 1 p.m. until the discovery of his body remains a nagging inconsistency.

A review of documents chronicling Fiske's investigation shows that investigators barely scratched the surface in their mission to retrace Foster's steps.

The only evidence of efforts in this area is revealed in a document stating that Fiske's investigators canvassed Foster's Georgetown neighborhood on May 10-11 to determine if anyone saw him on the afternoon of his death. The interviews turned up nothing.

But the documents don't show painstaking police work, such as interviewing personnel at restaurants he patronized, gas stations along various routes to the park, and finally, regular park visitors to Fort Marcy.

For example, Robert Reeves, a retired Army soldier who has been visiting Fort Marcy Park for over 20 years, was never interviewed by Fiske's staff. Reeves said last week he also had not been interviewed by Starr's staff. Reeves' intimate knowledge of happenings within the park include details about the man Fiske said found Foster's body.

Questions about hangouts or other areas outside the White House where Foster may have been on the day of his death are conspicuously absent from FBI statements of Mack McLarty, Webster Hubbell, Bruce Lindsey, and David Watkins—all part of the Arkansas circle that knew Foster well.

A brief mention in White House associate counsel William Kennedy's FBI statement mentions that Foster would, on rare occasions, eat lunch outside the White House at a nearby restaurant. But the interviewing agents didn't ask Kennedy to identify a specific restaurant.

The documents show that the last person to see Foster alive on the White House grounds was a uniformed member of the Secret Service, posted at station "E-4," at the first floor front entrance to the West Wing—which houses the Oval Office and various presidential aides' offices.

The officer at E-4 told the FBI that he remembered Foster leaving "about lunchtime," but couldn't remember the precise time.

But a White House law enforcement source who has reviewed the banking committee documents said that had Foster proceeded to exit the White House campus by going to his car, he would also have had to pass by another uniformed officer at guardpost "C-6" along the route to West Executive Avenue. The documents do not include such a statement.

Also, no documents indicate that officers posted at the Pennsylvania Avenue gate, post "A-5," were interviewed.

Contrary to popular belief, Foster's movements on the White House grounds would not have been captured by video camera. Foster's car also would not have been logged out.

An FBI agent assigned to Fiske's staff was questioned by Sen. D'Amato during hearings about Foster exiting the White House by car. He responded: "Senator, I don't believe the vehicle was logged out of the White House. I don't believe it was parked in the area where it would have been logged out of the White House."

Foster typically parked his car on the White House grounds in parking spots reserved for high officials. The parking area is located on West Executive Avenue, a street that runs between the White House and the Old Executive Office Building.

Foster noted his parking habits in a speech at the University of Arkansas Law School:

"When we leave work at night, we pull up to a large, heavy gate that surrounds the White House complex. While Secret Service guards slowly open that gate, I always look to my right . . ."

Leaving by that exit, Foster could not have been logged out, but he would have been noticed.

TRACE EVIDENCE

Documents show Foster left the White House about 1 p.m., but the trail ends there . . . until his body was discovered at Fort Marcy Park.

An FBI analysis of Foster's clothes shows carpet fibers of various colors all over his suit jacket, tie, shirt, shorts, pants, belt, socks, and shoes. The fibers were colored white, tan, gray, blue, red, and green.

This trace evidence indicates "Foster's body was in contact with one or more carpets on the day of his death," explained Vincent Scalice, a former crime scene expert for the New York City Police Department.

Fiske's staff acknowledged that they didn't attempt to match the fibers with Foster's office or home, something that several FBI sources have told the Tribune-Review was a major lapse in the investigation.

Scalice, who has 35 years experience in major homicide cases, says that "the first place you would check is where Foster was last seen alive—the White House."

Scalice said all the carpets have to be tested, not just in the West Wing, but in the residence and living quarters itself, and any buildings on the campus that Foster might have entered after exiting the West Wing.

Checking White House carpets may prove difficult, since Foster died almost 20 months ago and several carpets have been changed.

Since Foster's death, the living quarters on the second and third floors have undergone extensive redecoration, including several rug changes.

On the state floor, the Blue Room was completely redone.

Last month, Mrs. Clinton opened the new room to the press.

At the time, the New York Times reported, "Mrs. Clinton said that she had had a 'great deal of fun' while involved in the traditional work of replacing fading drapes and worn carpets in the oval-shaped space."

According to one law enforcement source, all rugs, despite the redecoration, should have been preserved in one of several secret warehouses kept by the government in the Washington area.

The Blue Room is an important area of inquiry because, according to several White House sources, it has been used by the Clintons, their friends and officials for small, informal lunches outside the hubbub of the West Wing.

There have been no reports Foster had lunch in the official residence.

If he had, he should have been logged by the Secret Service at the ground floor entrance with the White House Usher's office. He also would have passed a Secret Service agent stationed in the State foyer.

Noteworthy, however, is the White House "Memorandum For All Executive Residence Staff" obtained by the Tribune-Review.

The memo is dated, coincidentally on the day of Foster's death, and addresses the subject of " . . . the privacy of the First Family."

The memo, sent by Deputy Chief of Staff Roy Neel, reminded staff within the residence that "Discussions by staff members of the first family's personal activities of any kind, or any other matter which breaches their privacy, with anyone outside of the immediate staff is prohibited."

This directive is not unusual and is long-standing policy. But people familiar with the White House suggest that such a memo is usually distributed at the beginning of a new administration.

FISKE, FILES AND THE SAFE

On July 1, 1994, the New York Times reported that after the release of the Fiske report on Foster's death, "Fiske is still expected to issue a separate conclusion within 10 days about the handling of papers in Foster's office shortly after his death . . ."

But Fiske's report on the papers never materialized.

In fact, Fiske told Congressional staff members that his report would be delayed, and probably wouldn't be released until the end of August.

Fiske was fired August 4, and Fiske's delay of the report has remained something of a mystery to the public.

But Congressional sources have told the Tribune-Review that Fiske was stymied in releasing the report when Congressional investigators asked to pre-interview several White House officials who should have been familiar with activities relating to Foster's office and his safe.

Fiske's staff informed Congressional investigators in early July that several individuals had never been interviewed, even though Fiske was ready to issue his report within days.

"Fiske's staff called to ask who were several individuals on the list that we asked permission to interview," recalled one of the Congressional investigators.

Fiske wouldn't comment as to why the report was delayed, but said he recollected on or about June 20 that he had informed Congress that his hope of finishing the report before Congressional hearings was not possible, and that the investigation still had to continue.

But Congressional investigators insist Fiske was on the verge of issuing the report when his staff realized key people had never been interviewed. For example, Fiske's staff embarrassingly had never interviewed Charles Easley, the Office of Administration staffer in charge of security—including the safeguarding of safe combinations.

Easley was out of the office during the days nearest to Foster's death, but a well-placed source said Easley was aware of activities relating to the safe while he was away.

The source said a staff member of the White House counsel's office called Easley's office the day after Foster's death to request the

Continued on next page

Continued from page 83

combination to Foster's safe because "(associate counsel) Bill Kennedy needed to get into Foster's safe."

The combination was not given because Foster had taken the unusual step of authorizing no one but himself to have access to the combination.

When efforts by officials to gain access to the safe were first reported last year, White House Chief of Staff Mack McLarty denied the existence of a safe, stating in a lawyerly fashion: "I don't think there was a safe, as I understand it. To the best of my knowledge there was not."

The White House had apparently redefined the safe as a "file cabinet"—even though the depository had been registered with Easley's office as a safe.

In May 1994, Fiske had used his subpoena power to gather documents in Foster's office. Oddly, two weeks after the date Fiske's staff said they were to issue their report, Fiske obtained another subpoena on July 20. Why that subpoena was issued so belatedly remains a mystery.

According to the New York Times, the new subpoena called for documents "that reflect how . . . files were distributed" after Foster's death and files "it says were kept in a safe inside the office of Bernard W. Nussbaum . . ."

Although Fiske used subpoena power to gather documents, evidence also indicates he didn't use a full grand jury investigation into activities by officials involving Foster's office. Fiske would not comment as to whether he had used a full grand jury investigation.

An FBI statement by a White House aide included in banking committee documents indicate a special assistant to the President was asked only informally about the removal of documents from the office, not under oath. Additionally, sources say that key people such as Easley were not put under oath by Fiske.

The files in Foster's office are critical because they would give investigators a possible motivation for Foster's death.

The Foster files have been a focus of the House Committee on Operations. The committee, chaired by Rep. William Clinger (R-Pa.), has been investigating the files as they relate to Foster's connection with the Travelgate scandal.

According to a source on the committee staff, inventories provided by the White House of files in Foster's office list no files relating to the White House Travel Office. Because Foster was heavily involved in the Travel Office brouhaha—even mentioning it in his alleged suicide note—Congressional investigators believe the omission of such files strongly indicates that the documents had been "sanitized" before the official inventories were compiled.

Independent counsel Kenneth Starr has yet to release his conclusions as to activities related to Foster's office. His spokeswoman in Little Rock said she could not comment as to whether a full grand jury investigation is being employed to investigate the matter. ■

Editor's note: *Ruddy broke the story here that the failure to find Travel Office files was evidence Foster's papers had been "sanitized" after his death.*

Fiske Probe's Excavation Challenged

By Christopher Ruddy
FOR THE PITTSBURGH
TRIBUNE-REVIEW
APRIL 5, 1995

WASHINGTON—Doubts have arisen concerning the integrity of documents prepared by special counsel Robert Fiske's staff and the FBI in the investigation of the death of deputy White House counsel Vincent W. Foster Jr.

Two experts who worked closely with Fiske's staff and FBI agents searching the McLean, Va., park where Foster's body was discovered, have offered substantially different accounts of the events from what has been presented in official documents.

On April 4, 1994, 16 individuals from the FBI lab went to Fort Marcy Park "to conduct a search in the area where Foster's body was found," according to the Fiske report.

Searchers were looking for the bullet Foster allegedly had fired, bone fragments from a large exit wound and blood residue in the soil from a "large pool of blood." Neither the bullet nor bone fragments were found. The Fiske report gave no information about blood residue.

Their search, including their claim to have excavated the path where the body was said to have been found, had been cited as an example of the painstaking efforts made by Fiske's investigators to uncover facts surrounding the case.

EXCAVATION DISPUTED

But two members of the search team—Robert Sonderman, a National Park Service senior staff archaeologist, and Dr. Doug Owsley, a forensic anthropologist with the Smithsonian Institution—contradict that claim.

Sonderman accompanied the search party to ensure the historical site was protected and artifacts were preserved. Sonderman said he has extensive experience with metal detector searches and advised the FBI on how to lay out a search grid of the area. He was present when the ground was scanned by detectors and metal objects were flagged and subsequently unearthed.

Owsley's role was to assist in the search for bone fragments and to determine if such fragments were of human origin. He said he regularly works with the FBI.

Both men said that, because of their unique training and expertise, they spent the entire period of the search as an integral part of Fiske's team.

Both experts deny that the focal point of the investigation—the excavation of the pathway, including the area where the body was found—ever took place. They said there was superficial digging at the location—but only at specific flagged sites.

Sonderman also denies the search ended April 4, as noted in an FBI report. He said the project was unfinished by day's end and was therefore extended into the following day.

Concerning the search for bone fragments, Owsley said there "no reason" for digging, because these types of particles should have been on the surface or lightly covered by brush and the like.

As for the claimed sifting, he said, this amounted to largely "raking" the ground.

Page 47 of the Fiske report claims "the area immediately beneath where Foster's body was found was searched by digging and hand-sifting the soil and other debris. FBI lab personnel excavated to a depth of approximately 18 inches, searching the soil with various screening methods."

An FBI report in the Fiske documents also claims the area was excavated.

It reads: "The entire area of the path where the body was positioned was excavated down to approximately 15-18 inches, the soil and roots removed and then meticulously hand searched by various screening methods."

These descriptions clearly imply that at least 22 cubic feet of soil was unearthed—weighing more than a half-ton—on the pathway alone, and then carefully sifted.

But Owsley remembers no excavation and recalled no cutting or removal of the root stems that proliferate in the area. A recent examination of the area revealed that the root stems on the pathway were undisturbed.

"It was an intensive survey," Owsley recalls, but by no means the excavation that had been claimed. Sonderman also described the search as a "survey."

Owsley said the Fiske team concentrated its efforts not on the pathway where the body was said to have been found, but at the bottom of a hill where fragments might have been washed by rain and on the other side of the hill's crest, where bone material might have been thrown by the bullet's explosion.

"There was very little digging," Sonderman said. He told of Owsley's removal of "overburden," his term for the foliage and other surface material.

Sonderman remembered sifting of surface material only with a wire-mesh box with a 1/4-inch screen.

Sonderman confirmed Owsley's statement that no roots were cut.

"They (the FBI) worked around them," he said.

He added that investigators took great pains to protect the historic nature of the site and did not disturb the many root stems, even in the immediate area where Foster's body was said to have been found.

Asked if digging at the site went to the 15- to 18-inch mark claimed in the Fiske report, Sonderman was emphatic: "No way."

Nor, according to Sonderman, did the investigators seem to feel a need to dig deeply. He recalled FBI lab personnel saying the fired bullet should have been found either on the surface or no more than an inch or two below the surface.

A report in the Fiske documents with hand-written notations bears out Sonderman's recollection—indicating that numerous bullets recovered at the site were found at depths of 2 to 4 inches.

In all, Fiske's staff collected 12 modern-day bullets from the area, as well as dozens of Civil War artifacts.

Fiske, in his report, gave no explanation as to how so many metal objects could be recovered in an area the Park Police claimed to have searched.

Fiske, asked about the discrepancy between his report and what the two experts said, declined to comment. He did say he stands behind the accuracy of his report.

Fiske's was not the first search of the site.

In a deposition before the Senate Banking Committee, Sgt. Robert Rule of the Park Police said that two days after Foster's death he, another detective and two technicians searched 30 square yards of the area where Foster's body was said to have been found.

NO MINOR MATTER

Former FBI agent William F. Roemer Jr. believes the discrepancies between the Fiske report and the testimony of Owsley and Sonderman is no minor matter.

"I'd certainly get to the bottom of this," said Roemer, who is the most decorated of all living former FBI agents.

Roemer, with 35 years of

Continued on next page

Continued from page 85

investigative experience, doubts the Fiske report was deliberately falsified.

Still, "the discrepancy can't be ignored," he said.

Echoing those sentiments is Thomas Scorza, a former federal prosecutor and current professor of legal ethics at the University of Chicago.

"It's real serious," he said. "It's not a small matter. An excavation is a very specific maneuver."

Scorza said that while many were present the day of the search, only one person wrote the report, which should have been reviewed by one or more supervisory personnel at the scene.

In cases like this, he said, he likes to believe inaccuracies are a result of "incompetence" rather than purposeful misrepresentation.

He suggested that reports of this nature are sometimes embellished.

"As a bureaucratic thing, a supervisory person does it with the motive to make their work look more thorough," Scorza said.

He said it is essential that investigators for Fiske's replacement, independent counsel Kenneth Starr, interview everyone at the park the day of the search and ask them point blank, "What happened?"

Scorza said discrepancies of this type are "worrisome" in light of other discrepancies, such as the matter of blood found under Foster's body.

ANOTHER CHALLENGE

In January, the Tribune-Review reported on the discrepancy between the medical examiner's observation of blood under Foster's body and the characterization of those observations in the Fiske report.

A key part of the June 30, 1993, Fiske report notes that: "At approximately 7:40 p.m., Dr. Donald Haut, the Fairfax County Medical Examiner, arrived at the scene to examine the body. At that point, Foster's body was rolled over and those present observed a large pool of blood located on the ground where Foster's head had been. Haut observed a large exit wound in the back of the skull."

But in an interview in January, Haut, the only trained medical professional on the scene that night, gave a markedly different account, recalling that when Foster's body was rolled over, he observed a small amount of blood on the ground.

"There was not a hell of a lot of blood," he said, noting that "most of it had congealed" on the back of the victim's head. He added that what blood was visible, appeared "matted" to the back of the head.

According to pathology experts, a lack of blood could mean that the body was either moved to where it was found—or even that the deceased had died by means other than gunshot.

Haut's statement to the Tribune-Review, as well as a statement made to an FBI agent working with the Fiske investigators, indicates his observations may have been misrepresented in the Fiske report.

On April 12, 1994, according to Fiske investigation records, Haut told Fiske's FBI investigators that when Foster's body was rolled over, he saw "blood around the back of Foster's head," which he described as being "matted and clotted . . . the volume of which was small."

On the critical issue of the amount of blood on the ground underneath the body, Haut's statement contains no reference to having observed any blood on the ground.

This would indicate that FBI agents never asked Haut about the matter or that his response was omitted.

Starr is currently conducting a grand jury investigation into Foster's death and has been reviewing the investigations of both the Park Police and the Fiske group.

Both probes ruled Foster died of a self-inflicted gunshot wound fired near a Civil War cannon at Fort Marcy on July 20, 1993.

But both of these rulings have been challenged by a number of authorities.

The issue of whether the excavation of the site took place has an important bearing on the current investigation by Starr, according to a source familiar with the investigation.

Fiske has accepted the Park Police report that Foster's body was found on a dirt path directly in front of what is known locally as the "second cannon," though several witnesses claimed the body was actually found some 200 feet away, closer to the "first cannon" in the park.

Starr's investigators have not taken seriously the disputed issue of the body's location partly because they believe that the second cannon site—even though it seems inconsistent with photographs showing heavy foliage around the body—"has changed significantly," a source close to the investigation said. One factor cited for the change in vegetation around the second cannon site had been the Fiske "excavation."

But others familiar with the pathway said it has been a dirt path etched by root stems—virtually devoid of vegetation—for many years. ■

Prosecutor's Resignation Comes at Crucial Point in Foster Probe

By Christopher Ruddy
FOR THE PITTSBURGH
TRIBUNE-REVIEW
APRIL 6, 1995

WASHINGTON—The resignation of a key prosecutor for independent counsel Kenneth Starr challenges the integrity of a grand jury investigation into the death of Vincent W. Foster Jr., according to a Washington law enforcement source close to the probe.

The investigation had reached a critical stage by mid-March when associate independent counsel Miquel Rodriguez quit after he was stifled by his superior in his efforts to conduct a full grand jury probe, according to a source. Rodriguez's superior is deputy independent counsel Mark H. Tuohey III, who is viewed by many in the Washington legal community as being above reproach professionally.

Rodriguez's departure came at a crucial juncture.

The source said that by the time Rodriguez left, or shortly thereafter, Starr's investigative team had progressed in several critical areas:

■ Investigators had received new photographic evidence of a "significant" nature that was not available to investigators from the U.S. Park Police and the office of Starr's predecessor, former special counsel Robert Fiske.

■ Strong evidence had emerged that the 1913 Colt revolver found in Foster's hand—the alleged suicide weapon—had been "moved or switched."

■ Investigators had developed a clear theory that the body had been moved and had focused on the park's rear entrance.

Starr began using his Whitewater grand jury in early January to investigate Foster's death, which occurred on July 20, 1993.

Park Police and Fiske concluded Foster committed suicide. Fiske further concluded the body had not been moved and cleared officials of possible obstruction in the investigation.

Fiske had been criticized for not including Foster's death in his grand jury probe of the Whitewater affair.

The Starr investigation has turned up discrepancies in the testimony of police and rescue workers called before the grand jury, according to several sources.

Despite significant developments in the case, Rodriguez left because he believed the grand jury process was being thwarted by his superior, the key source said.

In a full grand jury process, a prosecutor has complete subpoena power to call witnesses, subpoena documents, and seek out wrong-doing at all levels.

Typically, prosecutors "work their way up," beginning with the lowest officials. Prosecutors are not supposed to exempt individuals or groups of individuals, such as police, from prosecution, according to a legal expert.

REPUTATION

Rodriguez, an assistant U.S.

Independent Counsel Kenneth Starr

Attorney from Sacramento, joined Starr's staff early last fall and had been the lead prosecutor on the Foster case.

Rodriguez, who is in his mid-30s, has approximately seven years' experience as a prosecutor and had gained a reputation as a hard-nosed, diligent prosecutor, especially on civil rights cases, said an FBI agent in California familiar with his work.

"He's the perfect lawyer for a case like this," the agent said, suggesting that if any cover-up existed, Rodriguez's cross-examination skills would be well suited for ferreting out the truth.

The agent also described Rodriguez as a "guy with a conscience. He could never play Pontius Pilate."

Rodriguez became critical of the investigation after he was denied the right to bring witnesses he deemed important before the grand jury, the source said.

Continued on next page

Continued from page 87

Rodriguez also became frustrated because of delays in bringing witnesses before the grand jury. He believed the delays could allow Park Police and other officials to adjust conflicting testimony.

A recent published report stated that by mid-March, after three months of proceedings, about a dozen fire and rescue workers had been brought before the grand jury.

Reached at his Sacramento office, Rodriguez confirmed he left the Whitewater probe and returned to his post with the U.S. Attorney's office on March 20. He refused to explain his departure.

"Ken Starr is a great man and a great prosecutor. Beyond that, I cannot comment on any aspect of the ongoing investigation," he said tersely.

Rodriguez also declined to provide biographical information on himself, such as his age or experience as a government prosecutor.

Tuohey confirmed Rodriguez's resignation, but said he couldn't comment on the reasons for the departure. He also refused to comment on the notion that Rodriguez left because he was not given full grand jury powers.

However, another person familiar with the Starr investigation has categorically denied the information provided the Tribune-Review as to the reasons for Rodriguez's departure.

"It's absolutely not true," the person said about Rodriguez being denied the right to call crucial witnesses.

"Absolute nonsense," the source said about allegations witnesses were being called too slowly.

Despite the contradictory statements of people close to the investigation, there are indications that a disagreement developed between Rodriguez and Tuohey.

According to the law enforcement source, Starr has given wide authority to his deputies, with Tuohey heading up the Washington phase and William S. Duffey Jr. in Arkansas. Starr has taken great pains to not interfere in their handling of the respective parts of the investigation, the source said.

Tuohey is a highly respected former federal prosecutor, who also served during the Carter administration as a special counsel prosecuting former Rep. Daniel Flood of Pennsylvania. He is currently a partner at the law firm of Reed, Smith, Shaw and McClay, where he handles white-collar criminal matters. In 1993-1994, he was president of the District of Columbia Bar Association.

According to several friends and associates, Tuohey is described as a congenial, fair, honest man.

Press accounts at the time of his selection by Starr last September noted that Tuohey's activism in Democratic Party circles helped answer criticism that Starr, an active Republican, would be unfair.

The Washington Post reported that Tuohey "is close to some Clinton Administration officials, including Associate Attorney General Jamie S. Gorelick, and last year hosted a party for Attorney General Janet Reno at his Washington home."

SIGNIFICANT QUESTIONS

Thomas Scorza, a former federal prosecutor in Chicago and a professor of legal ethics at the University of Chicago, said Rodriguez's resignation in the middle of grand jury proceedings could be significant.

Scorza said that "it's very unusual for someone above the working prosecutor (Rodriguez) to call the shots in the investigation." During his 10 years as a prosecutor in Chicago, he couldn't recall an instance where the actual prosecutor was limited in his powers.

Scorza also termed serious the allegation that witnesses were not expeditiously called before the grand jury.

"That's how a practicing prosecutor wants it done," he said. "If you're questioning several people about the same thing, you want to get testimony before the grand jury quickly. That's how you find discrepancies and you discover something and the dominoes begin to fall."

Scorza said that if he, as a prosecutor, found that he had been limited in his grand jury powers, he would resign.

"I'd also go public with it," he said.

Reports of problems in the Starr investigation surfaced in early January as Park Police officers were first summoned to testify.

A January 12 story by the Associated Press reported that lawyers for the Park Police had objected to Rodriguez's "tough questioning" of officers about their probe of Foster's death.

Several officers were upset because Rodriguez repeatedly read perjury statutes to grand jury witnesses, according to press reports of the proceedings.

"He (Rodriguez) was doing exactly what he should be doing," Scorza said. He based his remarks on personal experiences.

"The police always get upset," Scorza said of the prosecutor's repeated reading of the perjury statute.

He said it's necessary so witnesses don't later claim they didn't understand the significance of their testimony or the consequences of lying under oath.

Asked about his methods, Rodriguez said: "A law enforcement agent has to be held accountable to the same law as everyone else. If they aren't, faith and trust in a central institution in society is destroyed."

"There are some that say exposing corruption among police and officials is a bad thing because it weakens public confidence. In the short run, that may be true, but in the long term, it restores people's confidence and trust," he said.

PRESS REPORTS

January press reports about the grand jury proceedings and Rodriguez's handling of it seemed to exacerbate the rift between Rodriguez and Tuohey, the source suggested.

The Associated Press report detailing police anger over Rodriguez's questioning said, "Rodriguez's boss, deputy Whitewater prosecutor Mark Tuohey, acknowledged there had been problems, though he declined to discuss them."

The story went on to quote Tuohey as saying Rodriguez would continue asking the questions in the grand jury probe.

According to the law enforcement source, Rodriguez and several members of the staff were unhappy that Tuohey had spoken to the press. They interpreted his remarks as a violation of a federal mandate that grand jury proceedings remain secret.

Scorza said he found Tuohey's comments to be "odd," even if they didn't directly relate to the internal activities of the grand jury.

"Any prosecutor knows that when asked about anything relating to a grand jury proceeding, you can only say, 'I cannot comment on pending grand jury matters,' period," Scorza said.

Tuohey said he was not commenting about the grand jury itself, but on complaints made outside the courtroom by attorneys for the police.

"I responded to the AP that aggressive questioning sometimes causes friction," Tuohey said.

Some staff members, including Rodriguez, bristled over other press reports that the Foster probe basically had been concluded. Some people were concerned that political maneuvering was dictating the outcome of the proceedings, according to the source.

On the day grand jury proceedings in the Foster case began in January, a Scripps-Howard wire story reported that Kenneth Starr had concluded Foster's death was a suicide and was preparing to close the case.

Recently, the Wall Street Journal and USA Today reported that despite the preliminary aspects of the grand jury proceedings, Starr had concluded the case was a suicide.

Last month, the Tribune-Review reported on a similar occurrence in the early stages of the Fiske investigation into Foster's death. For example, the Wall Street Journal reported in April 1994 that Fiske had ruled the death a suicide and was set to issue a report.

Fiske did issue a report several months later, but documents released this year demonstrate that the most basic elements of the investigation had yet to be completed by the time the Wall Street Journal reported the case closed. ∎

Policy Dispute Led To Shakeup In Foster Probe

By Christopher Ruddy
FOR THE PITTSBURGH
TRIBUNE-REVIEW
MAY 3, 1995

WASHINGTON—The prosecutor and his top assistant assigned to investigate the death of White House deputy counsel Vincent W. Foster Jr. abruptly resigned earlier this year after sparring with their superior over how the grand jury probe of the case should proceed.

A Washington, D.C., law enforcement source close to the case says Miquel Rodriguez, an associate assigned to the office of Independent Counsel Kenneth Starr, called it quits when his supervisor, Deputy Independent Counsel Mark H. Tuohey III, allegedly:

∎ insisted that witnesses before a grand jury probing Foster's death be allowed to review evidence prior to testifying. Rodriguez, noting several discrepancies in the case, feared those previews would give witnesses time to rehearse and perhaps alter their testimony.

∎ refused a request from Rodriguez to decide which expert witnesses would be brought before the grand jury. Rodriguez wanted to summon independent experts—outside of the FBI—to explore inconsistencies in the case.

∎ interfered with Rodriguez's desire not to use FBI laboratory and forensic analyses for the case. Rodriguez was disturbed by previous FBI work and sought to use outside agencies, according to the source.

These new details have surfaced since the Tribune-Review first reported on Rodriguez's resignation last month. The report cited a number of reasons for his departure including the fact that Rodriguez believed he was not allowed to conduct a full grand jury probe and that witnesses

Continued on next page

Continued from page 89

were not being called quickly enough, allowing them to possibly adjust testimony.

On March 20, Rodriguez pulled up stakes in Washington and returned to his position as an assistant U.S. Attorney in Sacramento, Calif. His assistant, a paralegal, also resigned as a result of the disagreement with Tuohey, the source said.

Tuohey, former president of the Washington, D.C., Bar Association, is heading up the Washington phase of Starr's investigation of the now infamous failed Arkansas Whitewater real estate dealings. As part of that probe, Starr is delving into the death of Foster, a close friend and counsel to Bill and Hillary Clinton, both of whom were involved in the Whitewater deal.

This week, a source close to Starr's Arkansas investigation said Rodriguez departed as a result of a "personality conflict" with Tuohey.

Both Rodriguez and Tuohey have declined to comment on the departure. Starr's office has also declined to comment on the issue.

POLICY DIFFERENCES

The Washington source disagreed that Rodriguez resigned over personality issues.

The source said it was the mounting policy disputes between Rodriguez and Tuohey over the handling of the grand jury probe that eventually led to Rodriguez's departure.

After the grand jury probe began in January, Rodriguez had the investigation moving quickly, the source said.

"They (Rodriguez and his assistant) had people quaking," the source said. The case was so sensitive that even Tuohey was unaware of Rodriguez's daily plans to interrogate witnesses before the grand jury, the source added.

Soon, press reports surfaced that the Park Police were complaining of tough questioning by Rodriguez. Thereafter, Tuohey took a more active role in Rodriguez's day-to-day work, the source said.

One significant policy difference stemmed from Tuohey's alleged insistence that witnesses be allowed to review evidence before the grand jury, the source said.

Rodriguez, noting many discrepancies in the case, feared that previewing evidence would allow witnesses time to prepare and make their testimony agree with those who had already testified.

Rodriguez would not comment on this specific allegation. Tuohey also declined to comment.

WITNESS ISSUE

Perhaps the most serious disagreement between Tuohey and Rodriguez related to the issue of deciding which expert witnesses were to be brought before the grand jury to explain the inconsistencies and unusual circumstances of the case, the source said.

According to the source, Rodriguez made substantial progress in building a case that Foster's body had been transported to the park and that the gun found in his hand had either been "moved or switched" after the Park Police arrived.

Last week, the Western Journalism Center, a California nonprofit organization that supports investigative journalism, issued a report on the Foster case compiled by two former New York police homicide experts.

Vincent Scalice and Fred Santucci reviewed the crime scene at Fort Marcy Park (where Foster's body was discovered), along with numerous reports, and had laboratory analyses conducted by one of the nation's top forensic scientists, Dr. Richard Saferstein.

Their report concluded that homicide has not been ruled out in the death and that it was very likely that Foster's body had been transported to the park. The report also stated that the 1913 Colt found in Foster's right hand had likely been staged.

An official present at Fort Marcy Park on the night Foster died and who has testified before the grand jury, said he was shown enhanced photographs taken at the scene that suggested someone had moved Foster's hand.

Careful examination of the enhanced photos showed a glaring discrepancy, the official said.

Blades of vegetation protruded from between different fingers in separate photos—strongly indicating that someone may have moved the hand, thus tampering with the crime scene, the official added.

Rodriguez clashed with Tuohey over the issue of expert witnesses slated to testify to explain such inconsistencies before the grand jury, the source said. Rodriguez wanted to summon independent experts outside the FBI to explore inconsistencies revealed before the grand jury. He believed FBI experts were not interested in exploring inconsistencies, the source said. Tuohey wanted to use only FBI laboratory and forensic experts, the source added.

Rodriguez again declined to comment. Tuohey described the idea that he didn't want to have experts explore inconsistencies as "absolutely ridiculous."

THE FBI

According to the source, Rodriguez developed grave doubts about the FBI's ability to properly investigate the case. For example, important photographic evidence, said to be unusable by certain FBI experts, was turned over by Rodriguez to an outside agency that produced remarkable results.

Eventually, Rodriguez would refuse the use of FBI labs or forensic experts in the case—another point of contention with Tuohey.

The FBI's role in the Foster case comes late. Agents were first assigned to the investigation of Special Prosecutor Robert Fiske early in 1994, seven months after Foster's death on July 20, 1993. Starr was later named to replace Fiske to investigate the Whitewater affair.

Some controversy over FBI handling of the case has surfaced, for example with a confidential witness.

The confidential witness—also the man alleged to have first found Foster's body—charged that FBI agents had badgered him, and that his testimony, such as not seeing a gun in Foster's hand, had been misrepresented in the Fiske report.

A number of other issues involving the FBI have raised eyebrows inside and outside the bureau.

For example, some of the agents assigned to the Foster case had little or no practical homicide experience.

Also, two FBI agents who worked for Fiske testified before the Senate Banking Committee, which conducted a day of hearings related to Foster's death.

They drew several conclusions about the death—a function generally considered outside the investigative role of the FBI.

Several FBI sources expressed surprise that one of the agents during the Senate hearings dismissed the importance of trace evidence—multi-colored carpet fibers found on most of Foster's clothing. No effort was made to track the source of these fibers.

Homicide expert Scalice said "the highly suspicious fibers could be the most important evidence of the case."

Earlier this month, the Tribune-Review quoted sources as questioning whether an excavation said to have been conducted by FBI lab personnel at Fort Marcy Park actually occurred.

Statements made in FBI reports of the excavation were disputed by a Park Service archaeologist and Smithsonian anthropologist who were present when the excavation allegedly took place.

FBI interview statements contain numerous omissions on critical issues, like questioning Foster's associates about places Foster might frequent outside the White House.

A statement issued by former FBI Director William Sessions may explain Rodriguez's concerns about bureau behavior.

In February 1994, Sessions wrote that he had been fired the day before Foster's death, and that his firing effectively "compromised" the investigation of the death by the FBI.

The Justice Department gave jurisdiction in the investigation of the death to the Park Police over the FBI—a decision that has been widely criticized.

Sessions, known for his integrity and non-partisanship, also stated that his firing was the result of a power struggle that had begun before Clinton took office. That struggle pitted the FBI director, seeking to maintain the FBI's political neutrality, against the Justice Department and the White House.

Another development that may have affected the FBI's handling of the Foster probe in light of Rodriguez's difficulties was the resignation of the head of the FBI laboratory, Assistant Director John Hicks.

Hicks is highly regarded for modernizing the bureau's capabilities. Along with Sessions, he pioneered the FBI's entry into DNA analysis. Hicks retired early over several issues relating to the reorganization of the FBI implemented by Sessions' successor, Louis Freeh.

Soon after his appointment, Freeh quickly moved to reassign all special agents as specialists in FBI labs back into field investigations, sources confirmed.

Hicks opposed the reassignment on several grounds, including the fact that the removal left the labs staffed by technicians who he believed were more susceptible to political pressures.

Hicks, now affiliated with the Alabama State Crime Lab, declined to comment. Several bureau officials who served with Hicks on the Executive Committee confirmed the story. ∎

Starr's Grand Jury

By Christopher Ruddy
FOR THE PITTSBURGH
TRIBUNE-REVIEW
MAY 3, 1995

WASHINGTON—Independent Counsel Kenneth Starr's grand jury investigation of former White House Deputy Counsel Vincent W. Foster's death is ongoing, one source reports.

The bulk of former Starr associate Miquel Rodriguez's work was taken over by Starr's chief trial counsel, Hickman Ewing, a well-respected former U.S. Attorney from Memphis.

Recent news accounts have reported that Starr's office has been focusing its grand jury probe on documents removed from Foster's office, including a box apparently removed by a presidential aide.

But, the Washington law enforcement source said, the office issue was "a diversion" from the serious issue of Foster's death.

The source denied that the removal of the box was a new development and said its removal was known by Fiske's staff early in their inquiry.

According to the source, the internal problems among Starr's staff are partly a result of the "grand jury not knowing their full powers or how to use them."

An active and trained grand jury "keeps the prosecutors on their toes," the source said. The source stressed the importance of the grand jury in this case because of the gravity of the issues involved, and the fact that certain law enforcement agencies may not want full disclosure of the facts.

The source said the Foster case is basically a civil rights one since it challenges the government as to whether justice was properly administered in a politically sensitive case. The source suggested that Harvard-educated Rodriguez, noted for his handling of civil rights cases, was extremely well suited for the case.

Also, the District of Columbia, strongly represented by minorities and African-Americans sensitive to issues of civil rights and law enforcement agencies, should make for a grand jury less willing to accept law enforcement testimony at face value, the source added.

"No one has to explain to an African-American that the police or FBI can be politically pressured," the source said, noting the FBI's controversial record vis-à-vis the civil rights movement and Dr. Martin Luther King Jr.

Thomas Scorza, a former Chicago federal prosecutor and professor of legal ethics at the University of Chicago, suggests that difficulties between Miquel Rodriguez and Mark H. Tuohey III, if true, are "very serious."

He said he found it unusual that a supervisor would be telling a working prosecutor such as Rodriguez how to handle a case, or demanding a type of witness to be called.

Scorza agreed that some internal problems can be helped if the grand jury is not used as a "rubber stamp."

He said the grand jury "has the ultimate power" in an investigation, which it can exercise through a number of "controls" on the prosecutor to ensure an investigation is thorough and proper.

Scorza outlines some of these sweeping powers:

■ The active questioning of witnesses.

■ The ability to subpoena witnesses. As a practical matter, the grand jury can't prepare a subpoena, but can vote to do so. If the prosecutor refuses to consent, the jury can appeal to the supervisory judge.

Scorza said the grand jury has a legitimate right, for example, to have both Rodriguez and Tuohey subpoenaed and questioned under oath to see if any interference in the proceedings took place. They can also vote to have expert witnesses explore incon-sistencies.

■ The right to refuse to continue proceedings or to bring indictments.

■ The right to vote for indictments. Scorza said as a technical matter a prosecutor has to sign off on an indictment, and prepare the necessary forms, but nothing prevents a grand jury from voting indictments if they believe they discovered wrongdoing or a witness committed perjury. If the prosecutor doesn't comply, the jury can appeal to the supervisory judge.

"Just imagine if it comes out a grand jury voted to indict and the prosecutor refused to," Scorza explained.

■ The right to write their own report. If the grand jury believes the prosecutor was not thorough in certain areas, that inconsistencies were glossed over, or if it perceives any deficiencies, it can file a written report with the judge and ask it to be made public. ■

Missing Briefcase Could Be Key in Solving Vince Foster Mystery

By Christopher Ruddy
FOR THE PITTSBURGH
TRIBUNE-REVIEW
JUNE 13, 1995

Testimony would seem to indicate that a briefcase in the car of Vincent Foster was removed after U.S. Park Police arrived at his death scene July 20, 1993.

The briefcase, which may have carried important documents, was never listed on official evidence reports compiled by Park Police who conducted the first investigation into the White House deputy counsel's death.

Foster was found dead of an apparent gunshot wound to the head in Fort Marcy Park. His unoccupied car, a 1989 Honda, was found in the park's parking lot.

Several witnesses—before and after the arrival of the Park Police—have claimed they saw a briefcase in Foster's car.

Park Police spokesman Maj. Robert Hines said the police are sticking with their version that no briefcase was in the car. He suggested that witnesses may have seen something that they thought was a briefcase.

The briefcase issue became a focus of serious inquiry in January before a federal grand jury sitting in Washington to probe Whitewater-related matters.

Associate Independent Counsel Miquel Rodriguez was seriously pursuing several apparent inconsistencies in Foster's death and the subsequent police investigation.

Rodriguez resigned in March, according to sources, because he believed his superior, Deputy Independent Counsel Mark Tuohey, was not allowing him to conduct a full grand jury probe into Foster's death.

Rodriguez declined to comment on the case, referring all inquiries on the matter to the Independent Counsel's office.

FIRST WITNESS

The arguments over the existence of a briefcase first surfaced during the investigation by Robert Fiske, the original Whitewater Independent Counsel.

According to documents from the Fiske investigation into Foster's death, the first witness to observe Foster's car at Fort Marcy was a motorist who noted the car's Arkansas plates at approximately 4:30 p.m.

The motorist told the FBI last year that after exiting his vehicle for a brief time, he returned to his car and "he observed in this Honda a leather briefcase or leather folder on the passenger side seat."

Another witness, a van driver who Fiske claimed first dis-covered Foster's body and is now identified as CW, or the confidential witness in the Fiske report, reportedly told the grand jury that he, too, saw a briefcase in Foster's car.

According to a source familiar with the probe, at least two Fairfax County emergency workers present at Fort Marcy also testified before the grand jury they saw a briefcase in Foster's car.

Paramedic Sgt. George Gonzalez told Fiske's investigators, "The Honda contained a necktie, suit coat, and a black briefcase/attaché case."

Emergency Medical Technician Todd Hall also told the grand jury and Fiske's FBI investigators he saw a briefcase in the car, according to the source.

FOUR VERSUS FOUR

Another source familiar with new Whitewater Independent Counsel Kenneth Starr's probe admitted the briefcase discrepancy has not been pursued, stating, "Four witnesses say there was a briefcase, four say there wasn't."

The four officials swearing there was no briefcase were all Park Police officers.

But Rodriguez, according to a source, disagreed with that view, believing "the police had everything to lose and the four other witnesses had no reason to lie," the source said.

Thomas Scorza, a former federal prosecutor and lecturer of legal ethics at the University of Chicago, suggested the briefcase is "important, not in an isolated way, but in the context of other discrepancies."

"I wouldn't say, don't follow it, because it's four versus four on the witness stand," he said. "When you have a pattern of these discrepancies, a prosecutor should pursue the matter vigorously."

PHOTOS AND LEAKS

Other evidence indicated the presence of a briefcase. A Polaroid of Foster's car taken by Park Police shows a briefcase on the ground.

Early in the grand jury process, a high level source in the Starr investigation was quoted in an Associated Press report as detailing the probe's focus on the briefcase.

Continued on next page

Continued from page 93

At the time, Rodriguez told associates that he believed the leak, a violation of grand jury secrecy rules, had seriously undermined the investigation by giving officials time to possibly prepare testimony.

During grand jury proceedings, the police claimed the briefcase in the photograph was likely their own, a carrying case for crime scene equipment.

Further questioning by Rodriguez of the police revealed that their carrying cases are colored tan or silver. An enhanced Polaroid showed a black leather case, the source said. ∎

Foster Eyewitnesses Ignored

By Christopher Ruddy
FOR THE PITTSBURGH
TRIBUNE-REVIEW
JUNE 14, 1995

A couple present at Fort Marcy Park on the evening of Vincent Foster's death told the FBI last year that at least two individuals were in or around the White House aide's car shortly before his body was found.

The witness statements, which they claim were incorrectly recorded by U.S. Park Police, "were completely ignored" by the staff of former Independent Counsel Robert Fiske, a source close to Whitewater Independent Counsel Kenneth Starr said.

With the resignation of Associate Whitewater Counsel Miquel Rodriguez in March, Starr's staff has apparently also chosen not to re-investigate the matter.

The witness statements add to the several dozen inconsistencies and discrepancies in the suicide ruling, homicide experts say.

FIRST SIGHTING

Foster's body was found in the roadside park shortly after 6 p.m. on July 20, 1993—approximately five hours after he had left the White House West Wing.

No one saw him alive, as far as authorities are concerned, from the time he passed a Secret Service checkpoint at 1 p.m. that fateful afternoon until his lifeless body was discovered at Fort Marcy.

The first firm sighting of his car was at approximately 4:30 p.m., by a motorist who entered the small parking lot off the George Washington Memorial Parkway, according to an FBI report.

The motorist noted a Honda with Arkansas plates in one of the first spots in the lot, fitting the location and description of Foster's car.

The motorist also observed another car, probably of Japanese make, parked several spots past Foster's car. The car was occupied by an individual described as a male in his late 20s, probably Mexican or Cuban, with a dark complexion.

When the motorist left his car to urinate in some nearby woods, he said the male occupant left his car and followed him, making the motorist "feel extremely nervous and uneasy."

The motorist quickly relieved himself and left.

KEY STATEMENTS

Shortly after 5 p.m., a couple who have sought to keep their identities secret drove up to the park to enjoy a late picnic.

Both told Fiske's FBI investigators just over a year ago that when they entered the parking lot there was only one car parked in the lot, and their descriptions are generally consistent with Foster's 1989 Honda and its placement in the lot.

The female visitor told the FBI she believed that "a white male was seated in the driver's seat" of the vehicle. She said he had dark hair and "could have been bare-chested."

As the driver of the car, she had an unobstructed view of Foster's car, which was parked to her immediate left.

Her male companion told the FBI that he remembered the hood of the vehicle was up and a white male was standing near the hood of Foster's car. He was described as "mid to late 40s, appeared unclean and unkempt."

The male witness said he saw an unkempt man with long blonde hair standing near Foster's car after they had backed into a parking spot, giving him a clear view of Foster's car to his right.

The couple said they sat in their car until about 6 p.m., and then exited the car to have their picnic. They first learned of a problem, they said, when emergency workers stumbled upon them during a search for the body shortly after 6 p.m.

MISREPRESENTATION?

The Park Police report gives a decidedly different representation of their accounts.

The scene investigation report, prepared by plainclothes investigator Cheryl Braun, contains the only witness statements of persons found in the park after police arrived. That report cites the couple as having observed "a small car with a man without a shirt sitting in it," who the couple was quoted as saying "left shortly after their arrival."

The man with the long blonde hair who had the hood raised is described this way: "The final vehicle they observed was a light-colored older model that pulled in next to the deceased's vehicle." The driver then pulled his hood up, went into the woods for a short time and then left.

After being shown the Park Police statement of her account, the female witness told the FBI that the police statement was not true, and did not match her recollection of what she told them.

The police statement implies that two cars, in addition to Foster's Honda, were observed by the couple, who saw persons either in a car or with the hood up.

The FBI witness statements make clear that the male and female both saw only one car, apparently Foster's, and individuals in or around it.

In two interviews this year, the female witness told the Tribune-Review that she stood by her account to the FBI, which she said is consistent with her male friend's statement of seeing only one car parked in the lot.

The only other vehicle that parked in the lot while they were there was a white utility van. Fiske's investigators concluded the van driver was the first person to find Foster's body.

An older model car was driven into the lot, as noted in the police report, but contrary to that report never parked. The driver just turned and left, according to an FBI witness statement.

The female witness stated she has never been contacted by anyone on Starr's staff, nor has she or her friend been summoned before a grand jury.

A spokesman for the Park Police, Maj. Robert Hines, said Officer Braun was not available for comment on the case. He added that the Park Police stood by her report and the police report.

STATEMENTS OVERLOOKED

Fiske's 58-page report makes no mention of the witness statements, which were part of his investigation and released by the Senate Banking Committee this year.

According to a source close to the investigation, Rodriguez believed the witness statements were supportive of evidence Foster's body had been transported to the park.

No time has ever been nailed down for Foster's death, and the Fiske report concludes death could have occurred from the time Foster left the White House up until the time the body was found. ∎

Other Witnesses Still Unexplained

By Christopher Ruddy
FOR THE PITTSBURGH
TRIBUNE-REVIEW
JUNE 14, 1995

The couple who saw persons in and around Vincent Foster's car at Fort Marcy Park were not the only persons ignored during the investigation by Whitewater Independent Counsel Robert Fiske.

To date, no one can account for several men seen wearing orange vests in the park, as well as park visitors who entered after the police arrived.

According to a source familiar with the probe, several people entered during the night through a rear entrance and encountered Park Police. The police had not secured that entrance.

The officers also violated standard police procedure by not recording the names of the individuals who came into the park on the night of July 20, 1993.

And then there were the mysterious men wearing orange vests. A Park Police officer has acknowledged to Starr's inquiry that after police arrived at the park and well after the end of the workday, they discovered several men wearing orange vests who claimed to be park maintenance workers clearing a park trail.

The Park Police did not record their names or positively identify them.

Fairfax County rescue worker Todd Hall was among the first at the scene.

Sources in Whitewater Independent Counsel Kenneth Starr's probe were aware that he told the grand jury that when he first arrived at the death scene, he thought he saw a man wearing an orange vest running from the body on a footpath just below the slope where Foster's was found. The man, Hall reportedly said, was running toward the rear entrance.

During grand jury proceedings, Park Police claimed they were unaware of the second entrance. Prosecutors had evidence, however, that police were regularly stationed at the rear entrance during the Gulf War, since the entrance is directly across the street from the Saudi Arabian ambassador's residence.

Park Police spokesman Major Robert Hines said he was unaware of additional persons in the park and couldn't comment on the matter.

"Every investigation is not perfect. We are standing behind our investigation," he said. ■

Foster's Death: What and When Did the White House Know?

By Christopher Ruddy
FOR THE PITTSBURGH
TRIBUNE-REVIEW
JUNE 15, 1995

When it comes to the death of Deputy White House Counsel Vincent W. Foster Jr., the question remains: What did those in the White House know and when did they know it?

Another question: If Foster was not identified as a White House official until at least an hour and a half after police arrived, why were police officers associated with an elite federal unit on the scene within 45 minutes?

Evidence suggests that White House officials were informed of Foster's death on July 20, 1993, at least an hour before they claim to have been officially notified.

Recently, Whitewater Independent Counsel Kenneth Starr apparently reopened an examination into the time discrepancy. His staff questioned an Arkansas trooper who received a phone call informing him of Foster's death from a White House staffer before the White House claims to have been officially notified.

The time discrepancy, apparent from public documents relating to the case, was first investigated by Miquel Rodriguez, who was Starr's lead prosecutor probing Foster's death. The discrepancy was first reported by The London Sunday Telegraph.

According to a well-informed source, Rodriguez believed the time discrepancy was an important clue in unmasking a possible cover-up into Foster's death. Rodriguez, an assistant U.S. Attorney in Sacramento, would not comment on the case and referred all calls to Starr's office.

The Tribune-Review reported Rodriguez resigned from the prosecutor's staff in March because he believed he was not allowed to explore inconsistencies and discrepancies before Starr's Whitewater grand jury in Washington.

SPECIAL FORCES

By January of this year, as the grand jury began taking a cursory look into Foster's death, Rodriguez found evidence that police officers associated with the U.S. Park Police's special forces—an elite unit with close ties to White House security—showed up at the park by 7 p.m., the source said.

These officers have never been identified in the police report, congressional reports or any FBI report.

U.S. Park Police spokesman Maj. Robert Hines said he was unaware of the presence of such officers. He said the special forces unit was the police's "SWAT team . . . involved in sensitive duties."

Rodriguez apparently believed the introduction of these elite officers to a crime scene seriously diminished Park Police claims that the death scene did not strike them as unusual, and that the White House was not notified until 8:30 p.m.

SECRET SERVICE MEMO

Earlier this year, the Senate Banking Committee released documents related to the Fiske investigation into Foster's death, which was the original probe headed by Whitewater Independent Counsel Robert Fiske.

One document, a Secret Service memorandum, was written on the night of Foster's death, a minute after 10 p.m.

Foster's body was found by officials shortly after 6 p.m. in the small Virginia roadside park just seven miles from the White House.

The memo states that at 8:30 p.m. Lt. Pat Gavin of the Park Police contacted Lt. Woltz, a uniformed member of the Secret Service. This is the official version of how the White House learned of Foster's death.

Strangely, no member of the president's entourage would be informed for another 45 minutes, until about 9:15, while the president was on the "Larry King Live" television program.

And if the official notification was indeed made by Gavin at 8:30 p.m., other testimony then becomes inconsistent.

Cheryl Braun, then a Park Police investigator, told Fiske's FBI agents that she searched Foster's car at about 7 p.m. and found his White House ID, at which point she asked an unidentified officer to call Lt. Gavin, the police shift commander on duty that night.

The officer apparently failed to do so, and Braun said she herself called Gavin between 7:30 and 7:45 p.m.

Gavin was unreachable for comment. He did tell Fiske's FBI investigators that he notified the

Continued on next page

Continued from page 97

White House within 10 minutes of being informed of Foster's White House ID—which still would have made the official notification a half-hour to an hour before the time mentioned in the Secret Service memo.

Gavin also told the Sunday Telegraph that he was notified not by Braun, but by Park Police investigator John Rolla.

And Rolla gives still another story as to the time he discovered Foster was a White House official.

Rolla, in his sworn deposition before Banking Committee investigators last summer, as well as in his FBI statement of last year, said he searched the car after the death scene had been cleared and the body removed to Fairfax County Hospital.

"I believe I went through the passenger's door first and lifted up the suit jacket, observed the White House identification with his picture and name on it," Rolla said in his deposition, directly contradicting Braun's version of events.

Rolla was explicit in saying this search was conducted after the death scene had been cleared.

Fiske placed the approximate time of the removal of the body from the scene at 8:45 p.m.—meaning Rolla didn't begin his search until after the official 8:30 p.m. notification time.

Hines was unaware of any discrepancies involving the time the White House was contacted. He said if there was a delay, it probably occurred because investigators

"didn't think of suicide as a big deal."

He said police are trained to be sensitive to handling cases involving officials, but the officers, even after finding his White House identification card, were unaware of Foster's level at the White House.

TROOPER'S VERSION

The Telegraph also reported that in an affidavit, Trooper Roger Perry stated that on the night of Foster's death, while on guard duty at the Arkansas governor's mansion, he answered a call from Helen Dickey, an assistant to the Clinton family working in the White House.

Before being put through to Gov. Jim Guy Tucker, Dickey related to Perry that Vince Foster had killed himself.

"She told me that Vince got off work, went out to his car in the parking lot, and shot himself in the head," Perry recalled.

Perry, in his affidavit, states the call came from Dickey no later than 7 p.m. Arkansas time, 8 p.m. Washington time—a half-hour before the White House claims to have been notified.

But Perry believes, based on the recollections of others he notified after Dickey's call, her call may have come in much earlier, shortly after 6 p.m. Washington time.

Perry's recollection is buttressed by the sworn statement of State Trooper Larry Patterson and Lynn Davis, former head of the Arkansas State Police.

They both claim Perry contacted them immediately after receiving Dickey's call—and they both place

the time before 7 p.m. Washington time—a full hour before the White House claimed to have been notified.

Perry's recollection of Helen Dickey's account of Foster being found dead in his car—a story he had told long before the Secret Service memo was released—finds corroboration in the memo.

The Secret Service memo reads: "On the evening of 7/20/93, unknown time, U.S. Park Police discovered the body of Vincent Foster in his car. The car was parked in the Fort Marcy area of Virginia near the George Washington Parkway. Foster apparently died of a self-inflicted gunshot wound to the head. A .38-caliber revolver was found in the car."

Foster was found, according to officials, 700 feet from his car near an old Civil War cannon. Investigators for Fiske and Starr have deemed the memo's account "an honest mistake," according to one source.

Another source familiar with the investigation believes the "body-in-the-car" scenario may have been an initial attempt to cover up the unusual circumstances of death, considering Foster's body was found lying on a steep hill, in a neat position amidst dense foliage and brush. The source said it would be difficult to imagine that the circumstances of death of a high official would be so dramatically confused, and not verified by the Secret Service before being disseminated through the chain of command. ∎

Foster's Death Discrepancies Are Abundant: Did His Neck Suffer Trauma?

By Christopher Ruddy
FOR THE PITTSBURGH
TRIBUNE-REVIEW
JUNE 16, 1995

Independent Counsel Kenneth Starr's probe into the death of Vincent Foster has turned up some unsettling discrepancies in the case—including strong evidence that the White House aide may have suffered trauma or a wound to his neck.

Homicide experts say that in any investigation of a suicide, several inconsistencies and discrepancies should arouse suspicion.

In the case of President Clinton's close friend, the inconsistencies and discrepancies number in the several dozens.

"Freak things can happen in violent death," explained Vincent Scalice, a former New York City homicide detective. "But the laws of nature cannot be suspended and inconsistencies don't range into the dozens as in this case."

The Tribune-Review reported that Associate Independent Counsel Miquel Rodriguez resigned from Starr's staff after he was thwarted in his efforts to investigate such inconsistencies.

Rodriguez was unavailable for comment and his office in Sacramento referred all calls to Starr's Little Rock office.

In addition to the several dozen inconsistencies, here are some significant problems Rodriguez turned up:

NECK TRAUMA

Key elements in the suicide ruling have been official reports noting the absence of additional wounds to Foster's body and no signs of struggle at the crime scene.

An independent pathology team for Special Counsel Robert Fiske also reached that conclusion after reviewing the autopsy and Polaroid photos of the scene. The only wounds on Foster's body, according to official accounts, were an entry wound in his mouth and an exit wound out the back of his head—consistent with a self-inflicted gunshot wound.

But photographic evidence unavailable to Fiske's pathology team may have led them to a different conclusion.

Rodriguez and other prosecutors reviewed the original Polaroids never used by the Fiske investigation. These originals were enhanced by a specialized lab outside the FBI.

One enhanced Polaroid showed what "appears to be a wound, puncture or other trauma" to the right side of Foster's neck, the source said.

Two emergency rescue workers, trained in the identification of wounds and other trauma, said the neck appeared to have suffered trauma when they first arrived on the scene.

A Fairfax County EMS technician, Richard Arthur, who was present on the night of Foster's death told the FBI last year that "he noted what appeared to be a small caliber bullet hole in Foster's neck on the right side just under the jaw line about halfway between the ear and the tip of the chin."

Arthur has told the same story to Starr's investigators.

Lead Paramedic George Gonzalez told Fiske's investigators he thought he saw a bullet wound in Foster's forehead. After reviewing the new photographic evidence, Gonzalez told Starr's probe that the neck trauma is consistent with the appearance of Foster's body when he arrived at the scene, a source said.

"These wounds did not exist," said Fiske in his 1994 report. "The autopsy results, the photographs taken at the scene, and the observations made by Park Police investigators conclusively show that there were no such wounds."

PHOTOS DISTORTED

Investigators for Fiske said Arthur confused the wound with a contact blood stain on Foster's neck—a blood stain the FBI lab said was produced when Foster's jaw came into contact with his bloodied shirt.

An FBI blood splatter analysis identified the stain from a crime scene Polaroid.

But Rodriguez discovered that Fiske's pathology team, as well as the FBI lab, analyzed not the original photos, but third generation photos said to be distorted and obscured.

According to a well-placed source, the FBI, for unexplained reasons, first took Polaroid shots of the original 13 crime scene Polaroids.

After Polaroids were made of the Polaroids, the FBI lab then took 35mm picture shots of the second generation Polaroids.

It was the 35mm, third generation photos that were reviewed by the FBI and Fiske pathology team.

"Each time you make a copy, you *Continued on next page*

Continued from page 99

lose definition," Fred Santucci said. "Polaroids aren't sharp in definition to begin with."

Santucci, a former New York City police homicide expert, spent 15 years as a forensic crime scene photographer for the department.

"The only thing I can think why this was done," Santucci said of the use of third generation photos, "is because someone wanted to hide something."

Santucci said a 35mm shot should have been taken of the original Polaroid. Another method is to use high-tech computer scanning, which allows for enhancement with little distortion.

Park Police said that the crime scene photos taken by a 35mm camera were underexposed in the lab.

An autopsy prepared by a Virginia medical examiner makes no notation of wounds or trauma to Foster's neck. But a source who reviewed the autopsy photos said they show the right side of the neck depict "black crater-like indentions" where the scene Polaroid indicated trauma.

NO FINGERPRINT SET

Despite Foster's position as a high federal official, with appropriate security clearances, the government claims to have no set of fingerprints for him, according to two sources close to the Starr investigation.

The fingerprints would be important for the investigation because eight unidentified fingerprints were found on Foster's 1989 Honda, a palm print was found on a note torn into 28 pieces and two fingerprints were found on Foster's gun.

Despite the claims of having no set of fingerprints, the FBI lab reports attached to the Fiske report seem to contradict this. In one report the FBI lab stated that latent fingerprints did not match ones found on the fingerprint card of Vincent Foster.

The Park Police report states that during the autopsy "... fingerprints were taken from the victim ..."

A handwritten document in the police file states that on May 26 Fiske's staff acquired the fingerprint card [apparently from the autopsy] from the Park Police case packet. It was signed by FBI Agent William Colombell.

Apparently the autopsy fingerprint card was turned over to the FBI lab on May 31. The FBI stated it could make no identification based on those prints, since they were unusable.

The police and Fiske's investigations found no prints on any outside surface of the gun. During the FBI analysis for Fiske, the FBI found two prints, each under plates on the hand grip after they had been unscrewed.

Recently Starr's investigation has asked for an extensive search of Vincent Foster's late father's military records in St. Louis seeking his fingerprints in hopes of linking him to the gun.

The gun's ownership has been a glaring inconsistency in the investigation.

Both the Park Police and Fiske intimate the gun was passed on to Foster after his father's death. Yet, a grandson of Foster's father, intimately knowledgeable of his grandfather's gun, said the revolver did not match any he remembered.

MISSING POLAROIDS

Glossed over by the official investigation are missing Polaroids taken by the second Park Police officer on the scene, Franz Ferstl.

Ferstl said he took the photos almost immediately upon coming to the crime scene.

He told FBI investigators for Robert Fiske that he believed he took seven Polaroids.

The Park Police have accounted for only 13 photos taken by two other officers. According to one source, Ferstl told the grand jury earlier this year that photos he was shown of the 13 Polaroids didn't match the scene he remembered.

For example, Ferstl said when he first came upon the body it was lying on the ground with the palms of the hands up.

Current scene Polaroids show Foster's palms down.

A confidential witness who is said to have found Foster's body also claimed to have found Foster with his palms up.

Other evidence indicates Foster's hand was moved. New photographic evidence uncovered in the Rodriguez probe showed vegetation protruding through fingers that were different in another Polaroid of the same scene. ■

Ex-Prosecutor Can Show Apparent Cover-Up in Foster Death Probe

By Christopher Ruddy
FOR THE PITTSBURGH
TRIBUNE-REVIEW
JUNE 19, 1995

If former Whitewater Associate Counsel Miquel Rodriguez went public with his experiences as a lead prosecutor, it could be a major embarrassment to Independent Counsel Kenneth Starr's probe.

In March, Rodriguez left Starr's Washington staff as the lead prosecutor examining the death of Vincent Foster.

He returned to his position as Assistant U.S. Attorney in Sacramento, Calif. Foster, counsel to President Clinton, allegedly took his own life by shooting himself in the head.

According to a source close to Starr's probe, Rodriguez could detail apparent efforts to cover up several major inconsistencies in the case, as well as mishandling of the case by federal Park Police and Special Counsel Robert Fiske.

Rodriguez has refused to comment on the case, and recently has referred all press inquiries to Starr's office.

Among the more serious situations Rodriguez could address, the source said, are:

■ During the early part of Starr's investigation last fall, Starr's Deputy Independent Counsel, Mark H. Tuohey III, through remarks to Rodriguez and other staff members, informed them he wanted the Foster case to be concluded. Rodriguez understood from these remarks that he was expected to conclude that Foster committed suicide.

■ FBI agents assigned to Starr's staff sought to prevent a full independent probe into the death of the Deputy White House Counsel by refusing to do investigative work relating to the case requested by Rodriguez.

Rodriguez's objections to the manner in which he believed he was being forced to conduct his probe were chronicled in numerous memos-to-file which he circulated among members of Starr's Washington staff, the source said.

When Rodriguez insisted on conducting a painstaking review of the case, he met with stiff opposition from FBI agents assigned to Starr's probe, the source said.

STARR'S REVIEW

Details of the reasons for Rodriguez's departure continue to come to light, and provide some of the first glimpses of the Starr inquiry's handling of the Whitewater matter.

Within two months of taking the reins of the Whitewater probe in August 1994, Starr appointed Rodriguez to head up the Foster probe, which he promised would thoroughly review the work of Special Counsel Robert Fiske.

Fiske had been criticized in law enforcement circles and by several members of Congress for exempting the Foster investigation from his Washington grand jury inquiry.

On June 30, 1994, just a month before he was sacked by a three-judge panel, Fiske concluded in a 58-page report that the then-Deputy White House Counsel died on July 20, 1993, of a self-inflicted gunshot at the place he was found in Fort Marcy Park, Va.

But according to a well-placed source, Starr's mandate for a thorough investigation apparently conflicted with the desires of Tuohey, Rodriguez's superior.

Tuohey did not return a call for comment on the matter.

Tuohey, a former president of the District of Columbia Bar Association, has been heading up Starr's Washington phase of the Whitewater probe, and sources familiar with the probe say Starr has been unwilling to interfere with Tuohey's handling of the case.

Starr's appointment of Tuohey, an activist Democrat, was intended to offset criticism that Starr, a Republican, might use the inquiry for partisan gain. The Washington Post reported in 1994 that Tuohey "is close to some Clinton administration officials, including Jamie S. Gorelick, and last year hosted a party for Janet Reno at his Washington home."

Another factor that diminished Tuohey's appearance of independence was his friendship with former Special Counsel Robert Fiske. A source close to the probe believes that if Starr's inquiry found wrongdoing in the Foster case, it would be extremely embarrassing to Fiske.

FBI RESISTANCE

Rodriguez encountered opposition to his efforts in the case early on from FBI agents assigned to the Starr probe.

Starr's staff did not choose new agents to work with Rodriguez on the case, but kept the same agents to review their own work for Special Counsel Fiske. Notable was the lead

Continued on next page

Continued from page 101

FBI agent William Colombell. Colombell had been a senior agent working for Fiske in the Foster case.

He, along with Special Agent Larry Monroe, testified in Senate hearings in the summer of 1994 and concluded Foster's death was a suicide.

They also testified that their investigation found no major improprieties in the Park Police handling of the case. Monroe retired from the Bureau shortly after the Foster case was concluded by Fiske.

Several bureau sources have criticized the use of the two agents by Fiske before the Senate committee, since the agents were discussing conclusions outside the investigative role of the FBI.

Colombell came under fire after the release of the Fiske report by a confidential witness who claimed that Colombell and another agent had badgered him to alter his testimony.

One of Rodriguez's first requests last year to Colombell was that the FBI prepare a map of Fort Marcy Park, after he discovered to his astonishment that the Fiske investigation had drawn no survey map, the source said.

Colombell refused, the source said, citing the fact the case had been concluded by Fiske and was not to be reopened.

Rodriguez believed the map was basic to any investigation and important for a grand jury's understanding of the case.

Rodriguez also noted that a rear entrance to the park had been misidentified in the Fiske report as "For Pedestrian Access Only," when, in fact, vehicles are permitted to park there and regularly do so.

An aerial photo of the park also showed a maintenance trail that led to the area where the body was claimed to have been discovered. That trail has since been allowed to overgrow.

Rodriguez and Colombell remained at loggerheads for approximately three months, during which Rodriguez's requests for evidence and the questioning of witnesses were regularly denied. Eventually, Colombell was transferred from handling matters dealing with Foster's death.

Colombell, asked to comment on these issues, said it would be "unprofessional" to comment on the case, but did add that he follows this journalist's reporting, describing it as "mostly full of shit, and you can print that."

Colombell also suggested to this reporter in an unfriendly tone, "maybe someday we will meet."

The transfer of Colombell did not change the FBI stance toward Rodriguez's desires.

By the time Rodriguez left the investigation in March, no map of the park had been drawn, either for his use or for the viewing of the grand jury.

Also, the FBI had still to begin some of the most basic investigative elements of the case, such as conducting a door-to-door canvass of the many homes that surround and abut Fort Marcy.

Neither the Park Police nor Fiske's investigators had conducted the canvass, which police experts said should have been standard practice in a death investigation of this sort.

A source close to the probe has told the Tribune-Review that Starr investigators recently conducted the canvass.

"In a death investigation, time is everything. Time usually works against investigators," explained Vincent Scalice, a former New York City police homicide expert with 35 years of experience.

He found it "strange" that investigators would wait almost two years to do what police should have done in the hours shortly after Foster's death "when the events of the day are still clear in people's minds."

"Justice has to be administered expeditiously. If it isn't, then it hasn't been served," he said. ■

Grand Jury Examines Foster Matters

By Christopher Ruddy
FOR THE PITTSBURGH
TRIBUNE-REVIEW
JUNE 28, 1995

WASHINGTON—With Senate hearings into the handling of documents from the office of the late White House Deputy Counsel Vincent Foster set for mid-July, Independent Counsel Kenneth Starr's staff has been feverishly attempting to wrap up their investigation—which is already a year behind schedule.

This time last year, Special Counsel Robert Fiske was set to end his probe into the removal and handling of documents from Foster's office, giving a green light for the findings to be aired at congressional hearings last summer.

But within days of releasing his conclusions last July, Fiske balked and asked for more time. His report would have reportedly cleared White House officials of any wrongdoing, including Fiske's friend, resigned White House

Counsel Bernard Nussbaum.

Congressional investigators told the Tribune-Review the apparent reason for the delay was that Fiske's staff admitted to the investigators that several key White House officials had never been interviewed, and were unavailable for interviews by congressional investigators.

For example, Fiske's staff had never interviewed Charles Easley, the White House staffer in charge of safe combinations, including Foster's.

In an interview earlier this year, Fiske wouldn't comment on the delay, saying only that he needed more time.

Despite the long lag time given to Independent Counsel Kenneth Starr, who took over from Fiske in August 1994, sources familiar with the probe suggest that Starr's probe has been less than exhaustive.

"We were not given all the access we needed," one prosecutor familiar with Starr's probe said.

Another lawyer familiar with the inquiry said that all White House security personnel, including those in the Clinton's private residence, had not been interviewed by Starr's investigators, even though documents from Foster's office had been transported to the private quarters.

Three individuals who were working in the White House residence at the time of Foster's death, including one member of the Secret Service, told the Tribune-Review they had yet to be interviewed by anyone on Starr's staff.

Another member of the residence staff said they had understood that papers belonging to Foster had been stored in a converted office on the third floor of the White House residence.

Starr has been utilizing his Washington grand jury to review the handling of documents after Foster's death as well as the subsequent police death investigation.

SIGNIFICANCE OF DOCUMENTS

Papers taken from Foster's office shortly after his death have been considered a key element in unlocking the mystery surrounding his death. On the day of his death, Foster, according to official accounts, left his office at about 1 p.m. to violently take his own life at a roadside Virginia park just seven miles from the White House.

"That office, in any death investigation, would be considered part of the crime scene," said former Army criminal investigator Gene Wheaton. "Even more so because he died during the workday."

Wheaton, a retired 25-year veteran of the Army's Criminal Investigation Division who has handled federal investigations—including homicides—is an expert witness who has looked in to the Foster case for a confidential party. He says it would be "essential" for investigators to know what Foster was working on to determine a motivation for his death.

Wheaton suggests that the quickness by which officials sought to enter Foster's office and tamper with the scene should only "heighten investigator's concerns about the case."

The entire Whitewater scandal erupted on Dec. 20, 1993, when the Washington Times reported that three senior aides entered Foster's office just hours after his body was discovered on the night of July 20.

According to the Times, Park Police sources confirmed that Whitewater documents were removed from Foster's office. The White House quickly confirmed that Whitewater documents were among the first papers removed from Foster's office.

At the time, Foster was not only Deputy White House Counsel, but the Clintons' private attorney, privy to all of their dealings.

Since the Times report, the White House gave differing versions of what happened to papers removed

from the office. First, the papers were said to have been handed over to the president's attorney. Later, it was revealed that Hillary Clinton ordered the papers be put into a closet in the private residence, where they remained for a week until they were handed over to her husband's attorney.

Both Fiske and Starr have made a painstaking effort to reconstruct the papers as they were when Foster left his office for the last time.

But a number of experts believe that may be futile because of the long delay in securing and sealing the office by law enforcement officials, and because of the large number of people who entered the office without supervision.

Another suspicious aspect is what is missing from official inventories of the office.

"You become suspicious when papers relating to a hot-potato issue are not accounted for, and should be there," said Thomas Scorza, a former federal prosecutor and lecturer of legal ethics at the University of Chicago.

Inventories of Foster's papers compiled by White House staffers shortly after his death show no files relating to one "hot-potato" issue, the White House Travel Office brouhaha.

The White House has told congressional investigators the files relating to the Travel Office were in cabinets outside his office. But one investigator found that hard to believe because of Foster's intimate involvement in the case, and the fact that inventories of documents in his office showed files on cases he was intimately involved with.

The House Committee on Operations is expected to open hearings into the Travelgate matter this fall. Foster's files will also be examined during those hearings, according to a staff member.

ACCOUNTABILITY

A separate issue relating to the files is an effort by officials to deny

Continued on next page

Continued from page 103

federal investigators access to Foster's office.

On the night of Foster's death, the Park Police requested that the White House secure and seal Foster's office. When police investigators arrived at Foster's office the morning after his death, they discovered this was not done.

The investigators were also denied access by the White House.

The police returned the following day and were not allowed independent access to the office, but stood by and watched as Nussbaum searched the office. FBI agents were told to sit outside the office in a hallway.

"It's a very serious issue," said William F. Roemer Jr., former lead agent for the FBI's Organized Crime Strike Force in Chicago and the bureau's most highly decorated living agent.

Roemer suggested that apparent efforts to thwart a federal criminal probe by denying access to federal investigators "raised the possibility of obstruction of justice."

"It's the tail wagging the dog," he said, arguing that the incident is an example of increasing Justice Department and White House interference in federal criminal investigations.

"The office should have been sealed immediately after it was known he (Foster) died. In earlier days, the FBI would have pursued this vigorously," he said.

Army investigator Wheaton agrees with Roemer.

"Determining which papers were taken may be impossible. At this point, the grand jury may only be able to hold officials accountable for interfering in a criminal investigation," Wheaton said.

According to Scorza, the issue of possible obstruction of justice has to be determined by examining "the intent of officials at the time—was there a purpose or a hidden motive by officials in blocking access."

Park Police investigator Sgt. Pete Markland told the Washington Post earlier this year, "The whole search of that office was absurd," adding that he believed White House aides "obviously had something to hide."

Markland told the Post that Nussbaum claimed executive privilege in not allowing police the right to independently review the documents, which Nussbaum sorted himself.

"He should know better," Scorza said, adding that Nussbaum as White House counsel should have been aware that invoking executive privilege would mean that the documents "should have been sealed, each document initialed and catalogued and then handed over to judicial authorities for a determination."

Another matter the grand jury can weigh, Scorza said, was whether Hillary Clinton attempted to mislead investigators in "the very curious" way she "ordered documents from the office to the personal quarters."

Markland also told the Post that Nussbaum searched a briefcase twice declaring, "It's empty." Several days later, the White House claimed Foster's so-called suicide note was found in the same briefcase.

DELIBERATIONS

Whether the grand jury will bring indictments against officials for possible obstruction of justice is still an open question.

As a technical matter, prosecutors present indictments and must sign off on them. If a grand jury believes "there was intent to obstruct justice" on the part of officials, it has the right to vote for indictments without the consent of the prosecutors, Scorza said.

An indictment does not imply guilt. "It means there is evidence of a probably cause of a federal offense," Scorza said.

He emphasized that the grand jury does not decide on guilt or innocence, and that a trial is the fair and appropriate forum for that.

"If the grand jury were to hand down indictments in the case, I think they'd find a lot of people coming back to the witness stand to change their testimony," Wheaton speculated.

Aside from the serious issue of obstruction of justice in relation to the office, Wheaton believes that the grand jury also could seriously weigh indictments against officials for mishandling the death investigation of Foster "regardless of whether the case is a suicide or not."

Wheaton outlined some areas that the grand jury could review:

- Missing evidence—Crime scene Polaroids taken by a second police officer are missing and he says later photos don't match his recollection of the scene. Other 35mm photos were said to be underexposed in the police labs.
- Possible tampering with the crime scene—Photographic evidence supports contentions that Foster's hand was moved and the gun possibly tampered with after police arrived. Also, four witnesses, not members of the police, say a briefcase was in Foster's car. The police evidence report does not list a briefcase.
- Evidence suggests that X-rays taken at the autopsy are now missing. The autopsy report and the police report state X-rays were taken but the medical examiner states the X-ray machine was broken.
- Discrepancies in sworn testimony as to the investigation and activities relating to the case. ■

Gingrich Says Expect Hearings on Foster Death Topics

By Christopher Ruddy
FOR THE PITTSBURGH
TRIBUNE-REVIEW
JULY 13, 1995

What do the Speaker of the House, a former attorney general, and the former mayor of New York have in common?

All three believe unanswered questions about the death of Deputy White House Counsel Vincent Foster need to be fully explained to the public.

Last week House Speaker Newt Gingrich said on a New York talk radio program that the public is "entitled to a full airing" of the circumstances of Foster's death.

Gingrich's comments came after a caller to WABC's Bob Grant program, New York's most listened-to talk radio show, complained that Senate hearings led by Sen. Alfonse D'Amato would not cover questions about Foster's death.

"I was very struck by an article . . . in Investor's Business Daily," Gingrich told the caller, which he said was "stunning, raising question after question about Foster, and what happened there (at Fort Marcy Park)."

Gingrich said as a result of the article that he asked several committee chairmen in the House "to look into that."

"And I think you will be seeing some hearings on these topics because when you look at it there's just too much there to not try to find out what really happened."

On June 20, Investor's Business Daily, a national business newspaper, ran a cover story titled "The Odd Death of Vincent Foster."

The Investor's Business Daily story detailed the dozens of problems remaining in the Foster case, largely based on reports in the Tribune-Review and a report of two homicide experts prepared for the Western Journalism Center.

The article cited nagging problems in the Foster case, including:

■ Strong evidence that Foster's body was moved to the park, supported by the lack of soil on his shoes after supposedly walking 700 feet into the park, failure to find the fired bullet, and the lack of blood and blood splatter at the scene.

House Speaker Newt Gingrich

■ Indications that the body was not found at the site police claim.

■ Indications the 1913 Colt in Foster's hand was placed there, since powder marks on Foster's hand indicate neither hand was on the grip when it was fired.

■ The unusual location of Foster's eyeglasses, 13 feet from the body.

■ Discrepancies in testimony that indicate the White House was informed of Foster's death much earlier than claimed.

■ The resignation of the lead prosecutor examining Foster's death from the staff of the Independent Counsel, reportedly because he was thwarted in conducting a full probe into the discrepancies.

Gingrich's office did not return calls for comment. But U.S. Rep. Dana Rohrbacher (R-Calif.), who has himself been outspoken in raising concerns about the circumstances of Foster's death, believes Gingrich's comments reflect the Speaker "being a truth-sayer, speaking his mind and speaking honestly."

"Vince Foster might be dead, but he is not forgotten," Rohrbacher said, noting "not a day goes by that Foster's name does not come up on the floor of the House . . . that people are still talking that something is amiss here."

Growing skepticism about Foster's death appears to be spurred on by reports of apparent mishandling of the case by the Park Police, the FBI and the investigation of Independent Counsel Kenneth Starr.

Gingrich's comments also drew support from a prominent Democrat, former New York City mayor Ed Koch.

SUBSTANTIAL QUESTIONS

"There are some questions (in the Foster death case) that are quite substantial. I believe this is no minor matter," said Koch, who oversaw the nation's largest police force for 12 years.

Koch, an influential figure in the nation's media capital, hosts a radio program on WABC Radio and writes a newspaper column. He

Continued on next page

Continued from page 105

suggests that he would probably take the view that the death was suicide, but argues that the case "ought to be examined extensively to put it to bed, otherwise it will be with us like the Kennedy assassination."

Koch, for example, has pre-viously stated that carpet fibers and hairs found on Foster's clothing need to be investigated and that the public has a right to know Foster's whereabouts on the afternoon of his death.

He noted that, had a high ranking city official died under suspicious circumstances while he was mayor, he would have insisted on a public hearing. As for Starr's current secret grand jury probe, Koch said: "It is not good enough. The public is entitled to be filled in now, not 25 years from now."

Questions have persisted despite two federal probes into Foster's death. The Park Police ruled that Foster's July 20, 1993, death was a suicide. Special Counsel Robert Fiske issued a report in June 1994 also concluding that Foster committed suicide.

Former Attorney General Edwin Meese III, who served under President Reagan, took exception to the Fiske report, stating, "Obviously the questions that remained after the Fiske report have not yet been answered to the satisfaction of many people."

Meese agreed with Gingrich that the issues relating to Foster's death needed to be aired. "I think as long as serious questions remain, the public is entitled to a complete explanation of what occurred."

Some recent press reports have suggested that questions relating to Foster's death are solely the result of conspiracy freaks or Clinton critics. ■

Which Hubbell Was Telling the Truth?

By Christopher Ruddy
FOR THE PITTSBURGH
TRIBUNE-REVIEW
JULY 23, 1995

WASHINGTON— In testimony for the Senate Whitewater Committee last week, former Associate Attorney General Webb Hubbell gave dramatically different testimony about Vincent Foster's mental state in the days just before his death than what Hubbell told FBI agents working for Special Counsel Robert Fiske last year.

"I think, you know, we were all concerned. Vince had lost weight, had seemed to be depressed," Hubbell told the committee.

Late last month, Hubbell was sentenced to 21 months in federal prison after pleading guilty to mail fraud and tax evasion charges for bilking clients at his old law firm.

Hubbell was close to Foster, the Deputy White House counsel. The two, along with William Kennedy, were Rose Law Firm attorneys and colleagues of Hillary Rodham Clinton, who left Arkansas to join the Clinton Administration.

Hubbell and his wife spent the weekend before Foster's death with Foster and his wife, Lisa, vacationing on the eastern shore of Maryland.

Last year, discussing Foster's behavior and emotional state with Fiske's FBI investigators, Hubbell expressed a belief that, in hindsight, "the no time off from work was wearing on us all."

But Hubbell "did not notice Foster acting differently in the days or weeks before his death" reads an FBI statement based on the interview.

The FBI also noted, concerning Foster, that "Hubbell answered no to all questions concerning any headaches, loss of appetite or any kind of stomach trouble."

Yet Hubbell told the senators last

Former Associate Attorney General Webb Hubbell

week that Foster "talked about how tired he was, how down he was."

Drawing a vivid sketch of Foster's depression for the committee, Hubbell said he had even set up a meeting with Chief of Staff Mack McLarty upon his return the Monday following their weekend trip "to see what we could do to help our mutual friend."

"I think you know, we were all concerned. Vince had lost weight, had seemed to be depressed," Hubbell testified. [Fiske, like Hubbell, asserted that Foster had lost weight as a result of depression. In fact, records show Foster gained weight while at the White House. On December 31, 1994, Foster weighted 194 pounds. His autopsy showed a weight of 197 pounds—presumably not including the weight of several quarts of lost blood.]

He suggested to the senators that, in hindsight, it was evident that critical editorials in The Wall Street Journal and the blame Foster felt for the White House Travel Office affair had made "the disease . . . a lot worse than anybody saw." So much so, Hubbell recalled, that Foster suspected his phone was tapped. Hubbell never explained why Foster might have believed someone would want to tap his lines, and the suspicion wasn't even mentioned in his previous FBI statement.

In that statement, Hubbell described the weekend trip as "very relaxing." He made no mention of Foster having talked about depression or personal concerns, other than stating that Foster said he wanted to take more time off. Hubbell also did not mention his meeting with McLarty or his concerns about Foster on the day before his death.

In fact, Hubbell told the FBI Foster never talked about job stress. "Hubbell stated that he was not aware that Foster was experiencing any type of stress," the FBI investigators wrote. In the same interview, Hubbell recalled that "Foster talked about this great adventure in Washington, D.C."

The distinctly different accounts given by Hubbell to the FBI and to the Senate Whitewater Committee raise several serious questions.

For starters, which Hubbell was telling the truth? Was it last year's associate attorney general answering the FBI or this year's sentenced felon testifying before the Senate committee?

Thomas Scorza, a former federal prosecutor and lecturer on legal ethics at the University of Chicago, says that if prosecutors believe Hubbell's Senate testimony is clearly at odds with his statement to investigators, he could be prosecuted "even if they don't know which is true, since one has to be false."

Perhaps the most serious implication of Hubbell's new story, given under oath before a U.S. Senate committee, is that it impugns the integrity of Fiske's investigation.

None of Fiske's interviews relating to Foster's death, including those with Hubbell, were conducted under oath or before a grand jury. Fiske, apparently defending his use of interviews, stated in a footnote to his June 30, 1994, report that interviews were conducted under Title 18, Section 1001 of the U.S. Code. Section 1001 states that the intentional giving of false or misleading information to a federal investigator is "prosecutable."

But law enforcement experts say that "the hammer"—forcing witnesses to testify under oath with the threat of perjury charges—is a far better guarantor of getting the truth.

A prosecutor on Starr's staff, who requested anonymity, said that on about the same day FBI agents were interviewing Hubbell in Washington relating to Foster, Hubbell's lawyer was turning down requests by Fiske's office in Little Rock for credit card and other records. "If he wasn't cooperating in Little Rock, why should anything he said in Washington be believed?" the source asked. The source also said that Fiske had so "compartmentalized" his investigation that his Little Rock office didn't know Hubbell was being interviewed, and the Washington office was unaware of the request for his records.

If Hubbell gave a dramatically different version of events while under oath, what else would the more than 125 people interviewed by Fiske's investigators have told with the threat of perjury charges?

Fiske was sacked by a three-judge panel in the summer of 1994 and replaced by Independent Counsel Kenneth Starr. At that time, Fiske's failure to use his Washington grand jury to probe the death was the talk of Washington law enforcement circles.

Another significant issue that surfaces is the Fiske investigation's possible manipulation of witness statements in building its case that Foster's suicide was the result of depression directly related to the Travel Office affair.

A review of FBI interviews of Foster's friends and colleagues—similar to the interview in which Hubbell gave his first statement—prepared during the Fiske investigation and released this year by the Senate Banking Committee, show scant evidence that those around Foster detected "depression" or any behavioral or emotional changes.

Yet the depression theory became a cornerstone of Fiske's case that Foster committed suicide, particularly emphasizing the issue of the Travel Office imbroglio.

According to the Fiske report: "Those close to Foster have stated that the single greatest source of his distress was the criticism he and others within the Counsel's office received following the firing of seven employees from the White House Travel Office."

As the No. 2 lawyer in the White House, Foster was intimately involved in the Travel Office affair.

Yet in his FBI statement for Fiske in mid-April 1994, Hubbell made only passing references to the Travel Office, never connecting it with a depression. Hubbell described Foster as being "frustrated" and "unhappy" over the matter, stating Foster "didn't like the criticism being received on this issue."

Continued on next page

Continued from page 107

Fiske investigators, apparently needing more on Foster and the Travel Office from Hubbell to build the case for their report, interviewed Hubbell a second time in June 1994, solely on the issue of the Travel Office.

Again, Hubbell never linked the Travel Office matter with depression. He acknowledged only that Foster had overreacted to the case and was "upset."

Hubbell said he would not describe Foster's reaction as "anger," as he never saw Foster "blow up."

Hubbell's most dramatic statement in the interview was that Foster "got worse" by focusing on the matter, but he never stated that these office matters brought Foster to depression. "Foster was never concerned for his personal exposure on the issue," Hubbell told the FBI.

Fiske's handling of witness statements, and conclusions drawn from them, have already drawn some controversy. A key witness, who claims to have first discovered Foster's body and who is identified as CW (for confidential witness) in Fiske's report, has stated that FBI agents working for Fiske badgered him as many as 25 times to alter his testimony on such critical issues as whether a gun may have been in Foster's hand and the position of Foster's head at the scene.

According to a source familiar with Starr's probe, during grand jury proceedings earlier this year under Associate Independent Counsel Miquel Rodriguez, at least eight witnesses told the grand jury that their testimony in statements prepared for the Fiske investigation had been misrepresented by the FBI.

Rodriguez resigned in March. Starr has not continued the investigation into the serious issue of a possible cover-up of the death, a wholly separate issue from whether the death was a suicide. ∎

D'Amato Admits Questions Remain about Death of Vincent Foster

By Christopher Ruddy
FOR THE PITTSBURGH
TRIBUNE-REVIEW
AUGUST 19, 1995

In an apparent about-face, Sen. Alfonse D'Amato (R-N.Y.), chairman of the Senate's Special Whitewater Committee, now says "there are some open questions" relating to the death of Vincent Foster that will eventually be reviewed by his committee.

Foster, then deputy White House Counsel, died just over two years ago of a gunshot wound to the head, according to the U.S. Park Police.

"There is no doubt the initial investigation was botched," D'Amato told Charlie Rose, criticizing the Park Police's handling of the case on Rose's national television program earlier this week.

"His clothing was contaminated. The questions [are:] Where did he die? Did he have various stains on his clothes that would indicate that maybe the body was moved?" D'Amato said.

D'Amato's comments directly challenge the report of Special Counsel Robert Fiske, who concluded Foster committed suicide in Fort Marcy Park. D'Amato had previously accepted the Fiske report without criticism, and endorsed its conclusions after Senate hearings last summer.

D'Amato told Rose that his "strong feeling" was that Foster killed himself, but he had reservations about where and when Foster died.

Sen. Alfonse D'Amato

"There seem to be a number of questions that have been raised by some people, some who have expertise, that have not been answered," D'Amato said.

Earlier this week, D'Amato was

also on the Bob Grant Show on WABC Radio in New York City, promoting his new book "Power, Pasta, and Politics," and reiterated his concerns, adding that "it is my intent to raise the various questions that experts and others have raised" on the case.

D'Amato cited for Grant's listeners some of his questions:

"Did (Foster) die in that position? Was he dragged there? Was he carried there?"

"What about grass stains and other kinds of evidence that might be found on his clothing or on his shoes?"

"More particularly, what about powder burns? What about the gun? And the manner in which the gun was held? And the manner in which the gun was found?"

Most recently, Foster's death has been under review by Independent Counsel Kenneth Starr. D'Amato said he will await Starr's report and "then we will review and raise these questions."

D'Amato's comments further undermine Fiske's report, which has been challenged by two top New York City homicide investigators who reviewed the case for the Western Journalism Center, a nonprofit organization that supports investigative reporting. The investigators found "overwhelming evidence" that Foster's body had been transported to Fort Marcy Park, and that a 1913 Colt revolver had likely been placed in his hand.

D'Amato's questions about the case come on the heels of similar comments made by House Speaker Newt Gingrich, who last month said he was not convinced Foster committed suicide.

Both Republicans share wide public support for their views. According to a recent Time/CNN poll, 65 percent of the country has not accepted the government's ruling of suicide. Twenty percent of Americans believe Foster was murdered, 45 percent aren't sure. But a significant 45 percent believe the administration is engaged in a cover-up of the death.

"Question after question after question about Foster, and what happened there (at Fort Marcy Park) have not been fully answered," Gingrich said on Grant's program.

Gingrich later told a meeting of Washington reporters that "there is plausible reason to question whether or not it was suicide."

According to a member of Gingrich's staff who asked not to be identified, Gingrich is seriously pursuing the matter and has passed on a list of issues to the Government Reform and Oversight Committee, headed by Rep. William Clinger (R-Pa.).

Gingrich requested that Clinger locate a member of the committee with experience as a prosecutor to determine if hearings are warranted.

According to the staff member, Rep. Steven Schiff (R-N.M.) was selected for the task just before Congress went on recess and has not begun a review of the case.

Schiff, vice-chairman of the Government Reform Committee, is a veteran prosecutor, having served eight years as a district attorney in Albuquerque.

Schiff, through his spokesman, said he couldn't comment on the matter.

Clinger has been a staunch supporter of the Fiske report. Last year, when Rep. Dan Burton took the House floor to criticize the Fiske report on Foster's death, Clinger's office hastily issued its own report in support of Fiske.

Recently, Clinger has become a vocal critic of those who have raised questions about the case, and last month appeared on ABC's "Nightline" to debunk issues raised by critics.

For example, Clinger said multi-colored fibers found all over Foster's clothing, including his underwear, were simply the result of Foster's clothing having been mixed together in the same evidence bag.

The FBI lab report contradicts Clinger, indicating the FBI received the evidence in separate bags grouped as follows: pants and belt; shoes and socks; jacket and tie. The underwear and dress shirt were not identified. ■

D'Amato Says Foster Gun Position Impossible
Bullet Search Begins

By Christopher Ruddy
FOR THE PITTSBURGH
TRIBUNE-REVIEW
SEPTEMBER 14, 1995

WASHINGTON— Special White-water Committee Chairman Sen. Alfonse D'Amato (R-N.Y.) again challenged the official account of Vincent Foster's death, stating it was "impossible" for the gun to have remained in Foster's hand after the fatal shot was fired.

In addition, he said there are new questions about the death that need to be answered.

Foster, who served as deputy White House Counsel, died more than two years ago in what authorities ruled as a suicide. Foster, a former boyhood friend of President Bill Clinton, was found dead in a suburban Washington park with a 1913 Colt revolver clutched in his right hand.

"If indeed Vince Foster committed suicide, put the gun in his mouth—it's impossible for that gun to have been found in his hand," D'Amato said on New York's all-news WCBS radio.

"After the discharge there would have been a kickback and the gun would have jumped out—yet here it is in his hand," D'Amato added.

D'Amato's language is his strongest yet.

Last month, the Tribune-Review reported on questions D'Amato said he would investigate, such as the gun's position and whether the body had been moved to the park.

D'Amato also wants to know why soil and grass stains were absent from Foster's shoes after his trek through Fort Marcy Park.

In a new development, WCBS also reported that D'Amato would subpoena White House aide Helen Dickey. Arkansas state trooper Roger Perry has alleged that Dickey called him at the governor's mansion to notify him Foster had died in his car in the White House parking lot.

Perry also alleged that the call likely came to his post around 5 p.m. Arkansas time, at least 15 minutes before police said they officially found the body in Fort Marcy.

Perry's testimony, as well as corroborating testimony from others he called after hearing from Dickey, strongly impeaches U.S. Park Police and White House officials' statements that the White House was not informed of Foster's death for two-and-a-half hours—at or after 8:30 p.m.—after the police arrived.

D'Amato's renewed interest in the case is an about-face from his agreement last year with the findings of Special Counsel Robert Fiske who said Foster died at the spot he was found and no cover-up had taken place.

If the gun was moved or placed in Foster's hand or the scene tampered with, that raises the possibility of obstruction of justice, according to legal experts.

Last April, two former New York City police homicide experts, Vincent Scalice and Fred Santucci, issued a report for the Western Journalism Center stating that the gun had "likely been staged" or placed in Foster's hand after death. The experts noted that in their 50 years of combined experience investigating homicides, they had never seen a gun from a suicide positioned so neatly in the suicide victim's hand.

A Polaroid photo taken at the scene by the Park Police showed the gun in Foster's hand at his side, with the thumb still in the trigger guard and the barrel under his right thigh.

The Fiske report suggests Foster's thumb was trapped by the trigger mechanism and that the force of gravity forced the gun to fall naturally by his side.

But Scalice and Santucci, along with one of the country's top forensic scientists, conducted simulations at the official death scene at Fort Marcy Park and found that if Foster fired the weapon with the gun in his mouth and both hands on the gun, the explosive recoil would have forced Foster's arms and hands to flail outward—falling perpen-dicular to his body with his palms facing upward.

Police said his arms were found close to his sides with his palms facing down.

"It would really be a freak thing for the thumb to be caught in the trigger mechanism," Scalice said with some skepticism, but pointed out the other problems involved with the gun:

■ It has not been positively identified by the family as being Foster's.

■ It had no fingerprints on it.

■ It had no visible blood on it—though Foster was alleged to have pressed it deep against the back of his mouth.

■ No matching ammunition was found in his homes, and residues on the hands "demonstrate con-clusively he could not have fired that gun."

Sen. D'Amato's office did not

return calls for comment.

Scalice said another glaring problem is the fact that despite two searches that were labeled "exhaustive," the fired bullet was not found in the park.

This past Tuesday evening, FBI and Park Service officials were seen examining the Fort Marcy scene.

An FBI official asked this reporter to leave the area.

Within an hour, approximately six investigators left the scene, and shortly after, police put crime scene tape across the rear entrance. On Wednesday morning the front entrance also was closed with yellow crime scene tape.

Independent Counsel Kenneth Starr's office declined to comment on FBI activities at Fort Marcy, but Starr spokeswoman Debbie

Gershman did say the probe was "active and ongoing."

Last month, the Tribune-Review reported that Henry Lee, head of the Connecticut State Crime Lab, who had just finished testifying as a defense witness in the O.J. Simpson case, told Starr's prosecutors a third search would have to be conducted for the bullet. ∎

Police Failed to Find Keys to Foster's Car at Park

By Christopher Ruddy
FOR THE PITTSBURGH
TRIBUNE-REVIEW
SEPTEMBER 20, 1995

WASHINGTON—If Vincent Foster drove his car to Fort Marcy Park to take his own life, why didn't police find Foster's car keys in his pockets at the park?

Questions about the late deputy White House counsel's unusual and sudden death continue to nag Washington's political establishment.

Both House Speaker Newt Gingrich and powerful Banking Committee chairman Sen. Al D'Amato have suggested serious, unanswered questions remain as to whether Foster died in the suburban roadside park where his body was found.

Reports in the Tribune-Review, as well as a report by two former New York City homicide investigators, have suggested Foster may have died elsewhere and his body moved to the park.

Among the questions are the following:

■ Why was no soil found on his shoes or clothing, even though Foster was alleged to have walked more than 700 feet through the park from the parking lot to the spot where he was found?

■ Why did the FBI omit any mention of grass stains, which should have been apparent on his shoes?

■ How did multi-colored carpet fibers come to be found on almost every article of clothing, including his underwear?

■ Why did no one see him alive or hear the fatal shot in the park?

■ After such a violent death, how did his body compose itself into such a neat arrangement?

■ Why was the fired bullet never found?

KEYS NOT FOUND

To all of this add one more: the unusual circumstances of discovery of the keys to Foster's Honda.

According to official accounts, the car keys, as well as other personal keys, were found in Foster's pockets at the morgue, but only after White House officials arrived to identify the body and well after his pockets had already been searched fruitlessly at Fort Marcy Park by a Park Police investigator.

The report of former Special Counsel Robert Fiske, issued June 30, 1994—which concluded Foster died of a suicide at the park—states casually and without detail: "The keys to the car were found in Foster's pocket."

Typical of the Fiske report, it incorrectly implies the keys were found during the investigation at the park while failing to describe the strange circumstances of their discovery.

Senior police investigator Cheryl Braun told the FBI that while at Fort Marcy "she observed Officer (John) Rolla check the pants pockets, both sides and rear, in an effort to find identification or a possible suicide note."

Police officer Christina Hodakievic also told the FBI she saw Rolla check all of Foster's pockets.

Rolla, the lead investigator, described the results of his search of the pockets at Fort Marcy Park in a Senate Banking Committee deposition: "I searched his pants pockets. I couldn't find a wallet or nothing in his pants pocket."

Foster's wallet and other personal effects were found in his Honda but no keys were found.

The police then allowed Foster's body to be placed in a body bag and moved shortly after 8 p.m. by ambulance to Fairfax County Hospital morgue.

MORGUE SEARCH

The park police said they became puzzled about the absence of keys

Continued on next page

Continued from page 111

and decided to go to Fairfax Hospital to re-check the pockets. Around the same time, Associate White House Counsel William Kennedy and White House aide Craig Livingstone had gone to the hospital's morgue to identify the body.

Braun said when she rechecked Foster's right front pants pocket she found car keys.

Records show Braun found two sets of keys in a pocket that had already been searched by Rolla at the park—one ring containing the car keys and the other containing four door and cabinet keys.

"It sounds fishy," former New York City Police homicide expert Vincent Scalice said. He added that if police had theorized Foster had driven to the park to shoot himself but didn't find the key to the Honda "it should have immediately

aroused suspicion at the scene."

Scalice has 35 years homicide experience, specializing in examination and reconstruction of scenes where suspicious deaths have occurred.

Park Police indicated they believed they had overlooked the keys and went to the hospital to re-check the pockets.

Scalice said that doesn't add up. "You would want to re-search the death scene first, to see if they were thrown or dropped somewhere," he said, especially "since Foster's eyeglasses were found 19 feet from where his head lay."

Fiske said the eyeglasses "bounced" through thick foliage. But Scalice and two other experts determined it was physically impossible for the glasses to have been thrown that far after the shot was fired.

Records show the police did not search for the keys at the park again

but instead went directly to the hospital.

"Without putting your hand in the front pocket, two sets of keys should have been bulging from the pocket," he said.

He also said the pants should have been stretched as his body bloated in the summer heat, making the metal keys more apparent.

Just a freak occurrence?

A "Citizen's Independent Report" compiled by Hugh Sprunt, a Texas-based accountant who began investigating the death as an avocation on Internet bulletin boards, details dozens and dozens of discrepancies, including the one involving the keys, apparent in official documents.

"The sheer number of unusual circumstances and freak occurrences defy mathematical probability," Sprunt said, adding that the official suicide story "doesn't add up." ■

New Face Emerges in Probe of Foster's Death

By Christopher Ruddy
FOR THE PITTSBURGH
TRIBUNE-REVIEW
OCTOBER 20, 1995

WASHINGTON—Whitewater Independent Counsel Kenneth Starr has hired San Diego Chief Medical Examiner Dr. Brian Blackbourne to re-examine the death of Deputy White House Counsel Vincent W. Foster Jr.

Blackbourne told the Tribune-Review he began last month to review Foster's July 20, 1993, death.

Blackbourne joins noted forensic scientist Henry C. Lee, who has been studying the case since late spring.

According to a source close to Starr's probe, Lee's investigation is limited in scope—scrutinizing physical evidence such as Foster's clothing and several Polaroid photos taken at the scene.

Lee will not rule on whether Foster committed suicide.

Blackbourne, the source said, will be handling matters relating to the original autopsy conducted shortly after Foster's death, photographs taken during that procedure, and the report of a panel of four pathologists convened by former Special Counsel Robert Fiske.

The Virginia pathologist who conducted the first autopsy, and Fiske's panel, concluded Foster committed suicide.

But their methodology and

conclusions have been challenged by other experts.

"The (Fiske) panel of forensic pathologists looking into this I thought left a lot to be desired," said Dr. Michael Baden, the former New York City chief medical examiner who testified at the O.J. Simpson trial.

"Because they all didn't go to the (death) scene (and) only one of them interviewed the person who did the first autopsy, (the Fiske panel) tended to just adopt whatever was given to them," Baden said.

"I think Brian (Blackbourne) would be of the type that would want to get all the information necessary to arrive at a conclusion," Baden added. "You can't just adopt what the person who hires you says, or gives you."

Fiske's pathology panel included Charles Hirsch, medical examiner for New York City; Donald Reay, medical examiner for Seattle; Charles Stahl, pathologist with the Armed Forces Institute of Pathology; and James Luke, forensic pathologist with the FBI Academy. During 1994 Senate hearings, Dr. Hirsch said that only two of the pathologists visited the death scene at Fort Marcy Park, though all four certified Foster died at the spot where his body was found.

Starr's spokesperson in Little Rock, Ark., has stated the investigation into Foster's death "is active and ongoing."

"I haven't gotten any timetable from (Starr's office) at all," Blackbourne said in response to questions about when he would issue his report.

"I am waiting for some additional information from them, and I have been told to wait until I get all the information before I even consider a report," he added.

Blackbourne, a Canadian citizen, has been certified in forensic pathology for 26 years, and has headed the medical examiner's office for San Diego County for the last five years.

Before arriving in San Diego, Blackbourne was chief medical examiner for Massachusetts during most of the 1980s. He has strong experience in urban settings, having worked in both the medical examiner's offices in Miami (Dade County) and Washington, D.C., where he served as deputy chief medical examiner. His resume indicates that he has conducted over 5,200 medical-legal autopsies, including about 1,500 involving homicides and suicides.

Blackbourne has for many years served as a regular lecturer for the FBI Academy at Quantico, Va., the Armed Forces Institute of Pathology, and the District of Columbia's Homicide School.

"He's a very competent guy . . .

and I think a very good forensic pathologist," Baden said of Blackbourne. Baden suggested that Blackbourne has a "good all-around" background in pathology after serving in several large cities.

FOSTER AUTOPSY

Foster's autopsy was conducted by the deputy medical examiner for Northern Virginia, Dr. James Beyer. Beyer, 77, has conducted thousands of autopsies in his career, but in recent years has come under some criticism in ruling on suicide cases, including Foster's.

Last year, The New York Post and The Washington Times reported that Beyer had ruled incorrectly in the case of 21-year-old Timothy Easley, who Beyer said died of a self-inflicted stab wound. Easley's girlfriend later confessed to Easley's murder, but only after the family had another pathologist, Dr. Harry Bonnell, deputy chief medical examiner of San Diego, review photos they had taken of cuts to Easley's hand.

"The cut on the hand is definitely *ante mortem*, and I cannot understand how any competent forensic pathologists would miss it. It is a classical defense wound, suffered while trying to avoid the knife," Bonnell concluded.

In another case, the 1991 death of 21-year-old Tommy Burkett, Beyer ruled Burkett's death consistent with a self-inflicted gunshot. Burkett's alleged suicide was similar to Foster's—apparent death by a revolver fired in the mouth.

The Burkett family undertook a second autopsy and found that Beyer had failed to note that Burkett had trauma to his ear and abrasions to his chest, indications he may have been beaten first. Beyer also claimed to have dissected Burkett's lungs, but a second autopsy showed that procedure had never been done.

Several nagging issues relating to Beyer's autopsy of Foster remain:

■ **Missing X-rays**: Beyer's autopsy report indicates X-rays

were taken of Foster. But Beyer now says his X-ray machine was "inoperable." The police report quotes Beyer as stating "that X-rays indicated that there was no evidence of bullet fragments in the head." X-rays would help substantiate the written autopsy report.

■ **Exit Wound**: Fairfax County emergency medical technician Kory Ashford told the FBI last year that while he placed Foster's body in a body bag by grasping his shoulders and cradling his head, he did not see any exit wound—though the autopsy report said the bullet exited the top of the back of the head.

Ashford said he saw little or no blood, and didn't even wash his hands after the task.

Fiske claimed in his report that Foster had a large exit wound, yet the medical examiner on the scene told the FBI the wound was consistent with a low-velocity weapon. Foster was found with a high-velocity .38-caliber revolver. The lead police investigator said the wound was small.

Joe Purvis, a friend of Foster's and a Little Rock attorney, said last March that he was told by a staff member of Ruebel's Funeral Home in Little Rock that Foster had an entry wound deep at the back of the mouth, and an exit wound "the size of a dime" close to the neck at the hairline.

Though Foster's autopsy had yet to be released, Purvis' entry wound description was accurate, placing the hole deep in the back of the mouth. Beyer's autopsy notes a gaping exit wound, however, near the crown of the head.

■ **Trauma or Sign of Struggle**: Critical to any determination of suicide is a careful examination for additional wounds to the body, needle marks or other signs of a struggle. Beyer noted no such signs.

But a Polaroid picture taken at the scene and enhanced during Starr's inquiry before the grand jury earlier this year, showed what "appeared to be a wound, puncture or other

Continued on next page

Continued from page 113

trauma" to the right side of Foster's neck near the jaw line, a source said.

The photo, which was apparently never enhanced for review by Fiske's expert panel, finds some eerie corroboration in the statement made by emergency medical technician Richard Arthur, who told the FBI last year "he noted what appeared to be a small-caliber bullet hole in Foster's neck on the right side, just under the jaw line about halfway between the ear and the tip of the chin."

Blackbourne seemed perplexed when asked about the controversy over the scene Polaroid. "I am not familiar with any Polaroid, I'm not familiar with what you are talking about," he said.

■ **Drugs, Alcohol Analysis**: Blood lab work attached to Beyer's report indicates no drugs or alcohol were detected in Foster's blood.

Later the FBI analyzed the blood sample and reported to Fiske that it found trace amounts of an anti-depressant and Valium in Foster's blood, though Beyer's lab had tested for these very drugs.

Foster's doctor had prescribed an anti-depressant to help Foster with insomnia the day before his death. The discrepancy between the reports has never been explained, and Fiske never released the blood work report detailing the screens employed in his analysis. Starr's office also refuses to release the report.

"In a case like this I would want to test for all sorts of exotic drugs, ones not normally looked for," said veteran New York homicide expert Vernon Geberth, author of the authoritative text on death investigations, "Practical Homicide Investigations."

Other issues remain, such as the powder burns noted on the autopsy report and photos showing that both of Foster's hands were in the vicinity of the front of the gun when the .38-caliber Colt was fired. This would seem to indicate that neither hand was on the grip.

Seven leading experts, including Dr. Vincent Di Maio, say such a grip is inconsistent with suicide.

Blackbourne said he is reserving judgment on specific issues.

"I would rather not comment any further. I have only had one communication with the independent counsel's office. I think it's premature to discuss anything."

He declined to say whether he would recommend a second autopsy.

"Consideration of a second autopsy is an evaluation by a forensic pathologist that important information could be obtained from a second autopsy that was not addressed in a first autopsy," Baden explained.

Baden said he has made no judgment in the Foster case.

He added that a second autopsy shouldn't be "for trivial information, or a fishing expedition." He suggested that one legitimate reason for a second autopsy would be to retrieve tiny bullet fragments that are left behind in the head as the bullet breaks through the skull.

The recovery of such fragments could identify the type of bullet that was fired to see if it is consistent with the alleged suicide weapon "because the original bullet was never found," Baden said.

FBI agents have been engaged in an exhaustive search, the third one so far, and apparently have yet to find the bullet at Fort Marcy Park.■

Experts Say Foster 'Suicide' Note Forged

By Christopher Ruddy
FOR THE PITTSBURGH
TRIBUNE-REVIEW
OCTOBER 25, 1995

WASHINGTON—At a press conference in Washington today, an international panel of forensic handwriting experts—including one from Oxford University—will announce its findings that a torn note, said to have been Vincent W. Foster Jr.'s "suicide" note, is a forgery.

Strategic Investment, a Baltimore-based financial newsletter, and its editor, James Dale Davidson, have called the conference to issue the written findings of three experts that analyzed a copy of the note.

Twenty-seven pieces (the 28th piece was missing) of the note were claimed to have been found in the late deputy White House Counsel's briefcase almost a week after his sudden death on July 20, 1993.

If the forensic panel's assertions are true, it would indicate that someone engaged in a major cover-up of Foster's death and obstructed justice by hindering the investigation of the matter.

The U.S. Park Police originally determined that the note was written by Foster, and ruled his death a suicide. At the request of former special counsel Robert Fiske, the FBI lab examined the note and concluded it was authentic.

The methodology used by both the FBI and the Park Police to

certify the note, however, has been challenged.

Fiske relied on the note to help make his case that Foster was depressed in the last days of his life, particularly over apparent improprieties in the White House Travel Office.

The note begins, "I made mistakes from ignorance, inexperience and overwork," and from there rambles on about legal, personal, and office concerns on a single sheet of 8 1/2 by 11 legal paper.

Foster's wife, Lisa, told the FBI that she believed her husband wrote the note in the weeks before his death after she had advised him to document "everything 'they' did wrong." She told the FBI that she "did not view or read the note" until it was pieced together and shown to her.

The three forensic reports obtained by the Tribune-Review indicate that the experts came to independent conclusions that Foster did not write this note.

Reginald E. Alton indicated that, based on his comparison of a photocopy of the note with a dozen photocopied documents known to have been written by Foster, the torn note "is a forgery."

Alton has for 30 years lectured on handwriting, manuscript authentication, and forgery detection at England's Oxford University. In recent years he led a panel of experts that ruled on the challenged diaries of noted English author C. S. Lewis.

Alton's opinion has been sought by British police agencies and, according to his biography, he has testified in British courts as an expert witness relating to questioned documents.

Alton is currently Dean of Degrees at Oxford's St. Edmund Hall, its oldest undergraduate institution. Alton's findings will be particularly bitter for the president, since Mr. Clinton attended Oxford as a Rhodes Scholar, and has used the university's prestigious name as a significant part of his own credentials.

In his report Alton noted eight major discrepancies between the torn note and Foster's natural writing as "firm, open, rounded, with a consistent slight backward slope and an easy currency that joins letters with scarcely an interruption . . . is not consistent with (Foster's) writings . . ."

Scalice, a former homicide and identification expert with the New York City Police Department, has 22 years experience handling questioned documents and is a certified document examiner with the American Board of Forensic Examiners.

He has testified in numerous court cases relating to documents and has consulted with major firms and banks, including Citibank and Chemical Bank, as a document examiner.

"Look at the note, and just compare it with the flow of the letter the Park Police used to authenticate," Scalice said in an interview. "Even a lay person can see it's not a match."

Scalice added that he also analyzed the challenged document for specific letter characteristics and other patterns that indicate the note to be a forgery.

Offering a third opinion of forgery was Ronald Rice who heads New England Investigation of Boston and has 18 years experience examining documents and is board certified.

A consultant to the criminal unit of the Massachusetts Attorney General's office, Rice has worked on a number of celebrated cases, and was recently asked by CNN to examine notes written by O.J. Simpson.

Rice told the Tribune-Review that the note is an "artistic forgery." The forger, Rice suggests, took known writings of Foster and "either drew them, used a cut-and-paste method, or used a highly sophisticated computer scanning method."

Alton and Scalice also agreed that the forger created the torn note from known writings.

"A good forger always wants to mimic the real thing, rather than create a word," Scalice explained. "This is probably why the note never makes a reference to suicide. Foster likely had never written any such words."

"The flimsy investigation into the note parallels still the flimsy investigation of the death," Davidson said.

Davidson and his newsletter have criticized the handling of the Foster case by federal authorities.

Given the political overtones of the Foster matter, Davidson noted he strongly supported President Clinton in the past, having donated the maximum amount allowable to his 1992 presidential campaign, and has attended "renaissance weekends" and inaugural balls for then-Governor Clinton.

He said he hired the experts after he received information that the FBI and Park Police did not adequately review the note.

In his report, homicide expert Scalice said the torn note is "not consistent" with a suicide note, since it makes no mention of intentional harm, suicide, death, farewell, or expression of departure.

Scalice, also an expert in the identification of latent fingerprint impressions, said if the note was torn into 28 pieces without leaving any fingerprints, this "would be consistent with someone having worn gloves."

"Otherwise there should have been numerous latent impressions," he said.

Scalice and Alton both said finding of the note "torn" should have been a red flag for investigators that a forger may have been attempting to make a comparison of the document more difficult.

"Anytime a document is torn, mutilated, something spilled on it, suspicion should be aroused," Scalice said.

Continued on next page

Continued from page 115

The White House says that the note was found in Foster's briefcase at it was being packed almost a week after his death. Then-White House Counsel Bernard Nussbaum admitted he searched the briefcase two days after Foster's death and that he did not detect the torn pieces.

The Park Police in both private and public interviews have claimed that the briefcase was searched properly, and that the torn note was not in it during the official search conducted by Nussbaum.

Earlier this year Park Police detective Pete Markland told the Washington Post that he became suspicious when the note was later found in the same briefcase.

"Nobody could have missed that note in there," Markland told the Post. Markland never testified at Senate hearings this past summer.

POLICE, FISKE EXAMINATION

Despite apparent suspicions about the note, police apparently took a rather casual approach to its examination.

On July 29, 1993, the Park Police had Sgt. Larry Lockhart, an expert in handwriting for the U.S. Capitol Police, examine the note. Lockhart concluded that Foster wrote it.

Lockhart told the Tribune-Review that he has no certification as a handwriting examiner, but has developed a skill over a 15-year period.

He admitted that he used only a single document of Foster's known handwriting—a curt letter that Foster had written shortly before his death—to make the comparison.

"According to the federal rules of evidence you need at least four known writings to compare questioned documents, but usually an examiner wants as many as he can get," explained Ron Rice, who wrote the course on handwriting examination for the American Board of Forensic Examiners.

Scalice noted that in a homicide investigation police "would not normally accept a single document (for comparison purposes) from a family member. You'd want documents from several sources to make sure the police aren't given a forged document to compare another forged document."

Asked how many known writings he typically wants to make a comparison, Lockhart said his rule is "the more the better."

He said he made his opinion based on one document in this case because that "was all the police gave me."

Lockhart said when he examined the torn note he did notice a wavering in the writing "which could have been a tremble." He said that although he noted it to himself, "I didn't say anything at the time to investigators. There was something in the writing that indicated the individual could have been a manic depressant."

He said he later read in the paper that Foster was on medication and saw that as a possible reason for the "tremble." He was unaware that Foster is said to have gone on medication for insomnia the night before he died, and that the note was said to have been written days or weeks earlier.

Other experts say that a "tremble" could be a sign of hesitation—a forged document lacks the free-flowing style of the actual writer.

FISKE, FBI

The Park Police say that they did not use the FBI lab to examine the document because Foster had criticized the FBI by stating in the torn note: "The FBI lied in their report to the AG."

According to the report of former special counsel Robert Fiske, the FBI lab subsequently was brought in and "determined that the torn note was written by Foster."

Fiske used, like the Park Police, a single paged document offered by the family adding only two checks written by Foster for handwriting comparison purposes.

But a source close to the Starr probe said Fiske was imprecise in his report: the FBI lab found the two checks to be an "inconclusive match" to the torn note.

The FBI lab matched the note to the single paged document. The lab's reliance on so few documents in the case contradicts normal FBI procedures.

"The general guidelines is to have more 'known handwritings' rather than less," explained John Hicks, recently retired FBI assistant director and who oversaw the Document Unit.

"If I had to come up with a minimum number of (known writings) I'd want, I'd say 10," James Lyle said. Lyle, a former FBI special agent and unit chief for the Question Document Section who retired in 1993, said there "is no rule of thumb" except that analysts "usually want as many as you can get." ■

Editor's note: *The FBI actually used 17 checks written by Foster to compare against the torn note. All 17 were found to be an inconclusive match.*

'New' Evidence in Foster Case Would Strain Credibility

By Christopher Ruddy
FOR THE PITTSBURGH
TRIBUNE-REVIEW
OCTOBER 26, 1995

WASHINGTON—Don't be surprised if evidence suddenly surfaces "proving" that Vincent Foster Jr.'s lifeless body was not moved to Fort Marcy Park, the place where his remains were found, a law enforcement source here has told the Tribune-Review.

Federal authorities are said to be desperate to close the investigation into Foster's death of July 20, 1993. But proving that Foster died by his own hand in Fort Marcy Park has been a daunting task.

The source said that the investigation can be closed with credibility if "it can be demonstrated that Foster died in the park; that his body was not moved" to the park from another location. The notion that Foster's body was moved has gained some interest based on key evidence and the opinion of independent homicide experts.

A piece of primary evidence cited in hypothesizing that the body was moved are Foster's shoes.

The FBI lab found the shoes did not have a trace of soil on them—even though Foster allegedly walked more than 700 feet through the park to the spot where his body was found. No soil, and the FBI omitted any mention of grass stains that experts say should have been on the shoes as well.

The source said that the addition of "dirt and grass stains" on the shoes—while at this point raising the serious issue of evidence tampering—would be powerful evidence linking the late deputy White House counsel to the suburban Washington park where his remains were found.

FBI agents have been handling the investigation for Independent Counsel Kenneth Starr, and have had custody of such physical evidence as Foster's clothing and shoes. The source suggested that key evidence could be tampered with to help officials make the conclusion Foster was alive in the park, and then died there.

BULLET MISSING

The issue of the shoes would be muted if investigators had been successful in finding the bullet that caused the attorney's death. But that hasn't happened, despite tremendous effort.

The Park Police said they conducted a search; then came the FBI under former Special Counsel Robert Fiske. In early September, Starr had the FBI conduct its most exhaustive search yet, fruitlessly digging up much of the park.

Experts say that planting a bullet in the park would be a much more complicated task than simply tampering with the shoes.

Meanwhile, two former New York homicide investigators concluded in their own report issued last April for the Western Journalism Center that the "overwhelming evidence" indicated Foster's body had been transported to the park.

What evidence? The detectives noted the failure of almost two dozen people at the scene to note blood splatter above the area where Foster's head lay; the missing bullet; the statement of the medical examiner that the exit wound appeared to be "matted" and "clotted;" blood drainage tracks inconsistent with the position in which the deceased was found; and the finding of carpet fibers of many colors on most of his clothing and underwear.

Other circumstantial evidence, they said, pointed to a possible movement of the body. No one saw Foster alive at the park. Two witnesses in the park told the FBI that they saw two unidentified men in and around Foster's Honda just before the police arrived to investigate the death.

One man, with long blonde hair, was said to be standing in front of Foster's car with the hood up. Meanwhile, Foster's car keys were not found in his pockets at the park.

FOSTER'S SHOES

But the former New York homicide experts said the strongest indication the body was moved was the fact the FBI lab found "not one trace of coherent soil" on Foster's shoes.

The detectives also noted that the FBI lab didn't mention any evidence of grass stains on his shoes, which they said should have been apparent to the naked eye.

Even Mike Wallace of CBS television's "60 Minutes" took the test himself this summer, retracing Foster's steps through the park. He said he had found some soil on his shoes.

In March 1994, the New York Post reported that an emergency worker on the scene thought Foster's shoes appeared "very clean" for the circumstances. The Post also reported the Park Police had never conducted an analysis of his shoes and clothing.

Subsequent events corroborated those reports. FBI agents working for Fiske took possession of Foster's shoes and clothing from the Park Police soon after Fiske began his probe in 1994. Fiske asked the FBI

Continued on next page

Continued from page 117

lab to conduct the proper tests.

In a report dated May 9, 1994, the FBI, after conducting a microscopic analysis of Foster's shoes, found they "did not contain coherent soil."

Fiske downplayed the importance of this in his report by stating that "the FBI lab found small particles of mica on much of Foster's clothing, including his shoes." The tiny, silvery flecks of mica are found abundantly in Fort Marcy Park's soil. But the New York homicide detectives found soil always mixed with mica on shoes they tested.

They also noted that sand-like particles of mica are found covering vegetation all over the park. The detectives concluded in their report that mica particles on Foster's clothing, in the absence of soil, support a conclusion that Foster's body was lying on dense foliage and vegetation only—evidence still consistent with the body having been placed in the park.

MISSED SOIL?

Could the FBI lab have simply overlooked some soil on Foster's shoes? Despite the FBI's original search for trace evidence, so meticulous it yielded the mica flecks, authorities still could claim the sudden discovery of soil and grass stains—linking Foster to the park—as just a "simple oversight," said the Washington law enforcement source.

Other experts question how the FBI could have missed soil particles in their lab.

"I think it's very unlikely," John Hicks said. Hicks, recently retired as the Assistant FBI Director in charge of the agency's crime lab, explained that under normal FBI procedure the shoes would undergo rigorous inspection in the microscopic analysis unit, where the technicians are "very thorough . . . very, very thorough, and meticulous."

He indicated that the FBI lab, as a procedural matter, looks for minute particles of trace evidence, making it very difficult to simply overlook small amounts of trace evidence such as specks of soil. "They would use microscopes that magnify anywhere 30 to 100 times," Hicks, who is currently affiliated with the Alabama State Crime Lab, said.

Dr. Richard Saferstein agrees with Hick's evaluation. Saferstein, former head of the New Jersey State Crime Lab, is the author of the authoritative text on forensic science. Saferstein conducted the laboratory tests for the investigation by the former New York homicide detectives.

"The probability would be next to zero," Saferstein said of the FBI missing soil in the original analysis. He said shoes, unlike garments, are "probably the easiest surface to work with" for the laboratory collection of trace evidence.

The FBI's facility, however, has recently had its validity questioned. Last month Supervisory Special Agent Frederic Whitehurst with the FBI crime lab went public with charges that the FBI had altered, tampered or fabricated evidence in a number of important cases unrelated to Foster's.

Meanwhile, late last spring forensic scientist Henry C. Lee, who testified as a key defense witness in the O.J. Simpson trial, was brought in by Independent Counsel Starr.

According to a source close to the probe, Lee will evaluate physical evidence, including Foster's clothing, and several photos.

He will probably not make a determination whether the death was a suicide. But his findings will be key to learning whether Foster's body was moved to Fort Marcy Park. ■

Foster Case: Park Witness to Appear Before Starr's Grand Jury

By Christopher Ruddy
FOR THE PITTSBURGH
TRIBUNE-REVIEW
OCTOBER 29,1995

WASHINGTON—A man who says he was at Fort Marcy Park on the evening Vincent W. Foster Jr. died was served a subpoena last week to appear before Independent Counsel Kenneth Starr's Whitewater grand jury at noon Wednesday.

Since being served the subpoena, Patrick Knowlton appears to have been monitored around his Pennsylvania Avenue residence in Georgetown under a massive surveillance operation.

A week ago, Ambrose Evans-Pritchard of London's Sunday Telegraph reported details of Knowlton's account of a tie-in to the Foster case. Knowlton was apparently the first person to see Foster's automobile in the parking lot at Fort Marcy.

The Telegraph reported that Knowlton was "stunned" when he was shown a report in his interview with FBI agents working for former Special Counsel Robert Fiske. His statements had been falsified, the Telegraph reported.

Knowlton agrees with part of the FBI statement: that he arrived at the Fort Marcy parking lot on July 20, 1993, at about 4:30 p.m. Foster's body was found more than an hour later.

DETAILS AT THE PARK

Knowlton said that the first car he saw in the lot, a Honda, was parked to his immediate left and had Arkansas plates. He said he parked his car a few spaces from the Honda, and observed another car, a blue sedan with a young man sitting in it, who gave Knowlton what he said was a menacing look. Knowlton described the man as in his 20s and possibly Mexican or Cuban.

As Knowlton quickly relieved himself by a nearby tree, the Hispanic man got out of his blue sedan and stood leaning over the roof of the car.

Frightened, Knowlton said he quickly left the park, but mentally noted some of the contents of the Arkansas Honda, including a suit jacket and a briefcase. He called the Park Police later the same night after he heard on the news of Foster's death.

The police took a brief statement from him over the phone, which they included in their report though they spelled his name wrong.

But Knowlton told the Telegraph that a key statement attributed to him by the FBI during the Fiske investigation was "an outright lie." The FBI agents who interviewed him wrote, "Knowlton could not further identify this individual (the Hispanic-appearing man) and stated that he would be unable to recognize him in the future."

SHARP MEMORY FOR DETAILS

In point of fact, Knowlton said he

Proof positive the FBI lied? Witness Patrick Knowlton had drawn this composite sketch of the man he saw in Fort Marcy. His FBI statement says he couldn't further identify the man.

has a haunting memory of the man. With the assistance of a police artist provided by the Telegraph, Knowlton even produced a sketch of the man. The composite sketch was published in the Telegraph.

Knowlton, who owns a trading business, says—and his friends agree—that he has a sharp memory for details. Knowlton told the Telegraph that interviewing FBI agents Larry Monroe and William Colombell went to extraordinary lengths to convince him he saw a blue Honda of recent vintage with Arkansas plates. Knowlton insisted that he saw an older model brown Honda with Arkansas plates.

According to experts familiar with the case, Knowlton's testimony could be critical on several points:
Continued on next page

THE RUDDY INVESTIGATION **119**

Continued from page 119

■ If Foster did not commit suicide, Knowlton likely could positively identify the person somehow involved in the attorney's death. Key forensic and circumstantial evidence led two New York police investigators to conclude that "overwhelming" evidence indicated Foster's body was moved to the park. One source close to Starr's probe has suggested that the man Knowlton saw may have been there to "secure" the lot. A rear entrance to the park is close to where the body was found and could have, some theorize, been the actual point of the body's entry.

■ He possibly could demonstrate that the FBI covered up key elements in the case.

■ He posssibly could indicate that another car with Arkansas plates, similar to Foster's, was placed in the park to leave potential witnesses with the impression Foster was in the park earlier than he was. A nagging problem with the case is the large amount of unaccounted-for time—five hours from the time Foster left his office until his body was found.

Last Thursday, Knowlton said an FBI agent with Starr's office showed up at his door to serve him with a subpoena, one of several the agent said he had to deliver that day.

WITNESS BEING WATCHED

Since them, Knowlton has been aware that he is being watched.

"He called me and said that he and a female friend had been passed twice that evening by two men in a dark sedan who gave menacing looks at Patrick," reporter Pritchard said.

On Thursday night, this reporter visited Knowlton at his residence and noticed no unusual acitvitiy outside.

Knowlton appears to be a stable, credible professional. His friends in the building describe him as a rather normal person who seems beset in the middle of something larger.

He knows little of the larger issues of the Foster controversy and was unaware of the political overtones of the case. His foyer wall proudly sports a "Clinton-Gore" campaign bumper sticker.

Knowlton and a female friend recounted Thursday's events.

Knowlton said that while taking his daily walk for a newspaper, he encountered more than a dozen men, all wearing suits, who would be walking toward him or coming from behind, then would give him a sudden, purposed stare.

His female friend said he has no history of paranoia.

To verify Knowlton's account, he agreed the following day to take his daily walk with this reporter.

The surveillance was apparent, almost from the instant we exited his apartment.

He was approached again and again by the same men: dark suits, soft-soled shoes, each carrying a note pad or newspaper. And as they passed us, each gave a pointed, timed stare at Knowlton.

After crossing the first intersection, a man crossing the same street from the other side met us at the sidewalk. He looked at Knowlton and shook his head in an awkward gesture.

Another man, short and Middle Eastern looking, passed us and stared. After he passed, his walk slowed considerable and he made some comment to an African-American man casually dressed and carrying shopping bags—an individual we already had passed who had also given us "the stare."

The short man appeared aimless after passing us—a phenomenon repeated by the others.

Several cars appeared to trail us. In one white Honda with Virginia tags, two dark men with mustaches appeared to make no bones about their surveillance. They first caught our attention as we crossed the intersection, and both gave us a menacing stare.

The car entered a traffic circle, and instead of proceeding, circled back and came alonside, stopping in the middle of the road just yards in front of us. The occupants began to manipulate their mirrors to watch us along the sidewalk.

SIMILAR CIRCUMSTANCES

In all, at least two dozen and possibly three dozen people were encountered under similar circumstances from the time Knowlton left his apartment until he returned.

He said he recognized two of them from the day before.

We then took a drive around the block; no one appeared to follow us. But when we first entered the car, a pedestrian came alongside and noticeably checked the car's front and rear license plates.

Knowlton took out a camera and photographed the man, who quickly moved his hand toward his face.

After midnight that evening, Knowlton called Pritchard to say his apartment doorbell had been rung but no one answered when he asked who was there. Then there were four immediate knocks on the door.

Pritchard said that the license plate Knowlton noted from Thursday had checked out with a law enforcement source of Pritchard's as being a federal government vehicle.

His source suggested Knowlton was "being warned, or there was an attempt being made to destabilize him before he appears before the grand jury," Pritchard recounted.

Knowlton's lawyer has contacted the FBI to complain. There has been no return call.

STARR CATCHING UP

The subpoena is one indication that Starr may be playing catch-up; the Telegraph reported that three critical crime scene witnesses had never been called before his Washington grand jury—though Starr says he has been actively investigating the case for more than a year.

In addition to Knowlton, Starr had

never brought in two witnesses who said that when they entered Fort Marcy's lot they saw two men—not Foster—in and around his Honda just before the body was found. One man, described as having long blonde hair, was said to have stood in front of the car with the hood up, as was reported in the Tribune-Review months ago.

The failure to aggressively examine these major discrepancies seemingly corroborates earlier reports that Starr's lead Foster prosecutor, Miquel Rodriguez, resigned after being thwarted by his superiors in conducting a full grand jury probe into the death.

Starr's possible passivity with the Foster case seems to have taken some notice on Capitol Hill.

A leading Republican member of the Senate's "Whitewater" Banking Committee said Thursday night that he was "disappointed" with Starr's work, which he described as embarrasing. The senator, previously believed to have been a supporter of Starr's, said Starr is motivated by a desire to be on the Supreme Court. He added, as it stands now, that any notion of Starr getting on the court "is finished." ∎

Foster Case: Witness 'Treated Like a Suspect'

By Christopher Ruddy
FOR THE PITTSBURGH
TRIBUNE-REVIEW
NOVEMBER 5,1995

WASHINGTON—A witness who appeared before Independent Counsel Kenneth Starr's grand jury last week says he was given shoddy treatment by Starr's prosecutors.

Patrick Knowlton, a Washington businessman, was the first person to see Vincent Foster's Honda in Fort Marcy Park on the afternoon of July 20, 1993, when Foster died.

"I did the right thing," Knowlton told the Tribune-Review of coming forward to tell his story. "Instead of being treated with dignity and respect, I got treated like a suspect, a liar," he said of his grand jury treatment.

Starr's deputy, Hickman Ewing, told the Tribune-Review he was unaware of any problems Knowlton had during the proceedings. Ewing said Knowlton and his attorney are welcome to make any objections known to the staff.

He would not comment on specific matters raised by Knowlton. Ewing, a well-regarded former U.S. attorney from Memphis, said it is not uncommon for witnesses to complain about questioning. He added that the investigation has been handled in a "professional way."

Knowlton told Park Police shortly after the death, and later Special Counsel Robert Fiske's investigators, that he had stopped at Fort Marcy Park to relieve himself in the woods at about 4:30 that afternoon when he spotted a brown Honda in the lot with Arkansas tags. He also said a Hispanic-looking man glared at him menacingly as the man sat and then stood near Foster's unoccupied Honda.

The witness told the FBI he was frightened by the man and quickly left the park.

Knowlton was an anonymous figure in the case until two Sundays ago when London's Sunday Telegraph recounted his story. In the article, Knowlton said the FBI had misrepresented his statements, particularly by stating he "could not further identify this (Hispanic-looking man) and stated that he would be unable to recognize him in the future."

Knowlton backed up his statement to the Telegraph by helping a police artist draw a composite sketch of the man. The Telegraph published the sketch.

He told the grand jury last week that the FBI statement was a "lie," Knowlton said.

The Telegraph reported that Starr had never interviewed nor called before his grand jury the only civilian crime scene witnesses noted in the police report: Knowlton and two other witnesses who told Fiske's investigators that they saw two men, not Foster, in and around his Honda.

Apparently embarrassed, Starr issued subpoenas to Knowlton and several others after the Telegraph report—though his office had been telling the press in leaks that the case was all but wrapped up.

The Foster death investigation has been a Sisyphean task for Starr, a retired federal judge; each time he has tried to put his rubber stamp on the case to close it, something else, like Knowlton's testimony, has unraveled.

QUESTIONING

Knowlton said Starr's inquiry before the grand jury was led by assistant Independent Counsel Brett M. Kavanaugh. John Bates, Starr's deputy, was also present during the proceedings but did not ask any questions.

Bates is a 15-year veteran of the U.S. Attorney's Office in Washington.

Continued on next page

Continued from page 121

Knowlton said prosecutors spent a significant part of his 2 1/2 hours of questioning—as much as a third of his time—trying to ascertain who in the press he had spoken with and what he had told them. He was also questioned as to who in Congress he had spoken with.

He said that during the remaining time, the prosecutors seemed less interested in getting to the bottom of the misrepresentations in the police and FBI reports.

"I felt like they were trying to focus on my character," he said of Kavanaugh's line of questioning.

Questions about press contacts are not unusual in a grand jury setting, nor are challenging questions to determine one's credibility—though they can be perceived by the witness as attacks on his or her character.

But telling was the fact that Knowlton said at no point was his brief Park Police statement and FBI statement read back to him in its entirety to be reviewed by the grand jury. He said prosecutors never read back to him handwritten notes of FBI agents that should back up their statement as to what he said.

He said Kavanaugh quickly moved off the Park Police report when Knowlton began pointing out some obvious errors.

The police misidentified the Hispanic man as a "white male" and even spelled Knowlton's name wrong in their report.

Kavanaugh, a Yale Law School graduate, is a former clerk to Supreme Court Justice Anthony Kennedy. He is considered one of Starr's best and brightest prosecutors, and has been assigned significant responsibilities relating to the handling of papers in Foster's office. With the resignation of Starr's lead Foster prosecutor, Miquel Rodriguez, Kavanaugh was saddled with those responsibilities as well.

The scope of the case would be a daunting task for even a veteran prosecutor. According to his biography, Kavanaugh has never prosecuted a case before.

"If that's true, he should not be in there," said Jerris Leonard, questioning the decision to make a first-time prosecutor the lead interrogator in a case of this type.

As assistant Attorney General for civil rights during the Nixon administration, Leonard handled federal inquiries into the murder of two Black Panthers and the Kent State killings.

"The Foster case is very, very important to all people involved. An apprentice should not be trying an important case like this," he said.

Leonard agreed that Kavanaugh may be checking the credibility of the witness, but said it should be done in a way that does not attempt "to discredit" the witness before the grand jury.

Knowlton said Kavanaugh ended with a sarcastic question: "Why didn't you wait for someone to call you?" Knowlton said it implied he was some sort of publicity hound. In fact, Ambrose Evans-Pritchard of the Sunday Telegraph had sought out Knowlton. Starr's office only contacted Knowlton after the press report, though it has known of his identity over a year.

SAME AGENTS

Knowlton is now the second witness to claim that the FBI misrepresented his official statement and that interviewing agents went to great lengths to persuade him his original story was wrong.

The first witness is known as the confidential witness who came into Fort Marcy more than an hour after Knowlton left. The FBI and Fiske claimed he was the person who found Foster's body and who asked maintenance workers to call 911.

The confidential witness originally said that he did not see a gun in Foster's hand, that Foster's hands were palms up and that Foster's head was perfectly straight up. The Fiske report, however, states that the witness said a gun could have been in the hand and the head could have been tilted to the tight, explaining some unusual blood tracks.

The confidential witness said he was "badgered" by the FBI into making those statements.

His criticism has received attention from radio talk-show host G. Gordon Liddy and Republican U.S. Rep. Dan Burton of Indiana.

Though the confidential witness' statements were a key part of the Fiske report, federal investigators have since attacked his credibility, an apparent pattern for the investigators.

For example, a couple found in the park have been the subject of vicious comment that first emanated from the Park Police. The police said the couple, a man and a woman married to others, were caught having adulterous sex in the park. The motivation for the smear became more apparent when their witness statements completely contradicted the police version of events and the findings of Special Counsel Fiske.

Knowlton and the confidential witness were interviewed by the same FBI agents: William Colombell and Larry Monroe.

Starr brought the confidential witness before his grand jury earlier this year, but nothing has come of the testimony.

Monroe retired from the bureau shortly after the Fiske report was issued.

Starr kept Colombell as his senior agent, and the same FBI agents whose work has been criticized under Fiske, to review their own work.

HARASSMENT

Late last week, Knowlton and his attorney met with FBI agents working with Starr about concerns for Knowlton's safety.

"At first they didn't believe it, but seem to be taking it seriously," Washington attorney John Clarke said. Clarke is representing

Knowlton.

The Tribune-Review and London's Sunday Telegraph reported last week that Knowlton was being victimized by a surveillance operation. Knowlton took several pictures of individuals, including one of a man who took particular note of this reporter's license plates.

Also, the license tags to a white Honda that was trailing Knowlton and this reporter have been traced to an Arab man living in Vienna, Va. During a visit to the address, the Arab man who had followed Knowlton was found residing there. But the plates had been switched to a different car, a blue sedan, that was parked outside his home. He became visibly upset when he heard photos were taken, though he claimed he had not driven a white Honda and had not engaged in any surveillance.

In a related matter, the Tribune-Review reported last month that the FBI lab had compared handwriting on two checks written by Foster against the handwriting on a torn note found in his briefcase, and that the comparisons were inconclusive. The FBI lab actually compared the note to 17 of Foster's checks and found them to be an inconclusive match. ∎

Foster Death: Lee's Findings Questioned

By Christopher Ruddy
FOR THE PITTSBURGH
TRIBUNE-REVIEW
NOVEMBER 13, 1995

WASHINGTON—Forensic scientist Henry Lee has not yet issued his report on the death of Vincent W. Foster Jr., but has offered Independent Counsel Kenneth Starr's staff some preliminary findings.

Lee's opinions will bolster government claims that Vincent Foster's body was not moved to Fort Marcy Park, near Washington, D.C., a source close to the investigation told the Tribune-Review.

The source said Lee has informally told Starr's staff that he has reviewed some crime scene pictures, as well as some of the physical evidence, such as Foster's clothing. Earlier this summer, Lee visited Fort Marcy Park, the apparent death scene.

Shortly after his visit, Lee asked Starr to have the FBI conduct an exhaustive search of the park for the bullet. The search, which began in mid-September and ended over a month later, apparently did not turn up the slug fired from the .38-caliber Army service revolver found in Foster's hand.

Lee's hiring came in the wake of an independent report issued by two former New York police homicide investigators last April who concluded that the "overwhelming evidence" indicated Foster's body had been moved to the park.

The independent report cited, among other things, the failure of authorities to find the spent bullet, which they said should have been in the vicinity of the body.

The source said Lee will downplay the significance of the missing bullet while offering his own interpretation of key evidence to support the conclusion Foster killed himself at the park.

Lee's hiring also followed the resignation of Associate Independent Counsel Miquel Rodriguez, who reportedly found the FBI and its experts unwilling to fully investigate the case.

Starr's staff, according to sources, believes it can close the lid on the

Forensic Scientist Henry Lee

case by using Lee's report as the capstone of its probe. By knocking down arguments the body was moved, the Starr team hopes to create a "fire line" between those arguing Foster was murdered and others who have challenged the legitimacy of investigations by the police and former special counsel Robert Fiske.

Since Starr hired Lee last spring, Lee has been criticized for his testimony during the O.J. Simpson

Continued on next page

Continued from page 123

case. He was a central expert witness for the defense.

Meanwhile, the source close to Starr's inquiry told the Tribune-Review that Lee's still-unfinished report will contain some new, quite unusual evidence.

For example, Lee has told investigators that during a cursory examination of the death scene earlier this year, he found a skull fragment in the area in which Foster is supposed to have been found. Lee has not yet linked the fragment to Foster.

The failure of police or emergency workers at the death scene to note bone fragments under the head, or to find such matter after the body was removed—though Foster is alleged to have blown out a chunk of his skull—was one indication Foster may not have committed suicide in the park.

The police said they searched for the fragments and found none.

In April 1994, nine months after the death, Fiske's FBI investigators conducted an exhaustive search over a wide area of the ground in the park—utilizing extensive raking and sifting methods—and found no bone fragments.

Here are other factors Lee will offer the Starr team as evidence that Foster was shot at the spot he was found:

■ **FACIAL BLOOD**—Lee will interpret dark specks on Foster's face in a Polaroid photo as being blood. Lee will say the splattering is "consistent with the use of a high-velocity weapon fired in the mouth," the source said.

Foster was found with a high-velocity .38-caliber weapon in his hand with two high-velocity .38 bullets having been in the gun's cylinder. Lee's interpretation will counter suggestions Foster was shot with a low-velocity .22-caliber weapon, for example, and that the old .38 Colt was planted in his hand.

Dr. Vincent Di Maio, medical examiner for San Antonio, Tex., is considered one of the nation's leading authorities on gunshot wounds.

He agrees with Lee that had Foster placed the barrel in his mouth, the speckled material on the face would be blood. Gun powder marks, called stippling, would be present only if the gun was fired with the barrel outside the mouth.

Di Maio disagrees, however, with Lee's expected conclusion on the critical issue of the gun's velocity. Di Maio said the blood splatter is typically a result of "nasal spray" of blood emanating from the nose after the gun's explosion. Di Maio said such a spray is consistent "with any velocity gun," including a .22.

■ **BLOOD DRAINAGE TRACKS**—Lee will offer his opinion that blood drainage tracks found on Foster's face are consistent with Foster having been shot at the spot he was found.

A blood stain on Foster's face identified by the FBI lab will be determined to be the result of Foster's jaw having come into contact with a bloodied shirt shoulder. Lee told investigators he found a mirror blood stain on Foster's shirt collar from the shoulder area, supporting that conclusion.

The FBI said Foster's head, as the Polaroid picture shows, was found in a straight-up position, not tilted to either side. Lee will agree with the conclusion of Special Counsel Fiske that the stain is likely the result of the head having been moved by an emergency worker while checking for a pulse.

No emergency worker has admitted to moving the head.

Fiske's team did not make the claim the stain was caused by Foster's own movements after the shot was fired because, experts say, it would take time for blood to soak the shirt shoulder. Also, Fiske's pathologists claimed Foster's heart stopped beating immediately after the shot was fired, causing instant death.

Lee will also claim that the FBI lab misconstrued one blood track that their lab said flows from the right nostril to above Foster's ear by the temple area. That track has been cited as key evidence the body was moved, since Foster was found on a steep incline, and the track indicated blood would have moved uphill, against gravity.

Other experts suggest that Lee and others might be missing the most significant evidence of the case: that only blood drainage tracks were found on Foster's face, and not the excessive bleeding resultant from a gunshot to the head of a living person—a possible indication Foster's heart had stopped before the shot was fired.

At least three Fairfax County emergency workers told the FBI the death appeared suspicious because of the lack of bleeding.

Fiske's pathology team said the lack of blood was explained by the fact the bullet passed through the brain stem causing a "prompt cessation" of Foster's heart.

But other experts believe the small amount of blood could also mean that the gunshot cannot be accepted at face value as the cause of death.

"You'd expect the heart to continue beating for a minute or more," Dr. Martin Fachler said of heart activity after a shot is fired.

Fachler, former head of the Army's Wound Ballistics Laboratory, said such post-mortem heart activity should have left the face and shirt covered with blood. He said the heart stops beating when "it is deprived of oxygen" which occurs sometime after the shot. Impairment of the brain stops lung activity he said, followed, in time, by heart activity.

■ **BLOOD SPLATTER**—Lee is noted for his expertise in this area, and a source close to the probe said to "expect an O.J. defense" when it comes to Lee identifying blood splatter in the area above and around Foster's head.

The New York investigators concluded that if Foster had fired the shot at the spot he was found, as he sat down on a hill, with the bullet exiting the top of the back of the head, a "jet-like stream of blood, tissue and other material" should have been apparent to investigators on the leaves and foliage in the area above the head. Nothing like this was evident at the site.

Lee will argue that a dark-colored material he sees on leaves and foliage depicted in the Polaroid just above the head is, or could be, blood.

Lee was criticized by the FBI during the Simpson case for his speculative testimony that a blood pattern could have been from a shoe imprint.

His discovery of what he said is "blood" spatter will also be an advancement on Fiske's team of four pathologists who examined the same photo and noted no blood splatter in their report last year.

Lee's finds will also contradict the eyewitness testimony of 20 police, medical and emergency workers at the scene that evening who had clear view of the death scene, since the sun set late that summer night. Officials at the scene were interviewed by FBI investigators for Fiske last year. No one told the FBI of seeing blood on any vegetation.

And some specifically stated there was no blood or splatter on the vegetation around the body.

Lead Park Police investigator John Rolla stated in his official police report "There was no blood spatter [sic] on the plants or trees surrounding decedent's head." Rolla told Senate investigators that the only blood he saw was directly under the head.

Virginia Medical Examiner Dr. Donal Haut, who visited the death scene, told the FBI "no blood was recalled (having been seen) on the vegetation around the body."

Vincent Scalice, a former New York City police homicide expert who has reviewed the case, said that the large, jagged exit wound noted on the autopsy should have yielded "a flow of blood, significant blood, brain matter and gelatinous tissue in the area of the head. It shouldn't have been missed."

Fred Santucci, a forensic crime scene photographer formerly with the New York City police department, said that any finding of blood splatter from a picture "is suspect when no one saw it with their own eyes on the scene."

"The Polaroid is the worst quality photo for finding small drops of blood," Santucci said. Lee has been working with Polaroids, since the key photos taken on 35mm film were underexposed.

Lee has told Starr's investigators his review is limited in scope, partly because of the sloppy and incomplete work of the Park Police who originally handled the case.

The source familiar with the probe said that Lee's report will be critical of the FBI laboratory's handling of the case "implicitly or explicitly," but will spare the bureau the embarrassment of having overlooked serious evidence of foul play.

Apparently to bolster Lee's findings and to cover areas outside of his expertise, Starr hired San Diego Medical Examiner Brian Blackbourne to review autopsy findings in the case. Blackbourne has been closely associated with the federal government, having been a regular lecturer at the FBI Academy, the Armed Forces Institute, and the District of Columbia Homicide School.

Lee will not rule on whether Foster committed suicide, nor will he rule on a picture that shows possible trauma to Foster's neck.

Lee last month told an audience at the New York City University Graduate Center that he is overwhelmed with homicide investigations at his Connecticut state crime lab. So much so, he said of suicide cases reviewed in Connecticut, "If it looks like a suicide, we don't look at it."

Critics contend the Foster case remains open because the Park Police violated police procedure, which is to treat every suicide, no matter how apparent, as a homicide first. Apparently police procedure isn't followed in Connecticut either. ■

Foster Case:
Controversial Lee to Issue His Report

By Christopher Ruddy
FOR THE PITTSBURGH
TRIBUNE-REVIEW
NOVEMBER 24, 1995

WASHINGTON—Forensic scientist Henry Lee is soon to offer his opinions in the case of Deputy White House Counsel Vincent Foster. However, if his previous findings in high-profile cases are any indication, Lee's report is unlikely to lay to rest the issues surrounding Foster's manner of death.

Lee's appearance in August as an expert witness for O.J. Simpson's defense team has made the chief of the Connecticut State Crime Lab perhaps the world's most celebrated forensic scientist. And perhaps one of the world's most controversial.

Since late spring Lee has been preparing to issue a significant report for Independent Counsel Kenneth Starr relating to issues dealing with Foster's July 20, 1993, death. The Tribune-Review reported recently that Lee's findings from physical evidence will bolster government claims Foster died at the spot he was found in Fort Marcy Park.

According to sources close to the probe, Starr and his staff have been anxious to close their investigation into Foster's death in the wake of a cursory grand jury probe that took place earlier this year. They reportedly hoped Lee would do the trick. But criticisms of Lee since the Simpson trial have made that hope illusory.

Starr's then deputy, Mark H. Tuohey III, hired Lee after disclosures that primary Foster prosecutor, Associate Independent Counsel Miquel Rodriguez, resigned because of resistance from FBI experts to explore alleged problems in the case and the apparent unwillingness of Rodriguez's superiors to allow him to bring experts outside the FBI into the case.

Though Starr hired Lee knowing of his involvement as a defense witness in the Simpson case, Starr was apparently unprepared for the implications of Lee's controversial testimony there. In July, a source close to Starr's probe said Starr's staffers were under the impression that Lee would probably not testify at the trial.

However, Lee did testify and came under harsh criticism from FBI experts for his speculative testimony about bloodstain patterns found at the Ron Goldman-Nicole Simpson death scene.

For that reason, and the fact that Lee has limited the scope of his own inquiry, Starr hired the San Diego medical examiner to review the autopsy findings in the Foster case.

WEIGHING IN

While drawing sharp criticism from members of the scientific community for his Simpson testimony, Lee again has demonstrated his willingness to weigh in on controversial cases.

He has a powerful reputation in the legal and scientific worlds. "He's the best, the very best," Carla Noziglia, former director of the American Society of Crime Laboratory Director, told the AP earlier this year.

But, others, especially in light of recent events, are less impressed.

John Hicks, who retired in 1994 as an assistant director of the FBI in charge of its crime lab, suggested in a telephone interview last month that Lee's opinion is far from gospel.

Hicks, now working for the Alabama State Crime Laboratory, is highly respected in the scientific community, and under FBI Director William Sessions pioneered the bureau's entry into DNA analysis. Hicks has also supervised crucial scientific work that led to convictions in the New York City World Trade Center bombing.

Asked about Lee's role as an expert witness at the Simpson trial, Hicks said the defense "spent a lot of time building him up as to be the world's greatest, bestest and mostest," but suggested that he fell short of that billing.

Lee "must have been embarrassed," Hicks said, "when he had two (FBI) experts come in and basically point out that what he said with certain things were most certainly not what he said they were."

Hicks criticized Lee's interpretation of several imprints of blood patterns that enabled Simpson defense lawyers to bolster their case that the murders were accomplished by more than one individual. Lee, for example, argued that one blood pattern found on an envelope could have been made from a shoe different from the one prosecutors claimed Simpson wore the night of the killings. But during his testimony Lee said his judgment was not definitive as to whether it was a shoe print.

"When he said, for example, that this appears to be (a shoe print), he was very careful. He said, I see an imprint, it may be a shoe print, I don't know if it is or not, but if it is a shoe print it's not (Simpson's shoe)," Hicks said, recalling Lee's qualified testimony.

FBI agents William Bodziak and Douglas Deedrich took the stand in September to dispute Lee's findings; Lee did not retake the witness stand to counter their conclusions. Deedrich, an expert on fabrics, said some of the blood patterns were more likely the result of fabric impressions than shoe impressions. Deedrich called Lee's research "inadequate" and suggested it had been "irresponsible" of Lee to have made any inferences about the blood patterns.

Lee subsequently held a press conference in Connecticut to defend his testimony. He said he had drawn no specific conclusion about the stains, and that defense lawyers may have exaggerated the significance of his opinions for Simpson's benefit.

He told the press he was sorry to have taken the case because the hardships it had imposed on him and his family were "not worth it."

Today Lee appears uninterested in discussing his Simpson testimony. He declined to address the matter, or Hicks' criticism, with the Tribune-Review last month before giving a speech at the City University Graduate Center in New York, saying that any discussion of the O.J. case was off-limits.

"I don't want to talk about it," he said. And in an hour-long slide show of his most famous cases, the Simpson case was not even mentioned.

CREDIBILITY

Hicks said Lee's O.J. testimony had cost him credibility "with a lot of people in the forensic community."

"I think he is definitely a hired gun," Hicks said, a criticism frequently made of witnesses.

Lee does not take money for himself for his cases. But expert witnesses typically can call a higher price for their services from the defense than the prosecution, and Lee received a significant fee for his work on the O.J. case. Lee summarily gave the fee to a scholarship fund and to the state crime laboratory he heads.

Lee also says he works for neither the prosecution nor defense, but rather seeks to present scientific truth.

Others suggest Lee is also interested in prestige and attention.

"I think he has an ego as big as his resume," Dr. Richard Saferstein said, noting Lee's 50-page plus *curriculum vitae*.

Saferstein, former head of the New Jersey State Crime Lab, was a regular commentator on the Simpson case for Geraldo Rivera's talk show, and is considered a leading forensic scientist. He is author of "Forensic Science" (Prentice-Hall), the standard text in the field.

Saferstein, who conducted tests for two homicide investigators hired by the Western Journalism Center to review aspects of the Foster case, suggests Lee's success can be partly explained because "he is close to being an entertainer."

Hicks agreed with that assessment and suggested that Lee's powerful personality sometimes clouds the serious scientific issues involved in a case.

"Henry is a very personable person, and it's easy to be drawn in by Henry, he's full of . . . stories, very enjoyable, and sort of an exciting person to listen to."

CONTROVERSIAL CASES

For sure, Lee has been involved in some complex, seemingly unsolvable cases. In 1986, Lee helped resolve a Connecticut murder case involving a husband who had put his wife through a wood chipper to destroy her remains. Lee was able to identify minute fragments of her bones, teeth and other body parts, which helped police solve the case.

Though most forensic scientists confine themselves to the laboratory, Lee's generalist knowledge (he was a police officer before going into forensic science) has enabled him to be something of a Sherlock Holmes at crime scenes. He stresses during his presentation that he can be most effective when he visits the crime scene in its most pristine state: before it has been bothered by detectives and others.

Other controversial cases in which Lee has played a role:

■ The Levin killing, or better known as "the preppie murder" case of 1987. Lee was working for Robert Chambers' defense when Chambers confessed to the killing of young Jennifer Levin by strangulation during a sexual encounter in Central Park.

■ William Kennedy Smith rape case. Lee was said to have played the lead role in helping Smith get acquitted of raping a Palm Beach woman in 1991. Lee told the jury that had the young lady really struggled on the grass as she was raped, grass stains should have been apparent on her pantyhose. None were, and in court, he produced a handkerchief soiled with grass stains after he had rubbed it against the same area of grass.

Hicks called Lee's handkerchief experiment "outrageous," saying it did not follow proper scientific methodology, which would have entailed using the same fabric and making sure conditions, such as moisture, were the same.

Lee is apparently aware of such criticism, and during a recent speech answered his critics: "Give me a break, how many guys you know who carry panties in their pocket."

■ The still-questioned 1991 death of Danny Casolaro, a free-lance journalist found dead in the bathtub of a West Virginia hotel of an apparent suicide. His family contested that ruling and said Casolaro was working on an expose of corruption in the federal government. Lee reviewed the case and said the death, based on blood splatter analysis, was consistent with suicide. ■

Despite Evidence, FBI Ends Two Death Probes

By Christopher Ruddy
FOR THE PITTSBURGH
TRIBUNE-REVIEW
DECEMBER 10, 1995

WASHINGTON—The FBI recently moved to close the book on two inquiries into death cases that have received national attention. In both cases, bureau officials told parents of the decedents that investigators found no criminal wrongdoing, the Tribune Review has learned.

Both cases could have serious implications for current federal inquiries into the death of Deputy White House Counsel Vincent Foster and into allegations of narcotics trafficking in Arkansas while Bill Clinton was governor.

Thomas and Beth George Burkett were summoned just over a week ago to FBI offices in Tysons Corner, Va., to be informed that after an 18-month investigation the FBI had concluded their 21-year-old son, Tommy, committed suicide in 1991.

The Burketts had offered evidence that their son was murdered, a conclusion supported by a second autopsy. The first autopsy of Burkett was conducted by the same Virginia medical examiner who conducted Foster's.

Meanwhile, the parents of 17-year-old Kevin Ives met with FBI officials in Little Rock, the Arkansas state capital. In 1987 young Ives and his friend, Don Henry, were brutally slain and their bodies were thrown onto railroad tracks. Since then their deaths have been linked to narcotics trafficking at Arkansas' Mena Airport.

The apparent closure of both cases is no doubt welcome news to the Clinton administration as it enters an election year. If the FBI

had ruled differently on Burkett's death, for example, it would have seriously undermined the autopsy conclusions in the Foster case made by Dr. James Beyer, the deputy medical examiner for northern Virginia.

At about the time some FBI officials were meeting with the Burketts, FBI officials in Little Rock were meeting with Larry and Linda Ives, the parents of Kevin.

When the boys' bodies were found run over by a train, officials in Arkansas, including Gov. Clinton's medical examiner, Dr. Fahmy Malak, moved to rule the case a double suicide. After the Ives voiced objections, Malak ruled that the boys had died accidentally after smoking an excessive amount of marijuana.

Unwilling to accept that, Linda Ives pressed for a grand jury inquiry. The boys' bodies were exhumed, and a second autopsy found they had indeed been murdered: Kevin's skull had been crushed and Don had been stabbed repeatedly before their bodies were thrown on the tracks.

The grand jury determined the deaths to be murders, and suggested they were related to drug trafficking. The bodies were found near a known drug drop-off point for small planes, and some law enforcement authorities suggest the boys may have stumbled upon a drop.

Allegations that Gov. Clinton's administration had knowledge of drug trafficking at Mena airport have since surfaced, and some have questioned the failed police investigation in that light.

In their meeting, the Ives were told a story similar to what the Burketts were told: the FBI after a lengthy investigation had found no wrongdoing. The assistant special

agent in charge of the Little Rock office, William Tempel, told the couple that the probe was essentially concluded and a report would be passed up to Little Rock U.S. Attorney Paula Casey for final review.

Mrs. Ives said Tempel told her husband "in light of this, maybe it was time that Larry and I consider a criminal act had not occurred."

Flabbergasted by the statement, she and her husband walked out of the meeting. Mrs. Ives said she had already been told by the lead agent in the case, Phyllis Cournan, that the probe began running into resistance soon after investigators turned up links to Mena. According to Mrs. Ives, during the meeting Cournan admitted, "We all know drug drops took place by the tracks."

The case first came to the FBI's attention after the lead Saline County police detective, John Brown, told bureau officials that the police department was obstructing his probe. Brown also told the FBI that the bureau might have jurisdiction because the murders may have involved interstate drug trafficking or a political cover-up that violated the boys' rights.

Brown's investigation turned up evidence that police officials themselves may have been involved in the deaths. The FBI agreed to open an inquiry last year, Brown said, and he began working closely with Cournan on the case. Brown, too, said Cournan told him that she had encountered interference in the case from Justice Department officials and that she was afraid.

Brown, who today is chief of police in Alexander, Ark., said he was not totally surprised by the FBI ruling.

"To this day, no one, including the FBI, has interviewed any of the neighbors who live around the tracks where the boys were found," he said. "For the FBI now to say that no criminal act occurred is self-discrediting on their part." Tempel said he could not comment on a "pending" investigation. Cournan did not return a message left on her voice mail.

SECOND DEATH

The tale of the Burketts in Virginia is hauntingly similar.

"We were appalled," Thomas Burkett said of his and his wife's meeting with FBI officials, which lasted only several minutes. Burkett said William Megary, special agent in charge of the criminal division of the FBI's local office, opened the meeting by informing them the FBI had conducted a "long and exhaustive" investigation and found "nothing to indicate your son's death was anything but a suicide."

Mrs. Burkett said she quickly interrupted, challenging the FBI for having made a conclusion of suicide when the FBI repeatedly told the family during the long investigation that the bureau was only conducting a civil rights probe into the case.

The parents had indeed been told the FBI was not examining the circumstances or manner of death. But law enforcement experts say any civil rights probe of a death—examining whether local law enforcement agencies obstructed justice or engaged in a cover-up—would most likely have to include an investigation of the death itself.

An FBI spokeswoman, Susan Lloyd, speaking for Megary, said he told the Burketts that the FBI had investigated the death. Lloyd said the death investigation took place "because it's very difficult to separate a civil rights investigation from a death investigation because the two are so intertwined . . and the determination was that there was no cover-up by Fairfax (County) and also (the death) was a suicide."

The Burketts have incontrovertible evidence that they were told otherwise by bureau officials. The couple recorded their telephone conversations with the lead FBI agent in the case, Robert Posica. On the tapes, which were played for the Tribune-Review, Posica can be heard as many as a dozen times telling the parents, in an unfriendly and agitated manner, that he was conducting a narrow civil rights probe and not a death investigation.

On one tape Posica tells Mrs. Burkett that he has no desire to investigate whether the death was a suicide, or even to meet with the parents at any early stage of his inquiry. Eventually Posica did meet with them—a full five months after opening the inquiry.

In this meeting with the Burketts, Megary told the couple that the inquiry's records totaled some 1,800 pages. The Burketts were first told, however, that they could not see the case file. After they made objections, Megary suggested they "could try" to get the records by filing a Freedom of Information Act request, the Burketts recalled.

They told the agent they would not file any such request because previously filed FOIA request with the FBI are two years old and have gone unanswered.

Indeed, FOIA requests to the FBI typically take years to bear fruit. Lloyd was at a loss to explain the reasoning behind making the family wait other than to say it may be "standard operating procedure."

Despite the FBI's conclusion, the family has evidence that their son was murdered. A second autopsy, this one performed by the former medical examiner for Syracuse, N.Y., showed that Tommy Burkett's ear had suffered trauma, an indication that he may have been beaten. Also, a fractured lower jaw inconsistent with suicide was identified, and abrasions were found on the deceased's chest.

The first autopsy conducted by Beyer reported no such findings.

The second autopsy also noted that Burkett's lungs had never been dissected, though Beyer claimed in his report that the procedure had been done.

The victim's father said he saw one of the autopsy photos taken out of a file of photos by Beyer. But Beyer later wrote to the Burketts that only one autopsy photo was taken—a close-up of Tommy's face. If that is true, proper procedure was violated.

Beyer also said he took no x-rays. Thus, evidence from the first autopsy that would have identified the beaten ear or the broken jaw found in the second autopsy was either destroyed or missing.

The Burketts' meeting with the FBI did not last long enough for a discussion of the autopsy, but the parents said one official asserted "even the second autopsy supports a suicide."

Yet the family had other evidence of murder: Burkett was found with a .357-caliber Magnum lying on his hand after allegedly shooting himself in the mouth. No powder burns were found in the mouth. The parents found Tommy dead alone in his bedroom, but blood was found outside the bedroom, and neighbors said they saw visitors in the house on the day he died.

The evidence of foul play was compelling enough for NBC's "Unsolved Mysteries" program to air a segment on the death last year.

The family said Fairfax police quickly ruled the death a suicide and conducted little or no investigation. Last year, Fairfax spokesman Warren Carmichael said the ruling of death was made primarily on the basis of Beyer's autopsy.

But Beyer has consistently said he did not rule that the death was a suicide, only that it was consistent with a self-inflicted gunshot wound.

Lloyd said she was unaware of discrepancies with the original autopsy. She said the FBI conducted an extensive investigation that included 180 interviews as well as a review of the police case and the medical examiner's reports. ■

Pathologist, FBI Go Way Back

By Christopher Ruddy
FOR THE PITTSBURGH
TRIBUNE-REVIEW
DECEMBER 10, 1995

Dr. James Beyer, 79, the pathologist at the center of the controversy involving young Tommy Burkett's death, also has played a pivotal role in the Foster case. Though Beyer is employed by the state of Virginia, new information indicates he has strong links with federal authorities, particularly the FBI.

Authorities have assiduously asserted Foster's death to be a suicide, with primary evidence being Beyer's autopsy.

Bureau officials may have good reason to back up Beyer's findings.

For starters, Beyer has changed his story on significant aspects of the Foster case that could show the FBI played a greater role than admitted.

In an interview on Jan. 20, 1994—just six months after Foster's death and before any real controversy arose concerning it— Beyer said that an FBI agent and a Secret Service agent, in addition to Park Police, were present when he conducted his autopsy on Foster.

Yet the Park Police claim that only their officers were present, and Beyer has since recanted. The FBI has tried to distance itself from the handling of the initial death investigation by the Park Police, and has claimed FBI agents were not present at the autopsy or death scene.

Beyer's original recollection may also shed light on the lengths to which bureau officials have gone to absolve the Park Police of any wrongdoing. Since the controversy over the death, FBI agents have vigorously supported the suicide conclusion.

FBI agents have also testified that the Park Police made no significant errors in their probe, though outside homicide experts have found many.

Beyer stated emphatically in his unrehearsed interview in January 1994 that he had not ruled Foster's death a suicide, only that the death was "consistent with a self-inflicted gunshot." He said that in Virginia police authorities rule on the death. Beyer also stated he had never visited the death scene, did not review crime scene photos, and did not even know the caliber of the gun found in Foster's hand. Nor, he said, were any officers present who had been at the death scene; pathologists usually like to ask police questions to see if the body's state is consistent with how it was found. (The Park Police also violated their own procedures by not having such an officer present.)

The Park Police, and later Special Counsel Robert Fiske, relied heavily on Beyer's conclusions. During Senate hearings in 1994, Beyer again reversed his position 180 degrees, stating emphatically that he had ruled Foster's death a suicide.

In an interview last week, Beyer said FBI and Secret Service agents were not present at the autopsy, "I don't ever recall saying they were," he said.

Beyer also backed off a bit from his 1994 Senate testimony, calling the determination of suicide a "combined decision" made by him and the Park Police.

Asked how he could have reached that conclusion without the benefit of detectives who were at the scene, or photos of the scene, or even knowing the caliber of the gun at the time of the autopsy, he said he had several conversations with police after the death. Beyer also said the gun's caliber had "no bearing" on his autopsy.

Other pathologists, including the former medical examiner of New York, Dr. Michael Baden, disagree, suggesting such information would be important for any determination.

Another clue to understanding this puzzle of death may have been discovered by Miquel Rodriquez, former lead prosecutor on the Foster case under independent Counsel Kenneth Starr. Rodriquez resigned this year after heroic efforts to investigate the case were thwarted by higher-ups and FBI officials, the Tribune-Review has reported.

Rodriguez discovered that Beyer, far from being just an impartial state pathologist, has a long association with the FBI and lectured for many years at the FBI Academy in Quantico, Va. Beyer confirmed that he has worked with the FBI for 10 years or more. Beyer has also served as a consultant to the Pentagon.

Whether Beyer's connection with the bureau played a role in the FBI's handling of key cases is unclear, but the FBI's selective investigatory amnesia seems strange.

In two recent cases—Foster's and the deaths of the two boys—the FBI has apparently made its own rules, even dismissing two credible autopsies that in the real world show evidence of murder. No matter, the press has shown little interest in the case. The FBI's secret investigations have now ended with secret reports.

Likewise, in the Foster case, there has been no second autopsy. Any key forensic evidence such as blond hairs and carpet fibers found all over

Foster's clothing could have been from anywhere, one agent told a Senate committee.

To explain the weird circumstances of Foster's death, the FBI has even suspended the laws of nature: inanimate carpet fibers "jumped" onto his clothing; "bouncing" eyeglasses came to be found 19 feet from where Foster's head lay; his "frictionless" shoes picked up not even a speck of soil or grass despite his supposed long walk in the park; and "inverse gravity" allowed the stream of blood to flow uphill. ■

Did Clinton Counsel Take Part in Clean-up of Foster's Files?

By Christopher Ruddy
FOR THE PITTSBURGH TRIBUNE-REVIEW
JANUARY 9, 1996

WASHINGTON—Independent Counsel Kenneth Starr's grand jury heard testimony last year suggesting that former White House lawyer William Kennedy took part in a clean-up operation of Vincent Foster's Whitewater related files at the Rose Law Firm.

The testimony has taken on increased credibility in light of the release last month of Kennedy's notes of a Washington meeting in the fall of 1993 that some have interpreted as suggesting a need to "vacuum" or clean-up such files.

Kennedy's ex-wife, Gail, told Starr's Washington grand jurors in early 1995 that during the time when Whitewater *first* became prominent in the news, her husband, then associate White House counsel, had taken an unusual trip home from Washington to Little Rock, according to a source familiar with Starr's probe

At the time Kennedy made the trip, Mrs. Kennedy had not yet separated from her husband. The couple divorced in August 1994.

Kennedy, according to testimony, told his wife that he was taking a break to go hunting in Arkansas, the source said. At the time, Mrs.

Kennedy found that hard to believe, considering her husband's pressing duties at the White House.

Under grand jury questioning she said she had other reasons to doubt the hunting story, including knowing that during part of the trip he was at the Rose firm.

At about the time her husband was on his "hunting trip," Mrs. Kennedy told the grand jury, she spoke with a senior White House aide, also from Arkansas. The woman told Mrs. Kennedy in blunt terms her husband had not gone to Little Rock for hunting, but instead was at Rose cleaning up Whitewater-related matters.

Mrs. Kennedy refused to reveal the aide's identity under questioning from Brett M. Kavanaugh, a junior prosecutor for Starr, who, like Starr is, handling a prosecution for the first time.

After completing her grand jury appearance, Mrs. Kennedy returned to Arkansas, but was again pressed, this time by Starr's then-deputy, Mark H. Tuohey III, to reveal the name of the White House aide. She ultimately did so reluctantly, the source said.

Kennedy resigned from the White House inner circle Nov. 18, 1994. His notes from a meeting dealing with Whitewater-related matters a year earlier became the focus of an intense confrontation recently between the White House and the

Senate Banking Committee, which is probing the Clintons' dealings. Committee members sought the notes over claims of attorney-client privilege.

The November 1993 meeting took place with several White House officials and the president's private lawyer, David Kendall. Committee investigators were concerned the participants may have discussed administration plans to interfere with two federal inquiries into Whitewater-related matters after Foster's death.

The notes released by the White House last month show Kennedy wrote:

Vacuum Rose Law files WWDC (Whitewater Development Corporation) Docs—
subpoena
Documents—never go out
Quietly?

Republicans interpreted the notes to mean that participants at the meeting wanted to sanitize or remove any incriminating files relating to Whitewater stored at Rose.

In a statement released by the White House, Kennedy said that the use of the term "vacuum" in the notes referred to an "information vacuum" that had stymied Clinton aides in assembling data relating to the Whitewater partnership.

If prosecutors can prove that files
Continued on next page

Continued from page 131

were destroyed or concealed from investigators as a criminal probe was about to begin, those who participated could be charged with obstruction of justice.

Starr has brought no indictments on the basis of Mrs. Kennedy's testimony, or on any such information relating to the possible destruction of Foster's files from the time it became apparent that a special counsel was to be appointed in early 1994.

Recently, the Tribune-Review reported that Starr was aware of the existence of Kennedy's notes, but did not pursue basic prosecutorial tactics by challenging Kennedy's claims of privilege to have the notes released to his investigators.

Meanwhile, two Rose Law Firm couriers, Jeremy Hedges and Clayton Lindsey, testified before the grand jury in Little Rock in 1994. The couriers have stated publicly that they shredded a box of documents on Feb. 3—just after Robert Fiske's appointment as special counsel—marked with the initials "VWF," for the late Vincent W. Foster. Foster, at the Rose firm, and later the White House, worked on Whitewater matters for the Clintons.

Foster, like Kennedy, Webster Hubbell, and Hillary Rodham Clinton, were all senior members of the Rose firm—and all took senior positions in Washington with the new administration in 1993.

Kennedy left the White House under a cloud, himself the focus of intense press scrutiny for, among other things, his involvement in the so-called Travelgate affair. Early in the administration, Clinton functionaries sacked the long-time staff of the travel office, putting Clinton friends in charge. The White House claimed the regular travel staff was guilty of mismanagement and possible fraud.

Kennedy received a large part of blame for the fiasco, especially after he was fingered for summoning FBI agents to the White House to open an investigation into the Travel Office without proper authorization from the Justice Department or FBI officials.

Kennedy said at the time of his resignation that he was leaving to be closer to his children in Little Rock.

Within months, he also rejoined the Rose firm. ■

Aide Saw Foster Leave with Briefcase; Contradicts Official Claims

By Christopher Ruddy
FOR THE PITTSBURGH TRIBUNE-REVIEW
FEBRUARY 4, 1996

WASHINGTON—A White House staffer, among the last people to see Vincent Foster alive, has told federal investigators that Foster was carrying a briefcase when he left his office on the day of his death.

The account directly contradicts two federal investigations that have painted a scenario of Foster leaving his office without his briefcase.

In 1994, Thomas Castleton, a young staffer in the White House Counsel's Office—where Foster was a deputy—told investigators for Special Counsel Robert Fiske that when he saw Foster leave his West Wing office, Foster was holding a briefcase case, according to a source familiar with Fiske's probe.

Several witnesses who say they saw Foster's car in Fort Marcy Park on July 20, 1993—before and after the police arrived to investigate the discovery of Foster's body—also have apparently told Fiske's investigators they saw what appeared to be a briefcase or attaché case on the seat of Foster's Honda.

Castleton's testimony adds further weight to their observations. It also further fuels speculation that—as some investigators believe—a cover-up of the death may have been under way early on the night of the death and that the removal of the briefcase from the crime scene at Fort Marcy may have been part of the effort.

Official Park Police investigative and evidence reports make no mention of a briefcase, and several policemen have testified pointedly under oath that there was no briefcase at the scene, according to sources.

Castleton, since promoted to the Department of Justice's Office of Legislative Affairs, declined to comment on the matter for the Tribune-Review.

Despite the possible implications of Castleton's account, Fiske, in his June 1994 report on Foster's death, made no mention of Castleton's recollection of seeing Foster leave with the briefcase. Instead, he offered another account.

The Senate Banking Committee

signed off on Fiske's report after a single day of hearings in July 1994. The committee also released more than 2,500 pages of documents and FBI interview statements given to it for review by Fiske's staff.

Castleton's interview statement was not included in those documents that have been made public.

Castleton's interview statement, however, was included in material Fiske turned over to his successor. Fiske, the original Whitewater special prosecutor, was later replaced by Kenneth Starr.

FISKE VERSION

According to the Fiske report, Foster left work on the day of his death at about 1 p.m. after eating lunch in his office. Soon after that, he drove to suburban Washington's Fort Marcy Park, where he shot himself in the head with a 1913 Colt revolver.

The report addresses the issue of a briefcase. On page 26 is the following: "At about 1 p.m., (Foster) came out of his office holding his suit jacket, without a briefcase. He told (Linda) to Tripp (the top assistant) that there were still some M&Ms on the tray if she wanted them. He said 'I'll be back' and then left."

Foster never did return, leaving major questions in his wake for investigators: Where was Foster going? Why did it take so long for his body to be found (nearly five hours)? Why didn't anyone see him in the interim?

Two prosecutors told the Tribune-Review that if Castleon's statement about the briefcase had been accepted by Fiske's investigators, it would have raised the possibility of a cover-up (the improper removal of the briefcase from the crime scene) and of foul play in the death (where was Foster before he was found in the park?).

The only statement by Castleton in the material given to the Senate Banking panel is a brief one found in the Park Police report compiled shortly after Foster's death. Castleton told the Park Police that he "was present when Mr. Foster left the office after eating lunch and said 'So long.' Mr. Foster did not respond and seemed to Mr. Castleton to be 'in his own world,' focused and disturbed."

The written account of the Park Police interview with Castleton on July 22, 1993, makes no mention of any briefcase.

Yet the briefcase becomes an issue in the police interview that immediately followed Castleton's, the interview of Linda Tripp, executive assistant to White House Counsel Bernard Nussbaum. The police account of Tripp's interview has her "absolutely certain that Mr. Foster did not carry anything in the way of a briefcase, bag, umbrella, etc. . . . out of the office."

LIAISON OFFICER

The issue of the briefcase cropped up early last year during grand jury proceedings in Washington led by Associate Independent Counsel Miquel Rodriguez.

Rodriguez eventually resigned from Starr's staff to return to his post as an assistant U.S. attorney in Sacramento, Calif. The Tribune-Review has reported that Rodriguez's superiors thwarted his efforts to conduct a full probe. The stunted grand jury proceedings brought no indictments.

But two sources close to Starr's probe confirmed for the Tribune-Review that at one point their investigation had focused on the possibility that someone had returned the briefcase to the White House. The matter was not pursued after Rodriguez left.

During grand jury testimony, a ranking Park Police officer said that a "liaison officer" with the U.S. Secret Service was present at Fort Marcy on the night of the death. The presence of an additional law enforcement agent contradicts official records, the sworn testimony of some officers, and claims that the death investigation was handled solely by the Park Police.

During grand jury proceedings last year, at least four park policemen testified there was no briefcase at the scene.

However, Rodriguez had turned up photographic evidence of a black briefcase lying in the vicinity of Foster's car. The police said it was a carrying case for crime scene equipment, but during proceedings admitted that their cases are tan or silver, not black like the one depicted in an enhanced photograph.

Testimony also demonstrated that the briefcase found at Fort Marcy was not the leather satchel case found in Foster's office after his death, and one in which a torn note surfaced almost a week later. Foster was said to rarely, if ever, have carried that case.

Patrick Knowlton, the first witness to have spotted Foster's Honda in Fort Marcy's lot, told Fiske's FBI agents that he "observed in this Honda a leather briefcase or leather folder on the passenger-side seat."

Similarly, at least two emergency workers told Fiske's investigators and Starr's grand jury they saw a briefcase after the police arrived. Paramedic Sgt. George Gonzalez told the FBI, "The Honda contained a necktie, suit coat, and a black briefcase/attaché case."

Shortly after Rodriguez's departure, Starr effectively closed down the investigation into Foster's death, and no indictments have been handed up. ■

Grand Jury Witness in Foster Probe Taking Aim at FBI Tactics

By Christopher Ruddy
FOR THE PITTSBURGH TRIBUNE-REVIEW
FEBRUARY 8, 1996

WASHINGTON—A grand jury witness in the probe of Vincent Foster's death says investigators for Independent Counsel Kenneth Starr have gone to unusual lengths to question the credibility of his statements.

Witness Patrick Knowlton, a Washington businessman, said FBI investigators assigned to Starr's staff recently took him—under false pretenses—to Fort Marcy Park in an attempt to impeach his testimony.

The former White House deputy counsel's body was found at the park on July 20, 1993.

Knowlton's previous testimony has undermined FBI credibility.

He appeared before Starr's grand jury in November 1995 testifying that FBI agents assigned to former Special Counsel Robert Fiske "lied" in preparing his FBI interview statement.

For example, Knowlton's FBI statement said he could not identify a Hispanic-looking man he saw sitting, then standing next to Foster's Honda at Fort Marcy Park. Knowlton said he could identify the man.

Knowlton, along with others, says he saw a briefcase in the Honda. But Park Police have denied its existence and investigators have decided not to pursue the matter.

The Tribune-Review also reported that Knowlton said Starr's grand jury prosecutor treated him like a hostile witness before the grand jury, even asking him a graphic and embarrassing question of a sexual nature.

After his grand jury appearance, Knowlton said he was contacted by FBI agents assigned to Starr who said they were interested in a good-faith re-examination of his account. He said he met with FBI agent James Clemente and Coy Copeland, a retired FBI agent working with Starr, around Dec. 1 at Starr's Washington office.

According to Knowlton, he was asked to accompany the two investigators and a third man, identified as District of Columbia homicide Detective R. Jeff Green to Fort Marcy. Green was consulting on the case with Starr.

Knowlton was told they were interested in reviewing his story at the park. Knowlton agreed to cooperate.

He said he and the agents arrived at the park at just about the same time he did on the day of Foster's death—about 4:30 p.m.

After reviewing some aspects of the scene, Knowlton said that an African-American man appeared in the woods. He said agents, acting surprised, said he was the man some refer to as the "unofficial mayor of Fort Marcy."

The man was Robert Reeves, a retired Army veteran, who has taken an avuncular interest in the park. Reeves uses the park to exercise and assists the maintenance crew in keeping it clean.

Knowlton said agents suggested that he accompany them to say hello to Reeves. As they approached Reeves, Knowlton heard the homicide consultant ask Reeves, "Do you recognize this guy?'

Though he did not hear the response, Knowlton says it quickly became apparent to him that Reeves' presence was not a coincidence, but an attempt by Starr's FBI investigators to identify him as a regular park visitor.

"It infuriated me, unnerved me. It's not right. I'm just a citizen here to cooperate. Why should I be treated like I did something wrong?" Knowlton said.

If Reeves fingered Knowlton as a park regular or one of a number of gay cruisers who visited the park, it would have seriously undermined Knowlton's credibility. Knowlton had previously stated that he was neither a regular visitor to the park nor a homosexual.

Knowlton says he stopped at Fort Marcy on the day of Foster's death to relieve himself in the woods.

He added that he passed a polygraph test administered by a former FBI expert.

Knowlton said Reeves was obviously embarrassed by the encounter. He added that he believes the FBI and others visit the park that day, apparently to identify him.

Knowlton said that when they returned to the agents' car, he was informed that the car was low on gas. They drove to a nearby gas station in McLean, Va.

"The agent backed into the pump so the front window would face the station," Knowlton said.

He recalled the unusual maneuver allowed gas station workers to peer into the car window as he sat alone. He believed that this was another attempt to have individuals near the park identify him.

Knowlton was angered by the attempt and after discussing the day's activities with his lawyer, complained to FBI agent Clemente.

Clemente assured Knowlton and

his attorney that no one was called to be at the park and that it was merely coincidence that Reeves was present. He was assured he was not taken to the park under false pretenses.

When contacted by the Tribune-Review, Clemente declined to comment on the incident.

CORROBORATING ACCOUNT

Corroborating Knowlton's account is Robert Reeves.

Reeves, of Alexandria, Va., told the Tribune-Review that he was called by FBI agents, who spoke to his wife and requested that Reeves come to the park "to help identify if some was a regular visitor at the park." Reeves said that like any good citizen, he dutifully appeared,

Reeves' recollection of what happened jibes with Knowlton's. Reeves said he told the FBI that he had not seen Knowlton at the park before, and he was certainly not a regular visitor or cruiser.

Reeves, who has been visiting Fort Marcy several times a week for nearly three decades, said he first ran into FBI agents last fall just after the FBI had conducted an extensive search for the bullet that officials claim killed Foster. The bullet was never found.

"I was up there (at Fort Marcy) cleaning up after the FBI people had left six to seven bags of litter all over the park—Coke cans, chicken boxes," Reeves recounted. It was at that time that two agents came up to him and introduced themselves.

Reeves said he didn't get any of the agents' names, but they took his phone number. Weeks later, he was called to identify Knowlton, he said.

Jerris Leonard, a respected Washington attorney and former assistant attorney general for civil rights during the Nixon administration, finds the government's handling of Knowlton questionable.

"I'd be concerned that [Starr's investigators] continue to bang away at Knowlton," he said. "Obviously, they think Knowlton's testimony is pretty important. But why continue to question his credibility. Why not check out the leads he has given? Why not go after the officers at the crime scene challenging them on the briefcase?"

Starr's spokeswoman in Little Rock, Debbie Gershman, said she couldn't comment on the matter because the investigation is "active." Starr claims to have been investigating the case for the past year and a half. Despite that claim, Reeves, extremely knowledgeable about the park, told the Tribune-Review he has never been interviewed by the FBI. ■

Foster Case: Starr Investigator Sought Testimony Changes

By Christopher Ruddy
FOR THE PITTSBURGH TRIBUNE-REVIEW
FEBRUARY 11, 1996

LITTLE ROCK,Ark.—Two state troopers here claim an investigator for Independent Counsel Kenneth Starr tried to have them change their testimony relating to a critical aspect of the death investigation of Vincent W. Foster.

Trooper Larry Patterson said he met with three investigators from Starr's office shortly before Christmas. According to Patterson, the primary investigator, Coy Copeland, a retired FBI agent, spent 45 minutes "trying to trip me up, to find a problem in my story."

Patterson, a 29-year veteran of the Arkansas state police, found Copeland's questioning tactics unusual for a police investigation. "Usually the witness offers his statement of their account and then the investigator asks several clarifying questions." But Patterson says that was not the case here, where he believed Copeland was attempting to have his statement leave open the possibility that he was in error.

Patterson's recollection of the time he was notified of Vince Foster's death is a critical one. If true, it could indicate a cover-up of the late deputy White House Counsel's death was under way even before Park Police found Foster's body.

According to Patterson, on the day of Foster's death, July 20, 1993, he left work at his normal time, 4:30 in the afternoon. He said it takes no more than 20 minutes to commute home.

He vividly remembers entering his Little Rock apartment and "not changing from my uniform, not having a Coke or anything to drink and the phone rang."

"It was Roger (Perry)," Patterson said. "He said that he had just received a call from Helen Dickey that Vince Foster had blown his brains out in the parking lot of the White House." Dickey was then working as a staff assistant at the White House. Her duties included being a nanny for Chelsea Clinton.

Patterson placed Perry's call—which Perry said he made to Patterson *Continued on next page*

Continued on next page

Continued from page 135

moments after receiving Dickey's—definitely at no later than 5 p.m. Arkansas time "at the latest."

If that is true, that means Dickey knew about Foster's death about 15 minutes before Park Police even found—about 6:15 Washington time—the body at Fort Marcy Park in suburban Washington. It also means that the official account, that the White House was informed sometime around 8:30 p.m. or after, is not true.

DICKEY CALL

Dickey, who has since left the White House, signed a document that was released last year to the Senate Banking Committee indicating that she called Perry on the night of Foster's death, but sometime after 10 p.m., after President Clinton ended an appearance on the "Larry King Live" show. Dickey's statement appears to be sworn and notarized.

Trooper Perry, who was on guard duty at the Governor's mansion in Arkansas on the day of Foster's death, said he received the call from Dickey early on the evening of the 20th—contradicting her statement.

"Helen called crying, and she said, 'Vince got off work, went out to the parking lot and shot himself in the head,'" Perry quoted Dickey.

Foster was found dead that evening, not in his car, but on the side of a slope in a wooded park hundreds of yards from his car.

The Tribune-Review has reported that investigators for Starr have said that at one point they were examining the possibility that officials knew about the death much earlier, and the time of the official notification of death by the Park Police to the Secret Service—about 8:30 p.m.—may have been extended to allow for unnamed individuals to engage in a cleanup operation of Foster's office and possibly the crime scene before any law enforcement authorities, such as the FBI, could assert jurisdiction and secure the premises.

Patterson's account apparently supports Perry's account. Perry said he also called a former Arkansas State Police director, Lynn Davis, after receiving Dickey's call. Davis has also sworn he received Perry's call early on the evening of July 20—at about rush hour time, which is between 4 and 6 p.m. Arkansas time.

Investigators for Starr have apparently taken some interest in the matter.

During his questioning, Patterson said, he reviewed his simple story many times and Copeland proposed numerous "could of" or alternative scenarios to explain away the discrepancy, such as "Could you have stopped at the bank?"

According to Patterson, Copeland said, "I'm not trying to get you to change your story but . . . "

At which point Patterson said he interjected in frustration, "You damn well won't."

PERRY CHARGES

Similarly Perry, who also said he was interviewed by Copeland for over 1-1/2 hours, said the purpose of the interview was clear. "Copeland acted like he wanted me to change my story," Perry said.

Starr's investigators "wanted me to say it was possible Dickey called me at 9:15 or 9:30 Washington time, which would have been 8:30 Arkansas time. This was not possible," Perry said. He also said Copeland offered other possible scenarios as to what happened and seemed intent on having Perry admit he could have been mistaken.

Both Patterson and Perry suggested that Starr get phone records from the White House and the governor's mansion, since Tucker made several calls immediately after Dickey's call as well. According to the troopers, Copeland said the White House does not keep itemized phone records and that Tucker's records could not be subpoenaed because he was "under indictment."

The troopers' statements appeared to fit a pattern of controversy relating to the treatment of witness statements begun under the first Whitewater prosecutor.

A so-called confidential witness, the person who found Foster's body, has charged that FBI agents for Robert Fiske had badgered him to alter his testimony—asking him as many as 25 times if a gun "could have" been in Foster's hand.

Another witness, Patrick Knowlton, says FBI agents "lied" in his witness statement, and asked him dozens of times about matters relating to Foster's Honda where his account contradicted official's claims.

Commenting on the confidential witness's charge of badgering, former FBI Special Agent William F. Roemer said that repeatedly asking a witness the same questions or proposing alternative scenarios to a witness is inappropriate.

Roemer, the most decorated former FBI agent alive, said basically the interviewing agent asks the witness for his statement, then may ask some follow-up questions for clarification purposes.

According to a source, grand jury proceedings last year turned up numerous examples of witnesses indicating their statements to the FBI had been altered or mitigated.

For example, Fairfax EMS worker Todd Hall's FBI statement for the Fiske investigation stated upon finding Foster's body he "saw something red moving in the woods" and later: "Hall believes it is possible that he could have seen vehicular traffic" from a nearby road.

In fact, Hall said he testified that he told the FBI he saw a person running from the body and that FBI agents suggested the possibility that the person he saw was actually a car.

Copeland, reached at Starr's office in Washington, said he could neither "confirm nor deny" nor make any comment on the matter.

Starr's spokeswoman, Debbie Gershman, offered no comment saying the investigation was active.

Perry and Patterson said they have not been called before a grand jury to testify on the matter. ■

Make-up Artist Links Clinton to Possible Cover-up

By Christopher Ruddy
FOR THE PITTSBURGH TRIBUNE-REVIEW
FEBRUARY 14, 1996

WASHINGTON—It is said to be one of the closely guarded secrets involving the federal probes into the death of Vincent Foster.

And for good reason: it indicates to some investigators not only that a cover-up was under way early on the night of Foster's death, but also that President Clinton may have been linked to those activities.

The secret: a make-up artist for CNN's "Larry King Live" program has told federal investigators that she overheard a conversation indicating Clinton was aware of Foster's death before he appeared on the King show live from the White House library.

According to a source, the make-up artist came forward in 1994 to tell her story during the latter part of Special Counsel Robert Fiske's investigation into Foster's death.

The woman told investigators that as she was applying make-up to Clinton's face at the White House—shortly before the program's 9 p.m. air time—an unidentified male presumed to be an aide notified Clinton that a note had been found in Foster's office.

The president and White House officials say that he was not notified of the death until 10 p.m., over an hour later, by Chief of Staff Mack McLarty.

White House officials also say that no officials entered Foster's office until about 10 p.m. and that no notes or documents relating to the attorney's death were found or removed from the office that evening.

The young female make-up artist has told investigators that McLarty was present when the president was informed about activities in Foster's office. She was unable to identify the man who spoke with the president.

Her account was taken seriously enough that investigators had her review photos of White House staffers. She was still unable to identify the person, the source said.

The make-up artist, who has left CNN to work in CNBC's Washington bureau, told the Tribune-Review she could not comment on the matter.

"I usually don't discuss my clients and what goes on. It's not a good practice," she said.

Fiske issued his Foster report on June 30, 1994, concluding that there was no evidence of foul play or a cover-up of the death. The make-up artist's account was not mentioned.

A month later, two of Fiske's FBI investigators stated those conclusions for a Senate Banking Committee hearing. In neither instance did the make-up artist's account surface.

Sources close to the Senate committee probe of the death said they were not informed of the woman's claims by Fiske, or provided with her FBI statement.

Fiske released dozens of FBI statements to the committee, which have since been made public. The make-up artist's statement was not included in those released.

Her statement was considered credible by investigators because of other evidence that the White House knew earlier about the death than it claimed.

Her comments are also consistent with information gathered by investigators that an intruder alarm went off in the White House counsel's office, which includes Foster's, just after 7 p.m. on the night of his death—but well before the time the White House claimed it was notified by Park Police that Foster was dead. An alarm again went off after 10 p.m., but officials claim to have been notified by then.

OFFICIAL VERSION

During a press conference the day after Foster's death, conducted by Communications Director Mark Gearan and McLarty, Gearan laid out the official White House chronology of events.

During that time, Gearan had a testy exchange with reporters, who were incredulous about the statement that it took nearly four hours to confirm Foster was dead. Foster's body was found by Park Police just after 6 p.m. Police say a single gunshot wound to the head was self-inflicted.

Gearan said that White House security aide Craig Livingstone, a political appointee of the Clintons, was notified at about 8:30 p.m. of the Foster matter and that the White House's chief administrative officer, David Watkins, was notified about 9 p.m.

Gearan told the press: "Soon after the (Larry King) show began, we were pulled from the staff room, where . . . McLarty was informed of this—that it was an unconfirmed report. In the intervening 50 or so minutes, efforts were made to both confirm and to make preliminary calls . . ."

Confirmation, Gearan said, came at 9:55 p.m., and only then was Clinton told.

The president was finishing his first hour with King when McLarty informed him of a problem, and Clinton had to renege on his offer

Continued on next page

Continued from page 137

to King to continue for an additional half-hour.

According to Newsweek, Clinton asked McLarty, "What is it? It's not Hillary or Chelsea." The two went up to the residence quarters of the White House, where Clinton was told of Foster's death. "Oh no," the president reportedly cried out.

Calls to the White House and Fiske for comment on this story went unreturned.

The Tribune-Review has reported that investigators for Kenneth Starr, Fiske's successor, have said that at one point they were examining the possibility that White House officials knew about the death much earlier. Some investigators believed that the time of the official notification to the White House may have been extended to allow for unnamed officials to engage in an examination of Foster's office and possibly the crime scene before any law enforcement authorities, such as the FBI, could assert jurisdiction and secure the scene and premises.

Several points of evidence and testimony suggest that the long delay in notification of the death doesn't jibe with the facts. These include:

• Grand jury evidence turned up last year that members of the Special Forces, an elite unite of the Park Police closely associated with the White House security, were at Fort Marcy Park—where Foster's body was found—by 7 p.m. on the night of the death.

• Several accounts by police and emergency workers that demonstrate officials knew Foster was a White House official by 7 p.m. after searching his car early in the evening and finding his White House identification card.

These accounts directly contradict the testimony of other Park Police that they stumbled upon the ID after entering the car much later, at about 8:30 p.m.

• The sworn statements of two Arkansas State troopers that Chelsea Clinton's nanny, Helen Dickey, called the Arkansas governor's mansion earlier on the evening of the 20th—as early as 6 p.m. Washington time—to notify Gov. Jim Guy Tucker of the death. Officials say that Foster's body was not even found until after 6 p.m.

Additionally, London's Sunday Telegraph reported a Secret Service log shows that just after 7 p.m., security officials cleared a "MIG" group—a military intelligence group—into the White House West Wing. They met with presidential assistant Patsy Thomasson. Thomasson admitted to entering Foster's office later that night. The Secret Service told the Telegraph the MIG group's activities were classified.

The following clarification appeared in the Tribune-Review.

In a Feb. 14 article it was reported that a makeup artist for CNN's "Larry King Live," while preparing President Clinton for an appearance on the program, overheard remarks that could call into question an official version of circumstances concerning specifically when the President learned about the death of White House Council Vincent Foster July 20, 1993.

The makeup artist has subsequently disputed that report. While confirming that she has been interviewed by authorities about the matter, she denies overhearing anything dealing with Foster or sharing information with anyone that would be considered confidential, given her professional circumstances.

The author stands by his original report. ■

Chapter Six

Darkwater: Corruption, Drugs, and the Abuse of Power

Fiske Probes Clinton Link to Whitewater

By Christopher Ruddy
FOR THE NEW YORK POST
APRIL 20, 1994

A scenic Whitewater tract once set aside for Bill Clinton is under scrutiny by special prosecutor Robert Fiske, the Post has learned.

Federal investigators are studying Whitewater-related land transactions that took place in October 1980, just weeks before the then-governor's unexpected re-election defeat.

Chris V. Wade, an Arkansas real-restate agent, said FBI agents working for Fiske have interviewed him several times about the Whitewater parcel, known as Lot 7, and about contributions he made to Clinton's campaign.

Records examined by The Post appear to show that Wade bought Lot 7—Whitewater's most valuable tract—for a pittance, then sold it 24 hours later for a whopping $33,000 profit.

Fiske is investigating Whitewater and a failed savings and loan linked to the Clinton's to see if any funds were diverted to Clinton's gubernatorial campaigns.

Whitewater Estates was a land development project of Whitewater Development Co., a 50-50 partnership between Bill and Hillary Clinton and their friends, James and Susan McDougal.

Lot 7 was the largest parcel, comprising 28 acres of the 230-acre Whitewater Estates. It was among its most valuable because of its prime waterfront location on a hill overlooking the junction of the White River and Crooked Creek.

"It was the most desirable lot, a beautiful piece of land," recalls Dr. M.T. Bronstad of Fort Worth, Tex.,

who bought the site on Oct. 16, 1980.

Bronstad purchased Lot 7 for $35,000 through Wade, who was Whitewater's real estate broker. According to Bronstad, Wade told him the land belonged to "Governor Clinton," who "had kept the property for himself."

But deed records show that Bronstad bought the property neither from Clinton nor the Whitewater Development Co.

According to the warranty deed filed in Marion County Courthouse, the land was sold to Bronstad by "Chris V. Wade and Associates, Ozarks Realty Co."

Bronstad says categorically that Wade never told him he owned the property.

Court records show that on Oct. 14, Whitewater Development sold the property and deeded Lot 7 to Wade for $2,000, according to revenue stamps affixed to the deed. Wade in turn sold the lot to Bronstad the next day.

The Clintons and McDougals didn't receive a release from their mortgage obligation from Citizen's Bank until Oct. 16—the day after the land was sold to Bronstad.

Wade now says the revenue stamps on the deed were incorrect, and that he paid between $33,000 and $35,000 for the land.

He claims he bought the land simply "on contract" from Whitewater sometime before October and after Clinton had lost interest in it, and he was paying for it on a monthly basis. He would have received a deed when he made the final payment, Wade said.

Dick Wendel, president of North Arkansas Abstract and Title Co., a deed and title search firm, found that explanation unlikely.

"Generally, when there is a contract executed, there is a deed executed," explained Wendel, who is familiar with the Whitewater documents.

Wade says he turned over all his

Continued on next page

Continued from page 141

Whitewater papers to Fiske. He says they would substantiate his claim that he profited only "about $3,000" on the sale to Bronstad.

Jim McDougal says he can't remember "anything" relating to Lot 7 or Clinton's interest in it.

McDougal says he can't think why he might sell the property cheaply to Wade and that the price of $2,000 "must be wrong."

Wade admits to making campaign contributions to Clinton—usually under $1,000. He adamantly denies any funds from the sale of Lot 7 went into the campaign in the closing weeks of the hotly contested election, which Clinton lost to Republican Frank White. ∎

Editor's note: *Ruddy broke this story long before Wade became a figure in the case when he entered into a plea agreement with Independent Counsel Kenneth Starr.*

Suicide Disputes Common in Arkansas

By Christopher Ruddy
FOR THE PITTSBURGH
TRIBUNE-REVIEW
NOVEMBER 4, 1995

Challenged rulings of suicide, first in the case of Deputy White House Counsel Vincent Foster, are not unique in President Clinton's home state.

Any informed Arkansan can expound on "the boys on the track"—the unsolved murder of two Salina County boys, Kevin Ives and Don Henry, who had gone out spotting deer with flashlights one August night in 1987 and whose bodies were subsequently found run over by a train. Bill Clinton was then governor of the state.

Police told both sets of parents that the boys had committed suicide by deliberately lying on the tracks before an oncoming train.

One parent, Linda Ives, found that explanation totally unacceptable.

As a result of her protests, the state medical examiner, Dr. Fahmy Malak, looked into the case and ruled the death of her son "accidental." He suggested that high levels of marijuana found in the boys' blood indicated her son may have been in a stupor before lying down on the tracks.

But Linda Ives still wasn't satisfied, and so a grand jury was convened and ordered the boys

bodies exhumed.

An autopsy, the second performed, revealed that one boy had been stabbed and that the other's head had been crushed before the train ran over them. Further, the marijuana levels were found to have been exaggerated as a result of an erroneous test.

The foreman of that Salina County grand jury said, in an unofficial statement, that he thought the boys' deaths were related to drug trafficking—that perhaps they'd stumbled on something they shouldn't have.

As a result of the Henry-Ives ruling and similar ones, Malak came in for widespread criticism.

Even the distant *Los Angeles Times* picked up on his blundering, and in 1992 reported on the Henry-Ives case and one involving an Arkansas man whose body was found with five bullet wounds—but who Malak nevertheless ruled a suicide.

Just weeks before Clinton announced for the presidency, Malak was moved into another state job. But the controversy surrounding his rulings continues to swirl.

John Brown, a former Saline County detective who investigated the Henry-Ives case—he says he was forced to resign recently "because of official obstruction"— has a sobering view of the case. He

suggested that the boys' deaths, along with six other murders that followed, were linked to what is known as the Dixie Mafia.

"Gangs USA," a reference book on organized crime, describes the Dixie Mafia as an "informal association of white gangsters" that constitutes "one of the largest, most deadly and least-known gang systems in the United States," blanketing 16 southern states.

The organization originally specialized in "robbing banks, interstate theft, the corruption of public officials and contract murder," according to the book, but more recently has "turned to drugs, money laundering and firearms."

A former Little Rock-based FBI official said that the Dixie Mafia, while not as organized and tightly knit as the conventional Mafia, "can be more brutal" than the latter and less restrained and predictable.

Meaning that it would be not nearly so inhibited as its more famous northern counterpart about murdering, say, two innocent boys.

Gene Wirges, former editor of a rural Arkansas newspaper, is another of those who tend to raise an eyebrow at official declarations of suicides in high-profile cases there.

Wirges is author of the 1992 book "Conflict of Interests," which chronicled his experiences in trying to expose the pervasive political corruption in Arkansas.

"In 1985," wrote Wirges in his book, "a North Arkansas man was fatally shot, and (Dr. Fahmy) Malak ruled suicide; there [were] four gunshot wounds to the chest.

"In a 1986 case, Malak ruled accidental drowning; the family of the victim called attention to a bullet in the victim's skull that was overlooked.

"There were (numerous other) 'suicide' rulings (in at least six different counties from 1982 to 1990) and vehement complaints in each instance.

"In 1989, Malak ruled accidental death, saying a child had fallen from a porch—13 inches to the ground. Parents insist the child had been beaten to death."

Dubious suicide rulings are not, of course, limited to Arkansas; David Zucchino, a Pulitzer Prize-winning Philadelphia Inquirer reporter, for example, recently uncovered 40 such cases in the military.

Deserved or undeserved, Arkansas is rapidly acquiring a reputation for eliciting cynical quips and cynical looks whenever such finding are announced.

Prominent homicide expert Vernon Geberth says that staged deaths such as murders made to look like suicides are happening more frequently.

"In some parts of the country it's a license to kill," because, Geberth says, inexperienced local authorities can't tell the difference between a real suicide and a murder made to look like one. ■

Whitewater Probe Might Turn Toward Mystery Mansion

By Christopher Ruddy
FOR THE PITTSBURGH
TRIBUNE-REVIEW
NOVEMBER 25, 1995

With the dimensions of the 1994 Republican sweep not yet fully calculated, GOP staffers on Capitol Hill already are talking about expanded Whitewater hearings— hearings that would produce subpoenas to a cast of Arkansas characters who have lurked in Bill Clinton's shadow.

A name frequently mentioned is Dan Lasater, once a high-rolling bond dealer whose original fortune was made through the Ponderosa Steak House chain, which he founded and later sold at an immense profit.

Lasater was one of Clinton's biggest financial backers during the 1980's—a time when he was also the recipient of Arkansas state bond deals estimated at some $637 million.

During that period, the Clintons enjoyed a close personal relationship with Lasater, traveling on his corporate jet and vacationing at Angel Fire, the financier's 17,000-acre New Mexico resort.

Lasater's meteoric financial rise took a nose dive in the late 1980s when he became a known cocaine user (there are reports of his having openly dispensed it in bowls and ashtrays at parties). He was eventually snared by federal authorities, and in 1986 was convicted of cocaine distribution.

He served six months of a 30-month sentence; in 1990, Gov. Bill Clinton issued him a full pardon.

Though the origins of the Clinton-Lasater relationship are still murky, one version has it that their ties began at the Hot Springs, Ark., racetrack when Lasater met Clinton's mother, Virginia Kelley, an avid follower of racehorses, and Clinton's half-brother, Roger.

Roger Clinton—who would eventually meet the same fate as Lasater when he, too, would be convicted and incarcerated on drug charges—was given a job in the Lasater organization as his personal driver and "gopher."

Lasater, in turn, helped Roger pay off an $8,000 drug debt. Their relationship continues to this day.

Of late, Lasater has kept a low profile—so low that a June 1994 report on him in the Arkansas Democrat Gazette was wryly headlined "Address Unknown."

But his whereabouts are no secret to the residents of Paron, Ark., a sleepy hamlet in the Cockspur Mountains some 35 miles from Little Rock. They say that Dan Lasater, ensconced on a sprawling property there, is using their previously unnoticed little town as a hideaway.

That property has ties with the Rose Law Firm in Little Rock, in which Hillary Rodham Clinton was formerly a partner.

While some observers believe the property was intended as an additional presidential residence— the Arkansas Democrat Gazette, for

Continued on next page

Continued from page 143

example, reported it was rumored to be a "White House West"; and contractors who worked on it whimsically tagged it "Camp Chelsea"—there are strong indications something quite different might be taking place in Paron.

Natives of this tiny village of 350, initially euphoric over the idea of a presidential retreat in their midst, have since had second thoughts, especially concerning activities they feel are unrelated to normal presidential security measures.

"Everything is hush-hush," Paron postmaster Deanna Marbry said earlier this year. "There has been some airplane activity, and it's scary to us."

Hoyt Hill, former fire chief of Paron, said that his suspicions and those of his neighbors were aroused when the new owners of the property, identified on deed records as Southeast Investment Inc., purchased the heavily wooded 7,878-acre tract from International Paper Co. for $8.25 million.

Southeast abruptly made its presence known by padlocking the property's entrances—entrances that always had been open to neighbors.

Neighbors also noted the new property owners brought in radio-toting armed guards, who patrolled the wooded, undeveloped land on special "four-wheeler" motorcycles.

"Why guard timberland?" asked one Paron resident in a typical query.

At the time of Southeast's purchase in March 1993, employees of the company told Charles Cooper, an adjoining property owner, that the Rose Law Firm had purchased the undeveloped land.

Rose is among Little Rock's most prominent legal firms. Besides Mrs. Clinton, partners have included former U.S. Associate Attorney General Webb Hubbell and the late Vincent Foster, who was deputy White House Counsel.

Despite Lasater's ties with Rose and with Mrs. Clinton, the Federal Savings and Loan Insurance Co. hired the Rose firm in an action it took against Lasater. The agency, alleging improper activities between Lasater and Co. and an Illinois savings and loan company, sought $3.3 million from Lasater. Rose partners Hillary Rodham Clinton and Vincent Foster, in an apparent conflict of interest, were able to settle the case against Lasater & Co. for $200,000.

When construction of a mansion-like home began on the Paron property last year, signs were posted at the entrances ordering trespassers away. Would-be violators were warned the owner was the "Cockspur Hunting Club."

Simultaneous with this, residents said there was an increase in low-flying airplanes over the property.

Unlike the military aircraft that occasionally fly over the area, these were "small Cessna-like" aircraft, according to Hill. He said the planes typically fly through a pass in the Cockspur Mountains on Southeast's property, several miles from the main road.

"After the planes leave, 20 to 30 minutes will go by, and small trucks and jeeps leave the property at two different entrances," said Hill.

He added that neighbors, during a flurry of aircraft activity, had logged the details, which they then passed on to federal authorities.

Capt. Gene Donhan of the sheriff's department of Saline County, where Paron is located, acknowledged that his department had also received such complaints from Paron residents, but that he could not comment on them.

"We have passed the information to higher authorities," he said. He subsequently noted the complaints were directed to the Little Rock office of the Drug Enforcement Administration.

"These (Southeast) landowners are very secretive, and strange things go on," said Cooper.

Cooper's home is approximately 150 yards from Southeast's newly built "hunting lodge."

Cooper has been in a court battle with Southeast since last spring concerning Southeast's blockage of an access road leading to his home. He charged that on one occasion he was prevented from taking his 85-year-old mother to a hospital during an emergency. He eventually got a court order giving access to the road, and has settled all other controversies with Southeast out of court.

Cooper and other neighbors say that, in reality, Dan Lasater is the owner of the property. Cooper has met Lasater at the Southeast house, and Lasater is also frequently seen driving to the property or shopping at the local convenience store.

The Little Rock telephone directory has no listing for Southeast Investment.

In March, a secretary at Phoenix Mortgage Co., a Little Rock financial firm that was once owned by Lasater, said the firm still was taking messages for Southeast. Recent calls to Phoenix went unanswered.

Roger Clinton is also a frequent visitor to the Southeast house. Herschel Tarvin, who lives next door to the property, said he saw Roger Clinton drive up to the new house in late April. Other residents said they have spotted him in town. And Cooper said he recently saw the president's brother driving up the access road to that house.

According to state records, Southeast Investments is an Arkansas corporation formed in 1990.

The records show a Kenneth Shemin as president and sole proprietor of Southeast. Under Arkansas law, other owners and officers of a corporation may remain secret.

As to Rose's possible connection with the property, Ronald Clark, the managing partner of the law firm, wrote in a June 1993 letter to Cooper that the Rose firm "has no ownership interest or any other relationships with the property you described. . . ."

But Shemin, the owner of record, is a partner in the Rose firm, and state records reveal the firm acts as an agent for Southeast.

A call to Clark seeking clarification of this contradiction was not returned.

Further, county tax records for the property give the Rose Law Firm's Little Rock address. And in court papers related to Cooper's dispute with Southeast, Shemin answered for Southeast by identifying himself as representing the Rose Law Firm.

In a telephone interview, Shemin said he was the principal owner of what is described as the "Cockspur Hunting Club," and said the Rose firm had no connection with the property.

Shemin admitted the property was not used for hunting but, rather, was the site of "timber operations."

Shemin dismissed speculation about the property serving as a presidential retreat as "ridiculous; it borders on absurd." He attributed the rumors to the fact he and Mrs. Clinton were once partners in the Rose firm.

Shemin refused to comment on Lasater's connection with the property or with reports by Paron townspeople of suspicious activities taking place in the area.

The Arkansas Democrat Gazette reported that although Shemin is listed as president of Southeast, Lasater and Gerald Hannahs, the present owner of Phoenix Mortgage Co., are also partners.

Paron residents seem befuddled as to Southeast's investment objectives with the property, as well as with its ties to the Rose Law Firm.

Such curiosity was compounded when a representative of the Rose Law Firm made an offer to air-condition the local school.

Gerald Johnson, who recently retired as Paron's school superintendent, said he informed the firm the school was already air-conditioned except for the gymnasium. Johnson said the firm persisted in a "strange request" last winter to air-condition the gymnasium of the town's one school.

"The Rose law firm called us three or four times since then," Johnson recalled, somewhat baffled by the offer, since the school is not in session during the hot months of the summer.

At a school board meeting Johnson recommended that "we have nothing to do with it."

"Maybe we'd reconsider if they wanted to expand our library," Johnson said.

The new school superintendent David Smith, has written to the Rose firm seeking, instead, financial assistance for educational projects. To date, he has received no reply. ■

White House Bids for Immunity in Chef's Racism Case

By Christopher Ruddy
FOR THE PITTSBURGH
TRIBUNE-REVIEW
DECEMBER 8, 1995

A District of Columbia appeals court this week heard arguments from the Justice Department that federal equal opportunity laws do not apply to White House employees.

Justice Department lawyers told a three judge Court of Appeals panel that Sean Haddon, a former White House assistant chef, was not covered by the Equal Employment Opportunity Law, which forbids discriminatory practices. Haddon claims his dismissal was motivated by racism.

The intervention by the Justice Department has once again focused attention on an especially sensitive area in the Clinton administration, which critics charge has exempted itself from laws it seeks to impose on the rest of the nation.

"The idea of the EEO law is that people similarly situated ought to be treated the same," said Thomas Scorza, a professor of legal ethics at the University of Chicago. "It's hard to see why the White House as an employer should not be subject to the same law as other employers."

According to Scorza, the only exception should be the hiring and firing of personnel at "the highest policy levels."

"But you're talking here about chefs and staff members. I don't see the argument for not covering these people under the EEO."

Haddon, 38, an Atlanta native, began working in the White House kitchen in 1988, near the end of the Reagan administration.

In late March of this year, the Clintons fired the entire White House kitchen staff, ostensibly because of the first family's lack of fondness for the French cuisine that had been a staple of the kitchen.

In hiring Walter S. Scheib,

Continued on next page

Continued from page 145

formerly of the Greenbrier Resort in West Virginia, to head the new staff, the White House said it was seeking a more American cuisine.

But Rodney R. Sweetland III, Haddon's attorney, charges the staff change was largely a ruse to fire his client. He points out that all of the fired chefs—except his client—were immediately rehired, and that Haddon was, in fact, the resident expert on the American cuisine favored by the Clintons.

Sweetland says Haddon's difficulties stem from racism—and more importantly from the remedial action he sought.

In January 1992, Haddon, a white male, announced his engagement to an African-American woman whom he subsequently married in the fall of that year.

He alleges officials at the White House Usher's Office, which manages the residence and kitchen areas of the mansion, advised him not to marry a black woman and intimated adverse consequences if he did so. He also charges that his consistently "exemplary" job ratings suddenly plummeted to "satisfactory."

In an EEO-based lawsuit filed June 21, 1993, Haddon claimed he was passed over for promotion to *sous-chef* because of the marriage.

Haddon had pursued an informal process of mediation before filing his lawsuit, but the day before an investigation of his complaint was to begin, he was detained by the Secret Service on a charge that he had threatened the life of the president and his family. Haddon alleged that at least one White House official improperly used the FBI to bring false charges.

The Justice Department filed a motion to dismiss Haddon's EEO suit on the grounds that Title VII of the Civil Rights Act of 1964, which prohibits employment discrimination on the basis of race, sex and religion, does not apply to White House employees.

The Justice Department claims Haddon's suit should be dismissed on procedural grounds, arguing that even if he is covered by EEO law, it would be under the Civil Rights Act of 1991. The Act requires all EEO complaintants to first go through the Equal Employment Opportunity Commission, which Haddon has not done thus far. Sweetland believes that to do so would allow for potential White House interference in what he considers a politically directed body.

In a September 1993 ruling on the Haddon case, federal District Court Judge Stanley Sporkin agreed with the Justice Department that the White House is exempt from EEO law.

In seeking to overturn Sporkin's ruling, Sweetland told the appeals court that the Clinton administration, had departed from a long-standing pattern in past administrations. He presented the court with documents showing that the administrations of Nixon, Ford and Carter had either viewed EEO law as applicable or had voluntarily complied.

As for the Reagan and Bush administrations, Sweetland said they were never the targets of any complaints, so there were no applicable documents.

In addition to his EEO lawsuit, Haddon filed suit against the White House under the Freedom of Information Act when requests for documents related to the EEO action were denied. The Clinton administration claims the FOIA, like EEO law, does not apply to the White House.

Sweetland had harsh words about this.

"The Clinton administration is taking the standard of the Democratic Congress that was just thrown out. It's a standard of privilege—the Clinton administration believes it is above the law."

Sweetland cited not only the administration's policy of exempting itself from EEO law and the FOIA, but President Clinton's stance in the Paula Jones case.

In response to the sexual harassment suit filed by Jones against the president on May 6, his lawyers argued that he is exempt from all civil suits while he occupies the office.

On the evening of June 16, 1993, assistant chef Sean Haddon was dutifully cooking dinner for the nation's First Family.

He was working in the White House, but considering what Haddon was to experience later that night at the hands of the government's top police, it might easily have been the Kremlin.

Haddon was preparing a dinner for 25, a relatively small gathering in the White House.

"Two chefs could handle a dinner for 25 people easily," recalled Haddon, who first sensed something strange was afoot when the White House Usher's Office, which is responsible for managing the kitchen, inexplicably designated four chefs for the dinner—including one chef who was called in from the French Embassy.

Just as that outside chef entered the kitchen, Haddon recalls, "All of a sudden Secret Service agents were lining up in the hallway."

Next, four armed and uniformed members of the service called Haddon to the side and demanded to see all White House identification, which he was asked to surrender. He was escorted from the kitchen to one of the guardhouses on the perimeter of the White House grounds.

The baffled Haddon, still dressed in full chef's attire was brought to a back room, where he was interrogated by other Secret Service agents—who appeared equally baffled as to why a chef was being detained in a guardhouse.

After Haddon called his attorney, Rodney Sweetland, the Secret Service agreed to release him on the condition that he appear that evening at the Secret Service Washington field office on Connecticut Avenue.

THREATS ALLEGED

When he and Sweetland arrived there, they were informed by agents that two White House officials "have said that you threatened the life of the President and members of the First Family."

Haddon and Sweetland were dumbfounded at this accusation, and Sweetland suggested to the agents that this was out-and-out "retaliation" for an informal complaint he had filed with an Equal Employment Counselor. The counselor was to begin an investigation of Haddon's complaint the following day.

Who, then, made these charges against Haddon and what was the motivation?

The Secret Service could provide no answers, because the FBI agent handling the case, Dennis Scalimbrene, had passed the case along to the Secret Service without including the file. Haddon and Sweetland were told that Scalimbrene had locked the file in his desk and had gone home for the evening.

Thus was Haddon left facing grave but vague charges, filed by anonymous officials, with no chance to address himself to the essential issues. (Well after that frightful night, he would learn the specifics of his "threat": someone at the White House had made the bizarre assertion that Haddon was planning on smuggling a gun into the White House by somehow attaching it to the bicycle he rode to work each day.)

PASSES POLYGRAPH TEST

Faced with this Kafka-esque turn of events, Haddon was prompted to waive his rights against self-incrimination and call for a polygraph test, which he easily passed.

By 11:30 p.m. the next day, the Secret Service had concluded that the chef was no threat to the president or his family and he was allowed to return to his job a few days later.

But some nine months later, in March 1994, Haddon was dismissed. The treatment he'd been subjected to on that June 1993 night had received little press attention—and the matter of which person or persons in the White House seriously abused the power of that office had been largely glossed over.

Who had made the allegations against Haddon to the FBI? Was that powerful and feared agency used, as Haddon's attorney charged, for "retaliation" against the chef?

Asked to comment, Neil Lattimore, press secretary for Hillary Clinton's office, said he was unaware of current developments in the Haddon case, noting that he could not comment on "ongoing legal matters" anyway.

Susan Lloyd, a spokeswoman for the FBI's Metropolitan D.C. field office, confirmed that allegations had been made against Haddon to the FBI by White House co-workers.

Lloyd said the charges surfaced during a routine security check of Haddon's background.

"The investigating agent felt it was substantial enough to pass to the Secret Service because they deal with threats to government officials," said Lloyd.

Lloyd acknowledged that the claim made against Haddon turned out to be baseless.

Section 1001 of the Federal code states that it is a crime to knowingly lie or mislead a federal investigator.

Concerning this, Lloyd said that Section 1001 may not apply here because the claims could have been made "in good faith."

She admitted she was unaware of any FBI investigation of those who made the claims against Haddon.

TRAVEL OFFICE PROBE

If the bureau had in fact been used for political purposes in the Haddon case, it would not have been totally out of character at that time. On May 12, 1993, in what was to be a major scandal, the FBI was summoned by the White House to investigate members of the White House Travel Office—an act that the White House subsequently felt the need to apologize for.

In July 1993, a month after the Haddon incident, FBI head William Sessions was abruptly fired. A half-year later, in February 1994, Sessions charged that at the time of his firing, the White House together with its Justice Department arm had been in a "power struggle" with the FBI in an effort to undo its official politically neutral role.

Clearly the chef's assertion of his employment rights were of pressing concern to officials at the highest levels of the White House.

According to Sweetland, on May 28, 1993, a meeting was convened at the White House to discuss Haddon's EEO complaint—and the negative press coverage it could potentially engender. Attending that meeting was the head usher of the White House, Gary Walters, along with such top officials as Deputy White House Counsel Vincent Foster, the number two lawyer at the White House and Hillary Clinton's chief of staff, Margie Williams.

Following Foster's death two months later, a list of the contents of his desk and cabinet were compiled by a staff member of the White House Counsel's office. The handwritten document, which was turned over to the original special prosecutor in the case, Robert Fiske, lists one "notebook re Sean Haddon" and another document called "Executive Resident, EEO—Sean Haddon."

Haddon says his problems at the White House began shortly before Clinton arrived, but that they came to a head with the arrival of the Clintons because they delegated a great deal of autonomy to the White House Usher's Office.

CLAIMS RACISM

Haddon charges the office is racist and that when he, a white male, married a black woman he was subjected to racial taunts and

Continued on next page

Continued from page 147

was passed over for a promotion.

Sweetland suggests that the White House, run by an all-white Usher's Office that supervises a predominantly black servant staff, "is the last plantation" on the Potomac.

He and his client say that under the Clintons, the long-standing racism in the White House has worsened because of the distance they have put between themselves and the staff. Haddon contrasted that policy with that of the Bushes, "who treated everyone as a close member of the family."

"When the Clintons came, everything was through Gary," said

Haddon, referring to Gary Walters, the White House chief usher.

So careful were the Clintons to avoid personal contact with White House staff that Secret Service agents would send out advisories to computer work stations throughout the residence of the Clintons' impending movements in the house. This would give workers a chance to get out of the Clintons' path.

"We were told if they came down the hallway we would have to get out of the hallway," said Haddon in describing how White House staffers would scramble into the nearest room or closet as the president or first lady would move down a corridor.

Haddon has turned down

numerous offers from tabloid television to tell his story. He still has hopes of returning to his post at the White House, perhaps the most prized position to which any American chef can aspire.

LOOKING FOR WORK

Meanwhile he is looking for another job. Sweetland said the Clintons have not seen fit to provide Haddon with a letter of reference to help him obtain another position.

Concerning the false charges, Haddon has been caught in an endless pass-along-the-blame predicament between the agencies involved. ■

Senator Questions Hubbell Hiring

By Christopher Ruddy
FOR THE PITTSBURGH
TRIBUNE-REVIEW
MARCH 2, 1995

Whitewater special counsel Kenneth Starr has been asked to investigate whether the Department of Interior's move to rehire the wife of key Whitewater figure Webb Hubbell was a payoff designed to influence what he tells prosecutors.

Senator Lauch Faircloth (R-N.C.), wants Starr to examine why Suzanna Hubbell was rehired last month at a salary of $60,925 after an 11-month leave of absence from a politically appointed position with Interior.

"The action of hiring Mrs. Hubbell is very disturbing, and I believe this could influence the ongoing criminal investigation," Faircloth told the Tribune-Review Wednesday.

Faircloth said the hiring may have been done to indirectly benefit

Webb Hubbell and thereby affect his testimony before the independent counsel.

Faircloth, a member of the Senate Banking committee, which is reviewing Whitewater-related matters, recently wrote Interior Secretary Bruce Babbitt about his concerns. He asked Babbitt to provide his office with all information regarding the appointment, including "any communication between the Interior Department and the White House."

Webb Hubbell, the former associate attorney general and close friend of President Clinton, pleaded guilty in December to mail fraud and tax evasion. The plea bargain resulted from an agreement with the independent counsel.

The charges against Hubbell are related to his activities at the Rose Law Firm in Little Rock, Ark., where he and Hillary Rodham Clinton were partners. He is considered a major figure in the Whitewater probe because of his

close association with the Clintons and the possibility he has knowledge of White House interference in criminal referrals to the Justice Department relating to Madison Guarantee Savings and Loan.

Hubbell may also have knowledge useful in the investigation of possible obstruction of justice in the probe of the death of Deputy White House Counsel Vincent W. Foster Jr.

Hubbell's sentencing has been delayed until after he finished meeting with Starr and his staff.

In September 1993, Suzanna Hubbell was appointed special assistant to Babbitt's chief of staff at the Interior Department. She took leave of absence in March 1994 after her husband resigned from the number three position at the Justice Department, said Interior spokeswoman Stephanie Hanna.

Hanna said Hubbell was rehired Feb. 6 "at the same pay grade and same level, but with completely different duties." Her new position, special assistant to the director of external affairs, includes handling public affairs matters "with various constituencies served by the department," Hanna said.

"It's not a crime in this country for someone related to a person accused of something to have a job," Hanna said, irritated by the suggestion of impropriety made by Faircloth.

But a prominent legal expert, Thomas Scorza, disagrees with that stance and called Faircloth's charges "a legitimate concern."

Scorza said Hubbell is not simply accused of a crime, but is an admitted felon involved in a plea agreement. He said it would be proper for Starr to determine "if a benefit was conferred on Mrs. Hubbell as a payoff for (her husband) not to reveal too much to prosecutors."

Scorza, a professor of legal ethics at the University of Chicago and a former federal prosecutor, said conferring jobs and other benefits to an official's spouse has become a "modern kind of bribery" that is "very difficult to prove" since it often is done through "the most

intimate of conversations."

Debbie Gershman, spokeswoman for the independent counsel, said yesterday her office would have no comment on the matter.

Faircloth said he'll await responses from Starr and the Department of Interior before deciding on further action.

"It clearly can be an issue aired in Congressional hearings," he said.

Scorza said a proper review of the circumstances surrounding Suzanna Hubbell's rehiring would answer these questions: Is it a ghost job? Are there hidden benefits? Are there discrepancies in the stories of those involved in the rehiring? Had she planned to return to work at the time she took a leave of absence?

Scorza also characterized as "suspicious" the timing of her return to the Interior Department.

A grand jury convened by Starr in January is investigating the activities of the Park Police—an agency of the Interior Department—and the agency's possible mishandling of the investigation into Foster's suicide in 1993.

Scorza said there is the "possibility of internal interference" in the probe.

According to one source, Hubbell was questioned intensively by Starr for 10 hours one day about Foster. As the White House's man at the Justice Department at the time of Foster's death, Hubbell may have intimate knowledge of the actions of Justice, Interior and the FBI at that time.

The administration's determination to allow the Interior Department's Park Police to handle the high-ranking official's mysterious death has been widely criticized.

A Washington source familiar with the Hubbells suggested Suzanna Hubbell's return to work may have been related to the family's shaky financial situation.

According to the source, Webb Hubbell had difficulty landing a position at any of Washington's more prominent legal firms after resigning from the Justice Department.

During confirmation hearings for Hubbell in 1993, it was revealed he had debts totaling $570,000, including a $400,000 mortgage.

Efforts to reach Mr. and Mrs. Hubbell for comment were unsuccessful. ■

Arkansas Airport Project Criticized as Funding 'Scam'

By Christopher Ruddy
FOR THE PITTSBURGH
TRIBUNE-REVIEW
MARCH 19, 1995

A new airport planned for northwest Arkansas involving companies with close ties to the Clintons has drawn sharp criticism from surprising quarters.

Dubbed "Poultryport," · the publicly financed airport may benefit such private companies as Tyson Foods, the nation's leading

poultry processor, and the giant Arkansas-based Wal-Mart.

The airport is "really a scandal . . . a scam, using public money for private purposes," according to Ken Silverstein, who, along with Alexander Cockburn, wrote an expose on the project in the left-leaning newsletter Counterpunch.

Counterpunch, a 1,500-circulation semi-monthly newsletter, is published by the Institute for Policy Studies, a Washington think tank with close ties to Clinton administration policy-makers.

Titled "The Gang's All Here! Clinton, Tyson, Wal-Mart and the Arkansas Poultryport," the article charged that the airport's "prime function will be to ferry Tyson chickens to Japan and offer a hub for Wal-Mart's vast commercial operations."

The facility, officially known as the Northwest Arkansas Regional Airport, will be situated in the Ozark Mountains, in and around the town of Highfill, population 92.

The headquarters of both Tyson

Continued on next page

Continued from page 149

and Wal-Mart are within 30 miles of the proposed airport, but in different directions.

The Federal Aviation Administration said the regional authority is purchasing some 2,700 acres for the facility.

The airport will have the nation's second longest civilian runway, the longest being at Chicago's O'Hare Airport, at 13,000 feet.

The Counterpunch article charged that Jim Blair, a lawyer for Tyson—best known for advising Hillary Rodham Clinton in her profitable cattle-futures trading—was a charter member of a group seeking to have the airport built.

According to the article, the deal was recently consummated by one of President Clinton's top White House aides from Arkansas, Mack McLarty, counsel to the president. He is said to have lobbied Transportation Secretary Federico Pena to grant the Northwest Arkansas Regional Airport Authority $9 million from a discretionary fund that needed no congressional approval. Pena authorized the appropriation.

Edward Agnew, assistant manager of the airport division of the FAA's Southwest Region office, has been coordinating the project for the agency. He told the Tribune-Review the FAA gave approximately $12 million to the authority for land purchases last year and plans a similar amount this year for site preparations. Bulldozers might be moving into the area by summer, he said.

Agnew said it is projected the airport, scheduled for completion by 1997, will cost the federal government $90 million.

He denied the project was a payoff to the Tyson company, whose founder, Don Tyson, has been a principal supporter of Bill Clinton throughout his career.

"The project was conceived by two counties and five cities in north Arkansas," Agnew said. "Their goal was to have better capability than existed at the common airport at Drake Field."

The airport in Fayetteville, 35 miles from the proposed facility, is not sufficient for the region's needs because of terrain factors and lack of an all-weather instrument system, according to Agnew.

He pointed out that the initial grant for the facility, $600,000 for a planning study, came not during the Clinton administration but when George Bush was president.

Archie Schaffer, a spokesman for Tyson Foods, also denied any political considerations were at play. "Northwest Arkansas is growing. A regional airport is needed for the future of the area."

Counterpunch cited the airport's original feasibility study as benefitting the region's poultry firms, including Tyson: "If competitive air-freight rates were available, these companies estimate that Japan would become a boom market for U.S. fresh chicken products."

Concerning that, Schaffer said that shipping chickens there by air was "not economically feasible." He said that Tyson already ships to Japan, but by the cheapest means available: boat.

He also noted that the airport, as a freight center for Tyson, makes no sense, because the company's "23 processing plants are scattered all over the state" and would be of even less use to its 70 other plants in 20 states.

Counterpunch co-author Silver-

stein, referring to the scandals attendant to the Clinton administration, described "Poultryport" as "a classic case—the names are always the same."

The Tyson Foods chairman is the target of an independent counsel probe into whether he gave gifts to former Agriculture Secretary Mike Espy in exchange for relaxing federal regulations involving chicken processing. Espy resigned last year largely because of allegations relating to the investigation.

Tyson has been among Clinton's longest and largest financial supporters.

The Clintons also have close ties with Wal-Mart, and Hillary Rodham Clinton once served on the company's board of directors.

A spokesman for Wal-Mart did not return a call for comment.

Cockburn, a columnist for Nation magazine and perhaps its most left-wing voice, attributes Clinton's problems to "cronyism."

So does another well-known liberal writer, L.J. Davis, whose article in The New Republic last year on Arkansas politics may be the most detailed of any such work.

"It's a remarkable area for financial fraud," he said, referring to the state's insularity and the political domination by a few powerful business interests.

Based on many conversations he has had with liberals in the media, Davis said there is a "basic general disgust" with Clinton. "I can scarcely find anyone with a good word for him."

Silverstein agrees with the sentiment, commenting that Clinton "has been totally written off" by the liberal establishment. ∎

News Analysis:
Pieces Missing From Whitewater Puzzle

By Christopher Ruddy
FOR THE PITTSBURGH
TRIBUNE-REVIEW
MARCH 28, 1995

WASHINGTON—Don't be surprised if "Whitewater" revelations from the office of independent counsel Kenneth Starr exceed the expectations set by inside-the-Beltway cognoscenti.

In seven months, Starr has already surpassed the expectations set for former special counsel Robert Fiske by getting Webb Hubbell to plead guilty to two felon counts and act as a cooperating witness.

This January, Starr rode roughshod over Fiske's conclusions on Deputy White House Counsel Vincent Foster's death by convening a grand jury to look into the case.

Already, word is that Starr's Washington team has found several major discrepancies in testimony after bringing approximately a dozen police and emergency rescuers before the grand jury under oath.

On the Arkansas side, sources say to expect many more indictments.

Starr's staff is dealing with no ordinary set of scandals.

They touch upon both the president and first lady. What might be considered just shady business dealings, "Arkansas mores," as The New York Times termed them, remain totally unacceptable behavior for many Americans who hold high standards for the first family.

To be sure, Starr's staff has followed the money. The recent guilty plea of real estate salesman Chris Wade and the indictment of Neal T. Ainley, former president of Arkansas' Perry County Bank, for not reporting cash disbursements to Clinton's 1990 gubernatorial campaign, are indications of that.

Starr's investigation has kept a narrow focus on his jurisdiction, sources say, and hasn't gotten into the racier allegations that Bill Clinton's Little Rock was a modern-day Dodge City, complete with drug running, money laundering and murder—something that has proliferated through a spate of direct mail operators and a Jerry Falwell video.

Yet Whitewater has become a nagging boil on the body politic. And while it doesn't have the daily sensational reports of the O.J. Simpson trial, its cancer, relegated to the national sections of the newspapers, continues to fester.

If Whitewater is such a trifling matter, as its naysayers claim, why have its tentacles ensnared so many top officials: Bernard Nussbaum, counsel to the president; Hubbell, associate attorney general; Treasury's Robert Altman and Jean Hanson, not to mention missing characters from the Washington stage: Josh Steiner, William Kennedy III, Phillip Heymann, Michael Espy, David Watkins, Lloyd Bensten and, of course, Foster.

A post-scandal "autopsy" may someday demonstrate that the firings of 92 U.S. Attorneys and then FBI director William Sessions— the day before Foster's sudden death—were directly related to the amorphous scandal. Some Whitewater pundits believe the 92 attorneys were actually fired to cover the immediate firing of Little Rock's U.S. Attorney, who was replaced by Paula Casey, a long-time friend of Bill Clinton. Sessions has stated his firing led to a "compromised" investigation into Foster's death.

No, it certainly isn't a trifling matter. But it isn't a simple scandal, like bounced checks at the House Bank. Instead, it's something murky—like the ambiguous S&L scandal of the late '80s, with which Whitewater shares some connection. Remember, Clinton's partner, Jim McDougal, was chairman of the failed Arkansas savings and loan Madison Guaranty.

If one wanted to pick a scandal that would not stay on the public's radar screen, Whitewater the land deal would be it.

The 15-year-old North Arkansas land development deal is not going to tempt Oliver Stone as a prospect for his next movie project.

The problem with the Clintons, according to a White House source, is that instead of addressing any of the real issues, "they put the press on these wild goose chases; the McDougals, Madison, Whitewater." Inevitably, the press goes on the chase, and to the Clinton's chagrin, "it keeps blowing up on them. (The media) keep digging up different information and it doesn't go away."

What then is the real Whitewater story? The story may have been in the files of Vincent W. Foster.

BEGINNING OF WHITEWATER

To decide if the 50-50 land partnership deal between Bill and

Continued on next page

Continued from page 151

Hillary Clinton and Jim and Susan McDougal is a simple diversion, one must review Whitewater's rise as a national scandal.

Whitewater first surfaced in mudslinging during the 1992 Democratic presidential primaries. It went nowhere.

It was first reported in The New York Times in April 1992.

But, for the most part, the media ignored the story.

During the presidential campaign, it was not an issue.

After Vincent Foster died on July 20, 1993, it still was not raised as an issue.

The Clintons had been in office for almost a full year when on Dec. 20, 1993, The Washington Times ran a page 1 story headlined, "Clinton Papers Lifted After Aide's Suicide." The story detailed the late-night entry of three top White House aides into Foster's office on the evening he died.

The Washington Times reported, "the Park Police investigators familiar with the Foster inquiry say the Whitewater documents were among those taken from the office by White House officials."

Foster, in addition to being the number two White House lawyer, was personal attorney to the Clintons, privy to all their dealings.

So the key question remains: What were those White House aides looking for in Foster's office on the night of his death?

The question remains unanswered.

The White House took the unusual step of admitting that Foster was working on the Whitewater partnership papers.

"Whitewater Files Were Found in Foster's Office, White House Confirms," was the headline in the Washington Post two days after the Times ran its story.

At the time, the Whitewater deal was perfect bait for a hungry press believing some scandal on Foster's desk drove him to suicide.

It was an old scandal.

It had already been investigated by The New York Times and the Bush campaign and turned up no smoking guns. And, as Mrs. Clinton told the Associated Press just days after the Dec. 20 Washington Times revelations, "I am bewildered that a losing investment . . . is still a topic of inquiry . . . I just think what we've said is adequate."

If Whitewater is a diversion, then the deep, dark secrets of the real scandal could be buried with Foster or in files that were in his office.

ENTER MR. FISKE

No one could have imagined press reaction to revelations of Whitewater files in Foster's office at the time of his death.

Perhaps it was subtle and subconscious among the press: If a man commits suicide, violently and suddenly, without even saying goodbye to his wife and three kids, there must be something about Whitewater that drove him to it.

But a search of the Nexis on-line library for the word "Whitewater" shows that with the December revelations, the press reaction was seismic. Were the ever-growing number of news stories and editorials perhaps spurred by Foster's death or perhaps by a feeling among the press that stories like "Troopergate" were too easily brushed aside?

The press may well have overreacted and Whitewater may prove to be unconnected with Foster's death.

The cascade of press interest reached a feverish pitch in mid-January, when a reluctant President Clinton was dragged into having his attorney general select a special counsel. At this point, the independent counsel law had lapsed, and Attorney General Janet Reno would make the selection herself, not having to bring the matter before a three-judge panel.

At face value, Robert Bishop Fiske Jr. was a superb choice. A top-notch New York criminal Attorney, he once served as U.S. attorney for New York's southern district.

He was well received by Republicans and Democrats.

Beyond superficialities, there were obvious conflicts of interest that should have raised immediate red flags.

Fiske had a close professional relationship with White House counsel Bernard Nussbaum, himself a New York lawyer. Both had recommended each other for jobs.

According to press accounts, Fiske recommended to Nussbaum Louis B. Freeh to take over the FBI—whose selection was made without looking at any other candidates. Freeh is a long-time Fiske protege.

No matter that Nussbaum's involvement in Resolution Trust Corp. (RTC) contacts, or his entrance into Foster's office and later his refusal to allow Park Police to enter Foster's office, touch on some of the most sensitive issues relating to Whitewater. Fiske cleared Nussbaum of any wrongdoing.

Fiske had other conflicts. His New York firm represented International Paper Co., which had sold land to the Whitewater partnership.

Fiske had also successfully represented Bank of Credit and Commerce International (BCCI) figure Clark Clifford. The Wall Street Journal has argued that Whitewater was interrelated with the BCCI scandal of the 1980s.

By all appearances, Fiske had a full-fledged investigation underway by mid-February. By March, he had a plea agreement with David Hale, a key figure in the enlarging scandal.

Hale, a former Little Rock municipal judge, was charged with using his company to defraud the Small Business Administration of loans intended for minority and disadvantaged individuals. One of those loans was given to Susan McDougal. Susan and her husband, Jim McDougal, were partners with the Clintons.

But the McDougal loan was just one of a multitude of financial dealings, including the illegal use of SBA funds, in which Hale's company, Capital Management Services, was involved. A subpoena for documents in Hale's office identified 27 companies federal authorities suspected of wrong-doing.

According to one source, Hale could incriminate as many as two dozen individuals. He was treated as a star witness by Fiske and at that time was removed to a remote part of Arkansas and put under continuous FBI protection, an arrangement that lasted until shortly after Fiske was fired.

When Fiske was fired in August 1994, Hale had never appeared before a grand jury. Instead, he served as "a tour guide" for Fiske's team of prosecutors probing official corruption in Arkansas, according to a source.

In an interview last week, Fiske would neither confirm nor deny the story of FBI security for Hale, or whether he had been put before the grand jury. But he did say that in the prosecution of any case, a witness would be called only "at the stage of an investigation (when) testimony is complete and accurate."

FOSTER, HALE AND FISKE

At the same time, a parallel investigation was taking place in Washington. A grand jury was empaneled to review Resolution Trust Co. contacts relating to Madison Guaranty bank.

Exempted from both the Little Rock and Washington grand juries was the death investigation of Vincent Foster—though the fact that related files were in his office at the time of his death was a causal factor for the whole investigation.

Fiske's failure to use a grand jury in the Foster case is considered the major blunder of his investigation—and has been the talk of law enforcement circles in Washington since it was first revealed with the issuance of his report on Foster's death on June 30, 1994.

His failure to use a grand jury was first reported in "A Special Report on the Fiske Investigation into the Death of Vincent W. Foster Jr." published on July 18, 1994 by this author.

Instead, Fiske conducted what he described as a homicide investigation, headed by a former homicide prosecutor, Roderick Lankler. Like Fiske, Lankler, a Republican, is a noted New York attorney.

The Fiske team promised to explain the manner of Foster's death, and if it was suicide, the motivation.

In the end, Fiske's report was short on substance and long on puff, filled as it was with nearly a hundred pages of medical resumes, except the one for the medical examiner who actually conducted the autopsy.

Despite the Fiske report, great uncertainty about the death remained for two primary reasons: Foster's body was never exhumed, and Fiske did not use the power of subpoena behind the investigation.

The result of the less-than-rigorous investigation is that numerous holes appear in Fiske's report, which has likely led to Starr's recent convening of a grand jury into the matter.

Fiske concluded with certainty that "no evidence" indicated "Whitewater, Madison Guaranty, [David Hale's Capital Management Services], or other personal matters of the president or Mrs. Clinton were a factor in Foster's suicide."

Hale's linkage with Foster's death has been a matter of much speculation. A subpoena for documents at Hale's office was issued on the day of Foster's death. Fiske downplays its significance because the subpoena was actually served the following day and its contents were purportedly secret.

It is a large assumption by Fiske that in the clubby world of Arkansas' judicial system, and Foster's position as a top federal official, he would not have gotten wind of the issuance of the "secret" subpoena.

Recently, the Senate Banking Committee released a two-volume set of documents of the Fiske and police investigations of Foster's death.

Amazingly, the set includes no interview statement with David Hale.

Though Hale and his company were allegedly a major focus of Fiske's probe into Foster's death—and he concluded neither had anything to do with it—FBI agents testifying before the Senate Banking Committee seemed baffled when questioned about contacts between Hale, his attorney and Foster. In fact, the agents had promised to respond by letter after the hearings to the senators' queries on the matter.

In a letter dated Aug. 3, 1993, an FBI agent assigned to Fiske's staff responded to the Banking Committee that the staff "found no evidence that Foster" had information of the warrant.

Missing from the Fiske report is one important fact, according to a source close to the Fiske investigation. Just a week to 10 days before he died, Foster attempted to make contact with David Hale.

Why was Foster trying to contact Hale?

According to this source, both Hale and Foster knew each other on a professional basis. This omission in the Fiske report adds further weight to the argument that it was unbalanced, and its conclusions preordained.

Even though any information Hale had about Foster would not be subject to grand jury secrecy rules, Fiske said he could not discuss information gathered by the FBI relating to Hale.

Well before the search warrant for Hale's office was issued on July 20, many in Arkansas were well aware

Continued on next page

Continued from page 153

that federal authorities had been probing Hale and his company. Hale claims his company actually worked hand-in-hand with Bill Clinton's political machine—improperly giving loans at the behest of Clinton.

This month, a cover story in the Arkansas Democrat Gazette, "FBI Dangled Bait, but Hale Didn't Bite," reported that "a federal sting operation attempted to ensnare . . . David Hale several months before Hale went public with allegations about President Clinton . . ."

According to the March 11 report, in the summer of 1993, before the July 20 subpoena, an undercover FBI agent sought to involve Hale and his company in a $10 million money-laundering scheme. Hale declined to participate.

This report raises the question that federal officials may have attempted to entrap Hale early on in an effort to diminish his credibility before the subpoena was served and before Hale's allegations about Clinton surfaced.

Hale may have been a liability not just to Clinton, but to a number of figures in Arkansas, including the Clinton's personal attorney, Vincent Foster.

Some of the answers to the puzzling scandal may remain buried with Vincent Foster. But other answers, seemingly simple, were omitted from the results of Robert Fiske's investigation. ■

Starr Probes Money Laundering

By Christopher Ruddy
FOR THE PITTSBURGH
TRIBUNE-REVIEW
MAY 18, 1995

LITTLE ROCK, Ark.—Independent Counsel Kenneth Starr's probe into the Arkansas dealings of President Clinton and his wife Hillary appears to be straying far and wide from just the Clinton's 16-year-old land partnership deal known as Whitewater.

Arkansas state troopers who once provided security for then-Gov. Bill Clinton and his wife have been interviewed by FBI investigators working for Starr or have gone before Starr's Little Rock grand jury.

Troopers interviewed by the Tribune-Review say that Starr's investigators have been examining some of the more sordid allegations made against the Clintons during their tenure in Arkansas—allegations going beyond published accounts that Starr's probe had been limited to Whitewater and possible illegal contributions to his 1990 gubernatorial campaign.

According to the troopers, central issues they were questioned on by the Starr probe included:

■ MONEY LAUNDERING—Troopers were asked if they overheard discussions between the Clintons on the subject.

■ THE ARKANSAS DEVELOPMENT FINANCE AUTHORITY—Starr is probing whether the agency set up to help business expansion was used to pay off political friends of the Clintons.

■ MONEY AND GIFTS PERSONALLY RECEIVED BY CLINTON WHILE GOVERNOR—Evidence indicates that the areas of inquiry are not simply exploratory, but are being carefully examined by the grand jury.

One state trooper, who spent several years guarding the Clintons, testified before the grand jury last month and said he has been told it's likely he will be resummoned.

The trooper said the prosecutor questioned Clinton's relationship with an eastern Arkansas land developer and attorney who apparently benefited from loans from the finance authority.

The trooper said he was asked detailed questions about the Clinton's discussions about ADFA, as well as the Clintons' relationship with the two individuals who apparently benefited from loans granted by ADFA.

ADFA was the brainchild of Clinton, created in 1985 as a state bonding authority that would use bond proceeds to give to businesses for expansion and other groups in an effort to create jobs.

By the time Clinton left Arkansas for Washington in 1993, the agency had loaned approximately $719 million.

But the agency's role became controversial for Clinton during the campaign and remains so.

The Los Angeles Times reported in 1992 that Clinton received over $400,000 in contributions to his 1990 gubernatorial campaign from companies that had done business with ADFA.

Long-time Clinton critic Larry Nichols, a mainstay on talk-radio, and former marketing director for ADFA in the last 1980s, has claimed ADFA was used for money laundering. Similarly, authors Terry Reed and John Cummings in their book "Compromised: Bush Clinton and the CIA" have also alleged the development agency was used to launder drug money.

STATE POLICE

Starr's investigators have interviewed more than three dozen members of the Arkansas State Police who served on the Clinton security detail during the 12 years he was governor.

Trooper Roger Perry, who guarded Clinton for nearly seven years, said he was interviewed by four FBI agents working for Starr in March. He has yet to be called before the grand jury.

Perry said he was questioned intensively about contributions Clinton received that he had witnessed. Perry said it was not unusual for Clinton to receive cash—as much as $500—at fundraising events from individuals.

Another trooper who has been questioned before the grand jury said, "we received envelopes and cash all the time, at almost every reception he was at."

The trooper recalled that at the end of a reception it was not unusual to receive a sealed envelope from Clinton that he was asked to keep. The trooper said he typically handed the envelopes to Clinton's secretary in the Capitol building.

On one occasion, the trooper said he told the grand jury he was given an envelope "full of cash and checks" while at a reception in Denver in the late 1980s. He said it was one of the few times the envelope had not been sealed. The trooper said that while in the men's room during the reception, he looked through the envelope, noted one check made payable to "Bill Clinton" for $35,000.

None of the troopers could comment as to whether any of the money had been properly accounted for.

'AIR TYSON'?

Another area of inquiry was the troopers' knowledge of Clinton's relationship with chicken mogul Don Tyson of Tyson Foods of Springdale, Ark.

Investigators questioned the troopers about deliveries or pick-ups made from any of Tyson's planes at the local airport.

Perry said the pick-up of packages and envelopes for Clinton at the airport were "very routine for the troopers" and he remembers on several occasions meeting Tyson's corporate plane for a delivery. He said on one occasion he accompanied Mrs. Clinton on a Tyson plane.

Independent Counsel Donald Smaltz has been reviewing Tyson's relationship with former Clinton Agricultural Secretary Michael Espy.

Tyson is a long-time Clinton backer. In December of last year Time magazine reported that Smaltz had been investigating allegations made to a former pilot for Tyson, Joe Henrickson. He alleged that he regularly carried cash payments to Little Rock from Tyson's headquarters for Clinton.

Henrickson's charges, according to Time, have not been corroborated by other witnesses. Tyson Foods has denied the allegations and Time reported allegations that Henrickson was a fired employee of Tyson Foods who was exacting revenge on the company.

While Smaltz has said he is not investigating Clinton in the matter, a source familiar with Starr's probe said it would be in Starr's jurisdiction to investigate whether anything improper had taken place involving the Clintons.

Starr's Arkansas investigation appears to be leaving no stone unturned. One state trooper said in his career in law enforcement he had not seen a more thorough investigation.

The trooper said he was also surprised by the Little Rock grand jury. "They asked me at least a dozen questions on intimate details of the case," the trooper said. Typically grand jury members don't participate in interrogations. It is a sign of an active investigation.

Starr's use of the troopers is continuing. Another is slated to go before the grand jury this week. ■

Waco Prosecutors Join Probe

By Christopher Ruddy
FOR THE PITTSBURGH
TRIBUNE-REVIEW
JUNE 30, 1995

The staff of Independent Counsel Kenneth Starr's probe has become increasingly eclectic as time goes by.

In May, Starr's office hired O.J. Simpson defense team forensic expert Henry Lee to review the Vincent Foster death case.

This month, two U.S. attorneys who prosecuted the Waco-Branch Davidian case have joined Starr's Little Rock office.

The two lead Waco prosecutors, the husband-and-wife team of Ray and LeRoy Jahn (pronounced "Yawn"), were brought onto Starr's team as he attempted to bolster his staff with experienced prosecutors—apparently preparing for the prosecution phase of his Whitewater inquiry.

But, like the controversy that has swirled around the Waco case, that inquiry also has come to include the Jahns.

The Jahns have sterling resumes.
Continued on next page

Continued from page 155

As career prosecutors with about 25 years of federal service, they first gained recognition for handling the assassination case of U.S. District Court Judge John H. Wood in Texas.

The Jahns have spent most of their tenure as federal attorneys working in the U.S. attorney's office in San Antonio, though they served a brief stint as staff attorneys to FBI Director William S. Sessions in Washington.

Over the years, the Jahns have developed a close association with Justice Department officials in Washington.

When the Clinton administration needed experienced prosecutors to handle one of the most politically sensitive cases—Waco—the Jahns were selected.

Asked if the Justice Department played a significant role in the selection of the Jahns, former San Antonio U.S. Attorney Ron Ederer said, "There's no question about it, Washington was very much involved."

Ederer was the Bush-appointed U.S. attorney who served several months into the Clinton administration when the Waco incident began. The Jahns were tapped as the federal prosecutors for the case shortly after the Bureau of Alcohol, Tobacco and Firearms' Feb. 28, 1993, raid on the Branch Davidian compound.

"In the past, the Jahns have been successful as far as Justice was concerned," Ederer said.

Their close association with the Justice Department and their work on Waco, considered very important for the Clinton administration, appear to have posed no obstacle to their joining Starr's team, which has been investigating matters relating to the Clintons.

Former federal prosecutor Thomas Scorza, a lecturer on legal ethics at the University of Chicago, thinks the appointment of prosecutors close to the Justice Department "is something less than desirable" for an independent counsel's probe.

"It doesn't violate any rule of ethics and is not a conflict of interest," he said, "but it does seem picking prosecutors with strong connections to the Department of Justice is not the way to go."

Scorza noted that the "essence" of the independent counsel law was to have an independent investigation that doesn't answer to Justice or the president.

He believes that selecting prosecutors with "strong personal connections to Justice" undermines the spirit of the law.

Ray Jahn, contacted at Starr's Little Rock office, referred all questions about his appointment to Starr's press aide, but did say he did not see his association within Justice as a problem since "we're not the only people working here(on the staff) from Justice."

Starr's office refused to comment on the appointment of the Jahns or the matters they may be handling.

The couple's ties with Justice Department officials were strengthened, according to FBI sources, after their stint as aides to Director Sessions, even though Sessions' last years were marked by difficulties with Justice and the White House.

In 1993, Sessions was fired by President Clinton.

According to sources familiar with the Jahns' work at the FBI, the couple quickly aligned themselves with Justice Department officials after joining Sessions' staff in 1992. Sessions and his wife believed that it was an effort to undermine the director's position, sources said.

Eventually, Sessions asked the Jahns to return to San Antonio before their one-year contract expired.

Sessions didn't comment on the matter, but sources say Sessions and his wife, who were friends with the Jahns for over two decades, have fallen out and no longer talk to the couple.

WACO CASE

After the Jahns returned to San Antonio, they eventually tried the Waco case.

"They (the Jahns) have a reputation for taking a mess like the Waco case and making sense of it," Houston attorney Mike DeGuerin said.

DeGuerin was the lead counsel for the 11 Branch Davidian survivors brought to trial and charged with conspiring to kill federal agents.

After a seven-week trial in 1994, the prosecution took a "big loss" according to DeGuerin, when a Texas jury found the survivors not guilty on the prosecution's two main charges, including conspiracy to murder federal agents.

DeGuerin felt then that the Jahns handled the government's case fairly, but said "the jury just wasn't going to buy a conspiracy theory."

DeGuerin suggested the appointment of the Jahns to Starr's staff "raises some eyebrows."

The Jahns' handling of the Waco case has come under sharp criticism.

Author and columnist James Bovard wrote about the Jahns in a recent article titled "Feds Must Fess Up About Role in Waco":

"Federal Prosecutors were caught manipulating evidence at the trial. Prosecutors presented a transcript of tapes made from listening devices inside the compound in its last days, purportedly showing that the Davidians intended to commit suicide. But under cross-examination, the government's audio expert admitted altering the transcripts after meeting with the chief prosecutor."

Ray Jahn told the Tribune-Review that this allegation was a "bunch of beans" and said the defense team had full access to all of the tapes, amounting to over 100 hours of audio time, and the right to have them played.

DeGuerin, laughing, said while technically Jahn was correct, the defense team didn't have "200 people working the case" as the prosecution did, and the resources to examine all of the evidence thoroughly.

He said he was disturbed that the prosecution had omitted parts of the tapes that had the Davidians praying, and children screaming as tanks began knocking down the compound walls.

Sara L. Bain, forewoman of the jury and a San Antonio teacher, said she was concerned the prosecution was not "presenting all the evidence."

Bain cited the fact that a metal door, said by witnesses to have shown a barrage of bullets which the Davidians claimed demonstrated the ATF made the initial attack, was said to be destroyed in the compound's subsequent fire.

"The other metal doors were found, they didn't melt, some were even run over by tanks and were recovered," a suspicious Bain said.

DeGuerin agreed the door, a key point of evidence, was significant in its absence, but pointed out, "I don't think Ray Jahn has any idea what happened to the door." ∎

Indictments Against Former Clinton Partners in Offing

By Christopher Ruddy
FOR THE PITTSBURGH
TRIBUNE-REVIEW
AUGUST 3, 1995

LITTLE ROCK—Indictments against Jim and Susan McDougal, former Whitewater partners of President and Mrs. Clinton, are imminent, according to a source close to the investigation.

Barring any last-minute plea agreement, Independent Counsel Kenneth Starr plans to hand up indictment papers before his Little Rock grand jury, which the source said "could be in days, but certainly this month."

The McDougals will be indicted for financial dealings related to David Hale. Hale's Little Rock finance company, Capital Management Services, defrauded the Small Business Administration by improperly giving loans allocated for disadvantaged and minority-owned businesses to friends and business partners.

Hale entered into a plea arrangement with the original Whitewater prosecutor, Special Counsel Robert Fiske, last year. Sources in both Fiske's and Starr's investigation say Hale has been a credible, cooperating figure in the probe.

The main indictment against McDougal is very tenuously linked with Whitewater, the 50-50 partnership to develop 230 acres of land in northern Arkansas that the Clintons and McDougals began in 1978.

The indictment against McDougal will center around his ownership of Madison Guaranty Savings and Loan Association, which failed in 1989, costing taxpayers more than $60 million.

The indictment will allege that McDougal provided a loan to Hale's business partner as a front man for the benefit of Hale's company and McDougal's bank.

According to the source, Hale told federal investigators that the Madison loan was part of a scheme to defraud the SBA by artificially inflating his company's assets to give loans to friends and associates, as well as cover bad loans made by Madison Guaranty.

One beneficiary of Capital Management's loans was Susan McDougal, whose Little Rock advertising firm, Master Marketing, received a $300,000 loan. The loan was never paid back and published reports indicate some of the money made its way into Whitewater accounts.

The source said a report in the Arkansas Democrat Gazette on Aug. 28, 1994, detailing McDougal's transactions with Capital Management, closely mirrors the scheme to be presented in the indictment papers.

The August Democrat Gazette article elaborated on a series of transactions in 1986 among Hale, one of his business partners, McDougal and others.

According to the newspaper, Hale and his partner bought and sold a restaurant they jointly owned in Sherwood, Ark., increasing the property's value artificially. Using improper and favorable appraisals, McDougal's Madison Guaranty loaned Hale's business partner $825,000 to buy the restaurant from Hale.

Hale then took a significant portion of the proceeds from the sale and put them into his company to be used to qualify for matching SBA funds of $500,000 or more.

Hale used this new supply of capital, and SBA matching funds, to cover bad loans made by Madison Guaranty before bank examiners conducted an audit.

Though Starr is said to favor a plea agreement, sources close to the probe doubt that a plea agreement will be struck, since the McDougals are demanding full immunity. ∎

Clinton Indictments Unlikely

Starr's Hubbell Agreement Led to Resignation

By Christopher Ruddy
FOR THE PITTSBURGH
TRIBUNE-REVIEW
AUGUST 6, 1995

LITTLE ROCK, Ark.—Chances are slim that Independent Counsel Kenneth Starr will indict Bill or Hillary Clinton as a result of the Whitewater probe, sources close to the inquiry have told the Tribune-Review.

Starr, passing the first anniversary of his appointment this week, has found little substantive evidence linking the Clintons to wrongdoing relating to their Whitewater partnership, dealings with Madison Guaranty, or possible obstruction issues in Washington.

"At this time, it would take someone like (Jim Guy) Tucker or the McDougals to turn, and testify, against the Clintons," one source said, which would then allow prosecutors to "move up the food chain."

Clinton's main accuser has been David Hale, who maintains that Bill Clinton pressured him into making a fraudulent $300,000 Small Business Administration-backed loan to Susan McDougal.

While acknowledging Hale has been a credible witness, a member of Starr's team said "Hale versus the president is not going to fly," indicating more substantive evidence would have to be forthcoming to present to a grand jury.

But sources, critical of Starr's handling of the investigation, suggest the long delays in Starr's staff getting up to speed where the Robert Fiske investigation left off, the mishandling of Webster Hubbell's plea agreement and the problems in the Washington end of the investigation—highlighted by a major resignation—have all impeded a swift resolution of the case.

Starr's indictments of Arkansas Gov. Jim Guy Tucker and associates in June were more than six months behind the schedule set by Special Counsel Fiske's staff, which had planned a series of indictments for the fall of 1994.

Contrary to some expectations, Tucker has not sought a plea agreement behind the scenes as he awaits a decision on his motion to have the indictments thrown out, claiming Starr had no jurisdiction to indict him. Starr's staff is confident they will win the motion. Prosecutors also doubt Tucker would be cooperative under any circumstances.

The McDougals have demanded full immunity for a plea agreement, which is unacceptable to Starr.

Even if the McDougals were to testify against the Clintons, sources say, their credibility as witnesses would be seriously challenged.

Sources also suggest that getting individuals to cooperate in the future may be less than fruitful because of the mishandling of Hubbell's plea and the troubled investigation in Washington.

FIRST RESIGNATION

The first major policy dispute in Starr's staff led to the resignation of his chief trial counsel, Russell G. Hardin, last September, according to several Whitewater prosecutors.

Hardin, a seasoned former Houston assistant district attorney who was named Texas State Prosecutor of the Year in 1989, was hired by Fiske as his lead trial prosecutor.

Hardin was to have tried Hale for using his company, Capital Management Services, to defraud the SBA.

But Hale entered into a plea agreement with Fiske early last year. Hardin remained on the staff to try the next major case.

With Fiske's ouster in August 1994, Hardin was one of two prosecutors to continue with Starr's inquiry, and had agreed to try the probe's next major target, former Associate Attorney General Hubbell.

"Rusty (Hardin) wanted to go in with big guns against Hubbell, to nail him since the case was airtight and show others we weren't fooling around," one prosecutor familiar with the events in Starr's staff last year said.

Starr's staff had prepared a 38-count indictment against Hubbell, according to one source. Hubbell entered into a plea agreement in December, sparing himself "an extremely embarrassing trial," a prosecutor said.

As part of the agreement, Hubbell was charged on two counts of mail fraud and tax evasion, that entailed a 21-27 month term in federal prison, which could be reduced if he cooperated with the independent counsel (under sentencing guidelines, Hubbell's prison term would be the same for two counts or 38).

STARR OVER-ANXIOUS

Hardin had argued for Starr to play "hard to get" with Hubbell, who was seen as the first major target of the investigation, and one that could link the Clintons to wrongdoing in both Washington and Arkansas, sources said.

Hardin had successfully handled the plea agreement with Hale, when prosecutors went down to the wire to begin trial proceedings before a plea agreement was struck. The agreement was struck only after Hale had been debriefed for two weeks by investigators "as to what he knew and what he could give prosecutors," a prosecutor familiar with Fiske's probe said.

Instead, Starr, who had no experience as a prosecutor, and who served as federal judge and a well-regarded Justice Department official, was over-anxious to get Hubbell's plea and did not rigorously debrief him before entering into the agreement, two prosecutors familiar with Starr's probe told the Tribune-Review.

The process of agreeing to a plea "should be structured so the defendant has an overwhelming need to tell what he knows," one prosecutor said, lamenting that had not been the case with Hubbell.

"If Hardin had argued for this, he'd be exactly right," Thomas Scorza, a former federal prosecutor and lecturer of legal ethics at the University of Chicago, said.

"Typically a prosecutor wants to flip the smallest fish, the people at the bottom like an office secretary, to get higher ups," Scorza explained, "But Hubbell was a big fish, so a prosecutor figures he's going to be disinclined to give information. It's really important to hammer him at the early stage when the person is most vulnerable."

Scorza said that Starr could have, for example, tried to find additional charges, such as perjury, to increase sentence time, and use this as an additional lever.

Going easy on Hubbell though he failed to cooperate "is a sign to others not yet charged that the prosecutor is going to roll over, that you don't have to cooperate," Scorza said.

Another source in the Starr probe has disputed that Hardin left over a disagreement about dealing with Hubbell, and suggested he resigned solely because he was not allowed to choose the prosecutors handling the day-to-day case before the grand jury.

Hardin, in private practice in Houston, declined to comment on the matter, but did say he resigned several months earlier than planned.

At Hubbell's sentencing in June, Starr sought no reduction in sentencing, which was an indication of Hubbell's lack of cooperation. According to several sources, Hubbell provided no information that will lead to additional indictments.

One prosecutor pointed out that Starr's handling of the Washington side of the investigation may also have been a roadblock to cooperation from Hubbell and other witnesses.

Last March, Associate Independent Counsel Miquel Rodriguez resigned after he was apparently stymied in conducting what he felt was a full probe into Vincent Foster's death.

"Hubbell's probably a lot more worried about what happened with Foster than serving in prison," one prosecutor suggested.

After a year of investigation, Starr's office has come up with no indictment on the Washington end of his probe, and has shown no interest in "flipping" lower-level officials over apparent problems in testimony and evidence.

In other developments related to Starr's investigation:

■ Forensic scientist Henry C. Lee is currently on hiatus from investigating aspects of Foster's death as he consults for the O.J. Simpson defense team. Lee, who heads the Connecticut state crime lab, recently visited Fort Marcy Park in a suburb just outside Washington, the site where Foster's body was found.

■ Starr's staff plans to have the FBI conduct another search for a bullet at Fort Marcy. Two previous searches, first by the Park Police and then by the FBI under Fiske, didn't find the fired projectile—one of many nagging inconsistencies about the Foster-death scene.

■ Starr's Washington deputy, Mark H. Tuohey, plans to resign in September for a new position, as the Washington phase of the investigation winds down.

■ Starr has resisted efforts by the White House to issue a report on Foster's death, as Fiske did in June 1994. He will wait until the end of his Whitewater probe, a source said. ■

Opposition Mounts to Airport Ticketed for Clinton's Home State

By Christopher Ruddy
FOR THE PITTSBURGH
TRIBUNE-REVIEW
SEPTEMBER 6, 1995

A planned commercial airport for rural, northwest Arkansas—which would have the second-largest civilian runway in the nation—is being opposed by residents of local communities who view the airport as unnecessary.

Late last month, the Fort Smith (Ark.) Airport Board passed a unanimous resolution calling on the federal government to halt funding for the $144.6 million airport project.

The project, planning for which began this summer after receiving about $22 million in Federal Aviation Administration start-up money, will be centered in and around Highfill, Ark., which has a population of 92.

The FAA is slated to pick up 90 percent of the airport construction cost. The airport is to be completed by 1998.

Earlier this year, the Tribune-Review gave details about the pork barrel project slated for President Clinton's home state, and the fact that some of the president's prime supporters appear to be among the airport's biggest beneficiaries.

Department store giant Wal-Mart's headquarters is located just 30 miles from the proposed facility. Tyson Foods' headquarters is about the same distance from the site.

Hillary Clinton served on Wal-Mart's board of directors. Tyson Foods, the nation's largest chicken processor, is run by Don Tyson, a long-time Clinton political and financial backer.

Tyson's connections to the airport authority and the potential commercial use of the airport as a cargo hub for chicken freight resulted in the airport project being dubbed "Poultryport" by the left-wing newsletter Counterpunch, published by the Institute for Policy Studies.

The airport is "really a scandal . . . a scam, using public money for private purposes," said Counterpunch editor Ken Silverstein, who, along with Alexander Cockburn, wrote the story on "Poultryport."

The recent resolution by the airport board in nearby Fort Smith flies in the face of claims by the FAA that the project was the result of grass roots efforts of Arkansas communities and that airports such as Fort Smith's could not be expanded to handle growing demand.

In addition to Fort Smith, officials in Springfield and Joplin, Mo., and Pittsburgh, Kan., have voiced opposition to the project.

Opponents of the airport have found a powerful ally in Aviation Research Systems Corp., one of the country's most prominent airport and airline consulting firms.

The Colorado-based firm issued a report on the project last month. According to the Arkansas Democrat Gazette, the president of Aviation Research, Michael Boyd, described the airport as " . . . nothing short of a boondoggle (where) . . . the numbers have been cooked to show revenues."

In 1998, the year when the airport is scheduled to be completed, Aviation Research says that the per-passenger cost to use the airport will be $12.76—twice as much as the cost per passenger at nearby Tulsa International Airport.

Boyd, the Democrat Gazette reported, compared the proposed airport to Denver's recently built airport, which has fallen short of expectations. He said that Denver, at least, provides airline service, which would not be true of tiny Highfill, Ark. ∎

Clinton Security Chief's Murder Still Unsolved

By Christopher Ruddy
FOR THE PITTSBURGH
TRIBUNE-REVIEW
SEPTEMBER 26, 1995

At the Little Rock Police Department the murder of Jerry Luther Parks might as well have never occurred.

Odd, since the killing has gained folklore status on the "Clinton Chronicles," a video viewed by millions. The death is also a major selling point for direct-mail operators who hawk newsletters. Talk radio remains abuzz about the enigmatic death.

Today marks the second anniversary of the murder of Parks, the security chief of President Clinton's campaign headquarters in Little Rock in 1992 and 1993.

"I can't find him in my computer," Lt. John Hutchinson, Little Rock police spokesman said. "Are you sure it's a Little Rock case?"

Hutchinson, his memory refreshed about Parks, promised to check on the status of the case with his homicide unit.

The details of the murder are not in dispute: Early Sunday evening on Sept. 26, 1993, Parks was returning to his suburban Little Rock home, making a left turn on Arkansas Highway 10, when, without warning, a white Chevrolet raced into the intersection from behind.

An assassin jumped from the passenger seat of the Chevrolet and fired his 9mm pistol, hitting Parks at least seven times.

He died soon thereafter, his body sprawled across the highway. Parks's efforts to use a pistol he had begun keeping between the front seats of his car were apparently futile.

Despite several eyewitnesses to the killing, Parks's death remains unsolved.

"The case is at a standstill. The investigators have exhausted all their leads. There's no new information," Hutchinson reported after checking.

Hutchinson would not permit the detective handling the case to speak to a reporter, and a call to Little Rock police chief Louie Caudell was referred to Hutchinson.

FAMILY UNHAPPY

Parks, a former Arkansas police officer, private investigator and the owner of a security firm whose services were used by the Clinton-Gore campaign, left behind his wife, Jane, and 24-year-old son Gary. Neither is happy about the police's handling of the case.

Save two feature articles on the case in the Sunday London Telegraph by its intrepid Washington correspondent Ambrose Evans-Pritchard, Parks' death and the allegations made by the Parks family have been ignored in the mainstream press.

The Telegraph reported in March 1994 that Mrs. Parks and her son feared Parks had been killed because of incriminating information he had gathered on Clinton. Clinton's own relationship with Parks remains murky, though Clinton had appointed Parks to the state police's Board of Private Investigators and Security Firms in 1987. His company had a contract for security services at the building used by the Clinton campaign, and later the campaign contracted with Parks directly.

Parks, at the behest of an anonymous third party, had been keeping surveillance on Clinton for five years beginning in the mid-1980s when the governor's brother, Roger, lived temporarily in an apartment in the same complex as Parks. Mrs. Parks managed the complex and had an office that was once a bedroom in the apartment used by Roger Clinton.

"During the time (Mrs. Parks) worked next to Roger's apartment, she could hear the conversations in B107 very clearly," the Telegraph reported, adding, "Gov. Clinton was a frequent visitor." Parks told the Telegraph that drug use took place in the apartment often, and at one point she saw cocaine on a coffee table.

Mrs. Parks is suffering from multiple sclerosis and has declined to comment on the case to the Tribune-Review. Her friend, Little Rock attorney Harvey Bell, said her health condition is "serious" and she is under orders to "disengage" from the case and the controversy. As for the police's handling of the case, Bell said, "Nothing's been done."

Gary Parks, a former Navy submariner, still finds that irksome. Both he and his mother allege that an investigative file on Clinton compiled by his father may have led to his demise. They say that just weeks before Parks's murder, their home was burgled in a sophisticated operation that included cutting phone lines. Taken was the investigative file (which allegedly included photos) stashed in the master bedroom.

The Parks family seems to have some credibility with Sgt. Clyde Steelman, the detective handling the case.

"If they say that some files were missing, then I can tell you those files were missing," he told the Telegraph last year. "The Parks family aren't lying to you."

To be sure, Parks had dealt with a
Continued on next page

THE RUDDY INVESTIGATION **161**

Continued from page 161

number of shady characters through his business, casting a wide net over those who may have wanted him dead. The Parks family has offered no evidence to support insinuations about the president. The family has also charged that the Clinton connection had prevented a proper police investigation.

Lt. Hutchinson didn't deny the charge, saying in a plain-spoken manner, "I don't know." He also admitted that despite having witnesses, the police never completed composite sketches of the perpetrators.

FOSTER DEATH

Parks's murder took place just over two months after the suicide of White House counsel Vincent Foster on July 20, 1993. This would be simple coincidence, were it not for more allegations made by the Parks family.

Gary said his father became noticeably agitated immediately after Foster's death, and suggested just a day after the suicide that Foster had been murdered.

Parks soon began carrying a gun, even taking it with him to his mailbox. He also carried a cellular phone and checked in with his wife five or six times a day—something he had never done before. He changed his typical route home and began taking medication to sleep.

Parks, according to his family, had a major disagreement with the Clinton-Gore campaign, complaining he had not been paid for his company's services months after the election. Parks had borrowed tens of thousands of dollars to meet his payroll while his invoices to the campaign went unpaid, the family said.

Campaign officials claimed to Parks that he had in fact been paid. An inquiry into the matter, Parks told his family, indicated that someone had improperly diverted campaign funds, and with apologies he was promised full restitution.

Despite the promise, Parks's son said the payment didn't come easy, and led to some wrangling with the campaign in the months after Clinton was inaugurated.

How Foster possibly plays into this is unclear. What is clear is that Foster and Parks were well aware of each other. An associate of Foster's in Little Rock said that Foster had once recommended Parks as a private investigator.

Foster's death has been looked into by Independent Counsel Kenneth Starr, but a homicide investigation has never taken place as police procedure demands.

Starr, unwilling to fully investigate Foster's death, seems unlikely to begin examining Parks' murder.

A source close to Starr's investigation said that at the request of Mrs. Parks, one of Starr's Little Rock prosecutors met with her and Bell at a Little Rock McDonald's for coffee in the past year.

"It certainly should have been jumped on, if there's a hint that the two cases may be related," explained veteran homicide investigator Vernon Geberth.

Geberth, former lieutenant commander of New York's Bronx homicide task force, is the author of the authoritative text on death investigations, "Practical Homicide Investigation."

"If someone's telling they are related, I would expect it would be picked up as part of the investigation," he said, noting that federal authorities, having investigated Foster's death first, should have looked into the matter. ∎

Customs Service Falters with Drug Interdiction

By Christopher Ruddy
FOR THE PITTSBURGH
TRIBUNE-REVIEW
OCTOBER 8, 1995

WASHINGTON—The federal fiscal year ended just one week ago, and annual statistics being compiled by the U.S. Customs Service will show the amount of cocaine seized at our borders has plummeted by nearly 40 percent since President Clinton took office.

According to a Customs spokesman, in the first 11 months of Fiscal 1995 the federal service interdicted 144,000 pounds of cocaine.

At that rate, Fiscal 1995 will have produced the lowest amount of cocaine seized in the past five years, little more than half of the amount seized during the Bush administration's last fiscal year, 1992.

Experts and sources in Customs say the drop-off in seizures of cocaine—the Big Daddy of the illegal narcotics trade—is largely the result of a Clinton administration shake-up of Customs enforcement's senior staff, dramatic cuts of Customs enforcement budget, and de-emphasis of Customs' role in stopping illegal drugs at the nation's borders.

The changes come as statistics show the use of cocaine and other illegal narcotics is on the rise again, reversing a downward trend from earlier this decade.

"I would think that cuts in enforcement have resulted in an increase in the supply, distribution and usage of cocaine," said John Bellizzi, executive director of the International Narcotics Enforcement Officers Association, which includes agents of Customs and the Drug Enforcement Administration.

One high-ranking Customs enforcement official, requesting anonymity, told the Tribune-Review, "Enforcement people are all depressed because this administration does not want us to have authority, and doesn't want us to have operational money."

The source also indicated the numbers may be worse than they appear, having been boosted late this summer by one unusually large interdiction: a plane loaded with 24,000 pounds of cocaine in San Diego.

According to this year's National Drug Control Strategy, published by the White House's Office of National Drug Control Policy, a de-emphasis of interdiction at the borders began in 1993 after a National Security Council memorandum argued for "a shift away from past efforts that focused primarily on interdiction in transit zones to new efforts that focus on interdiction in and around source countries."

Soon thereafter, President Clinton signed a Presidential Decision Directive implementing the new policy, which some say has effectively clipped Customs' wings.

Of seven key areas where federal money is spent to control drugs, such as drug treatment and education, interdiction is the only area to have seen its funding cut.

"While all other agencies involved in drug interdiction will require additional resources in FY 1996, the U.S. Customs Service will not," reads the National Drug Control Strategy.

According to the Office of National Drug Control Policy,

Customs has borne the brunt of cuts in interdiction funding. The service's 1994 budget was $572 million; it will drop to $500 million under the president's proposal for Fiscal 1996.

The cuts have particularly affected Customs' aviation and marine units, which had been credited with earlier successes in cutting the drug flow.

Another indicator of failing enforcement is a precipitous drop in the number of drug-related arrests by Customs since 1992. For the first 11 months of Fiscal '95, Customs made 6,389 drug-related arrests, compared to 9,600 such arrests in the previous 12 months.

Customs itself seems unable to explain the drop in cocaine seizures.

"There's no figuring out the trends," said spokesman Dennis Shimkoski. He noted that marijuana statistics have gyrated over the past several years without any particular explanation. As to whether cuts in enforcement funding have thwarted efforts to interdict cocaine, he said he "couldn't speculate."

MEXICAN BORDER

The most telling sign of diminishing Customs enforcement efforts is at the Mexican-American border. The Office of National Drug Control Policy calculates that about 70 percent of all cocaine coming into the United States comes across that border.

Sen. Diane Feinstein (D-Calif.), has been the administration's fiercest critic on drug interdiction policy, particularly as it relates to California's shared border with Mexico. In a letter to Treasury Secretary Robert Rubin (Customs is an agency of the Treasury Department) in August, Feinstein pointed out that in 1993 Customs seized four tons of cocaine at the border.

But since Customs fully implemented a new policy in 1994, "not a single pound of cocaine was confiscated from more than two

million trucks that passed through three of the busiest entry points along the southwest border," Feinstein wrote.

That new policy, referred to as the "line release program," allows cargo shippers that are considered low-risk to be whisked through the border, bypassing inspections.

The program gives the special status to drivers and entire trucking lines that have gone through extensive background checks. Administration officials have promoted the program as consistent with the North American Free Trade Agreement, which calls for freer access across borders for signatory nations.

Earlier this year, Feinstein told the Los Angeles Times that the program had to be re-evaluated. She questioned whether "increased trade and reduced border control is worth increased narcotics shipments."

Feinstein spokeswoman Susan Kennedy said that since the senator made her criticism, Customs made "a number of refinements" to the program that the senator is reviewing.

Last month, Customs Commissioner George Weise slapped a moratorium on new applications for shippers and trucking companies to participate in the program. Weise admitted that the program has a defect: it allows smugglers to place narcotics on trucks that are part of the program.

As an answer to critic's complaints and a drop-off in seizures, this past February Customs initiated Operation Hardline, which added agents and introduced more rigorous inspections along the U.S.-Mexican border. Despite the media hoopla over Operation Hardline, sources familiar with Customs activity on the border said the emphasis remains on "trade and facilitation," and Customs enforcement personnel are not encouraged to do rigorous inspections.

Staffing at border crossings is still
Continued on next page

THE RUDDY INVESTIGATION **163**

Continued from page 163

said to be short-changed. At the El Paso station, for example, a source said the site remains 17 positions below its full authorization.

The lax Mexican border inspections are symptomatic of falling standards at all entry points, a ranking Customs official said.

Previously, inspectors conducted random checks of arriving air passengers, as many as 10 percent of any given flight. They also performed occasional "blitz" inspections, checking 100 percent of all arriving passengers from a particular plane.

For the most part, Customs has abandoned that system in favor of an Advanced Passenger Information System. Under the new system, passenger lists are checked against a Customs database of potential smugglers, and individuals are targeted for inspection before the plane even arrives.

But one official said the system is faulty because the database is incomplete and can't really predict potential smugglers. It also depends on foreign airline personnel inputting proper and honest information about the passenger's name and date of birth.

Concerns have been raised by a number of new administration proposals to relax border inspections, the most radical of which were in Vice President Al Gore's National Performance Review aimed at "reinventing" government. One proposal called for an open border between the United States and Canada.

In August, Customs announced that it had rejected some proposals, including the open border with Canada. However, some of the task force's proposals were accepted and are being tested at Miami International Airport, which has been designated as a "Reinvention Lab."

One idea that was first called "the upper-crust program" exempts first-class and business-class passengers from Customs inspections. One congressional staffer found the notion laughable. "What's stopping a drug dealer from buying a first-class ticket?" he asked, noting the small expense compared to the value of smuggled drugs.

While drug-transporting individuals—sometimes called "mules"—usually carry a small volume of drugs, their cargo is extremely valuable. A pound of pure cocaine can have a market value of $1 million. That price tag explains why "mules" have taken extraordinary means to hide drugs from Customs, for example by swallowing small condoms filled with cocaine.

The changes at Customs "are only one indication the Clinton administration is not making drug control a priority," said John Walters, who was acting director of the Office of National Drug Control Policy during the early days of the Clinton administration. "Clinton hasn't provided the leadership, and has cut monies, authorization and drug control as a priority across the board." ■

Starr's Probe Failed to Challenge Privilege Claims

By Christopher Ruddy
FOR THE PITTSBURGH
TRIBUNE-REVIEW
DECEMBER 24, 1995

WASHINGTON—As the Senate last week moved to seek judicial help in obtaining a set of Whitewater-related notes written by a White House lawyer, one key player in the confrontation went largely unnoticed: Independent Counsel Kenneth Starr.

The Tribune-Review has learned from a source familiar with the independent counsel's probe that Starr has continually accepted without question White House claims of attorney-client privilege since his inquiry began, including claims of privilege over the Whitewater notes written by then-Associate White House Counsel William Kennedy III.

Kennedy's notes of November 1993 were taken during a meeting with key White House staffers shortly after White House officials sought information relating to federal probes into a failed Arkansas savings and loan and a Little Rock lending company that granted fraudulent Small Business Association loans.

According to a source, Starr, following in the footsteps of his predecessor, Robert Fiske, has accepted without challenge claims of attorney-client privilege asserted by nearly every member of the White House Counsel's Office, including Kennedy and former White House Counsel Bernard Nussbaum.

Starr has also accepted such claims of privilege by others, including Susan Thomases, a New York lawyer who has been a chief factotum for Hillary Rodham Clinton. The claim of privilege has been used frequently to deny Starr both testimony and documents before his Washington grand jury, the sources said.

Though the White House ultimately caved in and agreed to hand over the Kennedy notes late last week, the administration continued to assert its right to claim privilege.

By going toe-to-toe with the Senate Whitewater Committee, Clinton's apparent strategy wasn't simply to protest attorney-client privilege with the Kennedy notes.

Rather, it was an attempt to protect an array of testimony and documents that have been withheld from the Independent Counsel's Office with Starr's acquiescence, according to sources familiar with the congressional probe as well as with Starr's.

Just Tuesday, the White House won an important concession when Starr signed a "no-waiver" agreement under which the White House would release the notes but Starr would agree that the White House has the right to withhold documents and testimony based on such a privilege. The House Banking Committee also made a similar concession later in the week.

The Senate committee, led by Sen. Alfonse D'Amato, refused to make such an agreement. That led to the Senate vote, which in turn led to the White House surrender.

Observers say Starr may have good reason to ink a deal with the White House agreeing to the privilege. If the Whitewater committee gains unfettered access to testimony and documents that Starr himself tuned a blind eye to,

and if the committee finds information leading to criminal indictments, then these revelations could be a major embarrassment to Starr.

Starr is a retired federal judge who never handled a prosecution before.

The Kennedy notes and other questions became an issue in his probe during the fall of 1994, just months after Starr took over the case from Fiske. That's when then-Associate Independent Counsel Miquel Rodriquez wrote a memo to his superiors stating that in the normal course of a prosecution, attorney-client privilege should be challenged. Rodriquez recommended that Kennedy and others be compelled to turn over notes and other information, but those recommendations were nixed by Starr and the rest of his team.

Starr has turned in no indictments in the Washington side of his probe even though it deals with some of the most sensitive aspects of his investigation: the death of Vincent Foster, possible obstruction of the death investigation, and possible obstruction of federal inquiries into Madison Guaranty, a failed thrift with links to the Clintons.

The Tribune-Review reported that Rodrigez resigned earlier this year after being thwarted in his attempt to conduct a full probe into Foster's death.

The failure by Starr to adequately challenge claims of privilege is just another indication his investigation has been less than vigorous, according to experts familiar with federal prosecutions.

"If the prosecutor just rolls over

on every claim of privilege, an investigation can be totally and completely thwarted," explained Thomas Scorza. Scorza, a former federal prosecutor from Chicago and a professor of legal ethics at the University of Chicago, was perplexed at the idea that the independent counsel has not challenged each and every claim of privilege asserted by witnesses—which Scorza said is standard procedure in a criminal procedure.

Whether the notes written by Kennedy fall under attorney-client privilege is a "very complicated" issue, Scorza continued. He said that during his tenure as a federal prosecutor "the grand jury practice was each time witnesses claimed the privilege, we would take the matter before the chief judge."

The judge, Scorza said, determines if the privilege applies. The judge has the right to uphold the claim or even selectively apply it to the point of examining a document sentence by sentence, according to Scorza.

Starr's failure to follow standard procedure and use the judge each time the privilege has been claimed is "highly unusual," according to the professor.

"A grand jury is entitled to every man's evidence, and a privilege is an exception to those general rules," Scorza said, adding that a prosecutor certainly does not want potential targets in a criminal probe to decide themselves if something is privileged.

"In an ordinary prosecution," he added, the prosecutor "requires people who claim privilege to put up or shut up." ■

Starr Terminated Washington Grand Jury, But Why?

News Analysis

By Christopher Ruddy
FOR THE PITTSBURGH
TRIBUNE-REVIEW
DECEMBER 29, 1995

WASHINGTON—An abrupt change of grand juries this year— that went unreported by the major press—may have major implications for the criminal inquiry of Independent Counsel Kenneth Starr into Whitewater-related matters and the death of Vincent Foster.

In about March 1995 Starr allowed his Washington grand jury to expire and replaced it with a new one, though he could have renewed the jury for another six-month term. The expired grand jury had been probing some of the most significant and sensitive areas of Starr's investigation for about a year, the Tribune-Review has learned. As a result of the move, Starr's prosecutors were forced to perform the tedious task of reviewing evidence heard by the previous grand jury and then rehashing it for the new panel.

Since new grand juries generally do not have the benefit of rehearing or even reading the original testimony, some experts believe that such a change causes jurors to lose the true flavor of a case.

In addition, it appeared the original grand jury would have completed its work in a very short period of time, if Starr had extended the panel's life. Starr was appointed independent counsel in August 1994 and took the reins of the Whitewater probe begun by Robert Fiske. In early 1994, soon after his appointment, Fiske had impaneled two grand juries, one in Washington and another in Little Rock. After Fiske was fired. Starr continued using the Fiske grand juries .

Under Fiske, the original Washington grand jury began probing issues relating to possible obstruction by administration officials of a Resolution Trust Co. investigation into links between Madison Guaranty, a failed Arkansas thrift, and the Clinton's Whitewater land partnership. Also, this grand jury reviewed issues related to the activities of White House officials after Vincent Foster's sudden July 20, 1993, death.

Starr incorporated Fiske's work into his own investigation and built upon it by using the Washington grand jury in investigate a key area Fiske had exempted from his grand jury: a review of Foster's death and the subsequent investigation. The Foster probe was led by Associate Independent Counsel Miquel Rodriguez.

The Tribune-Review has reported that during Rodriguez's handling of the Foster case before the Washington grand jury, major discrepancies surfaced between the official version of events surrounding Foster's death and the sworn testimony of several officials.

It also has been reported that Rodriguez resigned in March amid allegations that he was being hampered in conducting a full probe by his superiors and the FBI.

EXPIRING GRAND JURY

About the same time, Rodriguez was departing Washington in March to return to his position as an assistant U.S. attorney in Sacramento, the Washington grand jury term was coming up for renewal.

By then, the grand jury was two years old. It had been dealing with other matters since early 1993, and was assigned in 1994 to Fiske's Whitewater probe—giving it a remaining six months before its original term of 18 months was up.

Typically, Washington federal grand juries are seated for 18 months and may be renewed for six-month intervals at the discretion of the prosecutor and chief judge.

Fiske was fired just months after impaneling the grand juries, and Starr was appointed independent counsel on Aug. 4 1994, by a three-judge panel.

Starr picked up where Fiske left off and began using Fiske's grand juries.

With the Washington grand jury nearing the end of its 18-month term in the fall of 1994, Starr moved to have the grand jury renewed for another six months so the continuity of the probe would be preserved.

To seat a new grand jury at this point would mean that Starr's prosecutors would face the laborious chore of reviewing all the testimony gathered during the Fiske probe and then summarizing it for the new jury.

During the six-month extension, some of the most sensitive issues surfaced before the grand jury, sources close to the Starr probe have told the Tribune-Review.

Rodriguez took testimony from the U.S. Park Police, emergency workers and other officials examining Foster's death. Rodriguez soon after resigned in frustration, citing resistance from his superiors and FBI reluctance to investigate the case.

After he took over the probe. Starr retained the same FBI agents who worked for Fiske to review their own work.

Rodriguez's requests to FBI agents on the case fell on deaf ears.

For example, agents refused to have something as simple as a map of Fort Marcy Park drafted for jurors and witnesses.

Sources familiar with the grand jury at that time say that its members felt frustrated by both Fiske's and Starr's handling of the case.

Often, grand juries serve as a rubber stamp to satisfy prosecutors' desires, though occasionally these panels take an active role in an investigation and utilize their sweeping powers.

With Rodriguez gone and the witnesses all heard from in his limited grand jury probe into Foster's death, Starr was faced with renewing the grand jury for another six months. It was at this point that he decided to let the grand jury's term expire.

Starr has not given a reason for doing so.

His spokeswomen, Debbie Gershman, in Little Rock, said that she could not comment on any matter relating to the grand jury.

Historically, District Court for Washington grand juries serve no longer than two years.

But according to Jeanine Howard, grand jury administrator for the District Court in Washington, "a special grand jury"—which she defined as a grand jury assigned to an independent counsel—can be indefinitely renewed for six-month periods, as long, as the prosecutor and chief judge agree.

Howard said that special grand juries are typically renewed three times, giving them lives of about three years.

She recalls two recent special grand juries whose terms exceeded two years.

One reason for replacing grand jury, experts say, is because an investigation is destined to go for years, making it unfair to indefinitely tie up the time of citizens serving on the panel.

But all indications were that Starr's Washington grand jury was coming to an end and the major issues had been investigated with no wrongdoing found.

The resignation of Starr's deputy. Mark H. Tuohey III, in September was one indication of that possibility. Starr had appointed Tuohey, a Democrat with close ties to the Clinton administration, to head up the Washington probe. According to a source, Tuohey had accepted the job offer with a Washington firm in the spring of 1995, expecting the investigation would be wrapped up by the fall. Tuohey's associate, John Bates, was named deputy after Tuohey left.

Starr also had given a green light for Congress to hold hearings on issues relating to activities in Foster's office after his death—an indication that area had been cleared by his investigators. Starr's grand jury has been dormant for months on issues related to Foster's death, and Starr turned up no indictments

Yet, the grand jury was abruptly excused and a new grand jury impaneled.

With that done, Starr's prosecutors faced the task of reviewing evidence heard by the previous grand jury—though this was done in an abbreviated manner.

For this type of review, an expert or FBI agent will read transcripts and other documents relating to the original grand jury probe and give the new jurors his own interpretation of what the evidence and testimony means.

Typically witnesses are not recalled and the new grand jurors do not read the testimony themselves.

Another reason grand juries are sometimes allowed to expire is because members become bored and tired of the issues in the case.

Iran-Contra Independent Counsel Lawrence Walsh told the Tribune-Review his lengthy prosecution required several grand juries because "as a practical matter it becomes too big a drain on the jurors."

But that does not appear to have been the case with Starr's Washington grand jury.

Rodriguez, who said he was unaware of the change in grand juries, was surprised because the grand jury he worked with "was very interested in the testimony, demonstrative evidence and in further proceedings."

According to Thomas Scorza, professor of legal ethics at the University of Chicago and a former federal prosecutor, the changing of a grand jury "is not unusual." However, he said, most prosecutors don't like to have to transfer grand juries because "it's a large amount of work" and the process loses flavor for jurors who inherit "a paper case."

Scorza said he had not heard of a situation where a grand jury was expired to close down or reduce the momentum of an investigation. However, such a transfer, depending on the ethics of the prosecutors, could have such an effect, he said.

Starr's handling of his Whitewater probe has already raised some eyebrows. It was reported earlier this month that Starr had not been following standard prosecutorial procedure by not challenging claims of attorney-client privilege asserted by White House lawyers during the course of his inquiry.

In addition to the resignation of Rodriguez, Starr's trial counsel, Russell Hardin, resigned prematurely over a disagreement with Starr in handling the plea agreement with Webster Hubbell.

The criticism stemmed from the fact that Starr signed the agreement with Hubbell without adequately debriefing Hubbell and that Hubbell subsequently cooperated little with Starr's prosecutors. ∎

It's 'Desperation Time' For Clintons As Whitewater Trail Continues To Widen

Analysis

By Christopher Ruddy
FOR THE PITTSBURGH
TRIBUNE-REVIEW
MARCH 3, 1996

WASHINGTON—As the amorphous scandals related to the personal and official dealings of Bill and Hillary Rodham Clinton inexorably move forward, Washington insiders have told the Tribune-Review to expect more antics, desperation ploys and changed stories from the White House and fellow travelers.

Last week Senate Democrats threatened to conduct a filibuster to prevent Republicans from holding special Whitewater-related hearings past April 3.

Here are some other items from the Whitewater trail:

DAVID HALE

Former Little Rock Judge David Hale, as one federal prosecutor told the Tribune-Review, has been considered the "ace in the hole," first by Special Counsel Robert Fiske, and later by his replacement, Independent Counsel Ken Starr. Both Fiske and Starr have probed the Clintons' tangled Arkansas business dealings.

Hale is set to be Starr's chief prosecution witness this month in the trial of Arkansas Gov. Jim Guy Tucker and the Clintons' former business associates, Jim and Susan McDougal. Hale has alleged that Clinton coerced him into making a fraudulent Small Business Administration loan to Susan McDougal.

The Tribune-Review previously reported that Starr decided not to indict President Clinton on allegations made by Hale alone. As one prosecutor put it, "Hale versus the president won't fly."

But Hale will fly in the trial of Tucker and the McDougals. Speedy convictions of those defendants will be a bad omen for the Clintons and may convince other targets to "roll over" and cooperate with Starr.

Sources say Clinton's backers in Washington and Arkansas have been trying to damage Hale's credibility before he testifies. Senate Banking Committee Republicans rebuffed attempts by their Democratic colleagues to have Hale called before televised hearings in which inquisitors could rehash Hale's past wrongdoings.

Mark Stodola, a Pulaski County, Ark., prosecuting attorney, has decided to press ahead with state charges against Hale for insurance fraud. Stodala's moves have been played up in the Arkansas press, which, of course, will be read by many of the jurors who will make a judgment on Hale's credibility when he testifies against Tucker et al.

Starr objects to Stodola's actions, and in early February he issued a statement declaring it "highly unusual, if not unprecedented, for a state prosecutor to initiate separate criminal charges against an individual cooperating in an important federal investigation during the course of that person's cooperation."

Hale's sentencing is set for later this month, and his whereabouts have been something of a mystery.

This poses a problem for Stodola, who must serve Hale with a warrant.

Early in the probe, Fiske had some concerns for Hale's safety and assigned FBI protection to him. But FBI officials in Washington abruptly pulled the plug on that arrangement in 1994 between the time Fiske was fired and when Starr took day-to-day control of the probe.

"PRIMARY COLORS"

Life can initiate art. The anonymously penned political novel "Primary Colors" includes a James Carville-like character named Richard Jemmons. Jemmons, described as "manic, obsessive, very strange-looking, thin as a whipper," is obsessed with the 1989 cult film "Heathers," more specifically with one of its stars, Winona Ryder.

The "Heathers" plot is simple: Jason Dean, portrayed by Christian Slater, murders his fellow high schoolers by "suiciding" them—making the murders look like suicides. Dean has the art down to a fine process, including writing up "suicide" notes that don't necessarily refer to suicide but create a frame of mind indicating the victim just might kill himself.

Dean's girlfriend—played by Ryder—is bothered by two athletes whom Dean doesn't like, and he decides to "suicide them." He has her lure them into the woods, where they are murdered. He makes it look as if the boys are engaged in a homosexual tryst that ended in a double suicide. He even leaves a half-filled bottle of mineral water near the bodies, noting that if a guy doesn't "have a brewski in your hand you might as well be wearing a dress."

The police arrive and quickly determine suicide. Dean's maneuver is ingenious, the police have an easily buyable "script" to explain the unusual suicide of the two otherwise normal boys. The families have little desire to have the death investigated because an investigation would draw more attention to the supposed homosexuality.

Just as in the movie, Vincent Foster's body was found deep inside the wooded Fort Marcy Park, a well-known gay "cruising" area. A confidential witness told the FBI he found a half-filled wine cooler bottle near the body. After the death, Park Police were quick to fan speculation about the death by pointing out, off the record, to press and others that Fort Marcy was known for gay activity.

And just as in "Heathers," the first Park Police officer on the scene made an instant determination of suicide.

Of course, there is no evidence that Foster was homosexual or that he was ever in Fort Marcy alive or even knew of its existence. All of the forensic and circumstantial evidence demonstrates, according to some experts, that Foster's body was moved to Fort Marcy. If that is true, Fort Marcy may have been selected because it made for a nice script.

Some have pointed to a semen stain found on Foster's underwear, and noted in the Fiske report, indicating he may have been involved in a tryst before death. According to an FBI report, reviewed by the Tribune-Review but not yet released to the public, the FBI lab found a three to four inch stain of semen on the inside front portion of Foster's underwear. The expert said the stain could have remained on the underwear from a previous wearing and survived laundering. But he suggested the greater likelihood was that the stain was consistent with spontaneous ejaculation at death. Similarly, a urine stain was visible, though it was not tested.

MENA

The House Banking Committee, led by Republican Jim Leach of Iowa, has begun actively investigating goings-on at the tiny airport in Mena, Ark., in the state's northwestern mountains.

Leach is said to be looking into Mena's possible role as a conduit for narcotics shipped from Latin America during the 1980s, and whether Arkansas was a major center for money laundering.

New evidence may indicate that Leach's committee should determine whether smuggling is still going on at the seemingly sleepy airport.

Colorado-based journalist Scott Wheeler, who has covered the Mena story for several years and is considered an expert on the matter, says he has documentary evidence suggesting drug activity at the airport during the past year.

Wheeler, who continually photographs planes and their tail numbers at the airport, recently compared the numbers to official records in Customs Department computers. He discovered that a half dozen planes he photographed had tail numbers that had been illegally appropriated from legally registered planes. Wheeler said such funny business is cause for customs to seize a place, For instance, one turboprop aircraft he photographed at Mena just months ago has a tail number legally registered to a jet owner by General Electric Corp. Two other planes' tail numbers were not even found in Customs records, indicating they were in the country illegally.

Another Customs document obtained by Wheeler and shared with the Tribune-Review shows that in 1989 Dan Lasater, a friend and supporter of Bill Clinton, was the target of a federal drug probe. The record reads: "suspect in cocaine importation/distribution case— alleged; laundering of narcotics proceeds—alleged."

Charges were never brought against Lasater relating to this matter. However, in 1986 Lasater pleaded guilty to cocaine distribution charges. After serving a stint in a halfway house, he was reported to have found religion and become a changed man. In 1990, not a year after the customs file was created, Gov. Clinton pardoned his friend.

WINKING AT MURDER?

There is lots of evidence that since Bill Clinton fired William Sessions as FBI director, the bureau has been thoroughly politicized.

One shocking example is the FBI's investigative gyration concerning the 1987 deaths of two Arkansas teenagers, Kevin Ives and Don Henry. After their bodies were found on railroad tracks, apparently run over by a train, the state medical examiner decided the deaths were the result of a double suicide.

The case remained an unsolved mystery until Saline County detective John Brown discovered evidence pointing to possible police involvement in the deaths. Brown suggests the murders were related to the youths having been near a known "drug drop" location just outside Little Rock.

After encountering what he felt was obstruction from police officials, Brown turned to the FBI for help in 1994.

Late last year, FBI officials met with the parents of young Ives. Linda Ives told the Tribune-Review that Assistant Special Agent In Charge Bill Temple told her at the November meeting that she should consider "a criminal act had not occurred."

After the Tribune-Review published a report on the teens' deaths and the FBI's surprising

Continued on next page

Continued from page 169

conclusion, Little Rock's FBI Special Agent In Charge I.C. Smith took the unusual step of discussing the case with a local newspaper, the Benton Courier.

Smith told the newspaper that the FBI had never really investigated the case, but rather had tried to determine jurisdiction. This came as a real surprise to Ives' parents and to Brown, who worked closely with the FBI agent assigned to the investigation. Brown is now chief of police in Alexander, Ark.

Smith denied that Temple ever told Linda Ives that no criminal act took place. But a tape recording of a phone conversation with FBI agent Phyllis Cournan, who was present at the meeting with Temple, indicates otherwise.

"Basically, (Linda Ives) quoted (Temple) verbatim," Cournan states in the recording.

Smith also claimed there is "some doubt as to the causes of death," conceding only that "there may be some foul play involved."

Smith also took unusual aim at Brown, though not by name, when he told the newspaper that "one lawman . . . did nothing official to get at the truth" of the matter.

Brown said the attack on him by Smith may be rooted in the fact that Brown is being touted as a candidate for local sheriff.

The FBI, apparently, is endorsing his opponent. ■

Chapter Seven

The Documents Speak

The Documents

Herein follow excerpts from the actual official documents relating to the death of Vincent Foster and the subsequent investigations.

"SBCD" refers to the set of documents released by the Senate Banking Committee in 1995. "FR" refers to the June 30, 1994, report issued by Special Counsel Robert Fiske.

This outline is by no means exhaustive, but is intended to give the reader a general idea of the major discrepancies obvious from the official record itself.

The most exhaustive analysis of the official records is found in the Citizen's Independent Report by Hugh Sprunt. Copies of his report are available at cost by calling (214) 239-2679.

You decide if the official claims are supported by the evidence and testimony outlined in these pages.

1. THE BRIEFCASE

The official Park Police evidence report lists no briefcase found in Foster's Honda (SBCD 2193) or anywhere in the park.

But two civilian witnesses told the FBI they clearly saw a briefcase in Foster's car before the police arrived.

Patrick Knowlton, who first spotted the Honda, told the FBI (SBCD p. 1576):

```
stare at him.             stated, however, that upon returning
to the parking lot, he walked behind the brown Honda and peered
inside the vehicle where he observed a dark-blue jacket draped
over the driver's seat.  He further stated that he observed in
this Honda a leather briefcase or leather folder on the passenger
side seat.  He specifically recalls that this particular
briefcase or folder was darker than the interior of the vehicle
which, according to his recollection, was beige or light in
color.             further added that he specifically remembers
being surprised that anyone would leave a briefcase or folder on
the front seat of an unattended vehicle.  He could furnish no
other descriptive data regarding this vehicle or for that matter
the contents located within the vehicle.
```

The Confidential Witness who first found Foster's body also told the FBI he saw a briefcase (SBCD p. 1518):

```
distance of approximately fifteen to twenty feet.  He stated that
he clearly remembers that there was a four-pack wine cooler in
the front passenger floor of the car, he also recalls that the
interior of the car was blue in color and to the best of his
recollection, there was a suit coat or jacket and possibly a
brown briefcase in the car; he can't recall whether these items
were in the rear or front of the car.
```

After the police arrived, Fairfax County paramedic Sgt. George Gonzalez told the FBI he saw a briefcase in the Honda (SBCD p. 1351):

```
        After walking away from the location of the body,
GONZALEZ looked at the two vehicles in the park for further
identifiers related to the victim.  The Honda contained a
necktie, suit coat, and a black briefcase/attache case.  Based on
the manner in which FOSTER was clothed, GONZALEZ determined the
vehicle to have been driven by the victim.
```

The first police officer on the scene told Senate investigators he may have seen a briefcase (SBCD p. 968):

```
13      Q    Did you see a briefcase?
14      A    Possibly.  It doesn't stick in my mind right now.
15  I believe our concern at the time was if indeed this was a
16  suicide, that the department was going to be investigating,
17  a visual inspection of the car would determine whether or
18  not there may be a note in there, or some type of paperwork
19  or something, you know, if there was a connection between
20  the car and the person up the hill, maybe make that
21  connection.
```

Fairfax EMS Technician Todd Hall also told the FBI he saw a briefcase (SBCD p. 1162):

```
        Upon arriving at Fort Marcy Park, HALL noticed an
unoccupied brown car with the engine running parked in the lot.
He noted that the car was not parked in a space.  After coming
out of the woods, HALL noticed a second vehicle that contained a
suit jacket matching the trousers worn by FOSTER.  HALL noted
that the jacket was laying on the back seat of the car.  The car
was a foreign make, possibly a Toyota Corolla.  The car was
further described to be a 4-door sedan, light blue in color.
Also contained in the car was a briefcase; HALL believed FOSTER's
tie may have been in the car, but he was not sure.
```

2. TWO MEN IN AND AROUND FOSTER'S CAR

Special Counsel Fiske in his report states that a male-female couple, two Washington professionals, were in the park when the police arrived. Fiske said "Neither individual heard a gunshot while in the park or observed anything unusual" (FR p. 35).

Both witnesses said they drove into the park about 45 minutes before Foster's body was found. The female witness told Fiske's FBI investigators she saw a man sitting in Foster's Honda (SBCD p. 1470):

```
                         stated that she left work late afternoon and
in the company of a close friend,                  , drove to Fort
Marcy Park in her white Nissan      , arriving at Fort Marcy
Park sometime between 5:15 and 5:30 p.m.  To the best of her
recollection, she maintained that upon entering the parking lot
at Fort Marcy Park, she noted that the only vehicle in the
parking area was a relatively old (mid-1980's) Honda, possibly a
Honda Accord, either tan or dark in color, parked close to the
entry of the parking lot, adjacent to a path leading to the
Northern section of the park.         believed that this
particular Honda was parked with the front of the vehicle facing
the park area and to the best of her recollection, believes a
white male was seated in the driver's seat of this particular
vehicle.  Although she was extremely vague on the description of
this individual, she believed the occupant had dark hair and
could have been bare-chested.  After passing this particular
vehicle, she drove approximately mid-way into the parking area,
backing her Nissan      into a parking space.
```

The male witness said he saw a blonde-haired male standing near Foster's car with the hood up (SBCD p. 1474):

```
          They arrived at Fort Marcy Park at approximately 5:00
p.m.  As they drove into the parking lot, he observed a vehicle,
possibly a small station wagon or "hatchback" model, brownish in
color, parked to his left.  The vehicle was parked close to the
path leading up to Fort Marcy, with the front of the car pulled
into the parking space.  The hood of the vehicle was up and a
white male was standing in the vicinity of the vehicle.  He
described the white male as in his mid- to late 40's,
approximately six feet in height, medium build, long blonde hair
and beard, appeared unclean and unkept.
```

3. THE MENACING MAN

Fiske states that a witness, whose name is Patrick Knowlton, arrived at Fort Marcy and spotted a man sitting next to Foster's Honda in a blue sedan, who gave him a menacing look. He told the FBI he could identify the man, but here's what the FBI said in his witness statement (SBCD p. 1526):

```
proceeded into the park to urinate.  He further mentioned that
this male was staring at him making him,               feel
extremely nervous and uneasy.  He could not further identify this
particular individual nor his attire and stated that he would be
unable to recognize him in the future.
```

4. WHEN DID THE WHITE HOUSE LEARN OF THE DEATH?

The Park Police arrived at the park at 6:12 pm (SBCD p. 2252). Incredibly, they claim that they did not notify the White House until about 8:30 p.m. that evening.

A Secret Service memo written on the night of Foster's death states that call was received at 20:30 hours or 8:30 p.m. (SBCD p. 2076):

```
                                        UNITED STATES GOVERNMENT
                                        M E M O R A N D U M
                                        U.S. SECRET SERVICE

      DATE:       07/20/93    22:01 pm

      REPLY TO

      ATTN OF:  SA SCOTT MARBLE

      SUBJECT:  DEATH OF VINCENT FOSTER, DEPUTY ASSISTANT TO THE PRESIDENT AND
                DEPUTY COUNSEL (SEE ATTACHED)

      TO:       SAIC INTELLIGENCE DIVISION


      )N 7/20/93, AT 2130 HRS, LT WOLTZ, USSS/UD - WHB, CONTACTED THE ID/DD AND
      \DVISED THAT AT 2030 HRS, THIS DATE, HE WAS CONTACTED BY LT GAVIN, US PARK
      )OLICE, WHO PROVIDED THE FOLLOWING INFORMATION:
```

Seemingly supportive of this claim is lead Park Police investigator John Rolla's testimony. Rolla said he only learned that Foster was a White House official after he left the death scene and returned to the lot at about 8:20 p.m. Rolla told the FBI he found the White House ID this way (SBCD p. 481):

```
            Rolla continued by stating that after departing the
      death scene he returned to the Fort Marcy parking lot where the
      search of the 1989 Honda was being coordinated by Investigator
      Braun and photographs of the Honda were being taken by Officer
      Simonello.  Rolla, however, did physically observe the Honda and
      its contents stating that he noted a man's jacket, similar to the
      decedent's trousers, was neatly folded over the back of the front
      passenger seat and that further examination of the jacket noted a
      wallet inside the left pocket which contained, to' the best of his
      recollection, approximately $300 in cash.  While he did not take
      control of the material in the 1989 Honda, he does remember
      observing a White House identification badge with a photo of
      Vincent Foster located on the front passenger seat under the suit
      jacket.  Additionally he recalls a piece of paper in the vehicle
      with the names of what apparently were three Washington, D.C.
      physicians.  Investigator Rolla could furnish no information
      relative to the time the 1989 Honda arrived at Fort Marcy Park or
      any vehicle information which might assist in determining time of
      arrival at Fort Marcy Park.
```

Rolla told a similar story to Senate investigators in a sworn deposition (SBCD pp. 393-394):

> 10   Q   Did you get any keys?
> 11   A   I searched his pants pockets. I couldn't find a
> 12 wallet or nothing in his pants pockets. Later on,
> 13 Investigator Braun and myself searched the car. I
> 14 retrieved the jacket, retrieved the wallet, there was
> 15 identification, under the jacket on the seat was a White
> 16 House identification chain thing with a photo ID on it. It
> 17 wasn't really until then I knew that this was a White House
> 18 guy. We better call Secret Service. Again, not knowing
> 19 who he was, a million people work at the White House, so,
> 20 you know, obviously it was -- White House Communications
> 21 was what the ID said, so we weren't sure.
> 22   We searched the car and we were puzzled why we

Also supportive of Rolla's story is the chronology told to the FBI by Rolla's superior Lt. Patrick Gavin, who said he left the park by 7:30 p.m., after spending 30-45 minutes at the scene, without knowing that Foster was a White House official (SBCD p. 1555):

> LT. GAVIN stated that he stayed in the area for approximately 30-45 minutes, insuring that witnesses in the parking lot were interviewed and the vehicles in the parking lot were checked. By the time he left, the evidence officer, PETER SIMINELLO, had arrived on the scene. LT. GAVIN stated that he thought that the victim might possibly have been a government appointee because of the Arkansas tags. He noted, however, that the White House identification was discovered in the vehicle after he left the scene. To the best of his recollection, one of the detectives at the scene called him later in the evening, informing him that they had found White House identification for FOSTER. He stated that within ten minutes of receiving that call, he called the U.S. Secret Service, notifying them. LT. GAVIN stated shortly thereafter (within 5 to 10 minutes), MR. BILL BURTON, who identified himself as the Assistant White House Chief of Staff, contacted him by phone. LT. GAVIN stated that he asked for a callback number and was provided two numbers by BURTON; (202) 456-1414 and (202) 456-6797.

But the White House's version of events, supported by Rolla and Gavin, doesn't match other testimony that shows the police knew Foster was a White House official much earlier.

Fairfax paramedic Richard Arthur told the FBI that he saw Park Police gaining access to Foster's car when he returned to the parking lot, shortly before he left the scene. He left the scene no later than 6:37 p.m. (SBCD p. 1383):

```
          Once back in the parking area, the U.S. Park Police
took all the EMT's names.  He observed them gaining access to a
cream colored car with a suit jacket and tie in it, looking for
identification of some sort.  ARTHUR was on the scene
approximately 30-40 minutes.
```

And Senior Park Police Investigator Cheryl Braun contradicted Rolla by saying she searched Foster's car first, and then called Gavin to notify the White House. Braun said Gavin was notified by 7:30-7:45 p.m. (SBCD p. 561):

```
          Sergeant BRAUN advised that at some point, she and
Officer SIMINELLO went back to the parking lot to check the car,
adding that she took several polaroid pictures and Officer'
SIMINELLO took 35mm photos of the car.  She stated that she began
a search of the car and found a suit jacket with a wallet inside
and White House identification on the front passenger seat.
BRAUN stated that she advised another officer to call the Shift
Commander and inform him of this new development while she
continued to search the car.  She advised that approximately
thirty minutes passed whereupon she learned that the Shift
Commander had never been notified and she then, herself, called,
advising him of the White House identification at approximately
7:30-7:45 p.m.  Sergeant BRAUN stated that at about the time she
was completing the search of the car, the coroner and ambulance
arrived to remove the body and take it to Fairfax County Hospital
(morgue).  She advised that she did not learn until later that
MR. FOSTER was a Deputy White House Counsel.
```

In a sworn deposition to Senate Investigators, Braun told how she, not Rolla, went through Foster's Honda (SBCD pp. 502-503):

```
15    Q    Okay.  So you then go back to the parking lot
16  area?
17    A    Right.
18    Q    To look at the car?
19    A    Right.
20    Q    What do you find in the car?
21    A    I went through the car.
22         I found normal stuff in the car, sunglasses,

 1  photos, registration.
 2         I found on the front--
 3    Q    Do you remember who the registration was?
 4    A    Yeah.
 5         It was to Vincent Foster.
 6         On the front seat of the vehicle was the jacket
 7  which matched Mr. Foster's pants.
 8         It was like folded neatly on the seat.  Inside of
 9  the jacket was--inside pocket--was his wallet.
10         And as I recall, the credentials I thought were
11  tucked like not in a pocket but in the jacket like
12  underneath it or inside the fold of it.
13         And they were the White House credentials which
14  identified him as Vincent Foster and the picture resembled
15  the body that we had been looking at.
16    Q    Did the name Vincent Foster mean anything to you
17  at that point?
18    A    At that time, no, it did not.
19    Q    Okay.  But you saw White House credentials?
20    A    Right.
21    Q    All right.
22         Did that change anything about the way you were
                                                      24
 1  doing your investigation?
 2    A    Yeah.  Well, that means that notifications had to
 3  be made.
 4         So I had another officer make a notification to,
 5  or I asked him to make a notification, to our shift
 6  commander.
 7         And then I later found out that that notification
 8  wasn't made, so I made the notification to myself--or I made
 9  the notification myself.
10    Q    Whom did you notify?
11    A    The shift commander, who was Lieutenant Gavin.
```

When Fairfax County paramedics returned to their firehouse (before 7 p.m.) they were aware Foster was a White House official. Lt. Bianchi, their supervisor, told the

FBI that upon hearing of the White House connection he asked the paramedics to write detailed reports (SBCD p. 1365):

> BIANCHI was at Station 1 when the FCFRD personnel who responded to the initial call later returned to the station. BIANCHI heard two people who had been on the call, possibly TODD HALL and RICK ARTHUR, say that it had been a strange incident. BIANCHI also heard from the returning FCFRD personnel that the victim was deceased and had been employed at the White House. In particular, IACONE already knew that the victim had been employed at the White House when he returned to Station 1. When BIANCHI learned that the victim was a White House employee, he instructed HALL and IACONE to make their reports on the incident very detailed.

5. POOL OF BLOOD AND EXIT WOUND

On page 36 of his report, Fiske states that after Dr. Donald Haut arrived at the scene the body was rolled over "and those present observed a large pool of blood located on the ground where Foster's head had been. Haut observed a large exit wound in the back of the skull."

Yet, Haut in his statement to the FBI made no mention of the large pool of blood (SBCD pp. 1659-1660):

> In examining the back of the head HAUT describes the blood being clotted. Although the volume of blood was small, HAUT did recall that the blood was matted and clotted under the head. HAUT pulled on FOSTER's right shoulder turning him to the left in order to conduct his examination. HAUT recalls FOSTER's head being close to the summit of the hill, further noting that it was more on the slope of the hill than at the top of the hill.

Haut also never told the FBI that the exit wound was large. In fact he told the FBI that the wound was consistent with a low-velocity gun. (Foster was found with a high-velocity gun) (SBCD p. 1660):

> After examination of the back of FOSTER's head, HAUT believed that the wound was consistent with a low velocity weapon. HAUT recalled a separate case in which a .25 caliber rifle caused a much more devastating wound to the victim. HAUT did not feel FOSTER's demise was anything out of the ordinary.

Lead police investigator Rolla was also present when the body was rolled over. He told Senate Investigators he saw a small exit wound (SBCD pp. 401-402):

```
 9      Q    What about bone fragments?  Have you been
10   involved in cases where there were shootings and no bone
11   fragments recovered?
12      A    Certainly.  The size of the wound is not large
13   and bone fragments would be tiny.  You know, even the
14   FBI -- you know, much better than us, they had their expert
15   lab people, but, again, they searched basically an area
16   around his head.  I don't know how far bone fragments would
17   go.  I don't know.  I don't know where they are, I don't
18   know if they got stuck in the scene.  I probed his head and
19   there was no big hole there.  There was no big blowout.
20   There weren't brains running all over the place.  There was
21   blood in there.  There was a mushy spot.  I initially
22   thought the bullet might still be in his head.  Could have
 1   been the brain pushed up against that hole.  There's no big
 2   hole or big blowout in his head.
 3      Q    So the exit wound was small?
 4      A    Right.
```

Not mentioned in the Fiske report are the FBI statements of Fairfax EMT worker Kory Ashford, who placed Foster's body in the body bag (SBCD pp. 1347, 1559):

```
          ASHFORD and the driver of his EMS vehicle placed
FOSTER's body in a body bag for transport to the morgue.  ASHFORD
lifted FOSTER from behind the shoulders, cradling the victim's
head.  The driver of the EMS vehicle lifted FOSTER from the area
of his feet as the corpse was placed into the body bag.  ASHFORD
did not recall seeing any blood while placing FOSTER in the bag.
ASHFORD did not recall any blood getting on his uniform or on the
disposable gloves he wore while handling the body.  The name of
the EMS vehicle driver could not be recalled.
```

```
FOSTER.  ASHFORD did not recall receiving any assistance from
U.S. Park Police personnel in placing FOSTER's body into a body
bag.  ASHFORD was also unable to recall the name of the doctor at
Fairfax Hospital, who pronounced FOSTER dead.  ASHFORD did not
recall seeing any blood on the ground at the location of FOSTER's
body.
```

6. The X-Rays

The government has no X-rays taken of Vincent Foster during his autopsy. These would substantiate the nature of the exit wound. The Fiske report states that there were no X-rays because the machine was "inoperable."

The autopsy report says otherwise (SBCD p. 370):

5.	Bullet	Calibre	—	—														
	found:	Shotgun																

Photographs made: Yes ✓ No___   X-rays made: Yes ✓ No___

.MARKS: FOR PROFESSIONAL USE ONLY

The Park Police report quotes the medical examiner as having reviewed the non-existent X-rays (SBCD p. 2128):

> During the autopsy Dr. Byer noted that the bullet trajectory was "upward and backward" exiting in the center line of the back of the head. Dr. Byer stated that X-rays indicated that there was no evidence of bullet fragments in the head.

7. THE DEPRESSION

Fiske states Foster was clinically depressed, a state of mind that led to his suicide.

Oddly, Foster's friends and associates told the FBI they noted nothing unusual in his behavior before his death. For example, Webster Hubbell, longtime friend of Foster's, told the FBI he did not notice anything unusual with Foster before he died (SBCD pp. 1478-1479):

> Hubbell said that he was not aware that Foster was experiencing any type of stress. Foster never talked to Hubbell about missing the comfort zone of the Rose Law Firm where they had worked for more than 20 years. They just never talked about it one way or the other. Rather, Foster talked about being on this great adventure in Washington, D.C. Hubbell said he and Foster were very close to the President and First Lady and discussed with each other, prior to coming to Washington, that I'll go if you go. Hubbell believed that Foster thought that the option of going back to Little Rock or the Rose Law Firm would have been an acknowledgement of failure. This was during the time of the Travel Office situation. Hubbell said if you really

> want to understand Foster, to look at his recent speech at the
> University of Arkansas. He believed Foster wrote the speech
> after someone else had worked on it. Foster rewrote the speech
> himself on the plane.

> Hubbell described Foster in the following terms:
> reserved; not loud, held everything inside; loved his children
> more than anything, very close to them; had no weaknesses; very
> smart; quiet; meticulous in his work; spent time gathering facts
> before drawing conclusions; frustrated with White House Travel
> Office issues - attention in the media, unhappy with the FBI and
> internal report on the Travel Office matter; someone who worked
> until 10:00 to 11:00 p.m. each night and also on Saturdays and
> Sundays; hadn't gotten away from his White House work. When
> asked if he had observed any noticeable behavioral or emotional
> changes in Vincent Foster prior to his death, Hubbell said that
> in hindsight, he realized that the no time off from work was
> wearing on us all. Hubbell described a "once a week" dinner or
> "Arkansas night" frequently attended by Foster. Others who would
> often join the group included Deb Coyle (phonetic), Bruce
> Lindsey, Marsha Scott, John Emerson, Sheila and Burl Anthony and
> other out-of-town friends. Hubbell said Foster was a great
> friend, but not the life of the party. He did not notice Foster
> acting differently in the days or weeks before his death.

Foster's secretary, who had worked with Foster since he started at the White House, told the FBI she noticed nothing unusual in his behavior (SBCD pp. 1444, 1448):

> She viewed him as reserved, not depressed or unhappy. He could
> enjoy a joke with others in the office, but was a very hard
> worker and would ask people to "keep it down" if their talking
> disturbed him. The only time he seemed to be more agitated than
> usual was when he was under time pressures. He had a very long
> fuse, so it was relatively rare for him to show agitation. The
> Friday before his death, as he was preparing to go away for the
> weekend, he needed a long distance beeper to take with him and he
> and GORHAM had a misunderstanding that he needed it right away.
> He showed agitation at that time, but did not lose his temper.
> Even with hindsight, GORHAM did not see anything in FOSTER's
> behavior which would indicate a distressed state of mind. She
> recalled BETSY POND and LINDA TRIPP saying to her that FOSTER did
> not seem to be concentrating the morning of his death.

> FOSTER had not ever made any statements or comments to
> GORHAM indicating despondency and she had not noticed any
> physical changes in FOSTER from the time she started as his
> secretary to his death.

Yet Fiske asserted in his report, "Although no one noticed a loss of appetite, it was obvious to many that he had lost weight."

This assertion finds no corroboration in official medical documents, which show Foster actually gained weight after coming to work at the White House.

Foster's doctor told the FBI that on December 31, 1992, Foster weighted 197 pounds (SBCD p. 1676):

> FOSTER's weight in 1987 was 200 pounds. As of August 1990 he was 207 pounds. His weight on December 31, 1992 was 194 pounds and WATKINS had made a note that he was on a diet and exercising.

And the weight on the autopsy indicated he had gained weight (SBCD p. 364):

...opsy Authorized by: __Dr. Donald Haut — Fairfax County__		Persons Present at Autopsy:	
...dy Identified by: __U.S. Park Police Tag — 7/20/93__		James C. Beyer, M.D.; Dec. Morrissette, U.S. Park Po	

...jor. complete __X__	jaw _____	neck _____	arms _____
...or. color __pale red__	distribution: __posterior__		
• __48__ Race __W__ Sex __M__ Length __76½"__	Weight __197__	Eyes __hazel__ Pupils:	
...ir __greying black__ Mustache __no__	Beard __no__	Circumcised __yes__	Bo...

8. METAL DETECTOR SEARCH

The Park Police claim they conducted an extensive search for the bullet in Fort Marcy two days after the death (SBCD p. 2140):

OFFENSE/INCIDENT: __DEATH INVESTIGATION__	CASE NO: __93-30502__
INCIDENT LOCATION: __FT MARCY__	DATE: __07-20-93__
DISTRICT/FIELD OFFICE: __D2__	TIME: __1804__
REPORTING OFFICER: __FERSTL__	MCL#: __166__
C.I.B. INVESTIGATOR: __MORRISSETTE__	

RESULTS OF INVESTIGATION

On Thursday, 07-22-93 at approximately 1000 hours, myself and Tech Johnson responded to the area of Ft Marcy. Upon arrival we met with Sgt Rule and Detective Morrissette. We were led to the area of the death and proceeded to conduct a search of the vicinity with a metal detector. After a lengthy search for a bullet the results were negative.

Park Police Sgt. Rule in his sworn deposition gave more details of the search they claim was conducted (SBDC pp. 1277-1278):

```
5       Q    Were you present when that search was done?
6       A    Yes, I was.
7       Q    How big of an area was searched with the metal
8   detectors there?
9       A    If you come down from the cannons it is a fairly
10  open area and we felt that that area could reasonably be
11  searched with the number of people that we had --
12      Q    How many was that?
13      A    That day I believe there was, again, two ID
14  technicians and two detectives; myself and Morrissette
15  again.  And I think, again, it was Shelly Hill and Wayne
16  Johnson were the ID techs.
17      Q    So that's four all together?
18      A    I think it was four, to the best of my
19  recollection.  We looked at it and evaluated the position
20  that the body had been recovered.  The way we felt, having
21  already gone to the autopsy, we felt that the round was
22  going upward and felt that probably it was going to

1   continue on for some distance but that with the open area
2   behind where the body was laid out would be, you know, the
3   best place to be searched.
4           Beyond this open area it got into heavily-wooded
5   area and we felt that the probability of recovering the
6   round in that area in a reasonable time span would be
7   pretty small.  We searched this open area and I would --
8   geez..I tell you -- I would say maybe 30 yards by 30 yards,
9   that's just a big ballpark guess.
10          We searched that area and then what myself and
11  Detective Morrissette did, and I think the ID techs were
12  doing it also while they were finishing up, is check the
13  area of the trees, the visible area of the trees that
14  faced -- in other words, if the body was like this
15  (indicating) and the gunshot was believed to be going out
16  in this direction (indicating), we checked the areas of the
17  trees from, say, the ground up to see if we could locate
18  any impact point that the bullet may have struck these
19  trees because it was really pretty difficult to estimate
20  how much velocity this bullet would have when it exited the
21  body and obviously it exited the body, it wasn't recovered
22  in the autopsy.
                                                        16
1           We didn't find anything in either the visual
2   search of the trees or the ground and, again, you are
3   constantly hitting bottle caps and any little metal piece
4   in the ground, that's very painstaking, very laborious.  It
5   is not like the metal detecting at the beach that a lot of
6   people see.
7       Q    About how long did you guys spend doing this
8   metal detector search?
```

FBI agents working for Special Counsel Fiske visited Fort Marcy on April 4, 1994. They set-up an extensive area to be searched near where the police claim the body was found (SBCD p. 1905):

```
        The site had been previously surveyed and search grid
stakes positioned in order to measure the exact location of any
evidence recovered.  A five meter grid was set up and marked so
that none of the areas where the "missing bullet" could have
logically reached the end of its trajectory were omitted from the
search pattern.  Two and one-half meter grids had been set up in
the area where the body was positioned and all of this area was
examined thoroughly with metal detectors and by digging and hand
sifting/screening the soil and remaining debris.  The entire grid
area was systematically searched with metal detectors as well as
much of the surrounding areas adjacent to and below the grid.
```

The FBI evidence log shows they found numerous metal objects, including 12 modern-day bullets in grid areas the police claimed they had searched. Astonishingly, two cartridges cases, two casings and one bullet were found on or near the very path the body was found. Most items were found near the surface (SBCD p. 1910):

EVIDENCE RECOVERY LOG

LOCATION _FORT MARCY NAT'L PARK_   PERSONNEL _See attached list of personnel on scene._   PAGE _1_ OF ___

DATE _April 4, 1994_

CASE IDENTIFIER _MCZARK 290-LR-35163_

PREPARER'S ASSISTANTS ____ _Special Agent_ ____ _FBI LABORATORY_

#	DESCRIPTION	WHERE FOUND	RECOVERED BY	PHOTO	MARKING DIRECT = D INDIRECT = I	PAC M
1	1 Bullet	QUADRANT N10 E5	J.E. CORBY	YES	I	Plast
2	1 Bullet	QUADRANT N5 E5	J.E. CORBY	YES	I	Plast
3	6 CARTRIDGE CASES	QUADRANT N0 E10	J.E. CORBY	YES	I	Br. E
4	2 Bullets	QUADRANT N0 E5	J.E. CORBY	YES	I	Br. E

5	1 CARTRIDGE CASE	QUADRANT N0 E5	T.E. CORBY	YES	I	Br. E
6	1 Bullet	QUADRANT OO	J.E. CORBY	YES	I	Br. E
7	1 CARTRIDGE CASE	QUADRANT OC	J.E. CORBY	YES	I	Br. E
8	1 Bullet	QUADRANT S5 E5	T.E. CORBY	YES	I	Br.0.
9	1 Bullet	QUADRANT N0 E10	T.E. CORBY	YES	I	Br. E
10	1 Bullet	QUADRANT S5 E10	J.E. CORBY	YES	I	Br.E
11	1 Bullet	QUADRANT S5 E5	J.E. Corby	YES	I	Br. E
12	2 Bullets	QUADRANT S5 E5	J.E. Corby	YES	I	Br. E
13	2 CARTRIDGE CASES	QUADRANT S10 E5	J.E. Corby	—	I	Br. E
i	2 CARTRIDGE CASES	FOUND ON OIL NEAR PATH				
	2 shtshell casings	Below 2 QUADRANT	T.E. Corby	NO	I	Br. E
	1 Bullet	N5 E10				

Another indication contradicting police claims of an intensive search is the large number of metal civil war artifacts Fiske's team found during their search (SBCD pp. 1911, 1912):

```
                           GWMP
              Fort Marcy Artifact Inventory


         N0E0
               Harness, Hardware, Horseshoe (1), Ferrous

         N0E15
               Unidentified, Metal Object, Ferrous

         N5E0
               Hardware, Screw, Pitcock?, White metal

         N5E5
               Military, Button, w/ Eagle, Copper alloy

         N5E10
               Ammunition, Minie Ball, .57 Caliber, Lead
               Ammunition, Shot, Lead

         N5E15
               Coin, Penny, 1969, Copper

         N5W5
               Hardware, Nail, Common, Ferrous

         S5E10
               Hardware, Nail, Common, Ferrous
               Hardware, Nail, Unidentified, Ferrous

         S5E15
               Ammunition, Minie Ball, .57 Caliber, Lead
               Military, Button, w/ Eagle, copper alloy
               Hardware, Nail, Common (4), Ferrous

         S5E20
               Container, Barrel, Hoop (2), ferrous
               Military, canteen Lip, white metal

         N10E0
               Hardware, Nail, Rosehead, Ferrous
               Unidentified, Metal Object (Cog tooth?), Ferrous
               Hardware, Clasp, Haversack, Copper alloy
               Hardware, Wire, White metal

         N10E10
               Hardware, Nail, Common (8), Ferrous
               Hardware, Nail, Unidentified, Ferrous
               Hardware, Wire (3), Ferrous
```

<u>N10W5</u>
    Hardware, Nail, Rosehead (2) , Ferrous   **CONFID**
    Hardware, Nail, Common, Ferrous
    Hardware, Nail, Unidentified, Ferrous   OIC 0

<u>N15E0</u>
    Ammunition, Minie Ball, .57 Caliber, lead
    Container, Unidentified, Lid, White metal
Fort Marcy Inventory (cont)

<u>N15E5</u>
    Ammunition, Minie Ball, .57 Caliber (2), Lead
    Ammunition, Minie Ball, .69 Caliber, Lead
    Ammunition, Minie Ball, .57 Caliber, Lead

<u>N20E0</u>
    Toy, marble, Glass
    Ammunition, Minie Ball, .57 Caliber, Lead
    Hardware, Nail, Unidentified, Ferrous

<u>PATH BELOW GRID</u>
    Ammunition, Minie Ball, .57 Caliber, Lead
    Unidentified, Metal Object, Ferrous
    Hardware, Rivet, Haversack, Copper Alloy
    Ammunition, Cartridge Case, Brass
    Container, Can, Pull Tab (2), Aluminum
    Machinery, Plate, White metal
    Hardware, Nail, Common, Ferrous
    Harness, Hardware, Horseshoe, Frag, Ferrous
    Hardware, Spike, Ferrous

Appendix

The Daily Telegraph

- NEWSPAPER OF THE YEAR -

NO. 43,425

THURSDAY, FEBRUARY 2, 1995

Suicide is hard to sell

As the Whitewater investigation gains momentum, much may hinge on the suspicious death of a Clinton aide. In Washington, AMBROSE EVANS-PRITCHARD finds growing belief in a cover-up theory

Main picture: AMBROSE EVANS PRITCHARD

MORE THAN a year and a half has passed since the body of Vincent Foster was found in a secluded Virginia park near the headquarters of the CIA. Controversy about the highest ranking suicide in almost half a century should have subsided by now. Two investigations found no evidence of foul play, and the press has been almost unanimous in accepting that the Deputy White House Counsel shot himself in the mouth during a bout of depression.

But the mystery continues to fester. A growing number of people suspect that there may be a darker story behind the death of the handsome, soft-spoken man who accom-

Body of evidence: Chris Ruddy (above) believes Vincent Foster's body was found near here. Police say it was at another cannon. From top: Foster, William Sessions, Webb Hubbell, Kenneth Starr

MORE THAN a year and a half has passed since the body of Vincent Foster was found in a secluded Virginia park near the headquarters of the CIA. Controversy about the highest ranking suicide in almost half a century should have subsided by now. Two investigations found no evidence of foul play, and the press has been almost unanimous in accepting that the Deputy White House Counsel shot himself in the mouth during a bout of depression.

But the mystery continues to fester. A growing number of people suspect that there may be a darker story behind the death of the handsome, soft-spoken man who accompanied the Clintons from Little Rock to Washington. He was no ordinary White House aide, after all. One of the Four Musketeers from the Rose law firm, he had been mentor, law partner, and intimate friend of Hillary Clinton.

At the White House he had been the keeper of the secrets, managing the personal financial affairs of the President and the First Lady. Within hours of his death a high-level raiding party ransacked his office, removing a number of files, including the Whitewater papers.

The doubts are not confined to anti-Clinton enthusiasts. A member of the Foster family believes that *The Sunday Telegraph* that he no longer believes the official verdict of suicide. He suspects the death may have been a political murder with elements of government complicity. He says some other members of the family are increasingly willing to entertain that idea.

There are also murmurs at the Federal Bureau of Investigations. In a recent interview with the *Telegraph*, a high-level FBI source spoke about a cover-up by the US Park Police and voiced suspicions that the abrupt firing of FBI Director William Sessions on July 19, 1993 — the day before Foster's death — was in some sinister way linked. The man who took over as acting Director did not assert FBI jurisdiction over the case, leaving the investigation in the hands of a Park Police officer with no homicide experience.

Now it appears that the Whitewater special prosecutor, Kenneth Starr, is beginning to view the Foster mystery as the Rosetta Stone that can open up the Whitewater complex of scandals.

Last month his lawyers grilled Webb Hubbell — the confessed felon who once ran the Clinton Justice Department — questioning him about Vince Foster, according to sources in Little Rock. Starr also called a number of Park Police officers before a grand jury, read them the perjury statutes in a pointed manner, then interrogated them at length about discrepancies in testimony.

If we are really watching the unravelling of a colossal cover-up involving police officers, rescue workers, FBI agents, and the inner circle of the White House — a very big "if" — then much of the credit must go to a young Irish-American reporter called Christopher Ruddy who has been keeping the story alive in a lone crusade.

RUDDY has the right background for a sleuth. His father was a veteran of a New York police force. "My dad would never have looked the other way. That's part of what motivates me," he said. Before starting his career as a journalist he took a masters degree at the London School of Economics and then taught history in one of the toughest schools of the South Bronx.

It was Ruddy who broke the key stories in the *New York Post* last year that revealed that the rescue workers had doubts about the suicide theory. He reported that the paramedics were surprised by the lack of blood on the ground. There was no soil on Foster's shoes. The body was laid out "as if in a coffin". The suicide weapon, a Colt of

pre-First World War vintage that his family could not identify, was in his hand — always a red flag for experienced homicide investigators. The crucial crime scene photos were ruined by under-exposure.

"What we found out was that the Park Police never did a proper investigation," said Ruddy. The case was treated as a suicide from the beginning. The police did not bother to speak to nearby residents and failed to interview an old man who spends all day in the park and is a goldmine of information on everything that goes on there.

For a few weeks Ruddy, 30, was a star. But America's establishment press was not willing to pursue the mystery too deeply — nor was the *New York Post*, a gutsy, well-written tabloid. It is owned by Rupert Murdoch. As the first wave of interest in the Foster case subsided, Ruddy was pulled off the story.

The editor of the *New York Post*, Ken Chandler, praised Ruddy but said that there was a limit as to how far the *Post* could go in covering the story. He told one magazine: "The truth is, Chris Ruddy trod where others fear to tread. When you do that, you get criticism and scorn heaped upon you. When you're

writing about something you can't get answers to, you have to keep pushing, and he did."

Ruddy persisted. With the backing of the Western Journalism Centre, a California group that funds investigative reporting, he launched a guerilla campaign to get the story out. He published a document known as the "Ruddy Memorandum", attacking the report of former Whitewater prosecutor Robert Fiske, and chipped away at public apathy with a barrage of newspaper advertisements paid for by wealthy donors and grass roots fund-raising. In November he was employed full-time on the story by the *Pittsburgh Tribune-Review*.

He says the facts of the case simply do not point to suicide. Why were Foster's fingerprints not found on the gun? Why were no skull fragments found? Why was the gun in Foster's right hand when he was left-handed? Why was no attempt made to vacuum carpet fibres and blonde hairs found on his clothes? Why did the chief medical examiner claim there were no X-rays when he is quoted in the Park Police report talking about the results of X-rays? The list goes on. But the big question is over the

A member of the Foster family has said he no longer believes the verdict of suicide. He suspects it may have been a political murder

true location of the body. The police say that Foster was at the foot of a civil war cannon deep inside the park. This is the so-called "second cannon". But Ruddy says that two of the paramedics he interviewed last year located the body in a different spot, in an area of dense undergrowth 20 yards from the "first cannon". In a more recent interview, a medical examiner drew a map placing the body in the same spot. (The first cannon, interestingly, was recently removed from the park.)

CRITICS say his theory is preposterous. Twenty to thirty people saw the body that night. How could the Park Police get so many public servants to change their story? Why would they do so? What difference does it make whether the body was at the first or the second cannon?

Ruddy's answer is that the witnesses were not questioned under oath by the Fiske investigation, which is unusual, and most of them were never asked about the location of the body. As for the scale of the alleged cover-up, he argues that it shows the enormity of whatever it is they are trying to hide.

And what might that be? Ruddy prefers not to speculate, except to say it must be something more breathtaking than a 15-year-old property deal called Whitewater. As for Vince Foster, Ruddy is working from the assumption — until shown otherwise — that the man lost his life because of a refusal to compromise his honour and integrity.

Investor's Business Daily

"The Newspaper For Important Decision Makers"

irculation 209,000 | Published Nationally At Nine Plants By Investor's Business Daily, Inc. | Monday, November 6, 1995 | Los Angeles, California Volume 12, No. 146 ©1995

NATIONAL ISSUE

IS CBS KILLING THE MESSENGER?
'60 Minutes' Smears Skeptics Of Foster Suicide

By Thomas McArdle
Investor's Business Daily

For more than 25 years, CBS's "60 Minutes" has been the most successful news magazine on the tube.

Corrupt government officials, corporate charlatans, even violent criminals have been exposed before the 60 Minutes cameras. And longtime CBS News star Mike Wallace has the reputation as the program's most merciless, unfoolable interviewer.

This power can render a tremendous public service when 60 Minutes is right. But what if Mike gets it wrong?

In October, 60 Minutes took a look at the death over two years ago of Vincent Foster, the White House aide and financial confidant of the Clintons.

But rather than looking at the inconsistencies in the physical evidence in the case, Wallace took another tack. Targeted in Wallace's cross-hairs: Christopher Ruddy, a reporter with the Pittsburgh Tribune-Review who is the only journalist investigating the Foster case full-time.

60 Minutes contended there is but one reasonable conclusion: a depressed Foster shot himself through the mouth in Fort Marcy Park, where his body was found. Ruddy, who challenges that view, was presented as either a bumbling incompetent or a liar, his work the

Neither the U.S. Park Police, who were first on the scene, nor the FBI undertook a systematic investigation of the carpets in Foster's home or at his White House office. Mike Wallace neglected to mention these facts.

stuff of conspiracy theories.

Interview subjects whose views Mike Wallace agrees with came off as cool and dapper on screen. These included Rep. Bill Clinger, R-Pa., who headed a congressional investigation echoing the official conclusion, and James Hamilton, the attorney for Foster's widow.

The film shown of Ruddy, on the other hand, is edited from an interview of nearly three hours so that it appears he is fidgeting while being questioned, unsure of himself, nerdish.

But only days after the 60 Minutes story aired, Ruddy appeared on live television on the Washington-based Accuracy in Media program to respond to Wallace's criticisms.

There, unedited, Ruddy was sharp, quick, and in command of the facts — almost as if it had been someone else interviewed on 60 Minutes.

Apart from the portrayal of Ruddy, 60 Minutes also failed to live up to Wallace's own claim in the show: "We've dealt with the most important" questions in the Foster case and "we've examined the others."

In fact, many of the main anomalies of the case were not even mentioned.

■ Foster's car keys were not found on his person at the park, yet he is supposed to have driven to the park alone.

■ His eyeglasses were found 19 feet from his head, too far away to have been thrown off by the gunshot explosion, yet gunpowder was found on them, suggesting tampering.

■ Two witnesses saw two men at Foster's car with the hood up, before police arrived; the gun found in Foster's hand was never confirmed to be his.

Other questions were either skimmed over or misconstrued in the 60 Minutes piece.

■ Ruddy was the first reporter to reveal, earlier this year, that Foster was right-handed, not left-handed as first reported, incorrectly, by the Boston Globe. (The gun was found in Foster's right hand.)

Yet 60 Minutes implied that Ruddy, along with videotapes based on his

Continued on Next Page

LEADERS & SUCCESS

A '60 MINUTES' WHITEWASH?

From page 1

work, has been dishonestly or incompetently claiming that Foster was left-handed.

■ 60 Minutes allowed attorney James Hamilton to assert, unchallenged, that "Everybody that has looked at this ... every professional body, every government body" has concluded suicide at the scene where the body was found.

In fact, the Western Journalism Center, which partly funds Ruddy's work, commissioned a two-month investigation by a retired New York Police Department detective, Vincent J. Scalice, and a former NYPD forensic photographer, Fred Santucci, with lab tests performed by a the former head of the New Jersey state crime lab.

Their conclusion: the case is more consistent with homicide, not suicide.

60 Minutes did not contact Scalice or the other investigators and did not mention this private investigation.

Vincent Foster

■ The program also did not note that Whitewater Independent Counsel Kenneth Starr is re-examining the Foster death. At the time the program aired, the FBI had already spent nearly a month combing the area where the body was found, and was continuing to do so, in search of the bullet. This point was conceded by the program a week later in a correction.

In September, the San Diego chief medical examiner, Dr. Brian Blackbourne, was hired by Starr to re-examine the Foster case. He joins Dr. Henry Lee, a forensic scientist who worked on the O.J. Simpson investigation, also now working for Starr.

■ Wallace's interview with the medical examiner of Fairfax County, Va., Dr. Donald Haut, was one of the climaxes of the program.

Haut, who examined the body at the scene the day it was discovered, contradicted Ruddy's report that he told Ruddy there was not a lot of blood at the scene.

Wallace did not mention, however, that Haut also told this to the FBI. Haut "did not recall seeing blood on ... (Foster's) shirt or face and no blood was recalled on the vegetation around the body," according to the FBI report.

Ruddy has Dr. Haut on tape saying "There was not a hell of a lot of blood on the ground." Ruddy says he told Wallace he had the interview on tape, but instead of confronting Haut with the tape, or the text of his FBI interview, Wallace concludes: "Dr. Haut says Ruddy simply got it wrong." That is clearly not true.

The question of blood is important because a normal gunshot wound in the head from the kind of gun found in Foster's hand would be expected to produce tremendous bleeding, due to the heart not immediately stopping.

■ The presence of carpet fibers of seven different colors on Foster's clothes — including his underwear —were explained away by Wallace as "not significant ... anyone who walks on a carpet picks up fibers. ... And James Hamilton says that Foster's wife, Lisa (Hamilton's client), had just put new carpets in their home."

But neither the U.S. Park Police, who were first on the scene, nor the FBI undertook a systematic investigation of the carpets in Foster's home or at his White House office. The official reports do not indicate any search of the interior or trunk of Foster's car for trace evidence. Wallace neglected to mention these facts.

Wallace said, "since all of Foster's clothes were put into one bag, all of his clothes would probably have fibers on them." But Foster's suit and tie were found in his car and were bagged separately.

■ Wallace did not mention it on the air, but Ruddy says Wallace told him he found soil on his own shoes after retracing Foster's supposed footsteps; yet no soil particles were found on Foster's shoes.

Ideology may have something to do with the 60 Minutes report's shortcomings.

Both Mike Wallace and producer Robert G. Anderson refused to be interviewed for this article. The reason, a CBS News spokesman told *Investor's Business Daily*, was because it would give Ruddy, the Western Journalism Center and the others supporting Ruddy's work "more publicity and limelight than they really deserve."

Those promoting Ruddy's work are associated with conservative activism. They have run full-page advertisements publicizing the case and soliciting money in the New York Times and other major newspapers, including this one.

CBS News may also have a score to settle. Media magnate Richard M. Scaife, owner of the Pittsburgh Tribune-Review, was highlighted by 60 Minutes as a major source of funding for Ruddy's work and that of the WJC.

Mike Wallace

In the 1980s, Scaife spent $2 million helping General William Westmoreland sue CBS for a program accusing Westmoreland of misconduct and bad judgment in the Vietnam War.

James Dale Davidson, editor of Strategic Investment, a financial newsletter, and chairman of the National Taxpayers Union in Alexandria, Va., is one of the promoters of Ruddy's work.

He told *IBD* he has made no money from doing so. The WJC says it has sold only about a thousand of its videotapes on the Foster death.

Davidson angrily challenged Wallace "to get up on a platform and debate me on the points of contention he addresses in 60 Minutes, and the other unaddressed facts in this case before a live audience, where he does not have control of the editing capacity, at any place of his choosing."

Note A Forgery?

Meanwhile, there have been further developments in the case.

A Ruddy story last week revealed that the Park Police's ruling of authenticity regarding the torn-up "suicide note" found in Foster's briefcase relied on a sergeant from the U.S. Capitol Police never certified as a document examiner.

The FBI and the Fiske investigation only compared the note to a single document written by Foster and several checks Foster wrote.

Davidson's firm commissioned three handwriting experts to compare the note to 12 documents known to be written by Foster. The three all worked independently from one another over the course of three months. They included retired NYPD detective Scalice, an Oxford University historical document specialist with 30 years experience in forensic document examination, Reginald Alton, and a Boston-based Board-certified handwriting and forensic examiner, Ronald Rice, currently under contract with the Massachusetts state attorney general.

All three reached the same conclusion: the Foster suicide note is a forgery.

Sunday Telegraph

APRIL 9, 1995   . . .

Time riddle in Foster death

by Ambrose Evans-Pritchard

THE White House may have received an early tip-off about the death of Vincent Foster, the President's Deputy Counsel, long before the US Secret Service unit in the building was officially notified.

Evidence has come to light that members of the President's staff knew of Foster's death earlier than they have publicly stated, raising the possibility of a cover-up of the circumstances leading to his mysterious demise.

The official version of events says that normal procedures were followed and that the White House was first alerted when the Secret Service received a call from the US Park Police.

Foster, a former law partner of Hillary Clinton in Arkansas, managed the Clinton's personal financial affairs at the White House. He was found shot in a Virginia Park on July 20, 1993. The death was ruled a suicide by subsequent investigation by the US Park Police.

The US Secret Service office at the White House was told of the discovery at 8.30pm. But Arkansas State Trooper Roger Perry, who was on duty that night at the Governor's Mansion in Little Rock, has issued an affidavit stating that he learned about the death from a White House aide certainly before 7pm, Central Time, (8pm Washington DC time), and possibly much earlier.

The White House has refused to comment on the matter. A request for the relevant telephone logs under the Freedom of Information Act was turned down.

In a parallel development, *The Sunday Telegraph* has learned that the Park Police knew Foster was a White House official much earlier than previously supposed. A rescue worker said that by the time he left the park at around 6.45pm, everybody knew that the victim worked at the White House.

An investigation into the affair by Special Counsel Robert Fiske has been criticised for failing to call a grand jury which would have the power to compel testimony under oath. A new prosecutor, Kenneth Starr, has re-opened the investigation into Foster's death.

When did White House know?
— Page 23

explain the delay of one-and-a-half hours before notifying the Secret Service, which they should have done to comply with standard operating procedure? They say that there was a failure of communication.

The investigator who found the White House ID, Cheryl Braun, told the FBI that she gave instructions to another officer to pass on the word to the shift commander. This officer, who is never fully identified, apparently forgot to do so. She then made the call herself, she says, at roughly 7.30pm.

This still leaves almost an hour unaccounted for. In any case, the shift commander inadvertantly contradicted her story. He told the *Sunday Telegraph* that he was first informed by another officer on the scene, John Rolla.

The investigation of Special Counsel Robert Fiske last year never began to probe the glaring discrepancies in chronology. The shift commander, Lt Gavin, was not required to testify under oath. It remains to be seen whether the new investigation of Special Counsel Kenneth Starr does any better.

The *Pittsburgh Tribune-Review* reported this week that the Washington part of the Whitewater/Foster investigation, under the control of Democrat Mark Tuohey, is seriously compromised. The lead prosecutor, Miguel Rodriguez, resigned in March because the federal grand jury was unable to call witnesses and issue subpoenas.

If the White House received an early warning about Foster's death, why would it have been covered up?

One explanation is that a tip-off could have provided a window of time for pre-emptive moves. Papers that might have thrown light on any number of sensitive issues could have been removed or destroyed.

It is already acknowledged that Patsy Thomasson, the White House Director of Administration, went into Foster's office to remove documents later on the night of his death. Did anybody enter between 7pm and 8.30pm — that is, before the Secret Service claims it was notified?

President Clinton clearly had no advance warning. He was on CNN's *Larry King Live* from 9pm onwards, giving a cheerful account of himself.

His right-hand man, Webb Hubbell, did not know anything either.

He was having dinner with his family at the Lebanese Taverna when the Justice Department Command Centre contacted him with the bad news. It was already dark outside, clearly after 8.30pm.

Janet Schaufele, a young White House intern staying with the family, said that Hubbell was shattered by the news. After the dinner he couldn't remember where he had parked his car. Then he lost the keys to his house.

But somebody must have known. Somebody must have passed the word to young Helen Dickey. Who was it?

When did White House learn of aide's death?

By Ambrose Evans-Pritchard in Washington

WHEN did the Clinton administration first learn about the death of Vincent Foster, the deputy White House counsel and intimate friend of the First Family? Was it at 8.30pm on July 20, 1993, as the official version claims? Or was it really at about 7pm, an hour-and-a-half earlier?

It is not an academic question. If the exact time of notification was falsified, there must have been some purpose behind it. So far it is not clear what that might have been or who was involved.

Inquiries by the *Sunday Telegraph* have established, however, that an Arkansas State Trooper, Roger Perry, has signed an affidavit stating that he learned of the death suspiciously early, definitely before 7pm local time. (Arkansas is an hour behind Washington).

In an interview he estimated the call at 5.15pm — or 6.15pm in Washington DC, very shortly after the Park Police first discovered the body.

He claims that he was on duty that afternoon at the Governor's Mansion in Little Rock when a junior White House aide, Ms Helen Dickey, called to tell the Governor and his wife what had happened.

"She was kind of hysterical, crying, real upset," said Perry. "She told me that Vince got off work, went out to his car in the parking lot, and shot himself in the head'."

The wording is significant. It is very similar to the Secret Service memorandum on the night of the death which reported that the "US Park Police discovered the body of Vincent Foster in his car." The memorandum was wrong, of course. Or was it? When rescue workers and Park Police found the body after a telephone tip off at 6.03pm, Foster's corpse was deep inside a Virginia park. But the body-in-the-car version was the first one circulating in the White House that night.

After receiving the call, Perry telephoned several other people in Little Rock to relay the news. One of them was Arkansas State Trooper Larry Patterson. A second was Lynn Davis, a former US marshal and former commander of the Arkansas State Police. Both Patterson

> **'There is no doubt that police found Foster's ID before 6.45pm'**

and Davis have issued affidavits — which carry a penalty of perjury — swearing that they were told of Foster's death before 6pm local time. This would be a full hour-and-a-half before the Secret Service says it was notified by the US Park Police.

Dickey, a former nanny to Chelsea Clinton, is a member of the tight-knit 'Arkansas group'. She refused to answer queries about the alleged call to the Governor's Mansion. "It's going to have to go through the press office," she said. The White House press office, however, did not return repeated calls.

A Freedom of Information Act request for the telephone logs from the White House social office, where Dickey worked in 1993, was made on behalf of the *Sunday Telegraph* last year, but it was rejected without explanation.

It is possible that Perry, Patterson, and Davis are confused about the time, though they all seem certain that it was during the Little Rock rush-hour.

But there is another reason to doubt the official version of events.

People on the scene that night dispute a key element of the story put out by the Park Police. The shift commander on duty, Lt Pat Gavin, told the FBI that he notified the Secret Service within five to 10 minutes of finding out that Foster was a senior White House official. This would suggest he discovered the fact at about 8.20pm — that is, shortly before the 8.30pm call to the Secret Service.

But there is no doubt that the Park Police found Foster's White House ID on the front seat of his Honda Accord much earlier, probably before 6.45pm. The first medical examiner to see the body, Dr Donald Haut, told the *Sunday Telegraph* that everybody knew Foster was a White House official by the time he arrived on the scene at 7.30pm. "They all knew right away," he said.

A Fairfax County rescue worker, who left the park at 6.45pm, said: "We all knew that it was a White House official when we left." He is under a strict gag order, and asked not to be identified.

How does the Park Police

Statement of William S. Sessions

Editor's note: Underlining was not done by Sessions.

TO: Mr. Chris Ruddy
N.Y. Post
         February 2, 1994

Mr Ruddy: In Response to your Question about why the FBI had not been given the lead investigative Responsibility to investigate the Death of Deputy White House Counsel, Vincent Foster on July 20, 1993.

The Relationship between the White House and the FBI at the time of Mr Foster's Death should be looked at in the Context of Known events which had political implications.

A Power Struggle within the FBI and the Department of Justice, of long Duration, was ongoing at the time of President Clinton's innaugration. The White House Counsel's Office was the liaison between the President and the Department of Justice and its Component Agencies, including the FBI.

As a Deputy in the White House Office of Legal Counsel, Mr Foster was apparently Deeply involved in those Relationships and Events. The FBI in May and June of 1993 had already been involved

199

to Mr Kuddy:

IN THE "TRAVELGATE" AFFAIR THAT REERUPTED WHEN FBI AGENTS HAD BEEN SUMMONED TO THE WHITE HOUSE WITHOUT MY KNOWLEDGE.

THE WHITE HOUSE AND JUSTICE DEPARTMENT WERE CLEARLY IN A POLITICALLY AWKWARD POSITION WITH THE FBI "TRAVELGATE" INVESTIGATION IN JULY 1993.

Mr FOSTER'S DEATH CAME ON JULY 20, 1993, THE DAY AFTER MY TERMINATION AS FBI DIRECTOR BY PRESIDENT CLINTON AND JUDGE FREEH WAS PROPOSED AS THE NEW DIRECTOR. FLOYD CLARKE, THEN ACTING DIRECTOR OF THE FBI, HAD LONG BEEN INVOLVED WITH THE DEPARTMENT OF JUSTICE TO AFFECT THE POWER SHIFT AT THE FBI.

THE DECISION ABOUT THE INVESTIGATIVE ROLE OF THE FBI IN THE FOSTER DEATH WAS THERFORE COMPROMISED FROM THE BEGINNING.

THESE RELATED EVENTS WERE PERTINENT TO MY STATEMENT AT THE TIME I LEFT THE BUREAU THAT I WOULD NOT BE PART OF POLITICISING THE FBI FROM WITHIN OR WITHOUT.

200

Secret Service Memo

2076

UNITED STATES GOVERNMENT
M E M O R A N D U M
U.S. SECRET SERVICE

DATE: 07/20/93   22:01 pm

REPLY TO

ATTN OF: SA SCOTT MARBLE

SUBJECT: DEATH OF VINCENT FOSTER, DEPUTY ASSISTANT TO THE PRESIDENT AND
           DEPUTY COUNSEL (SEE ATTACHED)

TO: SAIC INTELLIGENCE DIVISION

ON 7/20/93, AT 2130 HRS, LT WOLTZ, USSS/UD - WHB, CONTACTED THE ID/DD AND
ADVISED THAT AT 2030 HRS, THIS DATE, HE WAS CONTACTED BY LT GAVIN, US PARK
POLICE, WHO PROVIDED THE FOLLOWING INFORMATION:

ON THE EVENING OF 7/20/93, UNKNOWN TIME, US PARK POLICE DISCOVERED THE BODY
OF VINCENT FOSTER IN HIS CAR. THE CAR WAS PARKED IN THE FT. MARCY AREA OF VA
NEAR THE GW PARKWAY. MR FOSTER APPARENTLY DIED OF A SELF-INFLICTED GUNSHOT
WOUND TO THE HEAD. A .38 CAL. REVOLVER WAS FOUND IN THE CAR.

SA TOM CANAVIT, WFO PI SQUAD, ADVISED THAT HE HAS BEEN IN CONTACT WITH US
PARK POLICE AND WAS ASSURED THAT IF ANY MATERIALS OF A SENSITIVE NATURE
(SCHEDULES OF THE POTUS, ETC.) WERE RECOVERED, THEY WOULD IMMEDIATELY BE
TURNED OVER TO THE USSS. (AT THE TIME OF THIS WRITING, NO SUCH MATERIALS WERE
LOCATED)

NO FURTHER INFORMATION AVAILABLE.

INVESTIGATION BY US PARK POLICE CONTINUING.

THE FOLLOWING NOTIFICATIONS WERE MADE BY USSS/UD - WHB:

DAVE WATKINS	DIR. OF PERSONNEL, WH
INSP. DENNIS MARTIN	USSS/UD
CRAIG LIVINGSTONE	WH SECURITY COORDINATOR
ASAIC PAUL IMBORDINO	OPO
DAD RICHARD GRIFFIN	OPO (BY ASAIC IMBORDINO)
ATSAIC DON FLYNN	PPD (BY ASAIC IMBORDINO)
SAIC RICHARD MILLER	PPD (BY ATSAIC FLYNN)
DIRECTOR MAGAW	DIR (BY DAD GRIFFIN)

THE FOLLOWING NOTIFICATIONS WERE MADE BY THE ID/DD: OIC 000818

ATSAIC LON WARFIELD	ID	2145 HRS	
SAIC STEPHEN SERGEK	ID	2155 HRS	
DAD DALE WILSON	PA	2205 HRS	00023
ASAIC CARL MEYER	PA	2207 HRS	

#1

201

An Independent Forensic Examination

of a Torn Note Allegedly

Written by Vincent W. Foster, Jr.

Prepared for Strategic Investment

James Dale Davidson, Editor

25 October 1995

Vincent J. Scalice

Vincent J. Scalice is a certified Questioned Document
Examiner with the American Board of Forensic Examiners.
Mr. Scalice began studying handwriting analysis over forty
years ago, and for the past 22 years has engaged in forensic
document examination as a specialty. He has testified in
hundreds of court cases on civil and criminal matters
pertaining to questioned documents. He has been retained by
numerous corporations and law enforcement agencies as a
consultant to examine questioned documents. He has conducted
forensic document examination for some of the nation's
largest commercial banks, including Citibank and Chemical
Bank.

In 1977, Mr. Scalice retired from the New York City Police
Department after 21 years of service as a detective first
grade with specialties in Identification, Latent Fingerprint
Analysis and Crime Scene reconstruction. Since his
retirement he has been Executive Director of Forensic
Control Systems of Staten Island, New York. He has served
as a Consultant to the House Committee on Assassinations
which investigated the deaths of President John Kennedy and
Dr. Martin Luther King Jr. He currently serves as chairman
of the Executive Board of Scientific and technical Advisors
for the American Board of Forensic Examiners.

R.E. Alton

Reginald E. Alton is a world-recognized expert on
handwriting examination and manuscript authentication. He
has 30 years experience in the field of forensic document
examination, and has lectured during this period at Oxford
University on handwriting and manuscripts, including the
detection of forgery and the identification of handwriting
to Doctoral and research students in the University of
Oxford. In recent years he ruled on charges that some
manuscripts of the late C.S. Lewis were a forgery. He
validated their authenticity. He has ruled on numerous
questioned documents and manuscripts--some of great monetary
value, including such noteworthy historical figures as
Donne, Shelley, Christina Rossetti, to modern day authors as
Oscar Wilde. He has been consulted by civil bodies and
British police authorities and has testified as an expert
witness in British courts on criminal matters relating to
questioned documents and anonymous letters and other
forgeries.

Mr. Alton, M.C., M.A. is an Emeritus Fellow of St Edmund
Hall, University of Oxford, and is currently Dean of Degrees
at St Edmund Hall, Oxford's oldest institution for
undergraduates. He was Fellow, Tutor and Vice-Principal of
St. Edmund Hall and has served as Chairman of the English
faculty, as well as lecturer at Pembroke, Jesus and Exeter
Colleges in the University of Oxford.

TRANSCRIPT OF NOTE

I made mistakes from ignorance, inexperience and overwork

I did not knowingly violate any law or standard of conduct

No one in The White House, to my knowledge, violated any law or standard of conduct, including any action in the travel office. There was no intent to benefit any individual or specific group

The FBI lied in their report to the AG

The press is covering up the illegal benefits they received from the travel staff

The GOP has lied and misrepresented its knowledge and role and covered up a prior investigation

The Ushers Office plotted to have excessive costs incurred, taking advantage of Kaki and HRC

The public will never believe the innocence of the Clintons and their loyal* staff

The WSJ editors lie without consequence

I was not meant for the job or the spotlight of public life in Washington. Here ruining people is considered sport.

---

* A transcript of the note prepared by the Park Police identifies this word as "legal."

The Torn Note

I made mistakes from ignorance, inexperience
and overwork.

I did not knowingly violate any law or standard
of conduct.

No one in the White House, to my knowledge,
violated any law or standard of conduct, including
any action in the travel office. There was no intent
to benefit any individual or specific group.

The FBI lied in their report to the AG.

The press is covering up the illegal benefits they
received from the travel staff.

The GOP has lied and misrepresented its
knowledge and role and covered up a prior investigation.

The Usher's Office plotted to have excessive
costs incurred, taking advantage of Kaki and ____.

The public will never believe the innocence
of the Clintons and their legal staff.

The WSJ editors lie without consequence.

I was not meant for the job or the spotlight
of public life in Washington. Here ruining people
is considered sport.

Q1

Foster's Actual Handwriting

VINCENT W. FOSTER
WASHINGTON, D.C.

6/18/93

can Exploration Co —

I am returning your check no. 04820598.
interests it represents were owned by
at father. As reflected by the enclosed
dt order these interests were distributed
my mother. As reflected by the enclosed
tclaim deed she assigned the interests
me.

Please revised your records

Sincerely

Vincent W Foster

FORENSIC CONTROL SYSTEMS
Private Investigations • Forensic Consultants

107 CEDARVIEW AVENUE
STATEN ISLAND, N.Y. 10306
TEL: (718) 979-0339
FAX: (718) 979-3261

October 6, 1995

James D. Davidson
Strategic Investment

Dear Mr. Davidson:

At your request I have examined a photocopy of the Questioned Document said to be written by Vincent W. Foster, Jr., with several photocopied exemplars identified as the known writing of Vincent Foster.

Q-1   begins as follows: "I made mistakes from ignorance, inexperience and overwork...".

Q-1   was examined and compared with several photocopied examplars.

K-1   is a note written by Vincent Foster on June 18, 1993, and used as the sole exemplar by the U.S. Park Police to certify Q-1 as genuine.

K-2   is a note written by Vincent Foster on his stationery and dated April 15, 1993. The note is signed.

K-3   is a single page document containing notes made by by Vincent Foster and found in the U.S. Park Police report.

K-4   are documents written by Vicent Foster relating to
thru   the Whitewater partnership and presented to the Senate's
K-10   Special Whitewater committee.

K-11   are various notes and docments containing the sign-
thru   ature of Vincent Foster and found in the U.S. Park
K-14   Police report.

PURPOSE

The purpose of this examination and comparison was to determine whether or not the document in question was actually written by Vincent Foster, Jr.

CONFIDENTIAL INVESTIGATIONS • FORENSIC SERVICES • CRIMINALISTICS
SECURITY & LOSS PREVENTION • FINGERPRINT IDENTIFICATION • DOCUMENT EXAMINATION   6

CIVIL & CRIMINAL   LICENSED & BONDED

208

RESULTS

As a result of comprehensive and thorough analysis of the
Questioned and Known photocopied documents under varying
degrees of magnification, I have arrived at the following
determinations:

1. Although some generalized degree of similarity exists
    between the photocopied questioned document with the
    known samples furnished, upon closer detailed examin-
    ation and comparison numerous marked differences have
    been noted throughout the writings.

2. Most of the execution, form and style of the writing
    contained in Q-1 is not consistent with the writings
    found in K-1 thru K-14. There are numerous inconsis-
    tencies found throughout Q-1 in regard to individual
    letter formation. Marked differences are noted in
    execution of stroke and the beginning of letter forma-
    tions. The document, Q-1, exhibits a style less conti-
    nuous and flowing than the writing contained in the
    known documents.

3. Based upon the above observation and comparisons of
    the photocopied documents I have formed the opinion
    that it is not possible to state that the questioned
    document was written by Vincent Foster. The document
    appears to be a simulation of Foster's writing result-
    ing in an unsuccessful attempt to produce a credible
    forgery.

ADDITIONAL FINDINGS

1. Q-1 is not consistent with a suicide note. It makes
    no mention of intentional harm to oneself. There
    is no signature and no date. Significantly, there
    is no mention of characteristic statements of depart-
    ure for loved ones, the putting of affairs in order,
    or a motive for suicide. The writer of Q-1 does not
    give any indication of clinical depression or apparent
    suicidal tendencies.

2. It is highly doubtful that the missing piece from
    Q-1 would have contained his signature.

3. Q-1, had it been torn by decedent into 28 pieces,
    should certainly have left numerous latent print impres-
    sions.

4. The use of only K-1 by the U.S. Park Police is not
    consistent with standard forensic document examination.
    Police should have obtained independent, additional
    samples of Vincent Foster's handwriting executed during
    the norman course of business and from other sources.
    Normally, in the course of a homicide investigation,

it would be improper for police to accept a single
document from a family member, and to form an opinion
based on same.

5. The use of a single document and a series of checks
   alleged to have been written by Vincent Foster by
   the FBI's Questioned Document section is not consistent
   with standard forensic document examination.

6. official reports omit any examination by the FBI of
   a psycholinguistic analysis of Q-1 compared with the
   known writings of decedent. This omission is serious
   considering the disjointed statements found in Q-1.

7. The long amount of time before Q-1 was found, and
   the unusual circumstances of its discovery, should
   have aroused suspicion that the time.may have been
   used to execute the fraudulent note. Also, the finding of the note in 28 pieces, one piece missing, may
   indicate an effort was made to further hider a comparative analysis.

SUMMARY AND CONCLUSION

The finding that Q-1 appears to be a forgery, coupled with
the additional findings one through seven, are all supporting
evidence that a proper homicide investigation is required
into the death of Vincent Foster.

Should you require additional documentation in the form
of graphic exhibits or charts to illustrate the basis for
these findings, please notify this office in advance and
allow time for preparation.

Respectfully submitted,

Vincent J. Scalice
Forensic Consultant
Document Examiner

VJS/mr

Telephone: Oxford (01865) 279000
Direct Dial: Oxford (01865) 2790 ....

Fax: Oxford (01865) 279090

Report and opinion by Reginald Ernest Alton

1.   I have examined photocopies of documents, each consisting of one leaf, and foliated l.r., in a different hand from the main body of the document, Q 1 and K 1 to K 12 inclusive. I am satisfied that K 1 to K 12 inclusive are, apart from foliation and printed or stamped material, all the work of one person who signed K 1 and K 2. The hand of K 1 to K 12 inclusive is that of a mature adult and the date of the questioned document Q 1 is close enough to the dates of the K group for the latter to be used to determine the authenticity or otherwise of Q 1.

2.   In my opinion, insofar as it is possible to come to a conclusion from photocopies, Q 1 is a forgery related to K 1 to K 12 inclusive because the forger was using parts of them as a model.

3.   The difficulties of this comparative study have been much increased by the fact that Q 1 has been torn and apparently crudely and inefficiently repaired. This process, whether deliberate or not, has obscured some of the continuities or discontinuities of the handwriting, and especially the lineation and layout which often, in their uncertainties, betray a forger's eye as it wanders from forgery to model.

4.   I have had in mind three axioms:
     (a) any letter form or ligature used by writers of a language at a given date is available for selection by any writer. Accordingly, the movements of the pen as it makes the letter and the general appearance of a document are of more importance than the presence or absence or even the frequency of individual letter forms;
     (b) slope, proportion (x - height: space: ascenders and descenders), degree of horizontal or vertical compression, roundness or angularity, pressure, characteristic movements of the hand, and the writing instrument itself all contribute to the general appearance;
     (c) writers of modern cursive hands can be divided into 'swaggers' [uu]
and 'archers' [mm] ⓘ

211

TELEPHONE: OXFORD (01865) 279000

DIRECT DIAL: OXFORD (01865) 2790 ....

FAX: OXFORD (01865) 279090

ST EDMUND HALL

OXFORD

OX1 4AR

5 .   Foster seems to have been a natural 'swagger'. He makes a series of minims e.g. nin (returning K 1 1.1), in and w with an even and rhythmic movement through a series of elegant swags. He rarely writes n or h with an arch.

The writer of Q 1 is aware of this habit but he fails to match Foster's usage or elegance. The incidence of arched n in the first eight lines of Q 1 is much higher than in the control documents. It is characteristic of a forger that the writer of Q 1 gets better at imitating this habit as he or she goes along.

6.   The uneven, uneasy and laboured nature of Q 1's swags for in can be seen in inexperience (1.1), individual (1.8) and in Clintons (1.17) as compared with what should be an exact match, Clinton's in K 9 (1.2).

7.   Even more revealing is another case which ought to produce an exact match and in Q 1 fails to do so: the word benefit, Q 1 (1.8 and 1.10) as compared with   K 11 (1.1) and K 10 (1.4). Foster makes initial minuscule b in one stroke (see also based, K 10 (1.5)).   Q 1 takes at least 2, possibly 3 strokes to reproduce the shape. In my opinion he is copying from K 10 for this word but has failed to understand the movements of Foster's pen.

8.   In a movement of the hand which is directionally the same as the swags Foster is a habitual writer of counter-clockwise loops or circles. This characteristic is visible in most appearances of the th ligature throughout K 1 to K 12 inclusive. In Q 1 the loops in this ligature either do not exist or are a mere thickening of the ascender of h.

9.   We see this movement not only in expected places e.g. round-backed looped d (see K 1 and K 2 and contrast did, lied etc in Q 1), but also in unexpected places e.g.   a in avoids and answering (K 7). In Q 1   minuscule a is an awkward 2 stroke letter; in K.7 a counter-clockwise loop closes the bowl in one stroke.

212

TELEPHONE: OXFORD (01865) 279000
DIRECT DIAL: OXFORD (01865) 2790 ....

FAX: OXFORD (01865) 279090

ST EDMUND HALL
OXFORD
OX1 4AR

Report...   Page 3

10.   The writer of Q 1 is generally uneasy about joining one letter to the
next e.g. o to l to a in violate (1.3) and especially l to a in the same
word (1.6). Contrast c to l to o in enclosed (K 1 1.5 and 1.7). This sort
of failure is characteristic of forgeries.

11.   There is much other detail which could be mentioned e.g. the of ligatures,
Q 1's failure to understand Foster's majuscule B (K 3) and majuscule I and J.

12.   In general appearance the hand of the authentic documents K 1 to K 12
is firm, open, rounded, with a consistent slight backward slope and an easy
currency that joins letter to letter with scarcely an interruption to the
flow of the hand. This is true whatever the different circumstances in which
the K group were written down.
In contrast the hand of Q 1 is slightly but clearly less open (slightly more
horizontally compressed); it has an inconsistent slope which, though often
backward in varying degrees, gives in total a more upright appearance than
K 1 to K 12 inclusive; and though it imitates letters and words from the K
group it fails to understand how they are made.

R E ALTON
18 September 1995

INDEPENDENT REPORT

in RE:

The Death of Vincent W. Foster, Jr.

Prepared for: **Western Journalism Center
April 27, 1995**

By: **Vincent J. Scalice Associates
Forensic Control Systems**

Report Prepared by
Vincent Scalice, S.C.S.A.
Forensic Control Systems
107 Cedarview Avenue
Staten Island, NY 10306

for

Western Journalism Center
P.O. Box 2450
Fair Oaks, CA 95628

RE: Confidential Investigation
Crime Scene Reconstruction
Vincent W. Foster Jr. (Deceased)

Case No. 2014/95

At your request, a Confidential Investigation was carried out by
this office in regard to the circumstances involved in the death
of Deputy White House Counsel, Vincent W. Foster Jr., whose body
was reported to have been found within the confines of Fort Marcy
Park, Fairfax County, Virginia, during the early evening hours of
Tuesday, July 20, 1993. The following is a detailed report of the
results of our investigation.

CRIME SCENE RECONSTRUCTION SEQUENCE

On Saturday, March 4, 1995, at approximately 2:00 p.m., our
operatives, Vincent J. Scalice, S.C.S.A.; Forensic Consultant,
Richard Saferstein, PhD., Criminalist, and Fred Santucci,
Forensic Photographer, arrived at the parking lot of Fort Marcy
Park and commenced this investigation.

Soil and surface conditions were dry. Temperature was measured at
41 degrees fahrenheit.

The operatives took the path which would have been closest to Mr.
Foster's car, and entered the main clearing of the earthen fort.
The operatives examined the ridge, or berm, immediately to the
left as they entered the clearing. Approximately midway along
the berm, the operatives noted the metal-concrete anchor which
secured the "first cannon." This cannon has been removed from the
park recently.

Approximately 50 feet past the first cannon site the operatives
noted a curve shaped hollow and a path going down the embankment.
This site has been identified in the Ruddy report as the true
location of the body's discovery on July 20, 1993. This location
herein will be noted as the cannon No. 1 area.

The operatives proceeded directly across the clearing, taking the
most direct path to the second cannon site. The site is hidden

216

from the main clearing, and is approximately 200 feet from cannon area No. 1.

The operatives reviewed the second cannon site, including the berm the second cannon overlooks, where the Park Police claim Foster's body was discovered. This site is referred to herein as "the second cannon site."

The operatives also noted homes along Chain Bridge Road which could be seen from the second cannon site.

The operatives then proceeded along an easterly trail which runs parallel to Chain Bridge Road to the park's rear entrance. The operatives noted that the entrance is for both cars and pedestrians, and identified the compound for the Ambassador of Saudi Arabia, as well as the compound's security camera that views the park's rear entrance.

The operatives then returned to the parking lot and met with a stand-in for Mr. Foster, identified herein as the model. The model is the same approximate weight and height as Mr. Foster.

The model put on a clean pair of dress shoes at the reported location of Mr. Foster's car. He then took the nearest path and proceeded to the second cannon site. He walked along the side of the path, avoiding walking on the freshly laid gravel path that begins at the lot and leads up to the entrance of the main clearing.

The model took the most direct route to the second cannon site. From the time he left the lot until he arrived at the second cannon site, the model was videotaped by Mr. Santucci.

The model thereupon removed the dress shoes, which were examined, bagged and noted by Dr. Saferstein. The model put on a fresh pair of shoes, dress socks, suit pants, and a white dress shirt.

The model then walked several paces down the second cannon site, and sat down on a root stem which forms a natural seat, as identified in the Fiske report. In a reclined position, the model's head laid approximately 10 feet directly in front of the second cannon's barrel. This is consistent with the Fiske report.

While seated the model was asked to place both hands around an imaginary gun placed in his mouth, and simulate firing the weapon.

During this time Mr. Santucci continued taking videotape, as well as 35mm photographs. Mr. Scalice took numerous Polaroids of the scene.

The model was asked to straighten out his legs and arms as he reclined on the path, as consistent with eyewitness descriptions

- 2 -

of how the body was found. Mr. Scalice had the model place his right hand and arm in a position closely resembling the polaroid that was released by ABC News. Similar Polaroid photographs were taken by Mr. Scalice for comparison purposes.

The operatives proceeded down the berm approximately 13 feet from where the body was reported to have been found to the point at which Foster's eyeglasses were said to have landed after being thrown from his body. Photographs were taken at this location.

The operatives noted that from the crest of the berm's hollow, the berm falls at an angle of approximately 25 to 30 degrees for several feet until it reaches the first section of the root stem. At that point, the berm falls away sharply at approximately a 45-degree angle. The abrupt drop in the slope takes place almost at the mid-section of the model's body, causing the body to appear curved around the slope, or bowed outward.

The model's upper body was then lifted up to examine the back of the head and the body was also allowed to slip for three to four inches on the incline, as noted by eyewitnesses. The body was then picked up fully. The model thereupon removed his clothing and shoes. The items were bagged and removed by Dr. Saferstein for further analysis.

Dr. Saferstein also examined soil conditions at the second cannon site.

The operatives then proceeded to the cannon No. 1 site and examined and compared the ABC News copy of the polaroid photo with conditions at this area. It was noted that at this location the body would have lain on a more gentle slope of approximately 25 degrees.

As a result of closer inspection of this site coupled with a detailed examination and comparison of the ABC photograph, obvious similarities were noted in regard to the plant life and vegetation throughout this area. Several leaves of a particular type which matched those contained in the photograph were found to be present at this location. Several of those leaves were collected, bagged and removed for further analysis and possible identification.

The operatives then returned to the second cannon site and thoroughly searched this area for similar type leaves. No matching leaves were found at this location.

The operatives returned to the parking lot at approximately 5:00 p.m., ending their reconstruction project.

In addition to the aforementioned crime scene reconstruction project, a detailed examination and evaluation was carried out in regard to the Fiske Report, as well as all attachments, including

- 3 -

218

F.B.I. laboratory and interview reports, U.S. Park Police reports, autopsy reports and Senate Banking committee testimony.

The following is a report of the findings and conclusions in regard to our investigation into this matter.

GENERAL FINDINGS

1. Movement of the Body

A high probability exists that Foster's body was transported to Fort Marcy Park from an outside location due to the following:

According to the Fiske report, Foster's shoes had not one trace of coherent soil on them or on his clothing although the 197 pound Foster had allegedly walked over 700 feet to the second cannon site. Although the heavy summer foliage may have covered much of the ground soil, other areas would have been traversed with exposed soil.

For example, a laboratory test conducted on one (1) pair of shoes (15017, worn by model) and walked simply several paces in the vicinity of the second cannon, revealed "significant quantities of soil in combination with vermiculite (mica) on both heels."

The shoes and clothing worn by the model at the park were closely examined and analyzed. Both shoes and clothing were found to contain soil mixed with mica.

These facts would be highly consistent with the fact that Foster did not walk to the spot where he was found, but was more likely transported to this location by other means.

Our laboratory analysis on a pair of shoes (65548) that had been walked from the parking lot to the second cannon site disclosed evidence of grass stains. It should be noted that the walk was carried out in winter weather (March). Had Foster walked this route on July 20, 1993, there would have been a greater likelihood of grass staining. The F.B.I. report omits any mention of grass staining whatsoever.

Officials claim that Foster's body was found on a path lying at the second site. If this were true, especially on a warm summer day, soil and other debris should have adhered to his clothing and shoes. The Fiske report indicates no traces of coherent soil whatsoever.

The position of Foster's body as described in numerous reports is completely unnatural with a suicide of this type. In agreement with the Fiske report the only likely scenario would be that

Foster was in a sitting position. In this position, however, it is not logical to expect that his arms and legs would have fallen

- 4 -

219

into a neat and orderly position. It is more likely that his arms would extend outwards at an angle to the body as a result of the discharge. The neat arrangement of his arms close to the body, coupled with the overall arrangement of the body itself, is not consistent with suicide.

The lack of extravated blood on the front of the body is inconsistent with death by intra-oral gunshot, which raises the likelihood that Foster's heart had already cessated and that death would have been caused by other means. Dr. Donald Haut, the Medical Examiner present at the scene when the body was rolled over, said there was little blood behind the body on the ground. This is consistent with the small amount of blood that had emanated from the entrance wound.

Haut said that blood had matted or congealed on the back of the head. This is an indication that the exit wound may have been covered if the body was moved.

Had Foster fired the weapon while in the sitting position and the bullet followed the trajectory described in the autopsy, exiting from the back of the top of the head, blood splattered brain tissue and other matter should have been visible above the head, on the surrounding ground or vegetation. No witnesses identified such matter as described and the lead police investigator saw none.

The inconsistent blood tracks and stain on Foster's right cheek, as mentioned in the F.B.I. report, cannot simply be explained by the fact that an emergency worker may have touched the head, for example, while checking the carotid artery. This further supports the theory that the body may have been transported.

2. Location of the Body's Discovery

The forensic evidence does not support the police and Fiske conclusion that Foster's body was found on the path directly in front of the second cannon site. This pathway has clearly been a dirt path edged by root stems. These root stems appear worn as a result of having been exposed for many years. A Gannett news report, published shortly after Foster's death, reported the path to be a dirt one.

Shoes and clothing worn by the model at the second cannon site were closely examined and analyzed. Dress shoes (15017) were found to contain significant quantities of soil mixed with mica. The pants were also found to contain soil mixed with mica.

Had Foster's body been lying at the second cannon site, especially on a warm summer day, soil and other debris should

have adhered to his clothing and shoes. The Fiske report indicates no traces of coherent soil whatsoever.

- 5 -

The second cannon site is not consistent with the heavy and dense foliage said to have been found all around the body. It is not consistent with description of the scenes polaroids, including the ABC News photograph.

The Fiske report notes heavy vegetation below the body extending to the location of Foster's eyeglasses, approximately 13 feet away. This also is not consistent with the barren area below the body at the second cannon site.

The cannon No. 1 site is consistent with the description of heavy foliage. It is consistent with the ABC News polaroid.

The ABC News Polaroid clearly shows evidence of a certain type of leaf, which has been found to be common to the cannon No. 1 area. This leaf has subsequently been positively identified as a species known as **Magnolia acuminata.** As a result of a careful examination and inspection carried out over a wide area in the vicinity of cannon No. 2, it was conclusively established that no leaves of this type were observed in or about this location.

The second cannon site has a slope whose angle of descent drops considerably to a point almost exactly where Foster's mid-section would have been. On the slope the model's body displayed a curved, or bowed appearance, with the abdomen clearly protruding. No mention of this characteristic position was noted in any of the eyewitness statements. The angle of the slope at the first cannon site is less pronounced and would not have resulted in any unusual or curved position of the body.

SPECIFIC FINDINGS

1. The Fiske report states that mica particles found on Foster's shoes and clothing, in the absence of soil, supports the conclusion that Foster had walked through the park. This conclusion is not logical due to the fact that shoes and clothing used in our reconstruction contained a mix of both soil and mica, as noted in our laboratory tests.

Our laboratory analysis of vegetation from the park also revealed "significant quantities of vermiculite (mica) and the absence of soil constituents." Therefore, mica particles found on Foster's clothing supports the conclusion that his body was lying on dense foliage and vegetation only. This fact is also consistent with the probability that his body had likely been transported to the scene.

The aforementioned conclusions are further supported by the F.B.I. report which notes mica being found not only on his shoes, but also on his shirt, pants, belt and socks.

2. Had Foster fired the gun at the second cannon site, it is conceivable that the shot would not have been heard by any of the

- 6 -

neighbors who reside in homes across the road. The barrel's position in the mouth may have produced a muffling effect, and traffic noise could have possibly further diminished the sound of the shot.

3. Had Foster fired the gun while in a sitting position at the second cannon site, the bullet, if it did exit the back of the rear of the head, could conceivably have cleared the berm behind him. However, after exiting the head, it is reasonable to expect that the velocity could have diminished considerably, thereby causing the spent projectile to fall closer to the body. Behind the body and above the crest of the berm is an open clearing area. On the other side of the clearing is a small berm, creating a natural barrier for the fired projectile. Failure to recover the spent bullet is consistent with the fact that the gun may have been fired at another location.

4. An important focus of this investigation should be placed on the park's rear entrance, as a possible means or method of transporting the body to the scene.

5. Carpet-type fibers of various colors which were found on almost all of Foster's clothing was clearly indicative of the fact that his body probably was in contact with one or more carpets at some point in time prior to his death. It is therefore logical to assume that such contact would have taken place at some other location prior to his being found in the park. This type of trace or transfer evidence should be considered highly significant as it would provide an indication of Foster's possible whereabouts or movements prior to him being found in the park. This evidence raises the possibility that his body may have been in a prone position, that his clothing may have been searched while in a prone position, and/or his body may have been transported while in contact with some type of carpeting.

It should be noted that nowhere in the reports is any mention made of any search or vacuuming in Foster's car for trace evidence. No carpet fibers were recovered from the interior of Foster's vehicle or the trunk area. The recovery of such evidence might have established whether or not Foster had in fact driven to the parking lot, or was transported in the trunk.

6. Foster's eyeglasses were reported to have been recovered approximately 13 feet below his body on the berm. The Fiske report notes that since the gunpowder was found on the glasses it meant that they must have been thrown from his head or shirt pocket after the gunshot. It is inconceivable for the glasses to have been thrown or bounced through foliage to the location where they were found. This would seem more likely an indication that the crime scene was tampered with.

7. According to the Fiske pathology panel, "Mr. Foster's index fingers were in the vicinity of the (front) cylinder gap, when

- 7 -

222

the weapon was fired." This conclusively demonstrates that neither his right nor left hand was on the hand grip when it was fired. This evidence is inconsistent with suicide.

In most cases of suicide, the gun does not remain in the victim's hand.[1] In addition to the unusual gunpowder soot found on the index fingers, we found disturbing the proximity of the right hand and arm to the right leg, the unusual deep position of the thumb in the trigger guard, the position of the gun barrel tucked under the right leg, the lack of any visible blood on the gun, the failure of the family to positively identify the gun's ownership and the failure to recover the fired projectile. These facts are all supporting evidence that a high probability exists that the positioning of the gun in the hand was staged.

CONCLUSIONS

All cases of suspicious death should be treated as homicides, until proven otherwise. Due to the circumstances involved in this case, the opinion has been formed that homicide has not been ruled out.

As a result of our investigation and reconstruction in regard to this case, we have concluded contrary to the conclusions arrived at in the Fiske report: the overwhelming evidence does not support the conclusion that Vincent W. Foster Jr. committed suicide in Fort Marcy Park.

Therefore, wholly separate from the issue of suicide or homicide is the obvious problem of the body's transport to the park.

Still another serious issue concerns the location of the body's discovery in Fort Marcy Park. Based upon the evidence made available and examined, it is more likely that the official location of the second site is not the actual site of the body's discovery. Evidence also indicates that the first cannon site is more consistent with the actual location of the body's discovery.

Signed:

Vincent J. Scalice, S.C.S.A.
Forensic Consultant
Crime Scene Analyst

Fred D. Santucci
Forensic Photographer
Crime Scene Expert

---

[1] Mr. Scalice and Mr. Santucci, in their combined experience of fifty years of investigating homicides, have never seen a weapon or gun positioned in a suicide's hand in such an orderly fashion.

- 8 -

LABORATORY ANALYSIS

Conducted by Richard Saferstein, PhD.

RE: Vincent Foster

The following articles were subjected to microscopic and mineralogical analysis:

1. One pair of red shoes (serial #15017). These shoes were removed from subject on 3/4/95 who was lying in cannon #2 area in Fort Marcy Park;

2. One pair of brown shoes (serial #12177). These shoes were removed from subject who walked from parking lot to cannon #2 location on 3/4/95 in Fort Marcy Park;

3. One pair of dark brown shoes (serial #65548).

4. Soil samples from cannon #1 and cannon #2 sites collected 3/4/95 in Fort Marcy Park;

5. White dress shirt removed from subject lying in cannon #2 site on 3/4/95 in Fort Marcy Park;

6. Socks removed from subject lying in cannon #2 site on 3/4/95 in Fort Marcy Park;

7. Pants removed from subject lying in cannon #2 site on 3/4/95 in Fort Marcy Park; and

8. Leaves recovered from cannon #1 area in Fort Marcy Park.

Conclusions:

1. Soil samples from both cannon sites are similar. Soils are characteristic of potting or planting soil. Soils contain a mixture of mica (vermiculite), peat, and organic soil (top soil).

2. Examination of red shoes (15017) shows significant quantities of soil in combination with vermiculite on both heels. Soil is consistent with potting or planting soils recovered from both cannon sites.

3. Examination of brown shoes (12177) shows small quantity of peat and organic soil in combination with vermiculite.

4. Examination of dark brown shoes (65548) shows small quantity of soil in combination with vermiculite. These shoes also show evidence of grass stains.

5. The white shirt was negative for soil constituents including vermiculite.

6. The socks were positive for flakes of vermiculite.

7. The pants were positive for peat and organic soil mixed with vermiculite. Vegetation was also present on pants.

8. Examination of leaves recovered from cannon #1 area shows significant quantities of vermiculite particles and the absence of soil constituents.

Prosecutor Joins Foster Death Probe

By Christopher Ruddy
FOR THE TRIBUNE-REVIEW
MARCH 26, 1996

WASHINGTON—A Tennessee federal prosecutor joined the Washington office of Independent Counsel Kenneth Starr Monday to review the death of Vincent W. Foster Jr.

Starr tapped West Tennessee Assistant U.S. Attorney Steve Parker to assist his Washington investigation, which has been examining the late deputy White House counsel's death, the Memphis Commercial Appeal reported late last week.

On July 20, 1993, Foster was found dead of an apparent self-inflicted gunshot wound to the head in a small road-side national park in McLean, Va. U.S. Park Police ruled the death a suicide, a ruling that was confirmed by Starr's predecessor, Special Counsel Robert Fiske, in a report issued on June 30, 1994.

Starr's appointment of Parker, 39, a former Memphis policeman, indicates Starr still has not accepted Fiske's conclusions. Parker's hiring also contradicts some press accounts that closure of the Foster case was imminent and appears to counter claims that Starr has been less than serious in investigating claims of foul play and a cover-up.

The Memphis paper stated that Parker, a 10-year veteran prosecutor, was selected because of his police background and his experience as a federal prosecutor dealing with homicide cases.

Hickman Ewing, Starr's deputy who has been leading the independent counsel's probe in Arkansas, told the Commercial Appeal that Foster's death "is one of the things being investigated insofar as Whitewater is concerned."

"There remains questions about Foster's death. Was it murder? Was it suicide? Either way, why?" Ewing said. Ewing is a former U.S. attorney from Memphis.

The appointment of Parker comes after continuing criticism of Starr's handling of the Foster case.

The Tribune-Review has reported on the resignation of Starr's original lead prosecutor, Miquel Rodriguez, who was probing Foster's death earlier last year after he was thwarted by higherups and FBI officials in conducting a full probe. Rodriguez returned to his position as an assistant U.S. attorney in Sacramento, Calif.

Rodriguez's rigorous probe ended with his grand jury cross-examination of about a dozen police and emergency workers first at the scene of Foster's death. Despite Rodriguez's departure, grand jury proceedings continued, though sources have stated they were for from thorough. The proceedings were led by Starr's then-deputy Mark Tuohey, a Washington, D.C., Democrat closely associated with the Clinton administration and another prosecutor who had never tried a case before.

Fairfax County medical examiner Dr. Donald Haut, who visited the death scene at Fort Marcy Park where Foster died, told the Tribune-Review he testified before Starr's panel after Rodriguez left in early 1994, and that he had spent approximately 20 minutes in the grand jury room undergoing what he said was perfunctory questioning by Tuohey.

Rodriguez had considered Haut a critical witness, as he was the only trained medical professional on the scene that night. But Haut's account of his grand jury treatment appears mild compared to witnesses who underwent cross-examination by Rodriguez.

One source said during Rodriguez's probe, no witness left before two hours of questioning, and one police official underwent as many as eight grueling hours of interrogation.

Legal experts say a prosecutor in a thorough grand jury probe will engage in intense cross-examination to find inconsistencies in a witness' statememt or to expose a possible cover-up.

FBI Challenged

By Christopher Ruddy
FOR THE TRIBUNE-REVIEW
APRIL 24, 1996

WASHINGTON—Susan Thomases, a key confidante to Bill and Hillary Clinton, says her official statement prepared by the staff of Whitewater Special counsel Robert Fiske is wrong and has raised new doubts about the credibility of such documents, according to a recent press report.

Thomases, a New York superlawyer, testified before the Senate Whitewater Committee earlier this year and raised the ire of some senators for her memory lapses about her activities after the death of Deputy White House Counsel Vincent Foster.

Thomases and her attorney told the Wall Street Journal that her official statement, prepared by FBI agents working for Fiske, incorrectly states her recollections about her contact with Foster in the last days of his life.

Thomases' attorney, Benito Romano, did not return calls from the Tribune-Review to explain the nature of the inaccuracies.

Fiske and his staff conducted about 125 interviews with Foster's friends and associates, as well as officials related to the original U.S. Park Police investigation of his death.

Fiske, using FBI agents assigned to his staff, followed Justice Department procedure by having statements prepared on the same form the FBI uses to compile information gathered during an interview. The forms are known as "FD 302's." While Fiske used these forms and FBI agents assigned to his staff, Fiske's investigation was not an FBI probe.

From those FBI statements and other evidence, Fiske issued a report on June 30, 1994, concluding that Foster had committed suicide.

Controversy over Thomases' FBI statement first arose in a report in the London Sunday Telegraph. The newspaper reported that Thomases' statements in a new book on the Whitewater scandal titled *Blood Sport* do not jibe with what she told Fiske's investigators.

The book details Foster's last days and states that Thomases met with Foster at a Washington boarding house just weeks before his death. According to Thomases, Foster was a close friend and confidante of hers who said that he was unhappy with his wife, Lisa.

In a telephone interview dated June 14, 1994, Thomases allegedly told the FBI another story.

In that statement she says that she last saw Foster over lunch the week before his death "with some other people in Washington." She said she had not noticed any change in his demeanor or appearance and that "his death came as a complete shock to her."

She said "she can offer no reason or speculation as to why he may have taken his life," according to the FBI statement.

The Journal reported that Whitewater investigators are looking into the discrepancy.

Thomases' claim that her official statement is incorrect joins a litany of problems in other statements taken during the Fiske probe. Fiske's replacement, Independent Counsel Kenneth Starr, recently announced the hiring of a federal prosecutor, Steve Parker, to review the investigation of Foster's death.

But sources familiar with the case suggest Parker's investigation may be hampered by questionable interview statements. Many of those statements, taken during the Fiske probe, have been used by Starr's staff as a foundation for additional investigations.

Thomases' claim adds to a growing list of problems:

■ Two witnesses, a male and female who were in Fort Marcy Park shortly before Foster's body was found, told FBI agents for Fiske they saw two men in and around Foster's Honda when they arrived, according to their statements. The female told investigators she saw a man, possibly barechested, sitting in Foster's Honda. The male stated he saw another man with long blond hair standing near Foster's Honda with the car's hood up. Despite those statements, Fiske, in his final report, inexplicably stated the couple saw "nothing unusual."

When a prosecutor for Starr's probe noted the couple's observations, agents assigned to Starr's staff re-interviewed the couple. The Tribune-Review recently reviewed those new interview statements prepared in January 1995. The male and female now state they saw no one in and around Foster's Honda. The female witness now claims not to have a clear recollection.

So far, various witnesses have offered contradictory accounts:

■ A confidential witness, who Fiske claimed first found Foster's body, has openly stated that Fiske's FBI agents "badgered" him into changing his testimony. He said he did not see a gun in Foster's hand. His statement indicates the gun could have been hidden by foliage.

■ Patrick Knowlton, a Washington businessman, is identified by the Fiske report as being the first person to see Foster's Honda in a Fort Marcy parking lot. Knowlton says he testified before Starr's grand jury that the agents "lied" in his statement about whether he could identify a Hispanic-looking male near the Honda. He also states that he was inaccurately quoted concerning his description of the Honda.

■ Last summer, the Tribune-

Review reported a glaring discrepancy between what Webster Hubbell told the Senate Whitewater Committee and his statement to the Fiske inquiry. During Senate testimony, Hubbell noted Foster was severely depressed in the days leading up to his death. His FBI statement to Fiske's agents gives a contradictory account. That statement says Hubbell told the FBI he "did not notice Foster acting differently in the days or weeks before his death."

■ The Tribune-Review has reported on grand jury proceedings headed up by Associate Independent Counsel Miquel Rodriguez in early January 1995. Almost every witness of the dozen or so first called testified under oath that their FBI statement contradicted what they remembered. One emergency worker, Todd Hall, suggested that investigators for Fiske asked leading questions.

Hall told the agents and grand jurors that when he first saw Foster's body, he also saw a man in a red vest running from away it. Yet, his statement reads "While inspecting the body on July 20, 1993, Hall believed he saw something moving in the trees surrounding the location of Foster's body . . . Previously, Hall thought he had seen either a bright orange or red color moving from right to left in the vicinity of Route 123. Upon discovering on April 27, 1994 (with Fiske's investigators) that there was a road in the area from which he previously thought he had seen movement, Hall believes it is possible he could have seen vehicular traffic on Route 123."

Hall reportedly told the grand jury that he specifically told Fiske's investigators he saw a person moving in the area, which was omitted from the statement, and that Fiske's agents had volunteered the

notion he simply saw a passing car.

In his report on the death, Fiske noted his probe did not use a grand jury for the Foster death investigation—though he employed grand juries for all other phases of his inquiry. Fiske noted in a footnote to his report that he relied on Title 18, U.S. Code, Section 1001, rather than take sworn grand jury testimony. Section 1001 states that making a false statement to federal investigators is a felony.

But legal experts say the statute is rarely used and were perplexed that Fiske, who had the opportunity to put witnesses under oath, did not do so. Fiske has not commented on the matter publicly and has not returned calls to the Tribune-Review. But Fiske has told some associates privately that he did not use a grand jury in the Foster death case because it would have been time consuming.

Prosecutor Moved to Firm with Whitewater Ties

By Christopher Ruddy
FOR THE TRIBUNE-REVIEW
AUGUST 7, 1996

WASHINGTON—A prosecutor who headed up a significant part of Whitewater Independent Counsel Kenneth Starr's probe now works for a law firm representing the Rose Law Firm, a Little Rock partnership linked to the Whitewater scandal.

In September 1995, Mark H. Tuohey III, a deputy independent counsel who led the Washington phase of Starr's inquiry for a year, resigned.

During his tenure with Starr, Tuohey remained a partner at the Washington offices of Reed Smith Shaw & McClay, a Pittsburgh-based firm.

Tuohey's departure from the Whitewater probe received little press attention. Also unheralded was the announcement that Tuohey would be leaving Reed Smith to join a firm with strong links to the Rose firm—Vinson & Elkins, a Houston-based organization with offices in Washington. Vinson & Elkins has represented the Rose firm in Whitewater matters involving Starr's staff and in Congressional investigations.

At the time of his resignation, Starr praised Tuohey, stating his work had been "superb."

Starr said Tuohey "led the day-to-day work of the Washington office" and served as a "valuable adviser to me . . . on all important decisions in both Washington and Little Rock."

The Rose firm has come under fierce scrutiny by Starr and Congressional committees because of its links to Whitewater:

■ Whitewater figures Hillary Rodham Clinton, Webster Hubbell, Vincent W. Foster, Jr., and William Kennedy were all partners at the firm before entering the White House. Kennedy, now a figure in the "Travelgate" and "Filegate" scandals, has since rejoined the firm.

■ Two Rose couriers allege that shortly after the appointment of Special Counsel Robert Fiske in 1994, their Rose superiors ordered them to shred certain Vincent Foster files. Other allegations surfaced that during the 1992 presidential campaign, Whitewater-related files were removed from the firm and never returned.

■ Rose represented Madison Guaranty, an Arkansas savings and loan chaired by Whitewater figure Jim McDougal. Madison failed, costing the taxpayers some $60 million.

According to Ronald Clark, managing partner at Rose, Vinson & Elkins continue to provide representation on several matters. Those matters have included: a "conflicts investigation" into the Rose firm's dealings with the Resolution Trust Company; subpoena and document production for the independent counsel and Congressional committees; and representing Rose partners and employees during questioning by FBI.

Rose itself has not been charged with any crime.

Tuohey, former president of the District of Columbia Bar Association and a former federal prosecutor, served as a special counsel during the Carter Administration, prosecuting former Pennsylvania Rep. Daniel Flood.

Several members of Starr's staff said that Tuohey, an activist Democrat, was appointed as deputy independent counsel to diminish criticism that Starr was too much of a partisan Republican to be fair.

Soon after his appointment, The Washington Post reported that Tuohey "is close to some Clinton administration officials, including Associate Attorney General Jamie S. Gorelick, and last year hosted a party for Attorney General Janet Reno at his Washington home."

WALLING OFF

There is no evidence that Tuohey joined Vinson & Elkins as a result of the work he did as prosecutor. There also is no indication that after his departure from Starr's office, he assisted Vinson & Elkins with information about the independent counsel's office.

"We definitely had a client-screening process at the time Mr. Tuohey joined the firm," said Angela Anthony, who handles media relations for Vinson & Elkins. Anthony said that as a result of the client-screening process, "any dealings Vinson & Elkins had with the Rose firm were kept completely away from Mr. Tuohey and his work."

Anthony said a client-screening process typically includes a written agreement outlining any work that a partner may or may not be involved with. Lawyers refer to these agreements as the "walling off" of a partner from potential conflicts.

Even with written agreements barring Tuohey from any conflicts involving the Rose firm while at Vinson & Elkins, experts in the field are not sure the matter has been put to rest.

No one says Tuohey had done anything illegal or violated any code of professional rules. Government prosecutors are afforded flexibility in joining private firms because of

Continued from page 1

the large number of potential conflicts that would cramp their ability to find jobs. But Tuohey's move to a firm connected with Rose does challenge ethical limits in some quarters.

"It doesn't violate capital "E" Ethics, rules that govern lawyers, but there are other considerations," said Professor Geoffrey Hazard of the University of Pennsylvania Law School, one of the nation's authorities on legal ethics.

Hazard suggests Tuohey's move to Vinson & Elkins and Starr's apparent acquiescence to that move, "raises serious questions." He believes Tuohey's job change violates "good sense and standards of prudence... start with the premise it looks bad."

He was surprised Starr simply did not tell Tuohey to go to another firm.

Hazard suggests that Tuohey's affiliation with a firm representing a player in the Whitewater investigation "creates suspicions" that hurt all parties involved as the inquiry continues.

Jerris Leonard, assistant attorney general for civil rights during the Nixon administration and now a Washington attorney agrees with Hazard. He says the matter is a "legitimate area of inquiry" for the press and public, especially in light of the sensitive nature of the case.

Leonard said that Starr should have filed a motion to disqualify Tuohey from the firm—not to prevent him from joining the firm—but simply to allow the matter to go before a judge and for all the details of Tuohey's new position to be laid out publicly.

Starr's office declined comment on the matter, but a partner at Vinson & Elkins told the Tribune-Review that Starr's ethics counsel, Sam Dash, had approved Tuohey's job change.

Tuohey was on vacation and unavailable for comment.

SECOND ANNIVERSARY

Monday marked the second anniversary of Starr's appointment as independent counsel.

To date he has brought no indictments on the Washington end of his investigations, though Republicans on the Senate Whitewater Committee stated in a June report that evidence warrants that the testimony of eight officials or Clinton associates should be reviewed for possible indictments.

The Washington side of the probe, as opposed to Little Rock, is the most sensitive part of Starr's investigation because of its proximity to the White House.

The Tribune-Review has reported that Miquel Rodriguez, Starr's lead prosecutor investigating Foster's death resigned in March 1995, claiming that Tuohey had hindered his investigation.

Rodriguez also complained in a letter to Starr that the Washington inquiry led by Tuohey was not following proper prosecutorial procedure by failing to challenge numerous claims of attorney-client privilege made by White House attorneys, who withheld documents or testimony from the investigators.

After Rodriguez returned to his position as an assistant U.S. attorney in Sacramento, Tuohey wrapped up the grand jury proceedings into Foster's death begun by Rodriguez.

Starr's office reportedly plans to issue a report on Foster's death later this summer based on the conclusions of forensic scientist Henry Lee and San Diego Medical Examiner Brian Blackbourne. Tuohey hired Lee shortly before joining Vinson & Elkins.

Starr's office has been investigating matters relating to the death of Foster and the actions by officials in the aftermath of his death, and, recently was asked by the Clinton administration to investigate aspects of the travel office and the FBI file scandals.

Though Starr has stated his investigation is active and ongoing, he has also commented recently that he may abide by a Justice Department practice of not making any significant moves during the upcoming election season. ■

New Expert with Old Ties Reviews Foster Report

By Christopher Ruddy
FOR THE TRIBUNE-REVIEW
AUGUST 14, 1996

WASHINGTON—An expert hired by Independent Counsel Kenneth Starr to impartially review official findings in the death of Vincent W. Foster Jr. is closely associated with a pathologist who already ruled on the case.

Starr's probe of the former deputy White House counsel's death remains open more than three years after Foster's body was found in a Northern Virginia park.

Starr reportedly is preparing to close the book on the matter by issuing forensic and other reports within the next several months.

One of those reports will be an independent autopsy review by Dr. Brian Blackbourne, a forensic pathologist who is San Diego's medical examiner.

Blackbourne told the Tribune-Review he has completed his report, though Starr's office recently returned it to him, asking him to make several revisions. He declined comment on those changes or other facets of the case.

The Tribune-Review first reported Blackbourne's appointment by Starr last year after questions were raised about the original autopsy performed by Dr. James Beyer, deputy medical examiner for Northern Virginia, and a panel of pathologists for Special Counsel Robert B. Fiske Jr.

Blackbourne, a Canadian citizen, is a seasoned pathologist with 27 years of experience. He has worked in Washington, Miami, and Massachusetts, and has conducted over 5,000 legal-medical autopsies.

Blackbourne's review of Beyer's findings, which supported the conclusion Foster died of a self-inflicted gunshot wound, will be the second review of the original autopsy. A second autopsy has not been done.

In 1994, an independent team composed of four noted forensic pathologists examined Beyer's work and issued a report to Fiske concluding that Foster died of a self-inflicted gunshot wound.

Starr's reasoning in hiring yet another pathologist remains unclear.

Also unexplained has been the extended length of time the case has been kept open by federal authorities.

Fiske's pathology team has come under some criticism and has been challenged by other experts.

"The (Fiske) panel of forensic pathologists looking into this I thought left a lot to be desired," former New York City Chief Medical Examiner Dr. Michael Baden told the Tribune-Review last year.

Baden said four of Fiske's pathologists certified Foster died at the spot where he was found at Fort Marcy Park, yet only two members of the panel visited the park.

Baden also noted that "only one of them interviewed the person who did the first autopsy. (The Fiske panel) tended to just adopt whatever was given to them. . . . You can't just adopt what the person who hires you says, or gives you."

The lead member of the Fiske panel was Dr. James Luke, an FBI pathologist who for 12 years was chief medical examiner for the District of Columbia. Luke was the only member of the Fiske panel to interview Beyer and was the only pathologist in April 1994 to assist the FBI in a search of the site where Foster's body was found.

Unreported at the time of Blackbourne's hiring by Starr was the fact that for a decade—from 1972 through 1982—Blackbourne served as Luke's chief deputy when they both worked for the District of Columbia.

Both Blackbourne and Luke describe their current relationship as "friends."

Blackbourne said his relationship with Luke had not precluded him from offering independent, objective findings, even though Luke had already officially ruled on the matter.

Blackbourne said there are only several hundred qualified forensic pathologists in the country and "everyone knows each other." Since his appointment by Starr, Blackbourne said he and Luke have met once for dinner, but did not discuss the case.

Luke, in a telephone interview, said the two had "made a point" not to discuss the Foster case during dinner, and that he had not recommended Luke for the job or consulted with Starr about the hiring.

Starr, through spokeswoman Debbie Gershman, declined to comment on the selection process that led to Blackbourne's appointment, or whether Starr believed it judicious to hire a pathologist closely associated with Fiske's lead pathologist.

"It's a curious choice," former federal prosecutor Thomas Scorza said about Starr's appointment of Blackbourne.

Scorza, now a lecturer on legal ethics with the University of Chicago, suggests that when an independent review has been conducted experts are usually hired "who can give you a dispassionate view of the facts... if you hire someone's friend, you can't expect them to stop being a human being." The same concerns could be cited if an expert is hired who is a known enemy of someone who has already given an opinion, he explained.

"I assume (Blackbourne) is a professional and well qualified . . . but it seems to me it is in Starr's greatest interest to hire someone who... has no personal connections to the case."

Blackbourne's appointment violates no conflict of interest rules, according to the American Academy of Forensic Sciences, but some believe that there are legitimate concerns.

"Obviously, one of the things that has to be considered with this kind of work (is) accuracy and validity and also the appearance of accuracy and validity," said a nationally prominent forensic pathologist who asked not to be identified.

The pathologist agrees with Scorza, adding that "the more arm's distance that there is (from the previous experts)" the more likely the public perception will be "there's no bias."

Since there is "a lot of subjectiveness to these reviews" decisionmakers or government agencies appoint pathologists with prudence who can give an "independent" examination, the pathologist noted. While he agreed there were no rules prohibiting Starr's appointment of Blackbourne, he said, "it's a common-sense judgement" that there is a problem.

The pathologist also claimed he heard there were concerns raised last year about the Luke-Blackbourne relationship.

"There was concern within Starr's group (about) whom to hire. There was some dissatisfaction initially with Blackbourne because of his relationship with Luke," the pathologist said. He said that the field of qualified forensic pathologists is large enough, numbering in the hundreds, who could have be brought in without a previous work or personal connection with anyone who has already ruled on the case.

Starr's hiring of Blackbourne took place after the resignation of Starr's lead Foster prosecutor, Miquel Rodriguez. One of the issues that led to Rodriguez's departure was his complaint that Starr's team was relying too heavily on experts closely aligned with the FBI or other federal authorities. Rodriguez believed the FBI had significant stakes in the original findings that Foster committed suicide and encouraged Starr to hire investigators and experts outside the FBI.

Starr apparently has not heeded that advice.

Blackbourne, as previously reported, has a long association with federal authorities and the FBI. For many years, like Luke, he lectured at the FBI Academy in Quantico, VA. Blackbourne, while deputy medical examiner in Washington, D.C., had worked closely with the

U.S. Park Police.

The Park Police handled the initial investigation into Foster's death. Blackbourne said he also trained park police investigators.

Blackbourne's appointment was seen as helping to buttress the findings of forensic scientist Henry Lee. Lee came under withering criticism after his testimony as a defense expert at the O.J. Simpson trial in 1995.

In another wrinkle to the questions rising from Starr's handling of the Foster case, the Tribune-Review reported last week that Starr's former deputy, Mark H. Tuohey III, joined a law firm representing the Little Rock-based Rose law firm in its Whitewater dealings before the independent counsel. Tuohey was involved in the selection of both Lee and Blackbourne.

In March 1996, after Tuohey's departure, Starr hired Steve Parker, a federal prosecutor from Tennessee, to once again review the case. Though Parker has homicide trial experience, he is also a close associate and protege of Starr's other deputy, W. Hickman Ewing, who had already weighed in on the case during the time of Rodriguez's departure.

Within weeks of Parker's appointment, the New York Times reported that sources close to Starr's probe said they had concluded their work with the case.

Fumbles Mar Whitewater Probe

By Christopher Ruddy
FOR THE TRIBUNE-REVIEW
AUGUST 29, 1996

The sentencing last week of three key figures in the Whitewater case appears to have been a setback for Independent Counsel Kenneth Starr's investigation of the scandal.

To prove wrongdoing by either President Bill Clinton or his wife, Starr needs cooperation from credible witnesses whose testimony world carry weight in a jury trial. But only one of the three defendants, Jim McDougal, agreed to cooperate and he is perhaps the least credible of the three.

Former Gov. Jim Guy Tucker, perhaps the most significant witness, refused to cooperate and received only probation and a fine. McDougal's wife, Susan, received a two-year jail term.

In August 1995, the Tribune-Review, quoting sources close to Starr's probe, said that indictments against Bill and Hillary Clinton were highly unlikely. This assessment was based on the fact that Starr has been unwilling to bring any indictment proceedings against the president by using David Hale's testimony alone.

Hale, a former Little Rock judge, has cooperated with Starr and has charged publicly that Bill Clinton pressured him into making a fraudulent, federally backed loan to Susan McDougal. It was Hale's testimony that led to the convictions of the Arkansas trio on fraud and conspiracy charges.

According to sources, Starr's team would not consider bringing charges against the president unless Hale's claims were supported by a credible witness, such as Tucker. But prosecutors were skeptical all along that Tucker would cooperate and any leverage they might have had with the threat of jail time was lost last week when federal District Court Judge George Howard sentenced him to four years' probation, with one and half years of home detention, which will still allow him to leave his home for work, church or medical reasons.

Tucker's sentence was one of the lightest handed out in the Whitewater scandal. Howard said he spared Tucker because sending him to a penitentiary would be "cruel as a grave." Tucker is said to have cirrhosis of the liver and will soon be in need of a liver transplant.

With Tucker having little reason to cooperate, Starr and his staff were left with the McDougals and they are well aware of the problems in using them as witnesses.

Jim McDougal has a borderline personality and has consistently told differing stories. Some jurors in the fraud and conspiracy trial said his testimony actually persuaded them to find McDougal, his wife and Tucker guilty on several counts.

As for Susan McDougal, prosecutors believe there are limits as to how much she knew about the scheme engineered by her husband. She has been indicted in California on charges of theft and fraud relating to her work as a bookkeeper for Nancy Mehta, wife of symphony conductor Zubin-Mehta.

HOLLOW VICTORIES

Starr's success this past May in gaining convictions against the three now appears to be a hollow victory, unless McDougal can produce hard evidence against the Clintons.

"The only way a guy like McDougal can be useful in a prosecution, since he has lied so many times, is if he has contemporaneous documents," explained Thomas Scorza, a former federal prosecutor and lecturer on legal ethics with the University of Chicago.

Scorza explained that only with such documentary evidence could a plea bargain be useful. "Then Starr's people can go before a jury and say, yeah this guy hasn't always told the truth, buy now you can believe him because here are the documents to prove that this time he's telling the truth" Scorza said.

Several factors diminish the likelihood McDougal will be a serious witness for the government. For instance, there has been no suggestion that the Clintons were involved in any paperwork relating to the illegal scheme. Unless McDougal kept tape recordings—which is highly unlikely—his testimony will prove useless where it counts—in court.

The uneven handling of plea agreements and sentencing by Starr and the court does not induce confidence in witnesses like McDougal who are considering just how much they want to cooperate with Starr. Since Tucker was given a light sentence for medical reasons, McDougal could cite health problems in quest of a similar deal. McDougal is also likely aware that Webster Hubbell, perhaps the most important witness to sing a plea agreement with Starr, failed to cooperate.

And of course Starr's key witness in the McDougal-Tucker trial was David Hale.

HARSH SENTENCE

Though Hale fully cooperated, federal judge Stephen Reasoner Howard gave him the harshest sentence so far handed down in the

Whitewater matter—a full 28 months in prison with restitution and fines totaling more than $2 million. Hale, it should be noted, has suffered two serious heart attacks in the 1980s, has undergone bypass surgery, and continues to take life-sustaining medications.

Hale's sentence was harsher than the sentence Howard gave Susan McDougal. While she received a two-year jail term, she will be eligible for parole in eight months.

Noted radio newsman Paul Harvey in a commentary last week said that "those who did talk (with prosecutors) were quickly silenced, and those who did not talk were taken care of."

Hale met with W. Hickman Ewing, a member of Starr's staff, in Little Rock, Ark., before beginning his jail term at a federal prison in Fort Worth, Texas. At that meeting Hale was told Starr's office had no plans to seek a reduction in the sentence.

However, following a story on Hale's dilemma in the Chicago Sun Times, Starr's office has done an about face, according to sources close to the inquiry. His prosecutors are said to be preparing a motion to have Hale's sentence reduced.

Despite his cooperation, Hale continues to suffer. He recently received a death threat and was transferred from the Fort Worth prison to a federal facility in Texarkana, Ark.

According to Starr's office, Tucker and the McDougals were all charged with and convicted of crimes that took place before Nov. 1, 1987—the date new, strict sentencing guidelines for white collar and other crimes went into effect.

Under the old guidelines applied in the sentencing of Tucker and Susan McDougal, the judge had wide latitude. Under the new Nov. 1, 1987, guidelines, the judge has almost no latitude in sentencing— even for health reasons. For example, former U.S. Rep. Dan Rostenkowski, though suffering from prostate cancer, was sentenced to 17 months in federal prison on charges of mail fraud.

While many judges like to generally follow the new, stricter guidelines for cases brought before them, even those that fall under the more lenient, pre-1987 policy, that was not the case here. The discrepancies with the two guidelines were brought home when the Washington Times reported that while Judge Howard spared Tucker jail time because of his need for a liver transplant, he sentenced Wallace Sims to 13 years in prison after his conviction on drug-related charges.

DIES IN PRISON

Sims, an African-American from Little Rock, was a quadriplegic. Despite testimony from some of the same experts who testified on Tucker's behalf, Sims was sentenced to jail and sent to a federal prison with medical facilities. Sims died three days after starting his jail term.

Sims obviously did not fall under the old guidelines. Even if he had, it's not clear whether Howard would have given him the same break as he gave Tucker and spared him a jail term.

While the old guidelines under which Tucker was sentenced are more liberal, they allow prosecutors to appeal sentences which are considered to be too light, according to Scorza. Starr's spokesperson was unavailable for comment as to whether the prosecutor planned to appeal the sentence.

If his previous actions are any indication, Starr will not appeal. During a hearing before Howard on Tucker's health, Starr's prosecutor did little to argue against Tucker receiving a reduced sentence. The Washington Times reported that Starr's prosecution "offered no witnesses, no statistics on how many such (liver transplant) operations had been performed on inmates and no opposition to the defense witnesses' often evasive answers on cross examination.".

Starr's apparent comfort with leniency is not out of character. A former federal judge, Starr has no experience as a prosecutor and before Whitewater had never tried a case. Some close to the probe say Starr still views his role as that of a judge rather than an aggressive prosecutor.

NUMEROUS MISTAKES

Starr's latest setback in Arkansas follows a string of fumbles:

Last month, a jury acquitted two Arkansas bankers on the most serious charges in an alleged scheme to shield several cash transactions made by Clinton's 1990 gubernatorial campaign from IRS scrutiny.

Some outside legal experts questioned why the case was brought in the first place, noting that it is extremely difficult to prove. Prosecutors have to demonstrate that not only did the participants scheme to shield the transaction, but that they did it to hide the matter from the IRS. The defendants claimed the transactions were done to keep Gov. Clinton's Republican opponent form learning of the transactions.

Starr has consistently failed to challenge claims made by lawyers at the White House and associates of the Clintons of attorney-client privilege. As a rule, prosecutors challenge every claim of privilege in court and leave it up to a judge where it's justified or not.

By failing to make such challenges, Starr has allowed the targets of his probe to dictate what matters are presented before grand juries.

At the sentencing of Webster Hubbell, Starr admitted that the former associate attorney general had reneged on his plea agreement and had never fully cooperated with prosecutors. According to several sources familiar with the probe, Starr never adequately debriefed Hubbell as to what he knew and *Continued on next page*

Continued from page 9

how he might aid prosecutors. This debriefing, according to the sources, must be done before any plea agreement is entered into.

Even though Hubbell failed to live up to his agreement, Starr has never taken any punitive actions against him, such as seeking additional charges. This inaction, according to Scorza, has given "a signal" to other potential witnesses that they do not have to cooperate.

Starr's handling of the Hubbell plea apparently led to the resignation of trial counsel Russell Hardin from his staff in late 1994.

FOSTER DEATH

According to sources, Miquel Rodriguez, Starr's lead prosecutor in examining the death of White House deputy counsel Vincent Foster, resigned in March 1995, after he was thwarted by his superiors in conducting a full grand jury probe into the mysterious death.

Starr's handling of the Foster case cuts to the heart of the practical handling of his prosecution and the integrity of his overall probe. Foster has been dead for more than three years and Starr has had jurisdiction over the matter for more than two years. With the full resources of the federal government, he still has offered no resolution.

Newsweek reports that Starr is a man of extreme ambition. With little press scrutiny of his handling of the Foster case, Starr may believe that anything he concludes will close the case, and keep him in good standing for future public positions.

With more than two years on the job and still no indictments having been handed down in Washington—despite Starr's promise that the major issues of the scandal would be before the American people before the presidential election—more and more people are beginning to realize they have been asked to swallow a pill with no real effort made to resolve the matter.

Recently, "Making Waves," a book by radio commentator Michael Reagan, son of former President Ronald Reagan, examines Starr's handling of the case and refers to it at one point as "another Fiske style cover-up."

Last year the Tribune-Review reported that Sen. Lauch Faircloth once considered Starr's biggest backer on the Senate Whitewater committee, indicated he had become embarrassed by Starr. After all, Faircloth was widely credited in having Starr's predecessor, Robert Fiske fired.

At the time, Faircloth said that Starr had been motivated by a desire to be nominated someday for a seat on the Supreme Court. Faircloth said that Starr's handling of the case had "finished" any chance of an appointment to the high court.

Book Review

Blood Sport: The President and His Adversaries

Simon & Schuster, pp 434, $25

By Christopher Ruddy
FOR DISPATCHES
APRIL 10, 1996

When I flipped open the hardcover to James Stewart's Whitewater tell-all, I came to the beginning—"The Prologue." I had high hopes for some riveting reporting. After all, Mr. Stewart is a Pulitzer Prize winner.

Then I read with dismay the first section of the Prologue, which unfolds on July 20, 1993 with the finding of Vince Foster's body in Fort Vince Foster's body in Fort Marcy Park by a Park Police investigator, John Rolla. Though only about two pages long, this opening contains no less than six significant errors.

On the first page of the book, Stewart makes reference to a Park Police Officer, Franz Ferstl. But Stewart spells his name wrong. Though a trivial error, a litany of errors flow from there. Stewart claims a man and woman were in a Nissan parked in the park's lot. Not true; they were found off a park trail. Stewart says Foster was found on a steep slope with his "feet resting on some exposed roots." Special Counsel Fiske concluded Foster sat on the worn, exposed roots, using them as a natural seat.

The medical examiner arrived "around 7 p.m.," Stewart claims. The Fiske report claims he came at 7:40 p.m.

Stewart accurately notes that after the body was lifted up. Rolla noted a "small hole in the back of the head." Stewart unequivocally accepts Special Counsel Fiske's

June 30, 1994 report on the death, but he cannot explain why Fiske states that Rolla, the medical examiner and others saw "a large exit wound."

I hurried back to the cover and re-read it: "Author of *Den of Thieves* and winner of the Pulitzer Prize." Errors of this number and type, which percolate throughout the book, can't just be chalked up to Stewart being a reporter on deadline. The author acknowledges that he had the help of two researchers.

Can a book that contains so many casual errors make any reliable conclusions? That's a good question for the reader to answer.

A cover story in the Arkansas Democrat Gazette pointed out that one vignette in Stewart's book involves Arkansas's Twin City Bank and its former Vice Chairman, Ed Penick. That section is filled with factual errors, the says, including getting Penick's title wrong.

Factual errors can have grave consequences. Stewart infers more than once that Foster shot himself with a silver gun Lisa Foster brought form Little Rock—which could be strong evidence indicating Foster did take his own life. Stewart has been propagating his "silver gun theory" on the talk radio circuit. He told a Washington audience recently that Foster's gun "was a vintage gun and I think it was basically silver."

Is Stewart aware that Foster was found with an antique, *black* Colt revolver? Is he aware that no one in Foster's family has ever positively identified that *black* Colt? Is he aware that Mrs. Foster told the Park Police that the gun found in Foster's

hand was not the silver one she thought it was?

Blood Sport has been acclaimed for deconstruction the Clinton's assertions they were just innocent, passive investors to their 50-50 partnership with Jim and Susan McDougal. This is not new. The Washington Times had already made that case.

Stewart never goes too far beyond the intrigue related to the land partnership deal. Making much hay of the land deal itself is ludicrous. Both Fiske, and his replacement, Kenneth Starr, have found little of interest in the Whitewater partnership and none of the more than a dozen pleas and indictments so far have been related to shenanigans relating to it.

None probably will, despite Mr. Stewart's heroic efforts to find some serious concern over a bank loan application in which the Clintons overestimated—or inflated—the value of their half of the partnership

Blood Sport presents no perspective and fails to see Whitewater as it is: an epicenter for a host of scandals that emanate from it. For example, *Blood Sport* fails to mention, or even examine, the significant Washington Times story of the shredding of Vincent Foster's documents at the Rose Law Firm just after the appointment of a Special Counsel.

Blood Sport's treatment of Vince Foster, as the glue which holds the book together, never explains how Whitewater became casual in leading to his death. It is not mentioned in the torn "suicide" note which Stewart makes much of. On
Continued on next page

Continued from page 11

ABC's Nightline, Stewart suggested that Foster committed suicide because of things relating to Whitewater too embarrassing to mention in the "suicide" note. His book never offers any evidence of this and later seemingly embraces Fiske's conclusion that Whitewater or matters related to Madison Guaranty played no role in the death.

Blood Sport's strong suit is its vivid portrayal of characters, detailing what no publication has before—the human element to this amorphous scandal. At times, he seems overly captive to his sources. For example, Stewart paints an unflattering picture of Hubbell, but accepts Hubbell's account, as he does his other sources, without question. Why should Hubbell, a convicted felon who reneged on his plea agreement, be believed? Why should Thomases, or Nussbaum or the McDougals?

No doubt, from these insider sources, Mr. Stewart puts together a stylistically well-written and coherent account of their stories, meshing them well with an overall chronology of the Whitewater affair.

Ambrose Evans Pritchard of London's Sunday Telegraph pointed out in his review of *Blood Sport* that the representations of Susan Thomases—his primary source—in the book, completely contradicts what Thomases told the FBI in a statement. Mr. Stewart states that he reviewed such documents.

These flaws have been eclipsed by the view that the author has given "tough" treatment to the Clintons over the Whitewater land partnership deal, and his harsh portrayal of the First Lady.

As Mr. Stewart tells it, it was the Clintons in the person of Susan Thomases who first sought him out, as a sort of hired gun to shoot down the President's critics. Stewart relates that the approach to him was first made in March of 1994 when the White House was besieged by

reports that Vince Foster was murdered. As Stewart tells it, he and the Clintons had a parting of company, at which point he was denied access, and went on to tell the real truth about the Clintons. But the story has to read that way if Mr. Stewart is to have any credibility. It is clear his access was only cut off to the First Family, not to other sources.

Thusly, while harping on the Whitewater land deal, he has at the same time been more credible in exoneration the Clinton White House in any wrongdoing relating to Foster's death or in the aftermath investigations—one of the chief reasons Miss Thomases came to him in the first place.

Coincidental to the time Thomases was showing up at his doorstep, my reporting at the New York Post on Foster's death had just peaked in March of 1994. Mr. Stewart devotes no less than four pages toward the end of the book to my work. Stewart smears me personally while knocking down the facts of the story in what has become a ritual formula first employed by Mike Wallace at "60 Minutes": ignore the serious evidence of wrongdoing, attack the story as just a partisan effort funded by right-wingers, and for a dash of credibility, rap the Park Police for concluding the case too hastily.

Dealing with me, Mr. Stewart thinks it deserving of the reader's rime to mention that at the Post, Ruddy was "always impeccably dressed in suit and tie, looking more like a Wall Street banker than his casually dressed colleagues."

I suppose the fact I wore a jacket and tie hurts my credibility—like the fact I drank coffee in the morning would. The insinuations become more nasty.

He suggests there has been racial overtones to my work, and points to the story I broke about a PBS documentary called "Liberators," which purported to show that two all-black combat units liberated the concentration camps of Buchenwald

and Dachau. That documentary was a hoax. While neglecting to point out to his readers that my ground-breaking reports were devastatingly accurate—so much so that PBS took the unprecedented action of withdrawing the film, he tries to cast my work with racial overtones, saying my work received "acclaim from some conservatives who saw the documentary as a liberal attempt to paper over divisions between (Jews and African-Americans)."

The truth was that my reporting was picked up not by conservatives, but rather, The New Republic, New York magazine, and such organizations as the American Jewish Congress. Purple Heart winner E.G. McConnell, a member of the all-black 761st Tank Battalion depicted in the film "Liberators," has publicly praised my work.

To buttress his insinuation of racism, Stewart then adds, "In another article, Ruddy attacked the New York school system's proposed 'Rainbow Curriculum,' intended to foster tolerance of minorities, including homosexuals." This statement is an out and out fabrication: I have never written an article about the Rainbow Curriculum, let alone one attacking it.

From there Stewart weaves a story line indicating my Foster stories started as part of a right-wing conspiracy. He says that conservative critic Reed Irvine of Accuracy in Media (he wrongly states Irvine has a program on CNBC) first put me on the story while at the Post. This is not true.

As a parting shot, Stewart records that I became "obsessed with conspiracy theories involving the death) which led to my termination with the Post because I "refused to work on any other topic." (Several stories totally unrelated to Foster were published after I began working the story, several others were submitted but were not published.)

Why, if my reporting on Foster's death is just nonsense, has so much effort been expended to sell the public on so many untruths about me and my work?

This targeting of me began at the New York Post by a media "critic" for the left-wing Village Voice who reported that I had been the editor of a publication that went into court-ordered bankruptcy. For weeks the critic made reference to me and this bankruptcy. I ignored it even though it was a total lie: the publication I worked for never went bankrupt, was always solvent, and was sold for a profit to another publication.

Despite the smear, I decided to ignore it, but the lie, like others, took root and bigger ones germinated.

Now some of them are being bound in book form. I wonder how the discernible reader will be able to discern fact from fiction in a book written by a Pulitzer Prize winner.

Starr Witness

The Whitewater independent counsel needs to make a deal to resolve the case.

By Christopher Ruddy
FOR THE CHICAGO SUN-TIMES
MAY 30, 1996

The guilty verdicts handed down this week by a Little Rock jury mark a significant turning point for the Whitewater scandal and give the independent counsel, Kenneth W. Starr, another opportunity to aggressively pursue the matter.

For now, Starr wins. But his victory has to be solidified with plea agreements, particularly with Arkansas Gov. Jim Guy Tucker, for the case to unfold quickly.

Starr's apparent success is dimmed by other news this week that has a direct bearing on his ability to prosecute future cases. Starr's chief witness, former Little Rock Municipal Judge David Hale, will enter federal prison Friday as a loser—and understanding Hale's plight may explain why the scandal will not unravel as quickly as some might wish.

Even though Hale fully cooperated, apparently at some risk, Starr stood silent when a federal judge, Stephen M. Reasoner, in Arkansas handed down a stiff sentence to his chief witness: 28 months in prison, restitution of $2.04 million, and a $10,000 fine with three years probation.

Last week, Hale met with Starr's prosecutors in Little Rock. They told Hale that Starr had no plans to ask to have the sentence reduced. Hale now has to reconsider how fully he will cooperate in the future. Already, on the advice of his lawyer, Hale has declined to testify before the Senate Whitewater committee.

There's little reason to blame Hale. Former Associate Attorney General Webster Hubbell signed a plea agreement with Starr in 1994, after pleading guilty to tax evasion and mail fraud. But Starr had to admit at sentencing that Hubbell never fully cooperated. For not cooperating, Hubbell was sentenced by an Arkansas federal judge to 21 months in jail and ordered to make restitution of $135,000—less of a penalty than Hale received.

Hubbell was a big catch for Starr's prosecution. An aggressive prosecutor might have made an example of Hubbell for breaking his word—such as filing additional charges against him—but Starr did not.

The importance of the stiff sentence handed down to Hale, and the way Hubbell essentially got off the hook, cannot be underestimated. The success of this prosecution, as is true with complex legal cases, depends on the prosecutor's ability to get key witnesses to cooperate.

Starr's prosecutors know that if they wish to prosecute President Clinton they will need to enlist the cooperation of Tucker—the most credible of the three defendants.

Tucker was found guilty on conspiracy and mail fraud charges and almost certainly will be jailed. He is to go on trial next month on additional fraud and tax evasion charges. Starr can "hammer" Tucker if he wants. But Tucker has to ask himself: If I plea-bargain and break my word, like Hubbell, can I get off the hook? If I bargain and fully cooperate, will my sentence be as stiff as Hale's? What is my incentive to cooperate?

It is too early to tell what the long-term result of the recent trial will be, though the convictions demonstrate one thing: The major media have gotten this story wrong. It is not about the 18-year-old land partnership deal known as the Whitewater Development Corp., where no criminality has been found.

The convictions indicate this case is more than a "garden variety" savings-and-loan scandal, as the Wall Street Journal once called it. The evidence demonstrates that the defendants—including a sitting governor—defrauded federally insured institutions to the tune of $3 million. Hale also has implicated the president in the scheme.

And these issues surfacing now in Little Rock may be less serious than the ones on the Washington side of Starr's probe. Remember, it *Continued on next page*

Continued from page 13

was reports that White House aides raided the office of Vincent Foster, White House deputy counsel and former law partner of first lady Hillary Rodham Clinton, on the night of his death and removed Whitewater papers that revived interest in the case. We now know there is much more to this scandal than Whitewater.

Uncovering the real scandal is another matter. Starr's lackadaisical handling of Foster's death investigation and related issues—for almost two years with no indictments—is just another indicator that no one should jump to conclusions as to how quickly this case will be resolved.

How to keep up with this unfolding story ...

THE TRUTH
ABOUT
VINCENT FOSTER

THERE'S ONLY ONE national journal publishing all of Christopher Ruddy's reports on the death of Vincent Foster and related stories. That publication is **DISPATCHES**, the Western Journalism Center's bi-weekly investigative news journal.

Call our toll-free number — **1-800-398-2225** to subscribe today for only $36 and get a full year of news, information and analysis you won't find in the establishment media — or send a check or money order along with the form below.